OF MYTH, LIFE, AND WAR IN PLATO'S *REPUBLIC*

Studies in Continental Thought

John Sallis, *general editor*

Consulting Editors

OF MYTH, LIFE,
AND WAR IN
PLATO'S *REPUBLIC*

Claudia Baracchi

INDIANA UNIVERSITY PRESS
Bloomington and Indianapolis

This book is a publication of

Indiana University Press
601 North Morton Street
Bloomington, IN 47404-3797 USA

http://iupress.indiana.edu

Telephone orders   800-842-6796
Fax orders   812-855-7931
Orders by e-mail   iuporder@indiana.edu

© 2002 by Claudia Baracchi

The paper used in this publication meets the mini-
mum requirements of American National Standard
for Information Sciences—Permanence of Paper for
Printed Library Materials, ANSI Z39.48-1984.

Manufactured in the United States of America

Library of Congress Cataloging-in-Publication Data

Baracchi, Claudia, date
    Of myth, life, and war in Plato's Republic /
Claudia Baracchi.
        p. cm. — (Studies in Continental thought)
    Includes bibliographical references and index.
    ISBN 0-253-33995-2 (cloth : alk. paper) —
    ISBN 0-253-21485-8 (pbk. : alk. paper)
    1. Plato. Republic.   I. Title.   II. Series.
JC71.P6 B33 2002
321'.07—dc21
                                    2001002950

1 2 3 4 5   07 06 05 04 03 02

Ai miei genitori

CONTENTS

CONTENTS

ACKNOWLEDGMENTS

A project that, not unlike the one presented here, spanned various lifetimes (various times in life, of life) and involved journeying to many places is the fruit of numberless encounters, exposures, and conversations. On this occasion I wish to mention with heartfelt gratitude the following mentors, colleagues, and friends: John Sallis, Idit Dobbs-Weinstein, Gregg Horowitz, Charles Scott, Walter Brogan, Jeff Bernstein, John Lysaker, and Victoria McGeer. This work would not have come together without what I learned from Dan Dolen. I wrote the concluding pages while looking at the ever-changing sky over the Adirondacks, as I was a guest at Carol and Richard Bernstein's summer residence. I thank them warmly for their gracious and engaging hospitality. Thanks also to Michael Weinman, Elena Tzelepis, Lisa Farooque, Russell Winslow, and my editors at Indiana University Press. While I owe almost everything to the circumstances in which I found myself and to the people, whether named or not, I had the fortune to meet, the responsibility (αἰτία) for all shortcomings in the work here offered is my own.

New York City
August 24, 2000

OF MYTH, LIFE,
AND WAR IN
PLATO'S *REPUBLIC*

Introduction

Der sog. Platonismus ist nur eine Flucht vor Platos Problem.

(Leo Strauss to Karl Löwith, June 23, 1935)

More Notes on Plato's Republic*?*

Yet another work on Plato, on that most universally recognized among the Platonic dialogues—the *Republic.* The *Republic* of Plato (so we call it, today, in this part of the world): a seminal text, inaugurating an epoch of which we are still witnessing the development—or is it a twilight, a closure, the coming to an end of its day? In virtue of its circulation and resonance since antiquity, one hesitates to consider this text as one text among others—even among other texts that have become canonical. One could indeed say that the history of the reception of this text, of the responses and reflections it engendered, coincides with the history of the formation of the Western canon (if it is one, and however its qualification as Western is to be delimited), with the history of Western philosophy itself, or even the history of the West tout court (however the sense of this history, perhaps the only history, may be understood). But other philosophical lineages, other modes and guises of philosophical πάθος, seem as well to be marked, in their emergence, by this text—this text so often in the vicinity of their inception. This text, itself in many ways coming from afar, echoing and gathering strange voices, has drifted to distant shores, to the East and to the West, along uncertain trajectories, undergoing translations into remote languages and times.

Still today, at the beginning of the third millennium of an era in which every year is said to be of the Lord, in this westernmost region of the Western world so removed from Europe (let alone from Greece) and yet, simultaneously, representing the culminating moment of a certain European (hence, Greek) projection, in this world whose accomplishments and self-enforcement sometimes seem to make the rest of the world, the other worlds, and that is to say, the world

1

as such in its manifoldness, almost disappear—still today, here, the Platonic heritage of which the *Republic* is an emblem is said to underlie our constructs and visions, whether obliquely or otherwise. And the stories abound telling how this is so—stories illuminating the disasters or the edifying programs resulting from such filiation, the way in which this text foreshadows and dictates, opens up a certain horizon of possibility and imposes losses and constraints.

In this tradition, certain authors will have denounced the problematic, even sinister legacy of the Platonic endeavor, the metaphysics there instituted along with its correlates, that is, the scientific-technological shift and the totalizing-totalitarian vocation. Others will have invoked the politico-constructive stratum in Plato's work, paradigmatically in the *Republic*, for what could be called "restorative purposes," in order to redeem the platitude of later times (which, merely because of their lateness, would by definition be marked by decadence), or even to envision alternative political solutions. At times the same author will have both denounced and invoked—both consistently pointed out the Platonic loss of primordial insight and surprisingly revived Platonic programs, for instance, the pattern of a just city—as if the Platonic discourse on the tripartite communal structure could readily be turned into a manifesto. Yet others, many others, for many generations, will have submitted this text to scholarly scrutiny of various kinds, from philological analysis to logical assessment, while further voices especially today will have called for an emancipation from this philosophical discourse and the order it legitimizes—as if this were one philosophical discourse among others, which could be simply set aside and disposed of; as if the wounds, the violence, the exclusions associated with a text like the *Republic* and the history it is said to inform could be healed by a gesture of denial or by the rhetoric of a new beginning; and as if this very rhetoric would not precisely reproduce the dangers it is claiming to overcome, etc. This text seems to be ubiquitous, unforgettable.

Yet, in another sense, this text is nowhere to be found, utterly forgotten. This text so public, so freely circulating, everywhere disclosed remains vastly silent, precisely in its availability—almost inaudible in the midst of the clamor that surrounds it. Infinitely reproduced, and this already means reduced, formalized, schematized, the *Republic* is also, quite significantly, buried. On the one hand, one witnesses the phenomenon of secondary discourses curiously alienated from the speaking of this text they claim to discuss—secondary discourses circulating often insubstantial myths about the *Republic*, myths hardly supported by evidence to be found in the text as such, made possible by a subtle, stratified process of selective reading and of dismemberment of the text into unrelated arguments. On the other hand, the text, repeatedly covered over and replaced, remains virtually inaccessible in its integrity, originality, and vitality.

Just as analysis, especially when lacking a reflective awareness of its own program and projective involvement, may obscure rather than cast light and discern, and just as a certain noise of commemoration may cover over that which is apparently in the process of being entrusted to memory (in this sense, commemoration would seem to exorcise that which is to be remembered and dispel the very possibility of remembrance), so writing may be a gesture of oblivion, distortion, erasure. As we know, this is also a Platonic intimation. It seems to be particularly illuminating in the case of the writing proliferated around and on the *Republic*—the body of writing that concerns itself with, and hence envelops, the *Republic*, while also quite crucially originating from the writing that the *Republic* itself is. In this sense the *Republic* of Plato appears gathered in a singular silence, closed off in an enigmatic muteness. One could even say that what goes under the rubric of Platonism is the locus of this muteness; that, subsequently, Plato and Platonism are not coextensive terms; and that, in the final analysis, the so-called Platonic tradition does not find its necessitating ground or justification in Plato's voice, of which the *Republic* is exemplary—not simply, not in this voice alone, not without any further qualification.

What follows is admittedly a study of this text. Yet another interpretive effort, yet another layer of scholarly labor—more notes on Plato's *Republic*. From a slightly different point of view, however, which would require a most inconspicuous adjustment, almost nothing, the present work can be glimpsed in its disinclination to confirm the logic of addition-accumulation, in its reluctance thus to contribute to the further accretion of the scholarly patrimony. In fact, this investigation presents itself as an attempt to effect something like a subtraction—to encourage a certain emptying, a certain hesitation to embrace all too customary assumptions. The present discussion would aim at providing one less version, systematization, or even simply interpretation of the Platonic dialogue. One less *Republic*, in sum. In order to try to begin to remember. Not that a similar excavation or de-sedimentation may finally lead to the recovery of the text in its integrity and let it speak purely according to itself. We would probably not be in the position of hearing, not even of imagining this, anyway. Rather, let it simply be said that the present writing is oriented less by the program of interpretation and construction than by the task of response, of a *rigorously responsive reading*. So that the text may speak—if not purely according to itself, then *out of itself*, in the space of this encounter—in this possible space neither its own nor, strictly speaking, mine.

The discussion offered here takes place in such intermediate space, where the text comes forth giving *itself as a task*, demanding to be heeded and accomplished, and is received through a rigorous exercise of reading, that is, according to a mode of reception and receptiveness always already at one with engagement. There is no reading that is "merely" reading, "merely" the repetition of what would, in turn, autonomously subsist in written form. That is why reading is at once responding. That is also why it is ultimately a matter of responsibility. However, the reading here presented consistently stems from a meticulous textual work—even when, in fact, especially when its articulations may be at odds with or openly question certain canonical versions of Plato.

But perhaps the thought of a "rigorously responsive reading" deserves further elucidation. Rigor is prevalently understood as a methodological virtue, as that thanks to which one does not let oneself be sidetracked, distracted, or detoured. In this sense, to proceed with rigor means effectively to pursue the intended goal, a goal determined before one set out to read. It means to begin with a project, with a set of criteria and commitments which will have to be articulated and ultimately to find confirmation. Rigor, then, makes responding, co-responding, co-responsiveness impossible. It involves a set of presuppositions which will have shaped and established beforehand the text to be read. One will find oneself before the text about which one will have *decided* already, the text literally constituted through such decision. Furthermore, one will have dissimulated the *creative* contribution of such a *reflective* mode, of such a decision, and re-presented one's approach as re-presentational and re-presentative—as unproblematically appropriate, adequate, and, what is more, objective. This practice appears to be quintessentially self-demonstrative.

But, besides assisting one in the carrying out of the textual conquest according to predetermined methodological strategies and goals, rigor can be a trait of involvement. It can characterize, indeed, inform receptivity, listening, letting in, letting be. It can sustain one—not so much in one's *effort* to listen or in the *disciplined cultivation* of receptivity, but rather in acknowledging, if not appropriating, the exposure, the receptivity, the listening occurring *before* and *beyond* all determination and intentional, disciplined approach. In this sense, rigor is less a matter of clearing, of making room for the text to come forth, than of letting go and allowing oneself to be attuned to, if not grasp, the essentially affective dimension of the advent and event of the text. Such attunement to and by the textual advent already harbors a response—a response springing out of the intimacy of a vastly unpredicted encounter.

A rigorously responsive reading, then, strictly speaking involves a certain, however qualified, not knowing—approaching a text in the lack of a pre-formed program projected in order to be realized, brought to be through and upon the flesh of what was for that purpose subdued and ignored. Such a reading involves both the toil of a careful frequentation of the text and a response to it formulated on this ground. It involves reading every line, every word—however irrelevant or surprising or extravagant they may seem. It involves rigorously acknowledging, taking the risk, and responding to that surprise or disconcerting extravagance without purposively selecting or editing. It requires the awareness that one will have been responding already, for responding begins with reading, that the condition of responsibility, of having to respond, cannot simply be evaded, and that the risk of the response is least of all avoided when one keeps oneself within the bounds of orthodoxy. It is in this way that rigor turns out to go hand in hand with dynamic involvement.

It is through such a dialogical play, too, that the question concerning who we are, could be, or might become—the question concerning, above all, human δύναμις—could receive further elaboration, if not an answer. Setting out to relinquish the desire for reductive and, at times, caricatured renditions of the text under consideration does not mean dreaming of suspending the projective dynamics operative in any encounter, of freeing the voices and experience that the Platonic writing harbors, *tout simplement*. Even dreamers, in fact, especially dreamers, are aware of the circles, strictures, and paradoxical shapes of the hermeneutical exercise. But it certainly means to lay bare a certain ineluctability of projection, along with the compulsion to reduce or caricature what (whom) is encountered. It means, then, indirectly to ask: To what end the positive, deliberate, even willful construction of doctrines that never were, of philosophical phantoms that recede whenever we draw close to what remains, to the written words, and read attentively? To what end the logical formalizations, the transcriptions according to anachronistic categories, according to categories tout court, and other such protective screens? What danger is feared or actually awaiting beyond such a defensive line? What is lost, what possibilities unknown, in such an avoidance of exposure? Whence the necessity, if any, of this posture of ours, of this posture of which we are heirs?

Or, to ask it otherwise: What function do the dominant readings of Plato serve, which, in the end, amount to one and the same, sharing as they do fundamental presuppositions concerning Plato, Platonic idealism, Platonic dualism, Platonic totalitarianism, etc.? What is it that is thereby made possible, enabled? Whence the power of the spell and hold of such prevalent narratives? Could it be that what is allowed, invisibly sustained, however remotely configured by such stories is an almost immediate perception of the world as standing reserve, the stance of domination and technologico-scientific mastery?

Génesis

The initial impulse for this work came from a concern with the role of myth in the Platonic texts and, more precisely, with the myth of Er concluding the dialogue on the πολιτεία. Thus, to a significant extent the present investigation comes as a response to the provocation of this strange text. The distance is, therefore, incalculable between the reflections articulated here and the position of those readers who have always already resolved what would count as "properly philosophical" in opposition to what appears to be corrupting, inessential, or, at best, ornamental. As Julia Annas, in a series of paradigmatic statements, puts it, for such readers the "Myth of Er is a painful shock," whose "vulgarity seems to pull us right down to the level of Cephalus."[1] Annas, indeed, concludes her account by observing: "The bulk of the *Republic* is Plato's most successful attempt. . . . Ideas that have powerful expression in the main coherent body of the book are presented at the end in a much cruder form, which Plato none the less believes can add to our understanding. And so the *Republic,* a powerful and otherwise impressively unified book, acquired its lame and messy ending."[2]

To this "lame and messy ending" the present study is dedicated. The discontinuity between the project developed here and the position and overall mode of investigation exemplified by Annas's assertions originates in a radically different response to the question of language, or, more accurately, in the tension between the acknowledgment and the denial of the question of language as such, as a question. It is a quite remarkable reluctance to acknowledge the irreducible opacity, questionability, and manifoldness of language which leads to remarks of this tenor:

> The insolubility of this problem is a good illustration of the difficulties that Plato runs into by using images to make a philosophical point. The imagery is apt to get overloaded, as happens with the Line, because Plato is trying to do two things at once with it. And the detail of the imagery tempts us to ask questions that cannot be satisfactorily answered within the terms of imagery; if we treat it with philosophical seriousness the image turns out incoherent. . . . Plato might well agree; he certainly warns us that he is providing *only* images.[3]

But is this providing *only* images, this providing which is limited to images, a merely accidental restriction, or, even, the fruit of authorial deliberation having no philosophical relevance whatsoever and to be ascribed to some "personal reasons"?[4] Could this otherwise "coherent" and "unified" text have been preserved from such an imaginative degeneration? Also, incidentally: whence the values of coherence and unity, unquestioningly projected upon the ancient text, as if having trans-historical validity? In many ways, the present inquiry displays the compulsion to show how the turn(s) to images, far from having an arbitrary, accessory, or even unnecessary character, disclose language as intrinsically and essentially imaginal.[5]

The question concerning the manifoldness of discursive modes and, in particular, the unique, ubiquitous, and perhaps unavoidable element of myth preserves its provocative force intact, especially in the light of the singular corpus it addresses. Indeed, raising the question of the discursive comportment characterizing Plato's texts means to wonder about the status of the discourses made possible by and inscribed within those founding texts. It especially means to wonder about the status of what goes under the heading of Western philosophy, namely, the variously intertwined Arabic, Jewish, and Christian (later on European, even American) lineages in whose context the Platonic reflection has been , taken up and systematically elaborated. It is, parenthetically, through such a systematic elaboration of Platonic motifs that philosophy has come to emerge as the demarcated field of a certain constellation of themes, as a discipline. At stake in such a line of questioning is the problematization of the purely representational, purely instrumental comportment toward language which essentially grounds the claims of an unaffected, nonaffective, safely separate exercise of reason—in its in(de)finitely many guises, to be sure, ranging from the project of philosophy as a positive science to dualism in its classical, that is, modern form; from the silent but unmistakable turning of the temporality of discursivity into the eternity of the system to the theological solution that, whether positively or negatively, exoterically or hermetically, offers the possibility of faith in the excess of and to language, that is, the possibility of reliance on, even decipherability of, such excess.

Of Myth, Life, and War

Of course, the concern with the essence and significance of discourse in the mythical mode, that is, on Plato's own terms, of poetry, or even of music, entails raising once again the ancient question of the relation between philosophical and poetic speaking—a "quarrel," a difficult διαφορά, ancient indeed, already for Plato (*Resp.* 607b). What the Platonic texts unmistakably betray is the fundamental function of mythical enunciation in the philosophical inquiry. In the paradigmatic case of the dialogue on the πολιτεία, virtually every major turn marking the development of the conversation seems to rest on a fictional proviso, whether clamorous or inconspicuous, on a story gently told, on a histrionic evocation of images which, in its nature, is no less questionable and wondrous than the wonders worked by the charlatans (the θαυματοποιοί) in the cave. The thaumaturgic power of calling forth a story appears to be one of Socrates' most remarkable resources. Images open up horizons within which the journey in λόγος continues to unfold.

This line of investigation leads to the consideration of myth in its poietic dimension, of myth as primordial making, as that which exceeds, precedes, and indeed founds the logico-contemplative moment.[6] But to speak of myth as originary making does not involve establishing myth as the ground, albeit inappropriable, of the properly philosophical effort. Not quite this simply, at any rate. Rather, to speak in such a way demands a radical rethinking of the meaning of ground and of origin. For to associate these concepts with ποίησις, with the ποιεῖν of myth means to set them in motion, to think ground as unstable and origin as multiple, as dynamically unfolding, as involved in sensibility and never constituting a pure beginning, a beginning from out of nothing.[7]

Such line of investigation is inaugurated once one orients oneself toward myth as *philosophically* relevant—not this or that myth but, although the consideration of myth will never have been an abstract affair, *myth as such*. Indeed, while the analysis of Platonic myths is all but underdeveloped (they have been the object of numerous and sometimes noteworthy literary, historical, morphological, even psychoanalytical studies), still today there seems to prevail a certain reluctance to acknowledge the significance of the pervasiveness of the mythical mode in the Platonic discourse. What seems to prevail, in other words, is a reluctance rigorously to pursue this ubiquity and reckon with its exquisitely philosophical implications. Then again, to do this would not simply modify the horizon of Platonic exegesis, the way we understand the Platonic text, but would rather alter the way in which we understand the horizon(s) disclosed by this text, the very task and orientation of philosophy itself—even ourselves.

In accord with what is said in the *Timaeus,* one of the central hypotheses underlying the present work is that myth (imaginal discourse) is the speaking of becoming, of what comes to be and passes away—in brief, *of life*. Such a genitive must be heard in its duplicity. On the one hand, myth gives itself as the discourse most appropriately addressing and articulating the theme of life. On the other hand, myth belongs to life—through myth life articulates itself and speaks.

Heraclitus said that "φύσις, nature the emerging, loves to hide." The question of life in its endless recurrence (in its generation and regeneration), the riddle that life is, seems to withdraw from language, hardly to lend itself to adequate formulation, only seldom and ephemerally allowing itself to be illuminated in discourse—seldom, to be sure, and especially in those modes of discourse more than others resembling gestures, movements, or singing, more than others drawing trajectories through the world. There appears to be a profound, if mysterious, intimacy between the cryptic emerging of life and the speaking of μῦθος. As if μῦθος (the ποίησις that μῦθος is) were a figure of life (the ποίησις that γένεσις is) or if, more precisely, μῦθος qua figure would be life's demand. The poetico-mythical dimension of the dialogue on the πολιτεία, thus, turns out to accompany the present discussion in oblique ways, less as the object of explicit analyses than as that, the attunement to which uniquely unveils and exposes otherwise inaccessible facets of the problem of becoming.

The focus on becoming in its exuberance and excess leads, in turn, to the emergence of a further related theme, namely, that of conflict and, more pointedly, of war. Alone, the concern with war pervasive in the Platonic dialogue, if scarcely studied, would warrant, in fact, call for an attunement to this motif and its thematization. But more importantly, as Heraclitus also intimated, there seems to be an essential connection between the broad configuration of becoming and the figure of war. In the course of the present inquiry, broaching the genetic question literally necessitated a polemic turn. For, as the discussion of life revolved around the issues of metamorphosis, dynamism, instability, and hence around the decay (the dying) inherent in the living, it became increasingly pressing to distinguish the destructiveness belonging in the cycles and revolutions of life from the destructiveness alternatively designated as evil, as violence, or even as disaster. This interrogation of war, then, made it possible to elaborate on the distinction between, on the one hand, the dying away that occurs as a mode of regeneration and, on the other hand, devastation in its barrenness, disconnected from the order of recurrence and preservation. Above all, such an orientation simultaneously casts light on the necessity and utter difficulty of this distinction.

For, indeed, along what lines is this difference to be captured and defined? What is the relation of war to the apparently ever-same cycle of life, death, and rebirth? Is war to be seen as that uniquely traumatic event shattering the order of the living, as that offense to life, that violation of its circularity perpetrated by an animal grown accustomed to standing erect, pointing skyward? Or is war to be counted among the countless ways in which this world, the locus of life, periodically undergoes unspeakable shocks and upheavals? Does war merely reflect, maybe even imitate, the natural outbursts and disasters throwing the world off balance? While these outbursts, at times characterized by extreme violence, in their very randomness disrupt the order of nature, they are recognized as belonging to nature. The inscrutable operation of random destruction, with no apparent finality other than itself, seems to belong in nature no less than its laws. The question would still stand, however, concerning this peculiarly human imitation, this imitation of nature which war would be. On the ground of what understanding of nature would such simulation take place? Or would humans mimic the ways of the world in the way children do, enraptured and absorbed in their playing? Such questions would lead one to wonder about the broader issue of the relation between humans and nature, of the place of humans in nature. More broadly still, one would be led to wonder about the place of intelligence (of νοῦς) in nature, in this world. This inquiry would unfold according to the underlying concern with the meaning and concatenation of terms such as cosmos, nature, life, animation—and the significance they have for a dialogue on the πολιτεία and on the just.

The Platonic text articulates the question of life or conflict by letting life or conflict shine through its own unfolding—by letting itself be the place of such shining. In a dialogico-theatrical fashion, that is, already, mythically, the text unfolds (as) the discourse of philosophy and simultaneously lets γένεσις speak through such discourse, showing the belonging of such discourse in γένεσις and its discourse. It reveals philosophical discourse as an inherently mythical matter, in its utterly singular enactment, dynamic character, and performative power.

Coming to terms with the dramatic-genetic dimension of the dialogues in its strictly philosophical relevance means, among other things, thoroughly questioning the assumption of a unitary, coherent doctrine resulting from the Platonic corpus. If the dramatic context does indeed affect the argumentative articulation in each dialogue, the doctrinal outcome of each conversation cannot have the value of a purely theoretical stance. The positions resulting from a dialogical exchange will never have been theses, stable propositions transferable from one context to the other and forming the coherent whole of Platonic philosophy. Rather, the developments and results of philosophical engagement prove to be inseparable from its conditions, material and otherwise.[8] Such are, rigorously drawn, the implications of the drama of philosophy, of philosophy as drama. It is also because of this that, in the present study, other dialogues are brought to bear on the *Republic* only occasionally and in a marginal fashion.[9]

Far from the impassible sequence of abstract formulations, the *Republic*, both the Platonic text on the πολιτεία and the community of inquiry, the πολιτεία therein envisioned, gives itself in its tumultuous, conflicted tentativeness—as a living, vibrant, even torn exercise in passing away.

Sunoptikón

Before laying out a schematic preview of the forthcoming discussion, a few remarks are in order concerning the proleptic text (*Proleptikón*). Strictly speaking without a title, outside the work proper, indeed, already there, anticipating the work, configuring the space in which the work will have taken place—this text should perhaps be understood as an attuning preparation. Although in a loosely digressive and fragmentary fashion, these preparatory remarks revolve around the opening pages of Book VII, that is, the discourse of the cave. This image, the womb from which the dialogue seems to have been expelled, will have occasioned the notes preparing the inception of the present work.[10]

An attuning ground is already there when something like an inquiry is to begin. Already there, inappropriable in its operation—the fecund, dark ground, the cave from which a primal image, like a sparkle, is released. Just as Socrates' elaborations in Book VII rest on Glaukon's ability to refer back to the image evoked, to imagine and envision it, to be attuned to and by it, so the study here introduced rests on the proleptic material preceding it.

Before beginning the discussion of the text, one will already have been speaking from within the text. One will have begun to prepare (for) the beginning of a discussion on the dialogue on the πολιτεία by finding oneself at the heart of this dialogue already—there, in its midst, speaking out of its navel (ὀμφαλός).

The themes broached in the proleptic pages are all extensively pursued and amplified in the ensuing work: the question of translation, transition, and conversation between utterly discontinuous and yet inseparable worlds (the visible and the invisible); the problem of the imaginal and mooded character of discourse and the subsequent question concerning the status of analogy; the issue of the manifold self-differing of life and the way in which the language of γένεσις (of motion and resistance, flow and rigor, change and fixation) can shed light on the structure of life in the πόλις (on the somewhat antagonistic interplay of δόξα-sophistry, on the one hand, and philosophy, on the other).[11] These and related questions, only pointed to in the *Proleptikón*, will in the present work receive a more thorough treatment. But attempting to find in the preparatory segment the traits of an introduction in the strict sense of the word would be in vain. That text is not an introduction in disguise. It does not in an orderly fashion lay out the themes later to be discussed, nor does it systematically anticipate or frame what is to come. The notes collected outside the work set the tone and the mood for what is to come. That they proceed less in the mode of argument than in that of performance—that they gesture, speak suggestively, by indirection—is far from being accidental, let alone a matter of authorial strategy. Indeed, it has to do with the impervious character of beginning as such.

The work whose inception is thus prepared, let it finally be pointed out, does not primarily focus on the central books of the dialogue. It does acknowledge the concentric structure of the dialogue; in fact, while mainly concentrating on the outer circle of Books I and X, it also analyzes at some length the more internal circle constituted by Books III–V and VIII. However, it does not provide a sustained or explicit thematization of Books VI–VII.[12] Only near the end, when a few suggestions are ventured concerning the intertwinement of justice, the good, and necessity, are the reflections on the good at the heart of the dialogue briefly addressed.

The text is subdivided into two parts. In the first part ("'Old women telling tales' [350e]: The City in View, the City Envisioned," Chapters I–II) the issue of generation is developed especially in its political implications, that is to say, in its significance with respect to the πόλις—the πόλις already in view and the πόλις imaginatively brought forth.

In Chapter I ("On Regeneration"), through an analysis of the inception of the dialogue, the issue of the possibility of regeneration in and of the πόλις is broached. The genetico-physiological metaphor is articulated here, already and unavoidably, in political terms. Indeed, the language of γένεσις will not have been brought to bear on the political sphere for merely heuristic or explanatory reasons. The language of γένεσις will not have been *applied* to the political, while at the same time constituting an essentially autonomous domain. On the contrary, it is crucial to understand that the language of γένεσις, that language in and through which γένεσις comes to mirror itself (to reflect on itself), will have been essentially *of the* πόλις—it will have belonged to it, spoken out of it, spoken of it, already.[13] It is such physio-logical and logo-political τόπος that the philosopher inhabits, with effects at once destabilizing and reviving.

Chapter II ("The Law of [Re]production") discusses Socrates' founding of the just city "in speech." In doing so, it underlines the aspiration to immobility which the Socratic elaboration paradoxically shares with the doxastic discourses it tries to deactivate. To be sure, whereas the doxastic fixation occurs through the unreflective confirmation of custom, the philosophical desire for stability manifests itself, quite distinctively, as the striving for eidetic purity. But a certain resistance to (and even denial of) the truth of becoming is common to both. This chapter exposes, in the first place, the Socratic preoccupation around issues of creation and procreation—his concern with the production of poetry as well as citizens and his systematic attempt to regularize both productive modes. However, Socrates also (and quite decisively) acknowledges the problems involved in such a founding and regulative approach to generation. Indeed, not only does it become apparent that the horizon of becoming eludes calculation, but, furthermore, it turns out that the just city cannot be preserved (cannot be separated) from the decay that such horizon ineluctably prescribes. Secondly, then, this chapter examines the implications of the impossibility of eidetic purity (i.e., separation) with regard to the question of justice.

The second part ("'A tale was saved and not lost' [621b]: Vision at the End of the Visible," Chapters III–VI) is dedicated to the analysis of the myth of Er in Book X, although, in all likelihood, its findings constitute only a propaedeutic to an encounter with this text of formidable difficulty. Here the exquisitely political concerns of the first part are taken up again and situated in the psycho-cosmological context of the myth. Life, invoked in its resurfacing (Chapter I) and disclosed as unmasterable (Chapter II), is "accounted for" in the final myth. In presenting the movement of souls (whose ἔργον, work, is ζῆν, living [353d]), the myth unfolds the circulation and self-regeneration of life. It is the story of souls envisioned and narrated by a soul. It results from the undergoing of a soul—analogously to the dialogue itself, which is narrated in its entirety by

Socrates the day after. A crucial issue discussed in this part of the work is the connection between war and the in(de)terminable recurrence of life, of life's cycles and returns. While the myth (and, perhaps, the philosophical passion it images) emerges as a kind of ψυχομαχία, it becomes pressing to investigate its relation to πόλεμος.

In Chapter III ("Preliminary Remarks in a Rhapsodic Form"), a few introductory reflections are put forth concerning the character of the ἀπόλογος of Er and the specific traits distinguishing the Socratic μυθολογεῖν from other modes of poetizing. Such a distinction is, to begin with, attempted on the ground of Socrates' arguments concerning poetry and the lie of μίμησις (especially those taking place in Books III and X). But, as becomes apparent in the course of this investigation, Socrates' own myth, too, is not free from the moment of lie and blindness he attributes paradigmatically to epic and dramatic poetry. It would seem, then, that a characterization of the Socratic narration in its exquisitely unique traits cannot be carried out on purely speculative, doctrinal premises. Rather, in following very closely the many turns of the Socratic reflection on this issue, it becomes clear that the distinctive feature of poetic utterance is less a matter of whether or not it harbors within itself the obscuring imitative element than a matter of the *comportment* adopted toward such element (which, indeed, appears to be ineludible).

Chapter IV ("War") is devoted to the theme of conflict. After all, the myth begins with the mention of Er who "died in war" (ἐν πολέμῳ). This image, furthermore, reflects a concern with war that manifests itself quite pervasively throughout the dialogue. The term "war" is in this context used equivocally, in part on the ground of the broad semantic range covered by the term πόλεμος and in part on the ground of Socrates' own loose terminological choices. At times it indicates the realm of becoming as a whole, according to a usage ranging from Heraclitus's saying on πόλεμος as the πατήρ and βασιλεύς of all to Proclus's remarks on γένεσις as the place of combat and tumult (*In Remp.*, I:17 f.). At other times it is used to indicate one of the modes of becoming, of its dynamic unfolding. In this sense it coincides with the broad domain of conflict, disagreement, contest, strife, faction (with the language of ἀγών, ἔρις, στάσις). The specifically discursive ἀγών would, on this account, be a mode of war in this general sense. At yet other times the term is used to name war proper, warfare, whose exclusive τέλος is destruction and termination. In this narrower sense, conversely, war appears to be a specific mode of conflict, of ἀγών—in fact, the most extreme one. War, strictly understood, is shown to be at once the apotheosis of motion and motivated by a deeply rooted (and twofold) resistance to motion. It appears to be that extreme agitation whose end is the stillness following the fulfillment of destruction, and whose origin is connected with the resistance (to movement and transformation) accompanying the institution of identity—whether psychological or political. In this chapter war is considered according to this broad range of signification and in its intertwinement with other modes of antagonism. Ultimately the various forms of conflict can be discerned in terms of their teleological orientations, ranging from utter destruction to deactivation, disempowerment, displacement, destabilization.

Chapters V and VI ("Vision," "[Re]birth"), with which the second part concludes, are dedicated to the journey to "a certain daimonic place" which Er is said to have narrated when he "came back to life." In particular, Chapter V analyzes the initial stages of the journey, in which what lies after death is articulated through images of fantastic brilliance. Chapter VI, on the other hand, discusses the moment of blindness, the utterly inappropriable interruption of vision at the heart of (re)birth—of the coming (back) into the light.

Vision in death, blindness in life, then—again, the question of the intertwinement of visibility and invisibility. Indeed, a blindness so radical that not even the one in whose narration death has become the locus of a wondrous imaginal proliferation utters a word about it. He may, at most, indicate it.

It's life that we don't understand, not death. This seems to be the indication of the myth. Far from fully illuminating the dark ground and accompaniment of the shining of life, this myth shows the shining of life pervaded by darkness, shows this shining in its mystery. The coming back of life and to life is not, cannot be, purely of light and to light—not even in myth.

Notes

1. Julia Annas, *An Introduction to Plato's* Republic (Oxford: Clarendon 1981), p. 349.

2. Ibid., p. 353.

3. Ibid., p. 252.

4. Ibid., p. 353.

5. On the nonrepresentational, nontransparent character of the specifically Platonic language, see Philip Merlan's "Form and Content in Plato's Philosophy," *Journal of the History of Ideas* 8, no. 1 (1947), pp. 406–30. One here would want to say of language as such what Merlan says of the Platonic idiom alone: "we shall have to insist also that the relation between Plato's philosophical truth and his written works is not the direct relation of content and form of communication. As far as essentials are concerned Plato explicitly denies the possibility of such a direct communication" (p. 429). On the connection between the imaginal-mythical thickness of language and the modality of reading, Merlan points out: "The more profound a myth, the more burning is our desire to understand it properly; but at the same time it becomes more and more doubtful whether we can interpret it at all and whether we shall ever be able to understand it properly. Plato's myths stimulate us. We listen attentively because we dimly imagine that if we

could interpret them, we should gain rich instruction. But we listen in vain; the only instruction we receive is the instruction how to listen attentively. Who would undertake the task of reducing to a sober and unambiguous doctrine the myth according to which our souls, before their fall, contemplated the forms of truth in a transcelestial region?" (p. 411).

6. On the embrace of myth, founding and enveloping the evolutions of λόγος, see Aristotle, *Metaphysics* Λ 8. At this crucial stage, immediately after declaring that "there is only one heaven" and before examining the aporetics of νοῦς, Aristotle puts forth a remarkable reflection that deserves to be quoted in full. "The ancients of very early times" (παρὰ τῶν ἀρχαίων καὶ παμπαλαίων), he says, "bequeathed to posterity in the form of a myth (ἐν μύθου σχήματι) a tradition that the heavenly bodies are gods and that the divinity encompasses the whole of nature (περιέχει τὸ θεῖον τὴν ὅλην φύσιν). The rest of the tradition has been added later as a means of persuading the masses and as something useful for the laws and for matters of expediency; for they say that these gods are like humans in form and like some of the other animals, and also other things which follow from or are similar to those stated. But if one were to separate from the later additions the first point and attend to this alone (namely, that they thought the first substances to be gods), one might realize that this was divinely spoken and that, while probably every art and every philosophy has often reached a stage of development as far as it could and then again has perished, these opinions (δόξας) about the gods were saved like relics up to the present day. Anyway, the opinion of our forefathers and of the earliest thinkers is evident to us only to this extent" (1074b1 ff.). (H. G. Apostle's translation was consulted, though not reproduced unaltered [Grinnell, Iowa: Peripatetic, 1966].) Notice how, in this passage, the motif of myth is intertwined with the dialectical strand of Aristotle's argumentation and with his alertness to hermeneutic-archeological difficulties.

7. This cluster of issues is consistently, if strangely, missed even by authors whose work, in other respects, so remarkably challenges the assumptions underlying the Western philosophical lineages. See (and this is only an instance) Philippe Lacoue-Labarthe and Jean-Luc Nancy's "The Nazi Myth," *Critical Inquiry* 16 (1990), pp. 291–312, in which the opening remarks on Plato, in spite (or because?) of their brevity, play a somewhat grounding role with respect to the later arguments. (Incidentally, this is a ubiquitous practice in the history of Western philosophy, whereby cursory references to the "Platonic" heritage function as the backdrop of later discussions—an enabling backdrop against which these discussions measure themselves, whether claiming to confirm or to transgress it.) In acknowledging the fact that Socrates never purely excludes myth and that, in fact, myth plays a fundamental role in the founding of the city, the authors keep treating myth as "an instrument of *identification*," "*the* mimetic instrument par excellence" (p. 298). The hypothesis that will be put forth here proposes instead that myth will never have been utilizable as an instrument (let alone as an instrument of identification), that myth as such does in fact disallow any program of identification (cultural, political, or otherwise), and that the text on the πολιτεία quite clearly *shows* this—albeit in spite of itself, of its attempts, and of its claims. This will be discussed especially in Chapter II.

However, it should be underlined already that a position which, like that of Lacoue-Labarthe and Nancy, overlooks the shaking, displacing, and transgressive character of myth, the impossibility of simply appropriating myth, mastering it, and setting it to work, a position which does not move beyond the analysis of Socrates' attempts at subjecting myth (attempts called "Platonic orthopedics"), as if this were the ultimate result of the philosopher's conflictual relation to myth—such a position entails (among other things) two related corollaries. In the first place, it establishes a certain continuity between the Platonic reflection and the "German tradition" (in classical philology, aesthetics, historical anthropology, and so on), even the Nazi ideology itself (p. 298). Secondly, this position ends up being perfectly consistent with the assessment of Plato characterizing such ("German") tradition and such ideology. Concerning the first issue, that of continuity: the privileging of λόγος attributed to Plato and the preference for μῦθος at the heart of Nazism (a preference that ends up being as instrumental and centered around λόγος as the position ascribed to Plato) amount, in the final analysis and at least on a formal level, to the same. For it is only on the ground of a priority of λόγος that the willful mastery over μῦθος could at all be envisioned and the poietic power of μῦθὸς turned into a technology. The alleged opposition of μῦθος and λόγος, thus, turns out to be no opposition at all, but a figure of assimilation or subjection. This much is acknowledged by Lacoue-Labarthe and Nancy as well. Indeed, the Nazi ideologues construe ancient philosophy (paradigmatically Plato) as their antithesis on the side of λόγος (the opponent to be vanquished by resorting to the resource of μῦθος) and simultaneously themselves repeat what they project upon antiquity thus constructed, namely, a certain "repression" of myth (p. 298)—for programmatically turning myth, even "mysticism," into deliberate self-assertion and self-enforcement constitutes a form of repression, if not plain extinction. Which leads to the second issue, regarding the consistency between Nancy and Lacoue-Labarthe's position and what they call the "German tradition": in these contexts, invariably, Plato is rendered as the thinker whose exemplary "cleanly drawn opposition" between μῦθος and λόγος (p. 297) and expulsion-instrumentalization (thanks to the privileging of λόγος) of μῦθος have to be "overturned" (to use Nietzsche's expression) or deconstructed. However, it would seem that an attempt at beginning to read Plato otherwise, as the Platonic corpus itself would require, would not be irrelevant to anyone setting out to understand the dynamics and inner logic of Nazism in its mytho-technological striving—especially if by Nazism one, following Nancy and Lacoue-Labarthe, does not designate "a past aberration" but a trait that "belongs profoundly to the mood or character of the West in general" (p. 312). Indeed, to attribute to Plato the simple opposition λόγος–μῦθος and the privileging of λόγος without any further qualification implies (1) reenacting the ideological operation by which an opponent is literally created in order to be deposed (i.e., is determined ad hoc, for rhetorical purposes) and (2) failing essentially to question such ideological framework. For a closer reading of Plato would reveal that *there* is no simple opposition between λόγος and μῦθος (even in terms of linguistic usage the two words are more often than not employed interchangeably) and that μῦθος, far from being the disposable counterpart of λόγος, shakes the order of λόγος and exceeds the very horizon of the opposition—with immense consequences for the task and character of philosophy. This much, nothing less, is at stake in reading Plato. On this question, see also Lacoue-Labarthe's *Typography: Mimesis, Philosophy, Politics* (Cambridge, Mass.: Harvard University Press, 1989), pp. 63–108 and passim.

8. This is emphasized throughout the present work, as is clear, e.g., from the resonance accorded to the dramatic setting in Chapter I or from the emphasis on the negotiations between Socrates and Glaukon in Chapter IV.

9. The references to other Platonic texts mostly occur in the footnotes, in order to

keep the main text focused on the *Republic*. At times, however, when a passage from another dialogue requires particular attention, its discussion is integrated within the main text. Because of the nature of the work that follows, references to secondary literature appear exclusively in the notes. This is far from unusual, even in classical philological works. In the context of philosophical exegesis there are authors who, strategically proceeding by indirection and relying less on the confrontation with other commentators than on the performative dimension of their own textual approach, almost completely suppress secondary references even in the footnotes (see figures as diverse as, e.g., Leo Strauss or Luce Irigaray). The stance reflected in this study is not nearly as extreme. However, the mention of scholarly contributions tends to be selective in character and mostly citational in function (i.e., theses exposed by other scholars are only seldom explicitly laid out and evaluated).

10. Like dark ink or the hollowness (privation, subtraction) of a carved tablet, the obscure womb is that through which, thanks to which, writing occurs. But to say this does not mean to think the womb as matter, as the potentiality of matter understood within the horizon of its opposition (and subjection) to a formal principle. That which effects the writing is not an external agent, a separate form-giving principle operating on matter from a distance. Rather, this effecting, this acting, still belong in the womb. As Giorgio Agamben, by reference to an image found in the *Suda* under the rubric of Aristotle, puts it: "The ink, the drop of darkness with which thought writes, is thought itself" ("Bartleby o della contingenza," in G. Deleuze and G. Agamben, *Bartleby: la formula della creazione* [Macerata: Quodlibet, 1993], p. 50, my translation). In this brief text, Agamben compellingly weaves together the themes of possibility, writing, and creation.

11. Motion and resistance, flow and rigor, change and fixation: these are not simply couples of opposites. Indeed, there is nothing simple to what is designated by these terms and to their dynamic, conflictual relation. With respect to γένεσις, each one of these terms presents a twofold significance. As will be suggested in the course of the proleptic discourse, in its many modes movement is of life just as it is of death, engendering just as it is dissolving. The same can be said of resistance and of each term in the remaining two pairs—at the limit, it can be said even of life and death. By analogy, this can be brought to bear on the pair of philosophy and δόξα-sophistry.

12. The readings of these books, most notably of the issue of the "divided line," developed by John Sallis (*Being and Logos: The Way of Platonic Dialogue* [Atlantic Highlands, N.J.: Humanities, 1986]) and Hermann L. Sinaiko (*Love, Knowledge and Discourse in Plato: Dialogue and Dialectic in* Phaedrus, Republic, Parmenides [Chicago: University of Chicago Press, 1965] and *Reclaiming the Canon: Essays on Philosophy, Poetry, and History* [New Haven: Yale University Press, 1998]) constitute definitive contributions on the subject and were a constant point of reference in the elaboration of this project.

13. Γένεσις may not be a matter of language, but γένεσις's self-mirroring or self-reflection is.

Proleptikón

At the heart of the dialogue on the πολιτεία Socrates addresses Glaukon as follows:

> Image, by likening (ἀπείκασον) it to a condition (πάθει) such as this, our nature (φύσιν) in its education and want of education. See (ἰδὲ) human beings (ἀνθρώπους) as though they were in an underground cavelike dwelling (ἐν καταγείῳ οἰκήσει σπηλαιώδει) with its entrance, a long one, open to the light (φῶς) across the whole width of the cave. (514a)[1]

Book VII begins with this twofold request—with the request of a double imaginative exercise. Glaukon is, in the first place, asked to form an image of our φύσις by reference to a certain condition, to a certain experience, namely, the experience of human beings in an underground dwelling. But *even before* forming an image of our φύσις, and in order to be able to do so, he has to envision the underground setting, to see the image of this dwelling in which a certain condition is undergone, to bring this vision forth—as strange as it may seem to him.[2]

It is, then, from out of and through this vision, thanks to the comparison with this image he has envisioned, that Glaukon can form the image of our nature. The envisioning of the cave, the lighting of the dark density of the ground (indeed, of the underground), the imaging of the otherwise inherently invisible receptacle, has a somewhat originary, originating character.

The envisioning encouraged by Socrates is not simply the seeing of a setting. Indeed, that which Glaukon should see and to which he should liken his image of our nature is a πάθος, that is, the experience of *life* in the cave. What Glaukon is asked to see (εἴδω), then, is essentially a condition, a kind of mood, an affection. The envisioning here at stake is not the envisioning of anything visual or visible. It is from out of the imagination of the imageless πάθος that the image of "our nature" may emerge.

The imaging of the cavelike dwelling and of its inhabitants is the medium through which the invisible is evoked. The visible, imaginal vessel carries the invisible with(in) itself. Indeed, a mood pervades and accompanies such imaging, is called forth and kindled by it. The image of the cave, then, is brought forth so that the invisible accompanying it may be indicated, a certain mood imagined, envisioned—that is to say, also, experienced. Such is the meaning of the seeing of a πάθος. Seeing a πάθος means experiencing the experience that πάθος is. "Seeing a πάθος" suggests a shift from vision as the act of seeing to vision as being seen—being affected, acted upon. Though such seeing by no means entails an undifferentiated con-fusion between experiencing and the experience experienced, it makes it arduous to think of vision as observation, as the contemplation from a distance whose self-contained, detached, and unaffected character would precisely allow for the corresponding isolation (that is to say, for the conceptual determination) of its object as such. (The possibility of conceptualization seems to be intimately and ultimately connected with a history of isolation and distance, of solitude, of interdependent solitudes . . .)[3]

This seeing, rather, means being in (experiencing) a certain mood, letting a mood come over one. Such a conclusion appears to be, among other things, in keeping with the crucial insight concerning the primacy of perception in its utterly passive character—that is, concerning the founding and simultaneously inappropriable character of sensibility.[4] Indeed, following through with the insight regarding the radically affective and receptive ground of experience involves recognizing the impossibility of a purely conceptual reduction of it, of subsuming it under categorial headings. Most importantly, according to this insight experience (the fundamental undergoing thus named), besides eluding the purely conceptual grasp, constitutes the primordially attuning, ineffably structuring environment of the conceptual effort.[5] This can be said even of the experience of vision, of seeing—this least sensible among the senses, this sense whose symbolism and terminology has systematically been borrowed to indicate conceptual procedures (the language of speculation, reflection, intellectual contemplation *is* the language of vision). It can be said especially of the vision of the invisible, of the seeing of a mood.

This seeing which attunes, this being in a certain mood, is what orients Glaukon's making of an image of "our nature," that to which he has to liken this image. Such a seeing is *decisive* with respect to the image-making. The movement of self-reflection (the presentation of "our nature"), far from occurring as self-representation, develops according to the uncertain indications of an imaging informed by (likened to) a mood. Such is the originary, originating, engendering character of mood. (But, again, the informing mood is in its turn called forth through an image—the primal image, namely, that of the cave.)

A primal image comes forth as if inhabited by the invisible—or, even, as if wrapped up in the invisible, surrounded by *this* invisible as if by an aura, stirring up a kind of tremor around itself in its appearing. According to this tremor, in the likeness of this invisibility, another image is made. But the structure of this intertwinement of visible and invisible raises numerous problems. For how is one to understand the transition and conversation between visible and invisible, this conversion from one to the other and back, this passage (passing) and this translation? How can the invisible be evoked or released through the visible? How can the invisible be the measure for the making of an image, indeed, of an image in its likeness? And, finally, what would likeness to the invisible mean? These questions are connected with the crucial issue of analogy and deserve a pause.[6]

The foregoing remarks imply a twofold range of consequences. First of all, the relation between the visible and the invisible comes to present itself as other than a simple opposition. Indeed, the undeniable contrast indicated by the two terms ends up assuming rather the character of a complex intertwinement, of the strange intertwinement of orders radically other to one another. Such intertwinement would have to be thought as an interdependence without correspondence or reciprocity—as the being bound together of orders that do not dissolve *in* and do not become commensurable *through* such bind. Secondly, then, the visible and the invisible thus bound together present themselves to thinking as essentially other than the categories of the sensible and the intelligible. Indeed, to the extent that it is the structure of a hierarchically organized opposition which essentially defines the relation between the sensible and the intelligible, and to the extent that it is within and in virtue of such structure that these categories are endowed with meaning, the visible and the invisible intertwined with one another in the way suggested above come to indicate a relation radically irreducible to the polarity of sensibility and intelligibility.

Suggesting the equiprimordiality, the interdependence, of visible and invisible and, furthermore, understanding the visible and the invisible according to the logic of a receptivity preceding (that is, exceeding) all logic make it difficult to secure the parallelism of analogy to a system of proportional calculation. Because none of the terms of the analogy is granted the privilege of priority, and because of the somewhat fleeting character of the terms involved, the ground and point of reference necessary to establish analogy as a calculable correspondence appears to be lacking. This, of course, opens up the possibility of an understanding of analogy less in terms of mathematical proportion than in terms of poetic simile and of the indicative, evocative force belonging to it. (Or this may even disclose the possibility for the interpretation of proportion itself, as well as of arithmetics and mathematics, beyond the horizon of pure calculation.)

Of course, one might wonder what remains of analogy when visible and invisible are thought of in this way, in a movement away from the hierarchized dichotomy of sensibility and intelligibility. One might ask what analogy has come to signify here, in the context of this discussion which (in abandoning the founding dichotomy and dichotomy tout court) seems purely to disfigure the terms on which analogy rests. But perhaps such a question is ill conceived and essentially flawed in its formulation. The issue at stake is not so much what, in following this line of reasoning, might remain of analogy, that is, of the assumption, inference, and calculation of an isomorphism between two or more items.[7] Rather, at stake is the origin, the formation of the procedure of analogy and the extent to which the strictly logical understanding of analogy may itself be what remains of a long and tortuous (hi)story. If anything, then, it would be analogy in its rigorously logical determination which would have to be considered as the mutilated fragment of a heritage sent across measureless distances and unfathomable temporal depths. In this sense, far from involving the protection of the conceptuality of analogy from that which a rigorously responsive reading may awaken in the ancient text and free, the task at hand might demand precisely pursuing the question concerning what analogy could have primordially indicated.[8] The possible deformation and disarticulation of the conceptuality of analogy through an encounter with the Greek text should be seen, even in its destructive traits, as a way of addressing the need for a deepening and a transformation in the understanding of what all too frequently goes without thinking.[9]

The words Socrates utters after the primal image has been brought to full fruition, too, call for a certain caution around the issue of analogy and warn against hasty conceptual appropriations of it. In urging Glaukon finally to realize the correspondence between that which has been envisioned and "our nature," Socrates variously underlines the epistemic fragility of his discourse and the role that desire plays in the conversation taking place:

> Well, then, dear Glaukon . . . this image as a whole must be connected with what was said before, likening (ἀφομοιοῦντα) the domain revealed through sight to the prison home, and the light of the fire in it to the sun's power; and, in applying the ascending upwards (ἄνω ἀνάβασιν) and the seeing of what is above (θέαν τῶν ἄνω) to the soul's journey up (ἄνοδον) to the noetic place (νοητὸν τόπον), you'll not mistake my expectation (ἐλπίδος), since you desire (ἐπιθυμεῖς) to hear it. A god doubtless knows (οἶδεν) whether it happens to be true. At all events, this is the way phenomena appear (φαινόμενα . . . φαίνεται) to me. (517a–b)

Immediately after these considerations, once the analogy between the underground world and this world has been granted thanks to the converging of both interlocutors' desires, Socrates proceeds to articulate his reflections on the good in the realm of the knowable. It is in the admission of such a correspondence, in the desirous agreement concerning this analogy, that the subsequent elaboration on the "idea" of the good is grounded. Such is the constructive and grounding (constitutive and institutive) force of analogy.

Philosophy, in this light, comes to resemble an analogical machinery. Yet, analogy appears to be sustained by desire, and not inherently and autonomously normative. Far from being otherwise secured, the analogical concordance, with its grounding and constructive power, is brought about through an accord of desires. This coming together of yearnings is that which surrounds, contains, and sustains the formulation of analogy and the subsequent conjectures that analogy grounds (i.e., the late fruits that analogy bears). The effectiveness of analogy basically rests on an analogy of longings, on an attunement of passions. This attunement (accord, concord, the analogy before analogy) is that in virtue of which analogical (philosophical) discourse can be ventured. This agreement, this coming together of desires, this desire to agree is that which allows for all bringing and joining together in analogy. The ground of analogy and its primordial essence is harmony, a coming together, a resonating of directions and strivings.[10]

Thus, according to the Socratic discourse, the institution of analogy takes place in the broader field informed by the logic of desire. In this context, the establishment of analogy and the articulation this makes possible cannot be a matter of knowledge. Socrates insists on this by delineating a contrast between the knowing (εἰδέναι) of "a god," on the one hand, and the desire bringing together the mortal interlocutors, on the other. Knowledge, rather, possesses a somewhat derivative character with respect to the fundamental experience of being-together. Not only can the divine dimension of knowledge be barely glimpsed by humans, but even this vaguest experience, this most uncertain grasping, is a relatively late fruit of the basic condition defining the being of humans. (Let it also be noticed parenthetically that, before beginning to develop the *idea* of the good, Socrates frames the discourse that is to follow with the proviso that this is the way *phenomena look* to him. The discussion of this most fundamental and strange "idea" is then, in an important sense, comprehended within the field of the appearing of phenomena and unfolded through the language of phenomenality. The insight concerning the highest idea—the invisible cause and governing principle of the intelligible realm as such—will have emerged out of the embrace of appearance.)[11]

❀

Through the mediation of the image of the underground, thanks to this *imaginal, attuning detour,* Socrates reflects on his own situation, brings it, as it were, before his eyes. The image he brings forth at first and the mood that comes over him allow him to catch a glimpse of himself, but not in the mode of quiet self-contemplation, not in the mode of self-representation, not according to that detachment from (transcendence of) self which allows for the constitution of self as the object of observation. Rather, he steals a fleeting vision of himself and his own condition from the advent of the primal image—an advent which, in turn, proceeds from out of him, or at least through him. That is to say, he steals a fleeting image of himself from that image and mood in whose coming into being he is implicated.

In a curiously autoaffective but not autistic Promethean gesture, Socrates gains an insight of himself that is neither purely granted and appropriable nor, evidently, purely inaccessible. This self-reflective insight lies somewhere in between the dream of pure, undisturbed self-reflection and the inarticulable silence of pure coincidence with self, that is, self-absorption. Socrates catches a glimpse of but does not position himself.

The image of the cave, then, makes it possible for Socrates to envision himself—or, better, for those who are involved in the conversation to envision themselves. Socrates himself, according to this envisioning, is primarily one of the many. After all, the image to be brought forth and likened to the πάθος of the primal image is that of "our nature," specifically with respect to "its education and want of education."

Upon experiencing the incipient emergence of the primal image, Glaukon makes manifest his perplexity: "It's a strange . . . image you are speaking of (ἄτοπον . . . λέγεις εἰκόνα), and strange prisoners." Socrates replies: "They are like (ὁμοίους) us" (515a), insisting on an analogy, on some kind of correspondence between the image he has brought forth (an image "without a place") and "our φύσις," that is, between the inhabitants of the underground world and "us." It is in the likeness of the image of that πάθος undergone in the cave, and through such likening, that "our nature" is at all imaged.

What characterizes the strange life of the many both in the cave and in the organism of the πόλις seems to be a certain being bound. More specifically, it seems to be a certain inability to turn around, a powerlessness with respect to movement, to a dynamic connection with the surroundings. There is a rigor, a stiffness, a staticity to their existence. They lack the δύναμις of κίνησις. More specifically, in the cave the many are in bonds, immobilized and "unable to

turn . . . their heads in a circle" (κύκλῳ δὲ τὰς κεφαλας . . . ἀδυνάτους περι-
άγειν) (514a). Analogously, in the πόλις the many are bound to given structures
and directions, compelled to conform to them, and lack the ability, the power,
to move freely beyond the bounds of the given, to wander astray and away from
communal demands.[12]

But the primal image does not simply mirror the structure of life within the
πόλις. Indeed, it also suggests an analogous structure at the level of the ψυχή.
The inability to move, which is somewhat promoted by environmental, sys-
temic dynamics, is not a purely external and contingent difficulty undergone by
the ψυχή. (One needs only to think, in an anticipatory fashion, about a decisive
clue provided by the text later, about the reluctance to move displayed by the
freed prisoner, the disorientation and the discomfort experienced by the prisoner when compelled to get up and walk.) The ψυχή in some way structurally
corresponds to that which it undergoes, to the world (the organism) in which it
participates.[13] In some way, the ψυχή is structured by what it undergoes while
simultaneously contributing to and structuring it. The ψυχή also crucially
shapes the conditions and circumstances of its own undergoing, that is, of the
world. In this way, then, the πόλις and the ψυχή belong together. These layered,
complex structures are held together by a bond of mutual determination, that is
to say, of complicity. The πόλις and the ψυχή are ciphers of one another. And
so are, primordially and essentially, politics and psychology. (Yet another articulation of the intertwinement of the visible and the invisible.)

The inability to move characterizing the condition of the prisoners in the cave
mirrors a certain inability to move which essentially belongs in the life of the political organism as well as in the life of the ψυχή. Such inability essentially (if
not exclusively) defines both the communal order of the πόλις and that of the
ψυχή. And it is not simply an incapacity for movement, but also an inability to
be aware of the possibility of movement and of movement in its range of possibilities. It is a kind of blindness, a condition due to eyes overfull with what is actually before them, to eyes indeed too full, too identified with the direction of
their sight. It is an inability to clear the space and make room, to receive inspiration or be affected by unexplainable presentiments, to attend to the disappearing or the loss accompanying the forced, total absorption in a unique orientation toward the world. It is the disappearing of the bonds themselves
through the identification (complicity) of the prisoner with them. In this way,
what may be denied, hidden, or dissimulated through the absorption in a unique
orientation cannot even become an issue. Such is the force of the totalizing tendency of actuality.

This overfullness, this saturation of the eyes which coincides with fixation, betrays a disquietude concerning emptiness, an inability to tolerate and even heed the void, a drive to exorcise the void. This saturation of the eyes is invoked to counteract, or even to heal and disperse the memory of an ancient *horror vacui*.

The inability to turn the head "in a circle" makes the prisoner unable even to divine the circular motion, to realize its possibility and power, to experience the cycle, the spinning of the wheel, and to situate herself within the embrace of this vast circling movement. Hence the attachment to (and the identification with) a given perspective, a given place and a given relation to the surroundings. Hence, too, the resistance to (and the unthematic but unrelenting denial of) motion and change. A primal, even primitive, sense of satiation makes the prisoners content with the spectacle of movement and unwilling themselves to move. Contentment is, in this sense, impairing. Inability and reluctance, powerlessness and unwillingness, belong together. Everyday routine practices, rituals and doxastic formulas, the psychological compulsion to grasp, to hold on to things, or unreflectively to accept the given and conform to it, are possible images of such tendency to staticity, of this peculiar and almost desperate faithfulness to fixed forms. In its most extreme version, habituation borders on absolute stillness, on a kind of rigor mortis.

And yet, at the same time, a kind of resistance to flux is necessary for anything to come to be, according to its order, to its law and rhythm. Life does not flow in a broad, undifferentiated course. It flows through shapes, forms, and configurations. *As* these shapes, forms, and configurations, it flows. But in order for shapes and forms and configurations to emerge as such, to come to a definite (if momentary) stand, the flow through them cannot be a purely eroding, dissolving, restless passing. Such a flow would have to be imagined as discontinuous and uneven, marked by moments of rest, of lingering, of hesitation. The emergence of any order, of organisms in their articulate and ordered complexity, would occur in a *friction,* in the engendering conflict of motion and the resistance to it, a kind of reluctance simply to move, simply to pass. The articulated and articulating movement of life would be what it is precisely through its divergence from itself, through the countermovement it harbors in its midst. This would be the formal structure of γένεσις, of becoming.

But the difficulty involved in such a statement is extreme. It would take a rather lengthy detour in order to unfold further the strangely twofold character of stillness in its death-bringing as well as life-giving traits and, hence, to consider the play of stillness and motion in light of the question of life. Such a detour is ventured here, with the awareness that this segment of the discourse may be especially, or most markedly, proleptic—indeed, ahead of itself, delineating hypotheses that will only later be examined in their emerging out of the Platonic text.

There is, then, a rigor in the midst of life.[14] The coming to pass of anything takes place between (is delimited by) the radical, ravenous in-stability of flux (movement in its excess, as death-bringing and destructive) and radical, lifeless staticity (both of which appear here as pure abstractions or, better, mysteriously give themselves as abstractions because of their inability to appear). Out of this crossing there unfolds the coming to pass of that which comes and passes. There is a stillness, a suspension, a crystallizing in the midst of mutability, in the flow of γένεϲιϲ and essentially belonging to it. For the realm of γένεϲιϲ is in be-tween—is a frontier, a threshold between worlds, a threshold on which, into which, worlds look.

There appears to be, then, difference at the heart of life, within life. Difference, that is, *from and of* life itself. This is what the light stiffness, the stillness engen-dering life's forms, that is, orders, intimates. The ordering, articulating move-ment of life occurs as a self-differentiating movement—in the flow still prevail-ing, a slight resistance, a hesitation, a momentary rest. Order, the in-forming through and as which life (γένεϲιϲ) unfolds, is born out of this dissymmetrical encounter, out of this dynamic interplay of movement and that which counters it. Order is the flowing in waves, the rippling and shivering of an otherwise smooth, indifferent surface. It is structure, cycle, rhythm, pulsation, and beat. It is the passing, moving stillness of life, the coming into being of what is, the com-ing to a stand while coming to lose it. Order (life): born of difference.

By reference to the realm of becoming, of γένεϲιϲ and γίγνεϲθαι, order has to be understood as the self-articulation of difference, as the orchestration of the self-differing of life, within which organisms (biological, political, or otherwise) emerge in their structural complexity and organization—if momentarily.[15] The realm of becoming is, then, the locus of the *arrangement* of beings, the place in which beings come to be and do not stay—each according to its proper rhythm. The sphere of γένεϲιϲ is the locus in which beings, in their emergence and dis-sipation, are organized, articulated in a polymorphous world.

The ordering (living, articulating) that the world itself is, resembles less a classifying, governing, and disposing of beings according to a fixed, preexisting model than a weaving together, a holding together of that which arises.[16] The ordering of the world would, thus, name the weaving together of beings. Even more precisely, it would name the coming into being of beings in their inter-twinement and as interwoven—it would name beings as weaving themselves with one another in their coming to be, finding their own ways through the tex-ture of the choral emergence into which they weave themselves and which they constitute. World: the intertwinement of beings, the belonging together of the differing, the ordering, the weaving (*ordo, ordiri*) of life, of the living. World (πόλις or ψυχή, κόσμος and hence ζωή—even λόγος, qua gathering) is essentially a matter of ordering. (That the harmony that the world itself is may not be representable, that the law of this ordering may not be calculable in any current sense of the term—this is already intimated by these remarks.)

The world is, thus, ordering—the structuring and ordering which take place at that tenuous threshold between flux and mineralization. At the heart of the world, of the orchestrating of order, of the flowing of life, is a stillness, a stopping of pulse, a freezing. This kind of transient paralysis is nothing extraneous to life. Rather, it is of the essence of life. It agitates the surface. It makes life what it is—a *flowing in shapes* and currents, a *flowing of shapes* and currents, *flowing shapes* and currents.

And yet. The countermovement which, in its intertwinement with the movement it counters, engenders shapes and configurations (i.e., which brings forth beings and is the very coming into being of beings) is not simply the same as the lifeless staticity of shapes persisting and insisting on their own preservation. It is not quite the same as that kind of fixation that paralyzes life, obstructing its flow and forcing it into preestablished patterns, that is, turning life into a permanent or premature withering. The countermovement of life, the momentary stability thanks to which beings come to a stand, the resistance to pure flowing which makes life manifest as ordering, cannot simply be equated with the lethal stiffness paradoxically accompanying the attachment to certain forms of life, with the resistance to transformation and to passing away, with the denial of the eroding flow of life. It cannot be simply reduced to that fixation which does not let (other) life come and does not let (this) life go.

Of course, while the difference distinguishing the engendering countermovement of life from the stiffening resistance bringing death must be preserved, the problematic status of such a distinction cannot be denied. Indeed, the intimacy and kinship between these modes of countering (between these ways of stabilizing), their virtual inseparability, and, moreover, their reversibility into one another make this distinction elusive and its character unclear.

Even the countermovement to and of life, then, is disclosed in its manifoldness, in the multiplicity of its modes.[17] The stability necessary for the emergence of shapes is not quite the same as the obstinate resistance that shapes oppose to the irresistible instability sweeping them away. Beings emerge in a contrast of movements, in a kind of holding back, in the friction of the countering. They are such friction. But the creative, engendering power of the countermovement to life and of life can turn into a stiffening: that is, the countermovement which follows as it resists, which belongs in the movement carrying it away and yields the transient stability of shape, can turn into that resistance which tends to utter staticity, to an obstinacy ceasing to belong in life, indeed, opposing life and falling away from it. Resistance as capacitation, as that which discloses the possibility and potentiality of ordering, can turn into resistance as denial, as rigidity and disorder. The order of life harbors the possibility of that which constricts and obstructs the flow of life.[18]

Thus, that which belongs most essentially to life belongs as essentially to death. Engendering can turn into a deadening—it *is* also a deadening. The fleeting order and just proportion of what is, the rhythm of emerging and passing away, harbors within itself disorder (i.e., the vocation to immutability), the disruption of rhythm, the denial of emerging and passing away.

But the reverting of the order of life into lifeless rigor, the corruption at work making the proportion unjust, the disorder corroding and carving order from within, may not be avoidable. Indeed, it seems to inhere, structurally and in-eluctably, in life. The creative, vital role of transient stability and the lethal, de-structive character of obstinate staticity are at one in such a way that their unity is constituted as dynamic interplay, that is, as movement and in movement.

The moment of lifeless rigor, in turn, is followed by decomposition. What is, having come to a full halt, having secured itself to its shape and hence in a sense accomplished its death, keeps dying in yet another sense—by moving through the agonizing stages of disintegration. The extreme rigor of actuali-zation fulfilled, with its exhaustion of possibilities, in turn meets its fate and becomes one with the disintegrating force of flux, of a certain λύειν (undoing, dissolving). The resisting shape falling away from life, its rotting away, the de-struction and dispersion of its order, are not extraneous to the movement of life. Indeed, through decay and dismemberment room is made, space is cleared, pos-sibilities are freed again.

In this way, then, the ravenous flow of life literally overcomes any and every resistance to transformation, thereby also reinstating (renewing) what was de-stroyed. In this way, life triumphs. This is not simply, however, a triumph over death, but more significantly a triumph of and through death. For, exceeding the countermovement which engenders what is, the ravenous flow is—death. Death-bearing life, in its dissolving flow, un-does its own fruits as it brings them forth, makes them grow through this un-doing, makes them fade away by un-doing their deadly rigor. Life triumphs—as "death-bringing." Such is the ex-tent of the self-differing of life.

❧

The inability to move characterizing the life of the prisoners in the world be-neath mirrors an analogous condition at the political as well as psychological level. Indeed, "an image of our nature in its education and want of education" has to be made in the likeness of the πάθος evoked through the image of the cave, that is, the πάθος defining the life of the underground prisoners.

The domain of the doxastic, of habitual everyday automatisms, of the unreflective acceptance of (and conformity to) the given was mentioned above as the political variation on the theme of the inability to move. It is evident how, in the context of the πόλις, the stability of δόξα is necessary for the constitution of a shared, common space. The stability that δόξα is allows for the coming together of the many into an organic and ordered structure, for the coming into being of the political gathering. Indeed, the constitution of the political space and the stabilization of δόξα are equiprimordial and interdependent occurrences. But, as may be the case, this engendering stability can (does) revert into a resistance to (denial of) life. The shared, common place becomes, then, commonplace. The πόλις as place of disclosure becomes a prison, a place of confinement. The twofold character of habit and δόξα is, thus, disclosed. Δόξα names both an element of stability and the possibility of staticity—it is essential both to the qualified stabilization involved in birth and to the crystallization involved in withering away.[19]

But there is more to the primal image than has been pointed out thus far. The impulse to move breaks through this immobile scene. There is an action taking place in the image envisioned. The primal image is itself an image in movement. A prisoner may be compelled to move, turn his head, and look around. Socrates intimates this possibility very cautiously, simply inviting Glaukon to imagine the release, the relief, and, literally, the return to life that would be experienced if anything of this kind were, "by nature" (φύσει), to happen (515c). How this release from bonds would occur, and what or who would inspire it and bring it about, is not said. But the freeing of the prisoner(s) is clearly linked to the call of the light (or even of its source), above and outside, whose driving force is close to irresistible.[20]

This liberation from bonds is also a kind of λύσις (515c), albeit not in the sense of utter dissolution, but rather of a loosening and setting free. Dragged along the upward way, forced to crawl toward the opening of the cave, the freed prisoner (say, Socrates) would experience utter distress, disorientation—would be overwhelmed by the sudden opening up of unsuspected horizons for the exploration of which neither his eyes nor his limbs would be prepared. Freed, in a sense, against his will, the prisoner is confused and in pain as he undergoes this sudden change in his condition. And yet, in another sense, this event would not be purely extraneous to him, not purely imposed on him by an external agent. Indeed, this event would have happened in virtue of an opening, of a possibility (a readiness) harbored within the crystallized life previously led. This happening would come to pass as that toward which the prisoner has a unique potential and as that through which the prisoner overcomes himself as such, opening up to a possibility that his actual condition could not simply exclude but certainly could not contemplate (admit) either.[21]

"Our φύσις" becomes even more strange. The field of the actual, in which life comes to a lifeless stillness, in which a kind of paralysis allows for the fixation of forms and their insistent duration, is pervaded by the possibility of change and motion. That immobility which manifoldly characterizes "our nature" also enfolds the possibility for its own disruption, possibility tout court, the agitating force that threatens any continuation and continuity and introduces dizziness into the image. Indeed, the possible occurrence of such a destabilization of a given equilibrium would equally be "by nature." It would be experienced as an insuppressible force dragging one away from one's fixed place, imposing the claims of light on one, forcing one to move without beforehand understanding why and how, disclosing life as transition, as passage, as uncanny striving, call, impulsion to follow. "Our nature," in this way, appears to be basically twofold.

The claim of philo-sophy is that which, in an important sense, introduces movement into the image and, thus, sets the image in motion. And yet, in another sense, movement is already taking place there, although in a way which contributes less to a dynamic unfolding of the life in that world than to the preservation of the utterly static, mechanically regular state of affairs. Movement is taking place behind the scenes, as it were. In the cave, indeed, "there is a wall, built like the partitions puppet-handlers (θαυματοποιοῖς) set in front of the human beings and over which they show the puppets (θαύματα)" (514b). Socrates continues in his evocation: "Then also see along this wall human beings carrying all sorts of artifacts, which project above the wall, and statues of men and other animals wrought from stone, wood, and every kind of material; as is to be expected, some of the carriers utter sounds (φθεγγομένους) while others are silent" (514b–515a). These "makers of wonders" in charge of the show are evidently able to move but do not share this ability with others.[22] Rather, the deceptive play they carry on has the function of keeping the others bound to the ground, of feeding their illusions, of filling their eyes and, thus, perpetuating their imprisonment. Those who do not share their ability to move produce, by their movement, immobility. These magicians and the prisoners essentially belong together. Together they constitute the closed and self-enclosed world of the underground.[23]

Both the movement of those who work wonders (keeping their power to themselves but also limiting their own range of possibilities, moving only along the wall, carrying artifacts) and that of those compelled to the ascent are by nature and define "our nature." But, whereas the former is essential to the fixation of the (para)doxical equilibrium of life in the prison, the latter movement presents a disruptive quality—it indeed threatens the very continuity and mechanical reproduction of the order established.[24] Those hiding backstage in the cave and the audience of prisoners they charm, on the one hand, and the one who is compelled to get up and move, on the other hand, are the figures of a dissymmetrical antagonism inhering in nature and in "our nature"—a nature which, therefore, appears to be not simply double but profoundly strange, as Glaukon had promptly remarked right away.

The cipher of the lover of light who, for some unspecified reason, is released from her bonds indicates a movement which, taking place in the world underneath, in the obscurity of the cave, exceeds the confines of that world, opens that world up—or, more precisely, discovers *in* that world the opening leading outside, the openness *of* that world to its outside. There seems to be—*already there*—an intuition, a presentiment of light in the midst of darkness. This ability to turn around, to move about, to gain bodily (and hence visual) mobility such a lover will *have to* share with the others and teach—whatever risk this may entail.

Notes

1. Here and for the rest of the present work the Teubner text is used. Allan Bloom's translation of *The* Republic *of Plato* (New York: Basic Books, 1991) serves as a point of reference. However, formulations diverging from Bloom's are not infrequently proposed. James Adam's commentary (*The* Republic *of Plato*, 2 vols. [Cambridge: Cambridge University Press, 1963]) has often been of assistance. As regards the other dialogues, in addition to the Greek and English texts in the Loeb Classical Library edition of the Platonic corpus, the following have been profitably consulted: Walter Hamilton's translation of the *Phaedrus* (London: Penguin, 1973), William S. Cobb's translation of the *Symposium* and *Phaedrus* (*Plato's Erotic Dialogues* [Albany: SUNY Press, 1993]), Francis M. Cornford's translation of the *Timaeus* (New York: Macmillan, 1959), and Giorgio Colli's Italian translation of the *Symposium* (Milano: Adelphi, 1979). In virtually all cases, however, the rendition of texts other than that on the πολιτεία significantly departs from the consulted translations.

2. This "even before" is of crucial importance. It points to what is required in order to begin—to the decision, orientation, and ability necessary to go on.

3. One here thinks of a history ranging from the Augustinian confessional monologues, to the Cartesian solitary meditator, to Husserl's soliloquy . . .

4. Consider, for instance, the two consecutive Socratic statements, near the beginning of the dialogue, concerning the attuning, proleptic character of education due to a certain priority of the perceptual and imaginative powers: "Don't you understand . . . that

first we tell tales (μύθους) to children? And surely they are, as a whole, false, though there are true things in them too. We make use of tales with children before exercises (γυμνασίοις)" (377a). "Don't you know that the beginning is the most important work (ἀρχὴ παντὸς ἔργου μέγιστον) and that this is especially so with anything young and tender? For at that stage it is most plastic (πλάττεται), and each thing assimilates itself to the model (ἐνδύεται τύπος) that anyone wishes to impress (βούληται ἐνσημήνασθαι) upon it" (377a–b).

5. The fact that this experience (the seeing of the cave and that which is thereby evoked) does not chronologically come first (the fact that this crucial moment in the dialogue between Socrates and his interlocutor does not open the text but occurs, rather, near the center of it) does not speak against the hypothesis articulated here. Indeed, it is important to underline that such an experience constitutes the "structuring environment"— not only of what chronologically follows, not simply of the later conceptual developments, but of the conceptual labor *as such*. As to the logic of the text on the πολιτεία, in fact, it should be noticed that the opening of Book VII, portraying the Socratic spell that makes Glaukon experience a seeing, is after all only a repetition of the inauguration of the text, in Book I—or a variation on the same theme. The thaumaturgy involving the evocation and vision of the cave makes explicit what is already operative since the very beginning. For does Socrates not, in that inception, address the listener or reader (perhaps even himself) by evoking a setting and an action taking place there, thus inviting those who hear or read his words to follow him and enter the dialogical *place* of inquiry? The attuning experience undergone by Glaukon and explicitly described mirrors ours, as we are caught by Socrates' initial words. Incidentally, let it be noticed that, in inducing (if not controlling) an attunement, an experience that grants and grounds the conceptual development proper, the present proleptic discussion is functionally analogous to Socrates' guidance. This *Proleptikón* stems from a certain attunement to (experience of) the text and has, in turn, an attuning, guiding function with respect to the development of this study.

6. On the theme of analogy, see Paul Grenet, *Les Origines de l'analogie philosophique dans les dialogues de Platon* (Paris: Boivin, 1948). In this study Grenet situates the Platonic "perception" of the fecundity of analogy with respect to pre-Platonic authors as well as Aristotle. In discussing the mythical, mathematical, and poetic dimensions of analogy, he makes it possible to pursue the philosophical implications of the irreducibly composite character of the analogical ὁδός.

7. The inference and calculation of a similarity between two items in a certain respect, indeed, rests on the *evident* (*ex videre*) similarity between the items in other respects. But this means only that inferring and calculating further similarities between the same items, that is, exposing more and more exhaustively and in detail their isomorphism, already presupposes the fundamental assumption of such isomorphism. It presupposes, that is, the faith in the predictability of what is as yet unknown by reference to what is known. It projects back a founding assumption in order, then, to infer it.

8. The discussion of μίμησις in the second part of this inquiry (Chapter III) should be seen as an elaboration of this issue, aiming to reawaken a more primordial insight into the meaning of such a philosophically crucial term.

9. Indeed, much is at stake in the decisions surrounding the question of analogy. For analogy plays a central role both in so-called analysis and in matters of (re)production (all production, qua imitation, involves an operative understanding of analogy). Pursuing an

investigation of the meaning of analogy may involve, among other things, shedding further light on analysis and production as well as, perhaps, on their inseparability.

10. The imperative mood of Socrates' address to Glaukon, the authority in virtue of which Socrates asks Glaukon to "make an image" and to "see," the claim to which Glaukon is exposed, the necessitating force governing the unfolding of the dialogue and Glaukon's initiation—these rest, then, on the invocation of a harmony of desires. The authority of a claim rests on the attunement of the listener to such claim. The force of an order or of a call rests on the openness of the listener to such an order or call. The call itself, as Socrates suggests, is called forth by one's desire to hear it (to become a listener), comes forth in such a way as to encounter this desire, and is informed, even dictated, by this desire (if it is to carry any authority at all). At a later point, in Chapter IV, this issue will be examined more closely. A certain powerlessness of the philosopher will emerge: Socrates having to make momentous concessions to Glaukon, having to acknowledge and even follow Glaukon's desire for the sake of the dialogue, which would otherwise become a philosophical monologue no longer reaching the other. Such agreement constitutes the ultimate ground of authority. At the same time, though, on such ground the authoritative tone tends to fade away. Indeed, a convening, an attunement of desires may make a command superfluous and turn into an exchange otherwise structured.

11. It should also be noticed that in Book VI, where this most crucial parallel between the good and the sun is first formulated, their analogy is situated within the framework of procreation. More precisely, it is elaborated by reference to the father's begetting of a son in his own likeness. Says Socrates: "[The sun] is the offspring (ἔκγονον) of the good, an offspring the good begot in a proportion with itself (ἐγέννησεν ἀνάλογον ἑαυτῷ): as the good is in the intelligible place (νοητῷ τόπῳ) with respect to intelligence and what is intellected, so the sun is in the visible place with respect to sight and what is seen" (508b–c).

12. The concern with the question of motion, and especially of circular motion (whether the migration of souls from life, to death, and back to life, the revolution of the celestial spheres, or intrapsychic revolution), informs the second part of the present text.

13. Or, rather, the ψυχή structurally *corresponds with* the world in which it participates. Or, again, the ψυχή is structurally co-responsive with the world. The structure of correspondence comes here to be understood in terms of interaction, of co-responding, indeed, almost that of epistolary exchange (mutual inscription).

14. Here the terms ζωή, φύσις, and γένεσις are used somewhat co-extensively. Indeed, if contemplated not as an abstract category but as the occurrence and recurrence of constant renewal, life (living, being alive) comes to include even what is called inanimate, involving it in the cycles of regeneration. In this light, life emerges as a certain elemental stir and exchange, as the turning of elements into one another, circulating in and out of organisms—air breathed in, nourishing (becoming) blood and sap; water absorbed, sustaining (becoming) the cellular environment; minerals becoming tissues, metabolic pathways, energy configurations . . . Catching a glimpse of life in its unfolding would entail, then, contemplating a certain convertibility and reversibility between the animate and the inanimate, their mutual infusion in variously complex patterns. Thus, ζωή coincides with φύσις, the upsurge of all that is, and γένεσις, the dimension of coming into being and becoming. Understood in this way, the cosmos itself is, as a whole, living, animated—as is suggested in *Timaeus* and numerous pre-Platonic teachings.

15. This understanding of order will be taken up again in Chapter II, in connection with the question of justice.

16. Once again, the present reflection (on the ordering of living and dying) is quite remarkably ahead of itself. It has not been made clear, yet, how such a view stems from the Platonic dialogue. Yet, alone the fact that, in the Platonic texts, cosmologies and cosmogonies are attempted only in the mythical mode (e.g., *Resp.*) or in the mode of a "likely (i.e., imaginal) discourse" (e.g., *Tim.*) should alert one that, according to the Platonic intimation, so-called natural or cosmic laws (principles of order) will never merely have been fixed, transcendent models—models ordering while remaining separate from the ordered. The qualified mythical-imaginal-doxastic rendition of cosmic order, above all, should alert one that such "laws" will never have been simply known, grasped, secured to conceptual permanence (i.e., to permanence tout court). But the point is even more extreme. For not only is the resorting to imaginal language symptomatic of a certain impossibility of eidetic separation, but, furthermore, separation will not have been stated in mythical terms either, not even as a fantasy. Suffice it to recall (to remain close to the text now under consideration) that the venture of the transcendence of the cave culminates with the return back into it, with yet another κατάβασις—a descent that Socrates himself will have acknowledged as necessary and will, therefore, have ordered. It is such circulation, such movement back and forth, between the inside and the outside, from below to above and back, which weaves together the world, indeed worlds—even the intelligible and the sensible. Indeed, the work that is to follow will in several ways and from different angles attempt to articulate (to allow for the self-showing of) the pervasiveness of becoming even in the striving to overcome it. That is to say, it will articulate, on the ground of the speaking and gesturing of the dialogue, the irrepressible surfacing of becoming in the midst of the passion for transcendence—the way in which becoming is never purely left behind, contemplated as a whole, captured in its purely formal truth from a separate and detached standpoint. For the moment being, however, this "especially proleptic" detour proceeds in the lack of a proper ground and defense for itself. It quite deliberately (or only self-consciously) advances while deferring (presently lacking) what would appropriately sustain and defend it.

17. Acknowledging the creative, vital role of stability as well as its manifoldness—acknowledging, that is, the self-differing movement operative at the heart of stability means overcoming the simple opposition between movement and staticity. Not all immobility is imprisonment.

18. In the resistance tending to utter staticity, that is, resistance as denial and obstruction of life, is prefigured one of the central traits of war. This will be seen in Chapter IV.

19. It is when δόξα has become lifeless, when it has come to an extreme rigidity, that the city's decay becomes most conspicuous. Another such crystallizing, paralyzing, hence destructive factor is inner faction. It may not be by coincidence that faction, the discord within the city which is degenerative, accompanied by a certain λύσις (λύειν), is designated by the term στάσις. Στάσις names that inner conflict, that tense equilibrium, between opponents which leads to a crystallized, hence decaying, condition—which, in other words, obstructs vital motion.

20. A light culminating in the illumination of σοφία. (Notice the component of τό φῶς, or φάος is, light, in the word σοφία. Notice also the proximity of the term ὁ

φώς, distinguished only by the accent—a term mostly used in archaic as well as tragic verse and meaning "human being," "mortal.")

21. Incidentally, it is in the reaction of the prisoner when the bonds are loosened that one can begin to catch a glimpse of the difference between λύσις (the movement of undoing) as liberation and as destruction. Indeed, the prisoner may openly undergo the change, respond out of a readiness to such change, a readiness harbored even while being a prisoner—in fact, qua prisoner. Or, conversely, the prisoner may rebel against change, affirm imprisonment, and from out of such resistance even try to kill the agitator or, in general, to annihilate the source of change. In Chapter II λύσις will be considered in relation to justice and injustice.

22. This "not sharing" seems to constitute the crucial difference between the philosopher and the sophist. The relation between philosophy and the work of the sophists (these agents of the self-enforcement of actuality) is examined in Chapter I.

23. The complex play of interdependence and complicity between the concealed makers of phantoms and their audience, the way in which prisoners and charlatans complement and supplement each other, are masterfully exposed by Luce Irigaray in "L'hustera de Platon," in *Speculum de l'autre femme* (Paris: Éditions de Minuit, 1974), p. 310 ff.

24. Notice, on the one hand, the taming, reduction, and containment of movement associated with the figure of the sophist and, on the other hand, the uncontrollable, irrepressible, even shaking movement of life evoked through the figure of the philosopher (almost a manifestation of the force of nature, however this may be understood).

PART ONE.
"OLD WOMEN TELLING TALES" (350 e): THE CITY IN VIEW, THE CITY ENVISIONED

> For what they are worth, all the Ephesians from youth upwards should hang themselves and leave the city to the children. (Her. 22 B 121)

I. On Regeneration

E' suo padre dunque che si ridesta in lui? Sono i figli dunque la
tomba dei propri padri? E' nella morte dunque che il padre si con-
tinua nel figlio? E' dunque così che anello si salda ad anello nella
catena delle generazioni?

Is it his father, then, who reawakens in him? Are sons, then, the
tomb of their fathers? Is it in death, then, that the father continues
in his son? Is it in this way, then, that ring is joined to ring in the
chain of generations?

(ALBERTO SAVINIO, *Il Signor Münster*)

The present chapter addresses the theme of political founding in Plato's dialogue on the πολιτεία. More precisely, the theme under consideration is that
of political re-generation—of a movement, that is, striving to re-constitute, to
re-configure, and perhaps surprisingly transform the communal organism
which is as such already in view. In this sense—let it be noticed already—founding does not appear as fully originary but, rather, as a matter of renewal, of a certain repetition. The task undertaken here, then, is following the way in which
the impulse (a daimonic impulse, let this be said by way of anticipation) to bring
life back, or to bring back to life, sustains the development of the Platonic text.
It is a matter of gaining an insight into the movement of regeneration vis-à-vis
the countermovement of the dying away of the city.

The dialogue in the course of which the founding of cities will be attempted
begins with(in) a city—a city already there, constituted, living. Thus, it is from
out of that which already is (that which already manifests itself in its configuration) that the founding discourse (the discourse both concerning and instituting beginnings) begins. Beginnings, it seems, proceed from that which is indefinitely anterior (and not simply in a linear, temporal sense); from that which
is not posited, but found and, as such, undergone.

This chapter shows how political regeneration is linked to a reformulation
of the questions of filiation, of descent, of heritage and transmission—in general, to the problematization of the automatisms (fixations) on which the continuity and stability of political life rest. In other words, political regeneration
has to do with the interruption of conventional appropriations of the inappropriable recurrence of life, with the acknowledgement of that which always already exceeds conventions, institutions, and the general establishment of the
πόλις. The strange, conflictual relation between the philosopher and the πόλις

is, thus, illuminated. The philosopher comes to appear as the de-forming and trans-forming force, the dynamizing impulse operative within the city, disrupting the closed circle of doxastic determinations and breaking through the fixity of necessity in its purely mechanical aspects. The figure of the philosopher, then, appears paradigmatically to indicate both the threat posed to political order and the possibility of the renewal of such order.

Going Down, or: In the Degenerating City

The time of the action narrated in the dialogue on the πολιτεία is the time of Athens's political decay. As the dramatic action unfolds, the city is dying. The λόγοι founding the just city, the conversation through which the just city is brought forth and defined in its growth, take place in the shadow of the corrupted city, of the city sinking down and perishing after having reached the highest moment of its development. The ascending movement of regeneration and the descending movement of degeneration, if at all discernible, are thus intimately connected.

More specifically, the regenerative, founding articulation originates *from out of* the corrupted city. This, in the first place, means that the inception (in λόγος) of the just city is rooted *in* the unjust one. The possibility of the dawning of the just city in λόγος is inscribed within the actual degenerating city. In other words, before the discursive elaboration of the city can begin, and in order for it to begin at all, the actual city must be encountered and acknowledged as such—as it is. The actual city must be followed in the descending trajectory of its corruption.[1]

The opening of Socrates' recollection of the dialogue that occurred the day before is well known: "I went down (κατέβην) to Piraeus yesterday with Glaukon, son of Ariston, to pray to the goddess (θεῷ); and, at the same time, I wanted to observe (βουλόμενος θεάσασθαι) how they would put on the festival, since they were now holding it for the first time" (327a). The narration, then, begins with a κατάβασις, with a going down. This descent is motivated simultaneously by a certain orientation toward the divine and by a quintessentially Socratic desire, a certain "theoretical" impulse, a wish to see, contemplate, observe—almost a curiosity. Going down to the port would appear to suggest a leaving the city behind, a journeying out of the city proper, venturing beyond its farthest periphery (as is the case in the *Phaedrus*). It would seem to designate a descent to the limit of the city and beyond, to that gate through which the city opens to the sea and to the flux of people, deities, customs, and goods from abroad. And yet, in an important sense, in going down to the port Socrates still remains within the city's walls and hence does not leave the city (Piraeus was connected to the city by the so-called long walls).[2] Κατάβασις, accordingly, designates a going *down with* the degenerating city, following the city's innermost movement. As a participating in the movement of the city even in its downward phase, κατάβασις comes to indicate a going deep *down into* the city, a descent yielding an apprehension of the most essential features of the city's becoming, of its arising and passing away. In this way the setting at Piraeus mirrors the city. The dramatic space captures the unique traits of the city and renders them allegorically (ἀλλοάγορεύω).

The port as the spectral image of the city, its bowels, dungeon, subterranean version, also prefigures the image of the cave.[3] Accordingly, the meaning of Socrates' κατάβασις acquires yet another facet: going down can now be more fully understood as a way of encountering the city and the citizens, who, from the point of view of the one living the life of philosophical passion, are but shades. (At 516d the philosopher will describe his situation by reference to the words with which dead Achilles addresses Odysseus in *Odyssey* XI. While referring to the hero's words, however, the philosopher will subtly subvert their sense. The Homeric hero would want "to be on the soil, serf to another man, to a portionless man" rather than ruling over the dead, over those whose mortal journey is over. The philosopher, too, would rather undergo the same servitude, but in order to avoid a certain kind of life, in order not to "live that way," in the midst of the competitions and games of power of those who, though virtually living, are dead to philosophy.)[4]

It should be noticed, however, that this ciphered rendition of the city, this translation of the actual degenerating city into a subterranean theater of the dead, somewhat sets the extreme and immediate dangers inherent in the corrupted city at a distance and describes them in a stylized, modulated fashion. While with the diaphanous figures of this nocturnal setting there can be a conversation, whatever obstacles may be encountered, in the daylight of the actual city, a few of the participants in this gathering (Socrates, Polemarkhos, Lusias, Nikeratos) will undergo political enmity in its otherwise devastating concreteness.[5] Piraeus is, then, the locus of the possibility of dialogue—of a dialogical involvement which, though in many ways marked by antagonism, considerably differs from the destruction, fracture, annihilation occurring when conversation is no longer possible, when the voices have been extinguished and silence (after the clamor of battle) reigns. The port far away from the citadel above indicates that self-distancing of the city (that spacing within the city) thanks to which the city may gain an awareness of itself and reflect (on) itself. The world beneath comes to appear as that from out of which the possibility of regeneration and growth offers itself.

The descent opening the dialogue already echoes the one by the Homeric hero celebrated in the *Odyssey*, but its character as well as the developments it makes possible mark a decisive turn away from Odysseus's experience and from the framework of the Homeric world. For the epic hero, the κατάβασις of which he retrospectively (and repeatedly) recounts (*Odyssey* XI, XXIII) is more properly a νέκυια, a ritual by which he summons and questions the dead, and thanks to which his fate is disclosed to him. Rather than remaining involved in the world below, the epic hero evokes this world, calls it to his presence, and instrumentally utilizes the insight it can yield. For him, the νέκυια is a function of the accomplishment of his heroic destiny.

But for the philosopher, instead, the descent preceding the creative blossoming of philosophy opens a series of arduous challenges. Before unfolding in terms of creative possibilities (or, even, as the disclosure of possibility as such), philosophy appears as an exercise in survival. Before the labors giving birth to the just city in λόγος, Socrates has to defend himself against the forms of intimidation and aggression he encounters down at Piraeus. Socrates continues his narration: "Now, in my opinion, the procession of the native inhabitants was fine; but the one the Thracians conducted was no less fitting a show. After we had prayed and looked on (θεωρήσαντες), we went off toward town" (327a). But the philosopher cannot come and go as he pleases, and when he is about to leave the world below he is held back. Like the force of an irresistible geotropism drawing or attracting him back into the earth, an injunction reaches him from behind which makes him turn and blocks his ascent. He recalls: "Catching sight (κατιδὼν) of us from afar as we were pressing homewards, Polemarkhos, son of Kephalos, ordered (ἐκέλευσε) his slave boy to run after us and order (κελεῦσαι) us to wait. The boy took hold (λαβόμενος) of my cloak from behind and said, 'Polemarkhos orders (κελεύει) you to wait'" (327b).

The insistence on the language of injunction here could hardly be more emphatic. An exchange follows between Socrates and Polemarkhos, which playfully but unmistakably mirrors the most common abuse of power, the use of force for the purpose of bending one's comportment, commitment, or direction. Exhibiting a certain suppleness, a readiness to comply, Socrates submits to the demand that he remain in the world below. The philosopher held captive, entangled in the network of the city, will have to conquer his way back, to make his flight possible. Compelled to go down into the earth and be a guest in the chthonian city, and simultaneously striving to go back where he comes from, he might eventually find in speech his way up, away from the subterranean city, toward another place, maybe the contemplation of the just city. But not quite yet.

Figures of Corruption, or: Against the Degenerating City

His κατάβασις has brought the philosopher to an intimacy with the degenerating city, to an acknowledgment and understanding of its becoming.

Such a comprehension, which entails a sharing, is a necessary moment in the emergence of the regenerative impulse. In this sense, then, the regenerative movement occurs from out of the movement of degeneration. As was pointed out above, this means, to begin with, that the inception of the just city is rooted *in* the unjust one. Secondly, however, the movement *out of* the degenerating city should also be understood as a movement *against* it, against its degenerative elements. Accordingly, the encounters with the figures of the actual city, besides having the character of an intimacy yielding understanding, will display the traits of conflict and fight. In order to find his way beyond the corrupted city, in order to bring forth the just city, the philosopher must first confront the guises and figures through which the actual imposes itself on him in the underworld city. He will have to break through the pretenses of the actual and its totalizing claims, to suspend and eventually to unhinge the logic of its self-enforcement. The warlike relation of actuality to possibility will, thus, be enacted.

The trial Socrates must face, in brief, consists in the confrontation with the structures informing life in the corrupted city, both at the level of ἦθος and at that of νόμος. The task basically involves the neutralization, or at least the deactivation, of whatever hinders the flight from the city below, that is, of whatever prevents regeneration from culminating in the founding of the just city. This hindrance is δόξα in its self-assertive articulations, in its falling back into unreflective automatisms—in brief, in its turning into authority. It is this stasis, the staticity of a crystallized equilibrium asserting itself, which essentially defines the city in its corrupted stage. This is the corruptive element within the city. Unrest, outbursts, even upheavals are the reactive counterpart of such an insistence on conservation.

Socrates encounters the degenerating aspect of δόξα as enacted by three exemplary figures and has to expose its naïveté, counteract its normative drives, tame the arrogance of its claims. A father, a son, and a master of λόγος, that is, archetypes representing vital functions of the political organism, are the three figures through which δόξα in its ossified, lifeless character presents itself to Socrates. (Let it be noticed, parenthetically, that none of these characters is, strictly speaking, Athenian.[6] Doxastic self-enforcement is not exclusively connected with the decay of any particular city. The problems faced by Socrates cannot be reduced to distinctive features of a specific community and, indeed, present themselves in their exquisitely anthropological dimension. Socrates' initial remark on the two processions—by the native inhabitants and by the Thracians—as being equally fine already situates him beyond distinctions pertaining to political or cultural identity/identification. The issues he is concerned with are politically least identifying. They are common in a sense that exceeds the communion defining a particular πόλις.)

In the dying city down below, the elders are absorbed in sacrificial practices, in order to secure for themselves a safe journey in the world of the dead. For they are made unquiet by those "stories (μῦθοι) about what is in Hades—that the one who has done unjust deeds here must pay the penalty there" (330d). Their relationship to the divine has shifted away from a primordial experience of the sacred as mystery. The gods have come to be unproblematically construed as those who dispense rewards and punishments in that other world. Those who were rapturously envisioned as the source from which the human race proceeded, those whose ways were never fully accessible to the mortals, to their awe and wonder,[7] are degraded to the rank of predictably severe parents—as if it were plain that such is their function; and as if, moreover, the evaluation of ἦθος in terms of prizes and penalties, which presupposes a fundamental insight into the essence of justice, were a matter readily disclosed and calculable. The understanding of the divine according to this logic of retribution eventually leads to a relation to the gods that resembles very closely a commercial transaction: the gods are offered gifts so that they may be well disposed toward the one who gives—whatever life this one led.

The invocation of the gods has become a matter of flattery, of seduction, of corruption, even. The gods' ineffable power, which was somehow involved in the generation of the city of their mortal children, is now that which the city tries to buy—that which the city *believes* it can buy. Such is the doxastic outlook of the old fathers in the degenerating city. Kephalos's concluding remark appropriately describes the tenor of relationships within the human community and of the community's relation to the gods:

> For this I count the possession of money most worthwhile, not for any man, but for the decent and orderly one (ἐπιεικεῖ). The possession of money contributes a great deal to not cheating or lying to any man against one's will, and, moreover, to not departing for that other place frightened because one owes some sacrifices to a god or money to a human being. It also has many other uses. But, still, one thing reckoned against another, I wouldn't count this as the least thing, Socrates, for which wealth is very useful to an intelligent man (ἀνδρὶ νοῦν ἔχοντι). (331b)

In spite of Kephalos's insistence on character, it turns out that, whether or not one is (as he puts it) "decent," or even "intelligent," wealth is crucial in order not to cheat or lie "unwillingly"—that is, in order to be just. To a reduced, trivialized understanding of the other-than-human (to which humans stand in relation) corresponds an analogously impoverished understanding of the human, of the meaning and implications of that mode of being which harbors νοῦς. Such assumptions tacitly but consistently shape and govern the practices in the city—and it is precisely to the extent that they are for the most part unreflectively carried out that these assumptions tend to present themselves as inherently unquestionable and self-evident.

Socrates, in fact, cannot engage Kephalos in a conversation. At Socrates' first sign of perplexity, leading to an attempt to assess the understanding of justice operative in Kephalos's views and practices, the latter withdraws from the dialogue in order to go back to his sacrifices. Justice is and remains for him a matter of telling the truth and giving back what was taken, without any further qualification—justice as the logic of transparent, calculable transactions, informing relations with humans and gods alike. Ethereal, almost disembodied, and elusive, at the end of this mortal journey Kephalos is by no means closer to philosophy than he ever was. In spite of his claims, he is by no means inclined to wonder and to consider the matter closely and thoughtfully. On the contrary, he is eager to transmit the λόγος to Polemarkhos, his heir and successor (κληρονόμος), and disappear (331d).[8]

In a strange way, however, Kephalos's fleeting apparition will have crucially marked the remainder of the conversation in its direction and focus. It was, to begin with, his presence (however qualified, a kind of spectral impression) that set Socrates on a certain course of inquiry. One will recall Socrates' initial address to the old man:

> For my part, Kephalos . . . I am really delighted to discuss with the very old. Since they are like men who have proceeded on a certain path (ὁδὸν) that perhaps we too will have to take, one ought, in my opinion, to learn from them what sort of road it is—whether it is rough and hard or easy and smooth (τραχεῖα καὶ χαλεπή, ἢ ῥᾳδία καὶ εὔπορος). (328d–e)

In this connection, Kephalos was then asked to report (ἐξαγγέλλω) how one lives at "the threshold of old age" (328e). The patriarchal figure opens onto another world, other places, and makes Socrates wonder about the course that all mortals may be called to follow. Kephalos's inability to speak as the ἄγγελος Socrates longs to hear discloses the space of the dialogue that ensues. As will become evident in the concluding part of the nocturnal conversation, it is precisely the wonder surrounding the journeys between worlds that will have animated the entire conversation—the question concerning the crossing "from this world to the other and back again," whether "by the underground, rough (τραχεῖαν) road" or "by the smooth (λείαν) one, through the heavens" (619e). But it will have taken a long dialogical voyage to lead to these final reflections on faring well (621c–d).

In the dying city the young inherit the belongings, the customs, and the laws of the elders. The sons inherit the substance (οὐσία) of the fathers. It is the law of succession established by mortals, and automatically applied to mortals, which determines one's lot. Unprepared and oblivious enough not to wonder about the origin of what is handed down to them, the heirs take on the wealth and the political power attached to it, and use both clumsily, in a dangerous game whose proportions and implications they do not fully comprehend. The process of alienation from the experience of the ancestors is deepened. At the same time, the experience of the ancestors, lost to the living (*if* this is living), no longer informing the ἦθος of the city from within, is formulaically appropriated, reduced to a set of prescriptions and laws unquestioningly enforced. The experience of the ancestors has turned into ancestral authority. This is what, at least initially, the persona of Polemarkhos makes evident.

Like his father, whose arguments he inherits, Polemarkhos does not appear habituated to the ways of philosophical reflection. To begin with, he defends a further impoverished version of Kephalos's definition of justice—a definition analogously grounded on the authority of poetic sources and of common sense, but deprived of any residual concern with the issue of truth: "it is just to give to each what is owed" (331e). At this juncture Socrates, in an attempt to break through the apparent obviousness of such a statement, introduces into the conversation the element of time—and the disruptive power time *always* carries in its folds as a possibility: madness. It may not always be just to give back what is owed, Socrates suggests. Circumstances change; what was previously deposited by someone could at a later time be harmful to him—if, for instance, he should now be "of unsound mind" (μὴ σοφρόνως) (332a). Polemarkhos is compelled to assent, and this represents a turning point.

By not withdrawing, by undergoing the shift brought about by Socrates (a shift that will not allow for a return to the previous unquestioning posture), Polemarkhos opens up the space of inquiry. Or, more precisely, he *opens himself up to* the movement of interrogation, that is, to both the acknowledgment of bewilderment and the subsequent work of investigation. Unlike his father, he makes himself available to questioning, vulnerable to the realization of not knowing. His initial position, submitted to closer scrutiny, begins to undergo transformation, reformulation, deepening—a process that proves to be as disorienting as the πάθος, described later in the dialogue, of the prisoner dragged out of the cave and dying to his previous life (*if* this could be called life). Indeed, "I no longer know what I meant," says Polemarkhos in the course of the argument (334b).

One of the crucial reformulations of Polemarkhos's view of justice involves promoting the advantage of oneself and of one's own friends, allies, and close associates, while inflicting harm on those who do not belong in this circle, that is, the enemies. In this connection Socrates articulates, for the first time in the dialogue, the distinction between being and seeming. It is human finitude, the fact of human fallibility, that discloses this difference; because, in judging and evaluating, humans make mistakes, things are not always what they are said to be, that is, what they seem. People may seem good and friends, while they are not (334c–e). Curiously enough, however, in order to question Polemarkhos's opinion Socrates does not exploit this discrepancy. He abandons it for the moment and, rather, proceeds to show the inanity of the logic of punishment in general, thus convincing his interlocutor that justice is never a matter of harming anyone, whether friends or enemies, apparent or genuine (335d). Before long, the "lord of war" is conquered and positions himself on Socrates' side. The son of the patriarch is adopted by the philosopher.

In the dying city ravenous wolves have become masters in the art of composing speeches.[9] They are not unaware of the derivative character of their art, but dissimulate it. They use as a tool the art made possible by a given tradition, but without acknowledging these roots and background, and actually thinking they can manipulate and dispose of that background thanks to which they are who they are. But they know that the art of persuasion or of contention, unconcerned as it may be with the contents it accidentally happens to promote, must at least ostensibly pay homage to the tradition and display an obsequious observance of its canon. In their speeches they need to refer to and defend the letter of that which is held most venerable, but their only aim is their own advantage and that of those they serve. Somehow remotely reminiscent of epic-heroic ruthlessness, these men "of many turns," too, act out of the assurance that they can do as they please. They skillfully exploit the inclination, incipient in the degenerating city, to appropriate the ancestral experience as a function and sanction of authority. This, in turn, deepens the paradoxical status of the forefathers, evoked to the extent that their names yield and confirm authority, and simultaneously reduced to mere simulacra, empty, silent, essentially severed from the life (*if* it is life) of the city.

The masters of λόγος utilize the power of their art to drive the many, to turn them around, to inflame or dissuade them, according to the orders of those in power. In the hands of powerful, avid rulers and of these cunning servants, the city, no longer the feeding-place or the allotted abode (νομός), has become a hunting territory. (Notice that νόμος, the term allegedly pointing to the distinction between the political organism and φύσις, is connected with νομός, which in Homer's idiom designates a feeding place for those roaming about, οἱ νομάδες, and in later authors such as Pindar and Sophocles indicates an assigned dwelling place. The turning from feeding place and shelter—an appropriately transient shelter, for those whose mode of being is essentially passing, roaming, that is, nomadic—into a hunting territory would, then, be yet another figure of political degeneration, of the city reverting to destructiveness, falling back into the specifically devouring aspect of nature. The νομός, the feeding place and assigned dwelling within which νόμος gave itself, becomes a place of terror, still in the name of νόμος.)

Thrasumakhos poses a more severe challenge than the previous characters. The combination of his vigor, of the violence of his intervention, and of his rhetorical skills makes of him a threatening adversary. But dialogue is not the element of the rhetorician. Neither being at home in conversation, nor being committed to it, Thrasumakhos manifests himself through aggression, scorn, and the formulation of abrupt, unscrutinized answers to the questions discussed. Pressed by Socrates, and only with extreme reluctance, he somewhat engages in an exchange.

It should be noticed that Thrasumakhos and Socrates tend to concur on an understanding of justice as somehow associated with τὸ ξυμφέρον: that which brings together, promotes gathering, nurtures development and sustains growth; in brief, what is called advantageous (339a). But the statement that justice is the advantage of the stronger seems obscure and eminently questionable to Socrates, who proceeds to take it apart by returning to the differentiation introduced earlier between being and seeming. It would seem that, to the extent that they are human, the stronger, too, make mistakes. They may judge something to be to their own advantage and make arrangements accordingly, but their evaluation may turn out to be fallacious. In this case it would appear that they do not know what is advantageous, but at most entertain opinions concerning what seems to be advantageous. But, then, would the stronger not end up ordering what is in fact disadvantageous to them? And, because what they order is, by definition, the just, would justice not come to coincide with the disadvantage of the stronger just as much as with their advantage? Furthermore, in what sense could those acting in this way be called stronger (339c–340a)?

Precisely in order to avoid the insinuation that the stronger may not be that strong after all, Thrasumakhos must reject Kleitophon's advice, namely, that he limit himself to asserting that justice is what the stronger believe to be advantageous. Underlining the importance of terminological precision, Thrasumakhos insists that the stronger, qua stronger, do not make mistakes concerning their own advantage. The sophist here depicted puts forth a claim to knowledge, not just a defiant celebration of belief or opinion (340c–e). Socrates, who will spend the rest of the dialogue trying to demonstrate that the stronger of whom Thrasumakhos speaks have no knowledge whatsoever of what is good for them (one can see the discussion of tyranny in Books VIII–IX, or even the whole so-called "epistemological" digression in Books VI–VII, with its radical delimitation of the possibility of knowledge, as further attempts to reply to the sophist), sketches here a first possible refutation.

Thrasumakhos's claim is countered by resorting to the example of the arts.

Socrates shows how the practice of any art, including the art of ruling, takes place for the sake of that to which it applies itself, not for the sake of the one who practices it. Just as the art of medicine fulfills itself in healing the patient and not the doctor, so the art of ruling culminates in benefiting the ruled, not the ruler. To this line of reasoning, Thrasumakhos can effectively oppose no further argument (343a). The most sophisticated, unabashedly artful, and apparently invincible articulation of δόξα is shown in its fragility when rigorously approached. But the conversation leads to an even more remarkable outcome. Thrasumakhos is evidently so caught up in the interaction that he eventually betrays himself and lets something appear whose dissimulation is one of the axioms of his profession.

As a rhetorician, he asserts whatever he asserts strategically—not out of sheer naïveté or unreflective improvisation. It is a part of his profession to be aware of the problematic character of his assertions, and deliberately to employ this awareness, not in order to reconsider his position (which in itself is irrelevant to him), but rather to polish his language, to make his claims more subtle, more cogent, more precise and calculated. In other words, his skill has to do with the occultation of anything that, in revealing itself as problematic, would stimulate further analysis. And yet, in the midst of the discussion he addresses Socrates with the following restatement of his view of justice:

> You are so far off about the just and justice, and the unjust and injustice, that you are unaware that justice and the just are really someone else's good, the advantage of the man who is stronger and rules, and a personal harm to the man who obeys and serves. Injustice is the opposite, and it rules the truly simple (εὐηθικῶν) and just; and those who are ruled do what is advantageous for him who is stronger, and they make him whom they serve happy but themselves not at all. And this must be considered, most simple (εὐηθέστατε) Socrates: the just man everywhere has less than the unjust man. (343c–d)

What is most striking here, especially in light of his earlier call to rigor in matters of language, is Thrasumakhos's inconsistent terminology. A double and contradictory definition of justice appears to be operative in his statement. This is evident, first of all, from the fact that the just and the unjust in the end emerge as identical. Justice, indeed, is defined as the advantage of the stronger and a personal harm to the one who obeys. Injustice, despite the fact that it is said to be the opposite, is presented precisely in the same way—as that which rules the "truly simple and just," who in obeying do what is advantageous to the stronger and make themselves unhappy. The problem of this double standard for justice is conclusively confirmed by the linguistic shift intimating that, in the end, it is those who obey who are "truly simple and just," and not the rulers. Indeed, Thrasumakhos adds, "the just man everywhere has less than the unjust man."

Justice, then, rather than signifying the advantage of the stronger, truly ends up being the condition of those who have less. And it is according to injustice that the advantage of the stronger is secured and promoted.

Thrasumakhos's logico-terminological inconsistency shows that he *does* perceive a distinction between being just and seeming just, although as a rhetorician it is his task to gloss over and actively to dissimulate this distinction. In fact, as a rhetorician in the service of those in power, he cannot ever let it be apparent that those who seem just (i.e., those who pursue their own advantage) may in fact be most unjust. As a rhetorician, it is appearances, what seems, δόξα, that he defends—although, as noted above, he must claim for δόξα the status of being, and for the discourse articulating it the status of knowledge. In other words, Thrasumakhos dissimulates the distinction between being and seeming (knowledge and opinion), not in order to espouse the side of appearance and to proclaim the arbitrary character of all assertions, but rather in order to present appearing under the legitimizing guise of being. In this way, on the one hand, being is brought to coincide with arbitrary determination and, on the other hand, the arbitrary may assert itself with the rhetorical force of the obvious, that is, of the unquestionable.[10]

It is noteworthy that the dialogical exchange with Socrates is for Thrasumakhos so unexpectedly disorienting as to provoke a slip that he, by definition, could not afford—a slip that is a betrayal of the ἦθος of his profession. What this slip reveals is the deliberately misleading character of his practice and, most importantly, a basic denial of any possibility of transcending δόξα. This denial, accompanied by a willful avoidance of a genuine engagement with the thought of being, furthers the self-assertion of δόξα as totality, as necessary and ineluctable. (Considered in this context the fact that Socrates raises the question of being should not be seen as a positing of being and appearing in their ultimate dichotomy. Rather, raising the question of being as irreducible, if not opposite, to appearing, means pointing to the finitude and instability of δόξα, reopening the indeterminate possibility of possibility itself, interrogating the self-affirmation of actuality as totality.)

An essential feature of Thrasumakhos's posture, willful dissimulation is crucially connected with an instrumental use of language. Speaking becomes a skilled deployment of rhetorical techniques, regardless of the commitment to truth. It is thanks to such skill that being is reduced to convention, or—which is the same—to οὐσία in the sense of monetary substance (linguistic usage is in this case especially revealing). To be sure, the philosopher's discourse, in its pursuit of the truth, may be just as obscuring—but not intentionally. A main distinction between sophistry and philosophy emerges through the difference between willful and inevitable concealment.

Revealing, as Thrasumakhos does, the programmatically deceptive character of sophistry (i.e., the annihilation of any discrepancy between being and seeming in order to attribute being to seeming) betrays a twofold ignorance which Thrasumakhos obviously cannot admit—the ignorance of what would be "truly simple and just" and, by the same token, of what would genuinely constitute one's advantage. For the sophist does perceive the noncoincidence of being and seeming, yet displays no commitment to a further understanding of it. This is perhaps why, at the crucial moment in which Socrates comes to associate injustice not only with κακία, viciousness, but also with ἀμαθία, lack of learning, something quite extraordinary happens. Socrates recalls: "And then I saw what I had not seen before—Thrasumakhos blushing" (350d).

However, disempowering Thrasumakhos's arguments amounts, at most, to depriving him of his weapons—and, even in this case, just temporarily. He cannot be easily turned away from his positions, practices, and habits and be otherwise persuaded. He cannot become Socrates' ally.[11] Hence, he represents a danger in a still more significant respect. When he first bursts out (after hunching up "like a wild beast," Socrates says), both Socrates and Polemarkhos get "all in a flutter from fright" (336b). Socrates, however, although initially overwhelmed (at least according to his account), moves against Thrasumakhos in order systematically to disallow his affirmations. But Polemarkhos *cannot* do this. Presumably the young, impulsive heir would never recover from the trauma. Were it not for Socrates' presence, he would be easily brought into Thrasumakhos's sphere of influence and would just as plausibly become his ally. Because of a lack of appropriate education, he is somewhat defenseless. It is easy to win his favors and support, and to manipulate him. Polemarkhos is in Thrasumakhos's power—in terms of Thrasumakhos's rhetorical supremacy and, subsequently, with respect to political deliberations. In rhetoric as well as in matters concerning the city, Polemarkhos, who has inherited political responsibilities along with his status and wealth, is Thrasumakhos's most immediate prey—he and a number of other young men sharing a similar condition in the hunting territory that the city has become.[12] The cultivation and orientation of the "young and tender" is what is at stake in the confrontation between the philosopher and the sophist.

Regeneration, or: Away from the City

Through the figures of Kephalos, Polemarkhos, and Thrasumakhos a vision of the dying city is articulated. In this city the experience of wonder seems to be ruled out. The θαυμάζειν constituting the philosophical πάθος is most foreign to the horizon within which the actual gives itself in its self-evidence and asserts itself as necessary. Having exhausted its capacity for growing, the city begins to die. In other words, the city begins to die when it can no longer see itself grow, when it sees its possibilities for development exhausted, that is to say, fulfilled, actualized. Through these encounters, Socrates takes the measure of the dying city and confronts it in its dying, in order to bring the just city forth—that is, in order to leave.

Socrates, whose name evokes the epithet "ruler of life" and whose art is that of μαιευτική, the art of assisting birth, will have to let life resurface in the midst of the realm of the shades. This will be his way up, his way of leaving. The whole first book of the dialogue on the πολιτεία can be seen as a threshold that the philosopher must traverse in order to be able to move on, away and upwards. The crossing of such a threshold marks the initiation of the philosopher and the beginning of the founding movement proper.

The going down into and with the degenerating city (apprehension) and the fight against the degenerative features of the city (conflict) finally make founding proper possible. The ascending movement of regeneration, culminating with the bringing forth of the just city in λόγος, makes it possible for the philosopher to articulate his way out of the place where he is detained. Regeneration, then, occurs *out of* the degenerating city in a third crucial sense: as a movement *away from* it, a movement of transcendence. The unfolding of the founding discourse, the movement away from the dying city developed in Books II–V, will be followed at a later stage in this work. Here it may suffice to consider the basic character of the founding discourse as it begins to emerge in Book II and to illuminate its connections with a few central developments in the dialogue.

In the city where the experience of wonder has become most foreign, something wondrous happens. Glaukon and Adeimantos manifest their desire to deepen their understanding of justice, to gain an insight into justice beyond the play of appearances and conventional views. Unlike Polemarkhos, they truly are too sophisticated simply to accept, simply to inherit the customary outlook handed down by the fathers. They, the sons of Ariston, resist the paternal traditional outlook precisely to the extent that they discern its ossification, its degeneration into common places mostly reflecting concerns with reputation (δόξα) and conformity (ὀρθοδοξία). Nor are they convinced by the wolves at once exploiting and furthering this ethical senescence of the city to their own advantage.

At the same time, they have not been fully persuaded by Socrates' previous refutation of these positions. The preceding discussion was for the philosopher a life and death combat. Now that his opponents no longer hold sway, Glaukon and Adeimantos provoke the surviving philosopher, ask him to say more, to speak on behalf of justice outside the framework of dispute and contention. Their repetition of the arguments that Socrates previously fought against represents, first of all, an important reminder concerning the force of δόξα, a warning against underestimating it. Secondly, it marks the transition from the conflictual dimension of the philosophical exchange to philosophy as a conversation with friends—from the dimension of ἔρις, or even of πόλεμος, to that of φιλία. These friends of Socrates now call for (βούλομαι, 358d), desire (ἐπιθυμέω, 367b), the creative labor of the philosopher.

Glaukon restates Thrasumakhos's position (that injustice yields all sorts of advantages and is the mark of the stronger), bringing its articulation to an unprecedented degree of refinement, seductiveness, and boldness. Adeimantos's discourse complements Glaukon's by subtly developing the view virtually contrary to that of Thrasumakhos, namely, the view valuing justice—but as a matter of mere seeming. "Fathers," Adeimantos begins, "say to their sons and exhort them, as do all those who have care of anyone, that one must be just." However, he adds,

> They do not praise justice by itself but the good reputations (εὐδοκιμήσεις) that come from it; they exhort their charges to be just so that, as a result of the opinion (δόξης), ruling offices (ἀρχαί) and marriages (γάμοι) will come to the one who seems just (δοκοῦντι δικαίῳ), and all the other things that Glaukon a moment ago attributed to the unjust man[13] as a result of his having a good reputation (εὐδοκιμεῖν). (362e–363a)

It is already evident that, with his discourse, Adeimantos effects a kind of regression and brings the discussion back to the conventional position Socrates encountered before Thrasumakhos came into play, that is, the position outlined by Kephalos's remarks and, at least initially, endorsed by Polemarkhos. Glaukon and Adeimantos's speeches taken together eventually show the coincidence of the two allegedly opposite positions.[14] Just as the rhetorician could never assert his position concerning the advantage of being unjust in the course of a lawsuit, but rather would have to formulate his address in the language of justice in order to win the cause, so the citizen knows that the appearance of justice, besides being required, is advantageous in the context of the city—and conforms to such a requirement even if in a thoroughly formal fashion. The connivance between common δόξα and ambitious arrogance, at any rate, was already apparent in the turn of Thrasumakhos's discourse considered above. The very possibility of rhetoric as the art of defending the appearance of justice, and eventually daring openly to declare the advantages of injustice, is rooted in (and sustained by) the degenerative turning of justice into a matter of mere convention. In this sense, the fathers are implicated in the coming into being of devouring and ravaging wolves.[15]

A second crucial issue that vividly comes into view through Glaukon's and Adeimantos's discourses is the plexus of political power (ἀρχαί), δόξα in its broad semantic range (as appearance, seeming, opinion, reputation, glory . . .), and familial or tribal bonds (involved both in the structuring and in the transmission of communal forms). Their mutual interplay and underlying unity constitute the framework within which can properly be understood the degenerative translation of justice into mere formality, that is, of community into administration. Such is the disenchanted, cogent account of the dying city, presenting the city in its most irresistible features in order to provoke the philosopher, to elicit a response from him.

Socrates, in awe, salutes Glaukon and Adeimantos's unexpected provocation with these words: "something quite divine (θεῖον) must certainly have happened to you, if you are remaining unpersuaded that injustice is better than justice when you are able to speak that way on its behalf" (368a). Something divine, something wondrous and ineffable, transpires through Glaukon and Adeimantos's comportment. For they were won over by Socrates and not by his opponent—although what compels them is in a way beyond λόγος. Indeed, though able to speak skillfully on behalf of injustice, they are not convinced and ask Socrates to address their perplexity. The philosopher's labor comes into being as a response to their (divine) injunction—or desire.[16] It is in response to this (divine) impulse that philosophy, after the danger, can begin to unfold in its properly creative power. The creative possibility of philosophy stems from both the philosopher's endurance and the philosopher's receptivity to something wondrous presenting itself in the form of a desire or of an invitation. (In this sense, *that thanks to which* the philosophical engagement unfolds is disclosed neither in terms of metaphysical truth nor in terms of epistemological certainty, but rather in terms of comportment, of ἦθος oriented to and by desire.)[17]

But how is Socrates to respond to the provocation brought forth by Glaukon and Adeimantos? Where should the turn away from the degenerating city lead? Would the movement of regeneration perhaps merely amount to the elimination of the corruptive features from the city?

At the heart of the city in which the experience of wonder is extinguished, something wondrous occurs to which Socrates responds. At the heart of the city of the fathers—and this represents a most remarkable turn—Socrates comes to envision a city in which familial and tribal structures, and the logic of transmission inherent in them, do not represent the fundamental principle of aggregation, and are, indeed, abolished.

This becomes clear in the course of the discussion illustrating how, in the just city, at least at the level of the guardians, the generation of children and the coupling of men and women would occur outside the framework of the family and of the couple, and hence parents as well as children would be in common (423e–424a). But the laconic account of the origin of the city already foreshadows this later development. The just city is of humble origin. Its founding in λόγος lacks epic grandiosity. The city is neither founded by heroic or divine deeds nor essentially based on the familial nucleus as its constitutive cell. Rather, the just city comes to be out of need, out of each human being's need for others. "The city, as I suppose," says Socrates, "comes into being because each of us isn't self-sufficient but is in need of much. Do you believe there is another beginning (ἀρχὴν) to the founding (οἰκίζειν) of the city?" (369b).

But once the structure on which transmission rests is disallowed, the very possibility of return and restoration becomes problematic.[18] The movement of regeneration taking place at the heart of the degenerating city, thus, does not amount to a nostalgic turn away from the corruption introduced by the predecessors of more recent generations, back to an imaginary city of the ancestors— heroes or deities. In other words, regeneration does not appear to be a matter of turning back to the city as it is said to have been, to the city freed from the corruptive elements and restored in its integrity. Regeneration is not an attempt at retrieving, revitalizing, re-authorizing, and preserving the tradition. The turn away from the degenerating city, this regenerative movement, ends up furthering the destruction of the city as it is, of the city as it is presently thought to have been, of the structures of communal living as one knows them (again, the strange embrace of life and a certain kind of destruction). The regeneration of the political ends up by contributing to the death of the πόλις, to the destruction of the political organism as (and where) one knows it.[19]

The understanding of procreation according to the conventional (νομικός) context of the paternal-filial relation and familial bonds, too, becomes problematic. Inheriting (κληρονομέω: being assigned, being allotted one's destiny, according to νόμος) comes to mean something quite different from the automatic transmission and reception of a purely ponderable (quantifiable) inheritance (riches, social status, political role). Nothing in the transmission and reception appears to be a matter of course. The later discussion distinguishing human beings into three main classes (according to the metal mixed in their soul at birth) is exemplary in this respect (414d–415c). It intimates that the belonging in these classes of the ψυχή is not simply an issue of transmission from generation to generation. That is why the origin of the rulers can, only and necessarily, be accounted for in mythical terms ("because we don't know where the truth about ancient things lies") (382d).[20]

The relation to and love for the ancestors (386a), whether the most recent or most remote predecessors, come to be quite different from a making them familiar, turning them into parents, bringing them into the family structure. The relation to them is not a relation to the source of authority—not, at least, if by authority one understands that which results from making available and readily intelligible what is neither purely available nor readily intelligible. Analogously, at a later stage the relation of the human race to the divine is shown as an issue not readily appropriable in terms of linear emanation from the divine, but rather as the task of an infinitely mediated, interpretive approach. It is Delphic Apollo, Socrates says at this point, who presides over "foundings of temples, sacrifices, and whatever else belongs to the care (θεραπεῖαι) of gods, daimons, and heroes; and, further, burial of the dead and all the services needed to keep those in that other place (ἐκεῖ) gracious." Socrates then adds:

> For such things as these we neither know (οὔτ' ἐπιστάμεθα) ourselves, nor in founding a city shall we be persuaded by any other man, if we are intelligent (νοῦν ἔχωμεν), nor shall we make use of any interpreter (ἐξηγητῇ) other than the ancestral (πατρίῳ) one. Now, this god is doubtless the ancestral interpreter (πάτριος ἐξηγητὴς) of such things for all humans, and he sits in the middle of the earth at its navel and delivers his interpretations (ἐν μέσῳ τῆς γῆς ἐπὶ τοῦ ὀμφαλοῦ καθήμενος ἐξηγεῖται). (427b–c)

The relation to the forefathers, deflected from instrumental and formulaic reductions, is inscribed within the perception of procreation, of relation to the source, as unfamiliar—as mystery.

Let it also be said, in passing, that it is in the context of this broad movement transfiguring the figure of procreation and descent that that other most sublime (extraordinary, indeed, exorbitant) paternity should be situated: the infinitely other, imageless father around which the dialogue as a whole revolves and from which it seems to emanate: the good.

The turn away from the city, then, leads away from the city as one knows it. And yet, in another sense, the turn away from the city never happened. The city was never left. A pure transcendence and overcoming of the city of the fathers appears to be impossible, and Socrates is still at Piraeus, talking in Kephalos's house.[21] But the limits of transcendence and the possibility of regeneration are intimately connected. For it is as foreign to the city below, and simultaneously as compelled to remain there, that Socrates can bring life forth in the midst of the shades—that regeneration *as transformation* (that is, as other than simple inheritance, as the complication of inheritance) can occur.

To understand more fully how, through the conversation down at Piraeus, Socrates disentangles himself and his interlocutors from the web of involvements with the dying city while remaining in its midst would imply a turn to the psychological stratum of the dialogue on the πολιτεία in the light of the shift taking place in Book IX.[22] After this conversation the souls of the listeners are no longer the offspring of their fathers.[23] The listeners and participants are reborn beyond the dimension of genealogical or familial belonging, no longer bound to the order inherited but free for possibilities of reconstitution—or perhaps not all of them, but only those who so desire. In response to this desire, in the midst of the underground city, Socrates leads life to reemerge.

Notes

1. The reflections presented in this chapter unfold out of a close analysis of Book I and rest on a consideration of this opening text not only as an integral part of the dialogue as a whole but also as having a fundamental preparatory function. Such an assumption is cogently argued for by Charles H. Kahn in "Proleptic Composition in the *Republic*, or Why Book I Was Never a Separate Dialogue," *Classical Quarterly* 43, no. 1 (1993), pp. 131–42. Contra K. F. Hermann, who inaugurated the interpretation of Book I as an early and originally separate dialogue (*Geschichte und System der Platonischen Philosophie* [Heidelberg, 1839], pp. 538–40), as well as more recent authors endorsing the same view, from Paul Friedländer (*Platon*, 3 vols. [Berlin: De Gruyter, 1964–75], vol. II, p. 45, vol. III, p. 55 ff.) to Gregory Vlastos (*Socrates: Ironist and Moral Philosopher* [Ithaca: Cornell University Press, 1991], p. 250), Kahn convincingly defends the view of "Plato's use of proleptic composition as an expository device that is characteristic of the artistic structure of the *Republic*" (p. 132). According to this view, "the myth of Er, the philosopher-kings, and the psychology of Book 4 are all plotted in advance and carefully prepared in Book 1" (p. 136). Parts of chapter 1 have been previously published as "A More Sublime Paternity: Questions of Filiation and Regeneration in Plato's *Republic*" in *Epoché: A Journal for the History of Philosophy* 6, no. 1 (1998). A discussion of these themes is developed in "Beyond the Comedy and Tragedy of Authority: The Father in Plato's *Republic*," *Philosophy 2nd Rhetoric* 34, no. 2 (2001).

2. See Indra Kagis McEwen's *Socrates' Ancestor: An Essay on Architectural Beginnings* (Cambridge, Mass.: MIT Press, 1994). While the explicitly philosophical remarks exposed here are at times based on too general and conventional premises, the analyses of architectural-urbanistic σοφία in its political significance and overall ordering power are of remarkable philosophical import. Concerning the issue of the relation between the port and the μητρόπολις (the mother-city) of Athens, see in particular Chapter IV, "Between Movement and Fixity: The Place for Order" (pp. 78–120).

3. Among other things, notice that, just like the cave, the nocturnal environment of Piraeus is lit by the light (φῶς) of fire—more precisely, by torches (λαμπάς). Indeed, the festival taking place at the port represents a variant of the λαμπαδεία or of the φωσφόρεια, festivities involving a torch procession and/or dedicated to one of the "light- (or torch-) bearing gods" (φωσφόροι θεοί). In keeping with the innovative inclination of the community of Piraeus, the celebration of the goddess is said to include, instead of a procession with torch bearers, a torch race on horseback (328a). That is why Socrates expresses surprise upon hearing this and calls it "novel." The festival, then, ritualizes the bearing and passing on of light—in the dark. It should be mentioned that, as a divine epithet, φωσφόρος mostly applied to nocturnal or cthonian deities, such as Hecate, Hephaistos, and Dionysos (at the mysteries, according to Aristophanes' *Frogs*, Dionysos was called φωσφόρος ἀστήρ, the light-bringing star). In the context of this dialogue, it

is important to underline the progression (yet another procession, in a way) from these subterranean fires, to the light of the sun, to the language of radiance and luminosity by which the noetic region, even the good, are presented. (See, e.g., 508d–509a, in which the glow of truth and being is said to light intelligence and in which, furthermore, the brilliance of beauty is attributed to truth, knowledge, and above all to the good.) Finally, see the reference to passing on the "torch (light) of life," in *Laws* (776b). Not unrelated to φῶς is the noun φώς, in archaic-poetic usage signifying a human being (e.g., Patroklos, a "godlike man" (ἰσόθεος φώς) [*Il.* XI.644]).

4. The complicated relation between the philosopher and the Homeric heritage is an important concern in the present project. Both Chapters II and III address this theme in its various facets. For an approach to the dialogue on the πολιτεία showing how certain traits of Homer's song are repeated, transfigured, and preserved within the Platonic text, see Richard J. Klonoski's "The Preservation of Homeric Tradition: Heroic Re-performance in the *Republic* and the *Odyssey*," *Clio* 22, no. 3 (1993), pp. 251–71. The highly qualified, elliptical manner in which the Homeric saying is retained and reenacted in Plato's text calls attention to a related issue, namely, the question of formal/formulaic retention of a heritage, as distinct from the keeping alive (saving) which manifests itself as engagement, however conflictual—as challenge, provocation, apparent rejection, distortion, and even destruction. More on this later.

5. Proclus interprets the environment of the port as a cipher of the realm of γένεσις, characterized by instability, frictions, and confusion—as the realm where Socrates' combat takes place against sophistry, the monster with "one thousand heads." But, in a typically Platonic fashion (by explicit reference to *Phaedo* 109b ff. and 111b, as well as *Phaedrus* 248a ff.), Proclus also draws a connection between the domain of becoming and the submerged life, that place and time in which the souls live as if beneath the surface of the water (*In Remp.* I:17 f.). The dialogue on the πολιτεία, too, analogously juxtaposes the symbolism of the sea, of marine and submarine life, to the domain of γένεσις. See Book X, where, after having established an analogy between the soul and Glaukos, now buried in the depths of the sea, disfigured, and nearly unrecognizable, Socrates speaks of philosophy as that longing and impulse (ὁρμή) which can bring the soul up, out of and away from "the deep ocean in which it now is" (611b–612a). In symbolic terms, then, the setting at the port presents a twofold significance. On the one hand, it can be identified with the fluctuating horizon of becoming, with the submerged world. On the other hand, it literally is the image of that which is situated above the surface of the ocean, of that which emerged from the depths and, though remaining in the proximity of the sea (indeed, before it), cannot simply be assimilated to it.

The image of the πόλις as a boat, in Book VI, should also be considered in this connection (488a ff.). Here Socrates depicts the perils to which a city is exposed in general (a frail vessel on stormy waters), but especially when governed by those who have no understanding of the elements, of the currents, of the sky, of the relation between the city and these—that is, those who do not even begin to envision the role and position of the city within the cosmos (see also *Laws* 758a, 961e ff.).

The recourse to such images is most appropriate in this dialogue taking place at the port of Athens, the city distinguishing itself, in so many respects, for its daring—the city that followed Themistokles when he had "the audacity to suggest that the Athenians should attach themselves to the sea" (Thucydides, *Hist.* 2.XXXVI.2). Thus, although in descending to Piraeus one will not have overstepped the city limits and will still be in

Athens, one will find oneself in a city that has dared to establish itself in its intimate relation to the ocean. Indeed, one will find oneself at the place of such conjunction. The port is not simply the place where earth meets the sea, but rather where the πόλις opens itself to the sea—and this means that the fluidity of the sea, its destabilizing impact on the land, will have a political no less than elemental resonance (as the Athenian notices, *Laws* 704a ff., especially 705a). The proximity to this element least of all allowing for political appropriation, measurement, and fixation will, at least in the order of the symbolic, constantly call into question any political plans (whether topographic or otherwise). Above all, it will jeopardize and problematize the establishment of boundaries, enclosures, and, hence, the very possibility of the delimitation of identity (cultural, political, etc.). More will be said about this at various later stages.

6. The master of speeches is introduced as being from Chalcedonia (328b). The patriarch, a merchant of arms, came to Athens from Syracuse, invited by Pericles—as his son Lusias says in "Against Eratosthenes" (*Lysias*, trans. W. R. M. Lamb [Cambridge, Mass.: Harvard University Press, 1988], pp. 226–77).

7. The procession of humans from the gods, through complex genealogies, primordially gives itself as a poetic insight.

8. One finds a quite different interpretation of the character of Kephalos in most of the literature on the topic. An exemplary case is found in R. L. Nettleship's *Lectures on the* Republic *of Plato* (London: Macmillan, 1901), where Kephalos's understanding of justice is considered as the "formula" in which "morality is summed up" (p. 16). By reference to Cicero, furthermore, Nettleship presents Kephalos as the one who cannot be questioned, as the venerable old man who is beyond all assessment. He even sees Kephalos's "simple utterances" as anticipating "some of the philosophical results of the body of the *Republic*" (p. 15 f.). Oddly enough, one finds not too dissimilar an understanding of this figure in Alexandre Kojève, who proposes an interpretation of Kephalos as the "'naturally' decent human being," as the father withdrawing into silence and, thus, remaining close to "'the voice of conscience'"—while "his 'sophisticated' son . . . gives impetus to the conversation about justice which the father avoids" (in Leo Strauss, *On Tyranny*, including the Strauss-Kojève Correspondence [New York: Free Press, 1991], p. 266 f.). For analogous positions see, e.g., Kahn ("Proleptic Composition in the *Republic*," p. 137) and C. D. C. Reeve, *Philosopher-Kings: The Argument of Plato's* Republic (Princeton: Princeton University Press, 1988), p. 7.

9. The allusion to the sophist as a wolf takes place at 336d. On the "unhealthy" and "unnecessary" presence of hunters in the city, see 373b. On the tyrant as wolflike, see 565e–566a. Related passages are 415e, in which the enemy "from without" is compared to a wolf, and 496d, in which the condition of the philosopher is described as that of a human being among "wild beasts."

10. There seems to be, then, an exquisitely ethico-political dimension to the question of being.

11. However, notice that, despite his intolerance with respect to Socrates' dialogical way, Thrasumakhos does not leave the scene. He remains, follows the development of the discussion, at one point even incites Socrates to say more (Book V, 450b). And in Book VI, when Adeimantos reminds him that his hearers (Thrasumakhos first among them) are not yet persuaded, Socrates replies: "Don't make a quarrel . . . between me and Thrasumakhos when we've just become friends (φίλους), though we weren't even enemies (ἐχθροὺς) before. We'll not give up our efforts before we either persuade him and

the others, or give them some help in preparation for that other life when, born again (αὖθις γενόμενοι), they meet with such arguments" (498c–d). Notice in this statement the anticipation of the theme of the return to and of life, with which the dialogue will end. Socrates' efforts to consolidate his friendship with Thrasumakhos and, in general, to persuade his interlocutors seem to exceed (while not excluding) the order of more or less immediate, quantifiable results. Socrates' attempts are for the sake of other lives and possibilities—unlikely as they may presently appear. The phrase "other lives" should not be understood naively, according to the model of temporal linearity, as indicating "future lives," or even an "after-life." Rather, what Socrates defends and tries to keep open is the possibility of transformation, the possibility of other possibilities, possibility itself—possible at any moment.

12. This is the first sign of a noteworthy (if inconspicuous) complicity between Kephalos and Thrasumakhos. In withdrawing and leaving his son alone, Kephalos disregards his responsibility to him and to the city. More on this later.

13. There is a divergence among different manuscripts here. Some give δίκαιοι, while more recent ones ἄδικοι. Given that the discussion at this point revolves around the ambiguity between being and seeming just (or unjust), the discrepancy may not present substantial implications. See Glaukon's observations at 362a–b.

14. This is the second, conclusive intimation of the above-mentioned complicity between the biological father and the sophist.

15. This is why, then, so much is at stake in the interpretation of Kephalos and of ancestral authority in general.

16. The sons of Ariston only make more perspicuous what already emerged in the case of Kephalos's son, namely, a condition of reflective starvation, a deprivation characterizing the rearing of the youth in the city. Socrates is compelled to heed their restlessness and cultivate their otherwise unfocused resources. Xenophon recalls in vivid detail a conversation between Socrates and Glaukon, showing how Socrates (because of his friendship with Plato and his uncle Kharmides, but also out of concern for Glaukon) used to reach out to the young man—while the latter's family was increasingly alienated by his ambition and youthful eagerness to participate in things political (*Mem.* III.vi).

17. The founding and fundamental character of the ἦθος of desire and, hence, the primordially ethical dimension of the philosophical discourse is underscored at crucial junctures in the dialogue, most notably in Book VII, during the momentous elaboration of the analogy "cave (fire) : visible world (sun) :: visible world (sun) : intelligible place (good)." As Socrates tells Glaukon, such continuous, ascending proportion is not granted by (grounded on) knowledge ("a god doubtless knows [οἶδεν] if it happens to be true"), but by the fact that "you desire to hear it" (ἐπιθυμεῖς ἀκούειν) (517b). Again, the importance of this cannot be emphasized enough.

18. That is why Leo Strauss's language of restoration, for example, in "On Plato's *Republic*," sounds somewhat questionable (*The City and Man* [Chicago: University of Chicago Press, 1964]).

19. In the *Philosophy of History* Hegel observes: "The principle of Socrates manifests itself as revolutionary against the Athenian state. . . . At this stage, in Athens, that higher principle which was the destruction of the substantial endurance of the Athenian state advanced in its development more and more." Most remarkably, Hegel connects this "revolutionary" character of the Socratic reflection with Socrates' δαιμόνιον, thus

disclosing the "rupture with actuality (*Wirklichkeit*)" as daimonic (*Vorlesungen über die Philosophie der Geschichte* [Leipzig: Reclam, 1924], p. 350 f.; my translation).

20. The issues of inheritance and transmission will be discussed further, particularly in Chapters V and VI.

21. This highly qualified movement of transcendence reveals at once an erotic dimension (the desire to leave) and a certain powerlessness (lack of δύναμις) characterizing the philosophical striving. The philosophical life, then, is not the life of θεωρία. Rather, it is the life defined by the desire for and the impossibility of θεωρία. The philosopher is simultaneously prisoner of and attracted to the city. Here, at the outset of the dialogue, one finds the first variation on the theme of the philosopher's never fully accomplished ascents, of the necessity for the philosopher always to come back to the city (to the cave, in Book VII; to embodiment, to this world, in Book X). The love of the city (of this world) appears as a certain limit imposed on the philosopher—or, better, on the love of σοφία itself. See John Sallis's discussion of the limits of transcendence (negativity), in *Being and Logos*, p. 447 ff.

22. The exchange between Socrates and Glaukon concluding Book IX should be recalled. Here, among other things, Socrates returns to the motif of something "quite divine," which in Book II he thought must have happened to the sons of Ariston: "'Then,' he said, 'if it's that he's concerned with, he won't be willing to mind the political things.' 'Yes, by the dog,' I said, 'he will in his own city, very much so. However, perhaps he won't in his fatherland unless some divine chance coincidentally comes to pass.' 'I understand,' he said. 'You mean he will in the city whose foundation we have now gone through, the one that has its place in speeches, since I don't suppose it exists anywhere on earth.' 'But in heaven,' I said, 'perhaps, a pattern (παράδειγμα) is laid up for the one who wishes (βουλομένῳ) to see and, on the basis of what he sees, found a city within himself. It doesn't make any difference whether it is or will be somewhere. For he would mind the things of this city alone, and of no other.' 'That's likely (εἰκός),' he said" (592a–b).

23. As was pointed out earlier, there is no Socratic authority without a certain concurrence of desires among interlocutors. This is in marked contrast with the functioning of paternal authority. See Socrates' remark in Book VII concerning the similarity between dogmatic convictions and parental influences: "Surely we have from childhood convictions (δόγματα) about what's just and beautiful by which we are brought up as by parents, obeying them as rulers and honoring them" (538c). In this connection, see Aristotle's remarks on λόγος as a father or friend who must be obeyed by the appetitive part of the soul (*NE* 1102b30 ff.).

II. The Law of (Re)production

The present discussion concerns Socrates' attempt to establish a city, the just city, on a ground other than that of δόξα—that is, of appearances, convention, and custom. Through this gesture, Socrates sets out to address the question concerning the essence of justice. This is, broadly understood, the twofold task Socrates undertakes in the dialogue on the πολιτεία and on the δίκαιος.

Such an attempt at founding a city that may be called just without any further qualification and at isolating justice in its essence takes place in spite of the circumstances pointed out in the previous chapter. Indeed, it was shown above that the articulation of justice occurs out of injustice and inseparably from it. Socrates, however, does not seem immediately to relinquish the dream of a purely just city and of a determination of justice at the eidetic level. At least initially, his response to the crystallization of δόξα brings about a similarly static vision: that of a city free from corruption and, hence, from decay—so purely just as to admit neither motion nor change. As the embodiment of the being of justice, such a city would enjoy perfect stability. It could be said that the ideal stillness of the just city presents itself as radically heterogeneous with regard to the self-perpetuation of the corrupted city. The latter, one could surmise, should be seen as a symptom of sickness, as an insistence on conservation which is out of joint with respect to the time of renewal and transformation. The equilibrium of the unjust city would be fragile and accidental, resulting as it does not from the unfolding of a harmonious configuration, but rather from the utter disorder of empty forms asserting themselves. Yet, quite remarkably, the two cities share a certain resistance to motion and dynamic development. At a fundamental level, they share a lifeless rigor.

In particular, the present discussion undertakes to show how, despite the regenerative vocation of the founding, at least in its inception this operation will demand a certain harnessing, even a bracketing, of life. Indeed, the calculation of life and of the living will turn out to be crucial to the founding of the just city and, hence, to the finding and capturing of justice in its eidetic purity. In the dialogue on the πολιτεία, the sustained discussions of issues pertaining to γένεσις, to the horizon of creation and procreation, clearly display the extent of Socrates' concern with the unstable, fluctuating emergence of life, with the mystery of generation and birth. These will be acknowledged and eventually celebrated in the myth concluding the dialogue. But, at this early stage, what is prominent is Socrates' determination to take precautionary measures against the inordinate power of life, to contain its potentially disruptive occurrence and recurrence.

The elaboration of the just city essentially rests on the variously antagonistic treatment reserved to the poets and on the project of complete control over reproduction—that is, on the possibility of subjecting and normalizing the genetic horizon in general. At this juncture, one observes a stark contrast between philosophy and poetry. Philosophy is at war against poetry—against ποίησις, the production of poetry as well as the reproduction (emergence) of life itself. Indeed, the role that the calculation of production and re-production plays in the founding, establishment, subsistence of the just city as well as in the determination of justice cannot be overemphasized.

But, even more importantly, the analysis presented here reveals the impossibility of Socrates' attempt—the impossibility of an attempt which, logically and in principle (i.e., according to λόγος), does not appear to be impossible. In order to problematize the entire project of political founding and conceptual determination, one does not need to press the issue of the mimetic quality of the just city (according to Socrates himself, the city brought to be in λόγος is a mere, albeit pedagogically indispensable, image of justice). To be sure, in so doing one would disclose the dubious character of a procedure arriving at eidetic determination through a mimetic (i.e., poietic) operation. But, alone, the mortality of the city decisively bespeaks the failure of the λόγος to accomplish its twofold project. Indeed, if followed in its life, the just city will eventually be seen in its decay—a decay not supervening upon the fulfillment of the city, but rather at work since the beginning, in the very coming into being of the city. The "just" city, then, will display a certain imperfect character of its justice, of the justice it images. But this already means that it will reveal a certain injustice of (its) justice. The discussion in the present chapter ultimately attempts to show how injustice is involved in the articulation of justice and how the problem of their interplay is not accidentally left unresolved in the dialogue.

The Magnified Letters of Justice

In Books II–V of the dialogue on the πολιτεία, Socrates calls the just city into appearance, makes his city come forth and shine through the λόγοι. He invites his guests and friends to enter this space evoked in and through speech— guides them into the city's walls and exhorts them to observe that organism in movement, to grasp the laws governing its life. By the end of Book IV the bringing forth of the just city "in λόγος," the task formulated earlier in the dialogue (369a), is basically accomplished.

It should be noticed, first of all, that the founding of the just city is undertaken solely for the sake of the investigation concerning justice. At the end of the founding effort Socrates will notice that, precisely because articulated by reference to the extrinsic dynamics of the city, the determination of justice which was achieved is merely "a kind of phantom (εἴδωλόν) . . . that is also why it is helpful" (443c). At that stage of the dialogue, after having attained a first provisional determination of justice, Socrates will readily dismiss that in virtue of which such insight was gained. He will do so by minimizing and dissimulating the importance of the path, the ὁδός that led to such realization. He will remind his interlocutors that the just city founded in speech is, after all, but an image, a figure, a ghost of justice. As such, it is but a stage in the ascent to the contemplation of the essence of justice—a ladder that must be left behind, discarded after the climbing. This will be the philosopher's reminder at the end of the founding exercise, once this undertaking has yielded what it can.

And yet, at the beginning of the enterprise, the founding of the city appears to be not so much a helpful stratagem, but rather the *condicio sine qua non* for something like an investigation of the essence of justice to take place at all. Indeed, according to Socrates' own words, the city (phantasmatic as it may be) comes first in the order of vision (of the vision of justice) and grounds that order as such in its further dimensions. The truth of justice is harbored within the city brought forth in λόγος and can be glimpsed only through the figure of the city. Far from being the derivative semblance of justice, then, the spectral city appears to be indispensable for the contemplation of justice. Even more precisely, it appears to be that through which justice originally gives itself to contemplation and becomes at all visible. This is the truth of the ghost town.[1]

The just city is brought forth as a *figure* of justice (just as the setting at the Piraeus functions as a figure of the decaying city). For it is only through the envisioning of such a figure that justice can be *found* and *captured.* Indeed, as Socrates points out at the outset, the investigation concerning justice "is no ordinary thing, but one for a man who sees sharply." However, he adds, "since we are not clever (δεινοί)" and don't see sharply enough to "read little letters from afar," it will be necessary to consider "the same letters . . . but bigger and in a bigger place . . . *if,* of course, they do happen to be the same" (368c–d; emphasis added).

The turn to the founding of the just city is precisely that through which justice can be brought closer, as it were, and made visible. Such is the unavoidable (necessary) detour which those must take who, like Socrates and his interlocutors, are not δεινοί enough to discern justice itself. Because of their structural myopia, of their short-sightedness, the construction of the city becomes that which, *alone,* can provide them with an access into the exceedingly distant, unreadable essence of justice. This is why, after surmising that there is "justice of one man" and, surely, "of a whole city too," Socrates concludes: "So then, perhaps there would be more justice in the bigger and it would be easier to observe closely. If you want, first we'll investigate what justice is like in the cities" (368e).[2] It is secondary, after all, whether the question of justice be observed in the human being (in the order of the ψυχή) or in the organism of the πόλις—whether, that is, this question be approached through a psychological or a political synecdoche. What is crucial is that the question of justice cannot be answered with a direct, unmediated turn to justice. Justice itself eludes the gaze, and insight into it can be gained only in terms of something other than justice, only by turning to something else (literally, by ἀλληγορία).

It should, then, be emphasized that a continuity is clearly implied between, on the one hand, the order of the essence of justice and, on the other hand, that which is other than justice, that in terms of which justice can be accessed, that is, the living πόλις. No separation or essential distinction is posited between them—no contrast between the invisible region of the objects of noetic contemplation and the visible domain of becoming in which the city belongs, between the immutable fixity of the eidetic and the fluctuating mutability of the "genetic."[3] The riddle of justice itself is simply written in letters too small and too far to be read. The nearsighted, looking out into the distance, can discern only confused, shimmering shadows—hence the necessity of observing the text of justice somewhere else, as it were, there where it is presented in a magnified version. The elaboration on the just city is such a magnifying device. No bridge between radically discontinuous orders is involved, not even a transliteration: the letters of justice are simply brought closer and to a "bigger place." (Notice, then, how the question of the essence of justice is posed in terms of reading, of interpreting the written signs of justice. Justice emerges as an originally signed matter.)

But, in this way, *finding* the essence of justice (for who would dare to say that justice could be founded, created, brought forth?) appears to be intimately intertwined with the *founding,* with the making, of the city. The determination of justice would be crucially involved in (indeed, indistinguishable from) the emergence and construction of the city. Even more precisely, the *destiny* of the eidetic would depend on the unfolding of γένεσις, on the becoming of the city. And finding, the discovering that discloses what is to contemplation, would no longer be clearly distinct from founding and in general from the deep involvement in becoming which characterizes all making (γένεσις, ποιεῖν).[4]

What does, then, the just city, the magnified image of the writing of justice, look like? How does its magnified text read? Down at the port, under the spell of Socrates' λόγοι, the guests gathered at Kephalos's house come to envision the spectacle of a city in accord with itself. In this city, differences harmoniously unfold according to the rhythm and necessity proper to them. Quite remarkably, the emergence of differences spontaneously and unproblematically flows into fixed configurations so as not to involve conflict, confusion, disorder, or division.

According to the Orphic and Hesiodic doctrines concerning the human races,[5] Socrates lays down the fundamental structure of the community constituting this πόλις. As is well known, he distinguishes three main classes of citizens: that of craftsmen and farmers, that of the auxiliary guardians, and that of the ruling guardians. The basic distinction, then, is between those who produce (whether by bringing forth crops from the soil or by making artifacts), thus supporting the subsistence of the city, and those who keep, those whose task is supervising, defending, and preserving the shape and structure of the communal organism from the attacks of enemies and time—in brief, from change.[6]

This political configuration, on the one hand, prepares and makes possible the subsequent elaboration of the structure of the ψυχή. Thanks to the isomorphism assumed since the beginning between city and soul, the threefold structure of the city foreshadows that of the soul. In this sense, then, the political magnifying prefiguration of the soul grounds the psychological discussion proper. On the other hand, though, the positing of the political classes presupposes a psychological ground, is secured to it and draws authority and validation from it. Indeed, in order for the subdivision into classes not to be a purely arbitrary, conventional gesture, there must be an essential link between political classes and psychological types (natural kinds: γένη).[7] The allotment of each citizen to one or other of the political classes must be exclusively based on the citizen's psychological constitution, on *who* the citizen *is*—not on privileges linked to birth or on other contingent, accidental factors. In this sense the image of the πόλις is but a projection emanating from the ψυχή, and all political order as well as political action have to be referred back to that originary ground, conformed to such ground, measured and evaluated in terms of it.

It is, then, the order of one's soul (the psychological kind one embodies) which necessitates the belonging in one class and ultimately determines the task to be taken up, the purpose to be fulfilled, and the role to be played in the city. Thanks to this unity of communal and individual purposiveness, furthermore, carrying out one's own task means to realize one's ownmost potential and, at the same time, to fulfill a vital function in the economy of the organism—hence to be in agreement with every other aspect of the πόλις, with the whole. Each citizen, says Socrates, "must be brought to that which naturally suits him (πρὸς ὃ τις πέφυκε)—one man, one job—so that each man, practicing his own, which is one, will not become many but one; and thus, you see, the whole city will naturally grow to be one (μία φύηται) and not many" (423d).

In the just city, then, all the citizens, men and women alike, mind their own task, and that alone. Everyone seems who (s)he is and does what is fitting to whom (s)he is. Everyone is self-possessed and quite transparent—to the others as well as to him- or herself. This is in fact crucial if the survival and continuity of the city have to be secured. As Socrates explains,

> That men should become poor menders of shoes, corrupted and pretending to be what they are not, isn't terrible (δεινόν) for a city. But you surely see that men who are not guardians of the law and of the city, but seem to be, utterly destroy an entire city, just as they alone can discern the crucial moment (τὸν καιρὸν ἔχουσιν) to govern it well and make it happy. (421a–b)

In order for the just city to subsist, in order for it to be at all thinkable, a fine attunement, or even the coinciding, of being, appearing, and acting is necessary. Any fracture between them must be healed. Being what one seems, and vice versa, seems to be connected with an ability to penetrate the secret of time, to divine its movement (and what is to unfold in such movement) so as not to be moved. It is such ability that allows one to perform one's task well.[8] The prescription, thus, is that one remain close to whom (s)he is. Such a coincidence and coordination would disclose one to oneself, give one back to oneself—resolve the ancient riddle (the one Oedipus faced in facing himself, that is, the sphinx) and satisfy Apollo's imperative. In this absolute proximity to oneself, in this reunion, one would see through appearances and smoke screens, straight into one's own being, far and clear. Finally, strange and wondrous (δεινός), with penetrating sight, one would know one's own as well as each one's own—with no mediation and hence no possibility of deflection, distortion, or dissimulation. The unity of being and seeming would make deception and lying, pretense and delusion, sorcery and other tricks impossible. Such coincidence of being and seeming would make the truth of human beings accessible—of those beings for whom and through whom the dislocation of being and seeming originally arises.[9]

Immersed in this magnificent clarity, relieved from confusion, error, faction, and treachery, in brief from the causes of degeneration—such would essentially be the just city, or even the essence of the city tout court. Indeed, as Socrates suggests, it may not even be "fit to call 'city' another than such as we have been equipping" (422e). This is the "perfectly good" city—"*if,* that is, it has been correctly founded" (427e; emphasis added). It is within these walls, in this "bigger place," that justice may reveal itself, be glimpsed at, perhaps even captured. It is now the philosopher's turn to chase his prey. "So then," says Socrates, "we must, like hunters, now station ourselves in a circle around the thicket and pay attention so that justice doesn't slip through somewhere and disappear into obscurity" (432b).

The surprising disclosure following this resolution is that justice has accompanied, unseen, the unfolding of the discussion from the start. Socrates now realizes this:

> It appears, you blessed man, that it [justice] has been rolling around at our feet from the beginning (ἐξ ἀρχῆς) and we couldn't see it after all, but were quite ridiculous. As men holding something in their hand sometimes seek what they're holding, we too didn't look at it but turned our gaze somewhere far off, which is also perhaps just the reason it escaped our notice (ἐλάνθανεν). (432d–e)

What is near, indeed, closest, escapes the attention of the one looking far into the distance. Justice was in the discourse since the beginning, but in the mode of concealment (λήθη). It is that which guided the development of the discourse, that is, the founding and elaboration of the city. It is "[t]hat rule we set down at the beginning as to what must be done in everything when we were founding the city" (433a). Socrates finally shares his insight:

> This—practicing what is one's own (τὸ τὰ αὑτοῦ πράττειν)—when it comes into being in a certain way, is probably justice. . . . After having considered moderation, courage, and prudence, this is what's left over in the city; it provided (παρέσχεν) the power (δύναμιν) by which all these others came into being; and, once having come into being, it provides them with preservation (σωτηρίαν) as long as it's in the city (ἕωσπερ ἂν ἐνῇ). (433b)

Justice, then, was crucially involved in the coming to be of the city and of what is in the city. An essential connection is here intimated between γένεσις and δικαιοσύνη—and justice appears (if fleetingly) as the law (the *potential* law?) of generation, as the ground of the power of coming into being, as intimately related to the possibility of generation, to the ordering and sustaining of generation. An even more direct link between justice and bringing forth is made explicit shortly afterwards, when Socrates intimates that justice *is itself* "this power (δύναμιν) which produces (παρέχεται) such men and cities" as those under consideration (443b).

But justice (which, thus understood, and in the most pregnant sense of the double genitive, is *of becoming*) is just as essentially linked to preservation, to keeping safe—to *saving*, even. Indeed,

> When one who is a craftsman or some other kind of money-maker by nature, inflated by wealth, multitude, strength, or something else of the kind, tries to get into the class (εἶδος) of the warrior, or one of the warriors who's unworthy into that of the adviser and guardian, and these men exchange tools and honors with one another . . . —then I suppose it's also your opinion that this change in them and this meddling are the destruction (ὄλεθρον) of the city. (434a–b)

Such "meddling among the classes" is "the greatest harm for the city" and "extreme evil-doing" (μάλιστα κακουργία). This is injustice (ἀδικία) (434b–c), crucially associated with quarrels, destruction, degeneration, and ultimately ignorance and lies.[10] Justice, then, appears to be doubly implicated in becoming: it informs the unfolding of becoming and constitutes the countermovement, perhaps even a certain suspension of such unfolding, that is, guards, protects, allows what has come to be to linger for a while, allots to each its own time. However, it does so, Socrates specifies, as long as it itself is there (ἕωσπερ ἂν ἐνῇ, 433b).

Later, in describing justice and injustice in the ψυχή by reference to his findings in the context of the πόλις, Socrates explicitly presents justice as the ordering of the living. Justice appears as the configuring operation whereby the soul is harmonized, unified, brought into accord with itself. The human who lives accordingly, Socrates says,

> doesn't let each part in him mind other people's business or the classes (γένη) in the soul meddle with each other, but really sets his own house in good order (εὖ θέμενον) and rules himself; he arranges (κοσμήσαντα) himself, becomes his own friend, and harmonizes (ξυναρμόσαντα) the three parts, exactly like three notes in a harmonic scale, lowest, highest, and middle. And if there are some other parts in between (μεταξὺ), he binds them together and becomes entirely one from many (ἕνα γενόμενον ἐκ πολλῶν), moderate and harmonized. (443d–e)

Such a human being, Socrates continues,

> believes and names a just and fine action one that preserves and helps to produce (ξυναπεργάζηται) this condition [of harmonized unity], and wisdom the knowledge that supervises this action (σοφίαν δὲ τὴν ἐπιστατοῦσαν . . . ἐπιστήμην); while he believes and names an unjust action one that undoes (λύῃ) this condition, and lack of learning (ἀμαθίαν), in its turn, the opinion (δόξαν) that supervises this action. (443e–444a)[11]

In this way, thanks to their magnifying imaginative effort (the just city was, after all, founded and envisioned through the λόγοι), Socrates and his interlocutors have caught a glimpse of justice and its opposite. In the founding of the city, "an origin and model (τύπον) for justice" was "probably" brought to light (443b–c).

The Circle of Growth

But here one should pause and reconsider once again the city whose most basic features have been recalled above. How is this city possible? What is necessary for it to come into being and continue to be according to justice? How can it avoid the injustice of falsity, corruption, and disintegration?

Calling this city into being required in and of itself quite a few portents and extraordinary measures. The discussion of this theme will be limited here to a few remarks on one of the most spectacular moments in the laying down of the city—the moment in which, with unheard-of audacity, the earliest stage of the founding of the city is withdrawn, dissimulated, and replaced by another account (414d ff.).

At the earliest stage of the founding, the cultivation of the soul through education, on the one hand, and the emergence of the three basic human types in their progressively clearer delineation, on the other, are shown in their simultaneous occurrence and mutual dependence. At a most primordial level, that is, the vision of the city develops out of the elaboration of this dynamic interplay between ψυχή and education. On the ground of the responses it elicits from the soul, education makes it possible to discern the three basic human types. In a way, these types begin to emerge as if simply awakened or un-covered, each according to its specific longing for learning. It is clear, however, that education is not simply a matter of dis-covering the psychological types. Rather, education is involved in the further definition and fixation of these types—and in their supplementation: that is to say, education will have subtly determined the manner of the awakening of the soul, interpreted and oriented its possibilities, guided them toward a certain end (destination).

Socrates is, of course, aware of the shaping, constructive, genuinely poietic power of παιδεία. He is aware of the way in which upbringing in general operates at the most fundamental level, indelibly affecting the soul, making the soul thrive according to its most proper potentiality or crippling it irremediably. For how volatile, how structurally fragile and defenseless, is the soul prior to and aside from education! And yet, in spite of this awareness, education is subsequently denied its generative role and reduced (or, perhaps, elevated) to the status of mere unveiling of self-subsisting psychic structures. In this way, not only is the ψυχή posited (in spite of the initial proviso, according to which it is thanks to the bigger letters of the city that the soul could be envisioned), but also, most crucially, it is viewed as totally free from the contamination of becoming, experience, education.

For the sake of such redetermination of education, Socrates impresses a new turn upon the development of the city. These are the words he has the audacity to utter to this end:

> I'll attempt to persuade first the rulers and the soldiers, then the rest of the city, that the rearing and education we gave them were like dreams (ὀνείρατα); they only thought they were undergoing (πάσχειν) all that was happening to them, while, in truth, at that time they were under the earth within (ὑπὸ γῆς ἐντὸς), being fashioned (πλαττόμενοι) and reared themselves, and their arms and other tools being crafted (δημιουργουμένη). When the job had been completely finished, then the earth, which is their mother (ἡ γῆ αὐτοὺς μήτηρ οὖσα), sent them up. And now, as though the land (χώρας) they are in were a mother and a nurse (μητρὸς καὶ τροφοῦ), they must plan for and defend it, if anyone attacks, and they must think of the other citizens as brothers (ἀδελφῶν) and born of the earth (γηγενῶν).
> . . .
> "All of you in the city are certainly brothers," we shall tell them in telling the tale (μυθολογοῦντες), "but the god, in fashioning (πλάττων) those of you who are competent to rule, mixed gold in at their birth; this is why they are most honored; in auxiliaries, silver; and iron and bronze in the farmers and the other craftsmen." (414d–e)

The boldness of this turn is at once astonishing and indispensable. In virtue of this device, the emergence of psychic structures is totally severed from the horizon of becoming, from dynamic involvement and development—psychic structures are secured to a transcendent determination and become, thus, what is one's own *by nature*.[12] The process of cultivation of the soul preceding this turn is made to recede toward the background and eventually disappear. In fact, the world as dynamic unfolding itself disappears. Little does it matter that this myth will not convince the present citizens. It will, Socrates says, determine the subsequent generations.

Out of the secret recesses of the earth rise fully developed adults, mature and educated, their weapons and tools already made (these humans are, by nature and divine artistry, armed). Adults such as these will have to become what they already are. Their living and growing will have been a persisting. This would be the degree zero of becoming, the point at which becoming would be resolved into the clarity of what is. Education will be a matter of reminding one of this. It is, of course, relevant that this effacement of education in its generative character is not itself effaced, that is, that Socrates so emphatically displays his effacing operation. It is especially relevant that this effacement appears through and as a myth.[13]

The earliest stage of the founding, in which the question of education was broached and its relation to the determination of the ψυχή shown, is covered over, superseded, replaced by a myth. This myth establishes the self-subsistence of psychological configurations, and their natural (that is to say, divine) origin. Besides showing how fundamental the element of myth is in the founding of the city,[14] this turn paradigmatically exposes Socrates' irreducibly twofold position with respect to myth (poetry). On the one hand, in the course of the conversation leading to the education of the citizens, Socrates has considered poetry with great apprehension. Worried by the tremendous power of poetry to seduce, to deform and transform, to influence in undesirable ways, Socrates insists on the necessity of driving it outside the city's walls. Poetry casts its spell on the soul, makes the soul visionary—by its uncontrollable bringing forth of phantoms and other delusions, poetry attunes the soul in ineffable, insidious ways.[15] As originary making (as a making whose originary dimension eludes mastery), poetry sets the tone and the mood, illuminates and frames the world. But it does so without authority. And it is out of ignorance that it speaks of the ancient and venerable things. Poetry is, in essence, falsity (ψεῦδος, 377a). Socrates' attempts to contain this dangerous discourse are relentless, and the early confrontation briefly considered here is exemplary in this respect.

On the other hand, the power of poetry to penetrate there where speeches do not, to harmonize the soul and move it, is precisely the precious resource that Socrates seeks to capture. Poetry is never quite driven out of the city, never simply rejected for the sake of the establishment of the proper education. Rather, as this segment of the dialogue illustrates, poetry is even instrumental to the grounding of education at a more fundamental level, that is, to the establishment of education as the propaedeutic to ἀνάμνησις. Along with Socrates' suspicion and hostility toward poetry, it is, then, necessary to notice his attempt at making poetry calculable and administering it—at keeping it, indeed, within the city, but tamed and in the service of the project of the founders—as if this were possible. As if poetry, the unemployable par excellence, could be usefully set to work.

For the city to come into being, and for its foundation to take place beyond the contingent realm of becoming, then, a quite divine intervention was necessary—in fact, an opportunistic utilization of the poietic power of poetizing, of making, of ποιεῖν. And what would be necessary to preserve this city?

The constitution of such a city must be safeguarded against the possibility of reverting into convention, into a simulacrum of itself, into a purely formal self-perpetuation. In other words, the patrimony of that constitution should not be lost in its transmission. The city was founded according to the immutable order of the natural (of the ψυχή, or, again, of the divine). Indeed, the city is based on so perfect a correspondence of becoming to its own immutable pattern that becoming tends to disappear from view, into a complete identity with its unchanging law. This absolute proximity of being and appearing must be defended. In its growth, the city must remain close to itself. After all, it should be remembered that Socrates' attempt at founding the just city in speech is not an exercise (let alone a game) carried out at an abstract level. Rather, it is also and significantly a response to the self-enforcement of sophistry (Thrasumakhos), to the authoritative ossification of δόξα, and to the complex of non- or pre-reflective familial and tribal commitments (Kephalos). The just city, brought into being as a response to the injustice of impostors and ravenous wolves feasting on the dying city, must tirelessly be guarded against them.

It is in light of these preoccupations that one should interpret the calculations for optimized procreation, the rearing of children in common (outside of the structure of the family), and the prescriptions concerning the proper acknowledgment of children who are essentially rulers even though they may be born from people of another class (and vice versa). All these measures are meant to keep the just city, generation after generation, as close to its first appearance as possible. The just city must grow without transforming itself, in a pure coinciding of development and preservation. In order to obtain this, the transmission of roles from generation to generation must remain exclusively based on being, on who one is, that is, on what human kind one embodies. And, of course, the very embodiment of human kinds must be controlled, so that the coming of kinds into bodies may be constant, always the same.

In the further elucidations provided in Book V, Socrates makes it clear that the jurisdiction over poetic creation and that over procreation are intimately intertwined—that, indeed, the former is essential to the exercise of the latter. The continuity and the conformity of procreation are significantly ensured by resorting to poetry. The lie of poetry, curbed and integrated into the political project, is employed as a φάρμακον at various stages of the founding discourse. The so-called "noble lie" discussed above is only the most outstanding illustration of this pattern. As Socrates reiterates here, "it's likely that our rulers will have to use a throng of lies (ψεύδει) and deceptions (ἀπάτη) for the benefit (ὠφελεία) of the ruled. And, of course, we said that everything of this sort is useful as a sort of remedy (φαρμάκου)" (459c–d).[16] However, at this juncture, Socrates proceeds to make explicit the connection between the poetic remedy and "marriages and procreations" (γάμοις καὶ παιδοποιίαις):

> On the basis of what has been agreed (ὡμολογημένων), there is a need for the best men to have intercourse (συγγίγνεσθαι) as often as possible with the best women, and the reverse for the most ordinary men with the most ordinary women; and the offspring (τὰ ἔκγονα) of the former must be reared but not

that of the others, if the flock is going to be of the most eminent quality. And all this must come to pass without being noticed (γιγνόμενα λανθάνειν) by anyone except the rulers if the guardians' herd is to be as free as possible from faction (ἀστασίαστος).

. . .

So, then, certain festivals and sacrifices must be established by law at which we'll bring the brides and grooms together (ξυνάξομεν τάς τε νύμφας καὶ τοὺς νυμφίους), and our poets must make hymns suitable to the marriages that take place. The number (πλῆθος) of the marriages we'll leave to the rulers in order that they may most nearly preserve (διασώζωσι) the same number of men (ἀριθμὸν τῶν ἀνδρῶν), taking into consideration wars (πολέμους), diseases, and everything else of the sort; and thus our city will, within the limits of the possible, become neither big nor little (μήτε μεγάλη μήτε σμικρὰ). (459d–460a)

This passage, in its programmatic character, occasions a number of considerations.

The political prescription is such that the πόλις may be stabilized in its ways and proportion, that it may subsist intact, growing neither bigger nor smaller. This counteracts the expansionistic thrust impressed earlier upon the newly born city by Glaukon, who had brought the aristocratic passion for luxury to bear on the founding (372d ff.). Such an emphasis on the control of growth clearly echoes the earliest vision of the city, where the citizens were said to enjoy "sweet intercourse with one another (ἡδέως ξυνόντες ἀλλήλοις), and not produce children beyond their means (οὐχ ὑπὲρ τὴν οὐσίαν ποιούμενοι τοὺς παῖδας), keeping an eye out against poverty and war (πενίαν ἢ πόλεμον)" (372b). It may even seem that the overall operation of containment, control, and fixation of the just city is oriented toward that previous political model, as if attempting to approximate it as nearly as possible.

However, in contrast to the first city, which was envisioned in its healthy simplicity, harmoniously integrated in its environment, and entertaining peaceful relations with surrounding peoples, the just city is critically organized around a preoccupation with faction inside and war outside. Its very hierarchy reflects the urgency of these problems: the class of auxiliary warriors is required to fight wars against foreign enemies, that of wise rulers is necessary to watch over domestic affairs. To protect this city from inner turmoil and divisiveness, to preserve its peace and allow it to abide unchanged, it is necessary sharply to demarcate its interiority, to isolate it from becoming, to keep out all factors of destabilization and change. But this means to identify, on the one hand, this city with order and concordance, and, on the other hand, what lies outside such city with chaos. This city persisting in its freedom from faction is at the same time constantly readying itself for war. To perpetuate this peace means to project disagreement, horror,

and conflict outside—such is the cost of eidetic purity, that is, of political conservation, let alone conservatism. This is why the exercise of mastery over sexu-
ality and procreation, which is essential to the continuity of the city, here is explicitly disclosed in its link with both war (with regard to which the calculation
of the appropriate number of *men* is fundamental) and internal discord (to avoid
which the rulers must operate unseen, behind the scenes).

It is also remarkable that the community of utter transparency, within which
all veils would be lifted and nothing would stand in the way of the direct perception of what is, should be achieved and preserved crucially through the administration of the φάρμακον of lies and secrecy, that is, through concealment.
It may well be the case that poison and remedy indicate the same; that that
which in certain circumstances kills, at other times, in other respects, and in
different proportions may cure; that there is no way ultimately to discern revealing from veiling. But what, then, of the eidetic-ideological program? Is it
not becoming apparent that, precisely on Socratic terms, injustice is at the heart
of the allegedly just city—that the pursuit of justice discloses the extent of the
intimacy, of the inseparability of justice and injustice? Indeed, in the opening of
the present discussion it was underlined that the corrupted city and the city
brought forth by Socrates share a similar quest for stability, a certain crystallization of life in its shapes, and a rejection of metamorphosis. It is now apparent, moreover, that the Socratic psycho-political construction, haunted by an ignorance it tries to dissimulate through deliberate deception and the exploitation
of the power of poetry, can hardly be called just without qualification. For, as was
mentioned above, injustice is repeatedly associated with lack of learning and
lies. In its passion for self-assertion by such means, the Socratic city is, on
Socrates' own terms, far from a model of justice in its uncompromised essence.

For the moment, though, Socrates does not focus on the increasingly
aporetic character of his discourse. In spite of all obstacles, he limits himself to
tending to his "flock," this "community of pleasures and pains" (462b) where no
one utters the phrase "my own" (462c). Why should the coming into being and
enduring of such community be problematic, if, indeed, it is possible "among
other animals (ζώοις)" (466d)? Thus wonders one who has undertaken to divine the laws of the living (specifically of the human mode of living), to make
intelligible the truth of humans, to wrest this truth from life, in the name of life,
as an interpreter and spokesman (προφήτης) of life.

A systematic control over production and reproduction, over poetic as well
as physiological γένεσις, over the "genetic" in general, then, is that out of which
the just city is born and that which secures its constancy. "And hence," Socrates
promises, "the regime, once well started, will roll on like a circle in its growth"
(424a).

Of Life: The Dictation of the Muses

Book VIII of the dialogue marks a dramatic shift. Although dramatic, however, this shift does not strike one as surprising or sudden. Indeed, it comes after having been announced in various ways, after having been consistently prepared in the course of the bringing forth of the just city "in λόγος." Because of the injustice variously involved in the coming into being of the just city (namely, the lie surrounding its origin, the surreptitious denial of its becoming), it is no wonder that this city, too, should pass away—and that this passing should be proclaimed by what was repressed, covered over in the founding of the just city.

The way in which Socrates introduces this shift is similar, in its register, to many preceding references to poetry. He addresses Glaukon with the following question: "Do you want us, as does Homer, to pray to the Muses to tell us how 'faction first attacked,' and shall we say that they speak to us with high tragic talk, as though they were speaking seriously, playing and jesting with us like children?" (545d–e). In spite of its irreverent tone, though, this address is going to lead to a quite novel development. Socrates is preparing to speak of the decay of the just city—of the degeneration which, even for the just city, is necessary and unavoidable. This is what the Muses, having been invoked and now speaking through Socrates himself, have to say:[17]

> A city so composed is hard to be moved (κινηθῆναι). But, since for everything that has come into being there is decay (γενομένῳ παντὶ φθορά ἐστιν), not even a composition such as this will remain for all time (τὸν ἄπαντα μενεῖ χρόνον); it will be dissolved (λυθήσεται). And this will be its dissolution (λύσις):[18] bearing and barrenness of soul and bodies (φορὰ καὶ ἀφορία ψυχῆς τε καὶ σωμάτων) come not only to plants in the earth (φυτοῖς ἐγγείοις) but to animals on the earth (ἐπιγείοις ζώοις) when revolutions complete for each the bearing round of circles (περιτροπαὶ ἑκάστοις κύκλων περιφορὰς ξυνάπτωσι).[19] . . . Although they are wise (σοφοί), the men you educated as leaders of the city will nonetheless fail to hit on the prosperous birth (εὐγονίας) and barrenness (ἀφορίας) of your kind (γένους) with calculation aided by sensation (λογισμῷ μετ' αἰσθήσεως), but it will pass them by, and they will at some time beget (γεννήσουσι) children when they should not. For a divine birth (θείῳ γεννητῷ) there is a period (περίοδος) comprehended by a perfect number.[20] (546a–b)

The turn is spectacular—truly, a coup de théâtre. Even the just city must decay. It will not simply endure through all time, that is, defeat time, annihilate it. Its rulers will not master life, penetrate its receptacles, grasp the secret of its cycles and, in virtue of this, establish and guard the measure for human generation. This inability, far from accidental or contingent, is announced as insurmountable—at least for these humans beings educated through the founding discourse. (But then, again, these would be the best among humans, or so it appeared to those involved in this dialogue.)[21] It is for essential reasons that these best among human beings under Socrates' guidance will fail to understand the revolutions of time and to capture the number of the timely conception of humans. With "calculation aided by sensation" they, however wise, cannot accomplish such a task.

The Muses proceed to describe how the number of human generation would be obtained.[22] Then they continue unfolding the irreversible degradation of the city:

> This whole geometrical number is sovereign of better and worse begettings (γενέσεων). And when your guardians from ignorance (ἀγνοήσαντες) of them cause grooms to live with brides out of season (παρὰ καιρόν), the children will have neither good natures (εὐφυεῖς) nor good luck (εὐτυχεῖς). Their predecessors will choose the best of these children; but, nevertheless, since they are unworthy, when they, in turn, come to the powers (δυνάμεις) of their fathers, they will as guardians first begin to neglect us by having less consideration than is required, first, for music (μουσικῆς), and, second, for gymnastics; and from there your young will become more unmusical (ἀμουσότεροι).[23] And rulers chosen from them won't be guardians very apt at testing Hesiod's races (γένη) and yours—gold and silver and bronze and iron. And the chaotic mixing of iron with silver and of bronze with gold engenders unlikeness and inharmonious irregularity (ἀνομοιότης ἐγγενήσεται καὶ ἀνωμαλία ἀνάρμοστος), which, once they arise, always breed war and hatred (ἀεὶ τίκτει πόλεμον καὶ ἔχθραν) in the place where they happen to arise. Faction (στάσιν) must always be said to be "of this ancestry." (546b–547a)

Because of a certain limit in their cognition, the rulers will be unable to reckon with time and to administer procreation accordingly. The καιρός, the proper moment for the work (or even time as the dynamically unfolding structure of what is), will elude them—and they will operate literally "aside" from it, in an increasing divergence from it. Being unable to grasp the unity of time and the order of the living (indeed, time as such order), they will be unable to keep dissolution, that is, injustice, at bay. The error made through calculation aided by the senses will engender untimely offspring increasingly prone to be betrayed by sensation—confusing gold with bronze, silver with iron, no longer being able to discern the Hesiodic kinds. From this disorder will come hatred, war, and the unrest destroying the city from within.

In spite of all the worries concerning the possibility, in principle, of the just city, in spite of all the efforts to show how the city is perfectly possible from a logical point of view, the just city turns out to be possible only in a highly qualified sense.[24] It is possible in its limits, in its passing away—and hence, not as purely just, not separate from injustice and corruption, not free from the λύειν of injustice.[25] The unjust cities which become visible out of the degeneration of the just one are not *other patterns* alongside the pattern of the just city. They are, rather, the *other possibilities* harbored within the just city, its other faces temporally released—almost a trace of δύναμις at the heart of actuality. This distance from itself, this seeming what it is not (and vice versa), marks the limit of the just city, its mortality[26]—*but also its life.*[27]

And lie, mutability, error are at its heart, and injustice at the heart of justice. Or perhaps the speaking of the Muses necessitates an other understanding of justice, of justice not in its remoteness from the living, but as encrypted in the living. The riddle of the ψυχή, far from being made transparent through the image of the πόλις, is resolved into another riddle—into the disclosure of the living in its aporetic structure. Thus dictate the Muses, in a saying which is no longer ancillary but which irrupts, irrepressible, in the midst of the calculating discourse.

"And we'll say that what the Muses answer . . . is right (ὀρθῶς)," says Glaucon. Socrates' reply unhesitatingly emphasizes the compelling, binding quality of such "correctness" and attributes to it the status of necessity. "Necessarily," he says—"for they are Muses" (547a).

Dia-logical Necessity

What emerges in this discussion is an irrepressible return of life, an irruption of life (in its death-bringing fluctuation) in the midst of the discourse aiming at controlling it. This irruptive movement eventually undoes the politico-eidetic construction, a construction that can be seen as a reactive reply to the blind self-enforcement of convention witnessed in Book I. But such a reaction, precisely qua reaction, shares many of the same problematic features observed in the unreflective exercise of δόξα. Analogously to the latter, it is above all, in its passion for mastery, life-denying. The movement of life destabilizing such reactive discourse points to a community (enacted in the very unfolding of the dialogue) whose ground is neither mere appearances, in the sense of convention and custom, nor ideal fixity. This community (this other πόλις) is rooted in δόξα otherwise understood—in the shared seeming, appearing, surfacing of phenomenality. For δόξα (appearing, seeming) will never simply have coincided with the manipulation and formulaic reduction of appearing observed in the city below. Phenomena will never simply have coincided with convention or reputation.

Such an upsurge of life casts light on an other kind of necessity—not the necessity of Socrates' λόγοι, but a necessity imposing itself on the λόγοι and on Socrates. Such an incidence of necessity shows the impossibility of what appeared, in λόγος, to be possible. What thus emerges is a nonlogical, extra-logical order of necessity—an order of necessity which one would want to think in conjunction with life. Excessive to the horizon of logicality (which alleges to be the horizon of all horizons, endowing the claims it grounds with the status of universality), this order of necessity is similarly excessive to the domain of contingency (which is but the counterpart, complement, and projection of the logic of universality).

The inability of Socrates and his interlocutors properly to determine justice (that is to say, to found the perfectly just city, the city which would not be exposed to decay) is only later, in Book VIII, disclosed as a limit structurally inherent in human beings. At this stage the Muses announce that such cognitive insufficiency is not an accidental feature of this particular dialogical circumstance. They disclose this lack as necessary (in the sense of unavoidable) and as exhibiting a necessitating function with respect to the development of the dialogue. Such powerlessness having a necessitating power demands the explicit acknowledgment of the heretofore repressed element of mortality—of the mortality of the just city, too.

But this means that earlier manifestations of this powerlessness (e.g., Socrates' having to resort to the analogy between πόλις and ψυχή because otherwise unable to discern justice, or taking other allegorico-mythical detours) cannot be reduced to a matter of mere contingency. They may not simply be seen as contingently necessary. (While one may envision different mythical-iconic courses to follow, *that* one must take a circuitous path to the issue at stake is inevitable. For one does not have a vision allowing for a more direct perception of the subject matter. This is why, among other things, the mythical-imaginative element is never simply separable from λόγος, never too remote from it.) Just as these manifestations of powerlessness cannot be reductively viewed as necessary and necessitating solely in the order of contingency, so they cannot be viewed (in an equally reductive way) as pertaining to the order of universality. They do, indeed, compel assent as soon as they manifest themselves: no one present challenges Socrates' imaginal turns, neither in their occurrence as such nor, most importantly, in the specific courses they happen to draw. No one questions, for instance, the appropriateness of Socrates' psycho-political analogy. This readiness to follow shared by everyone involved in the dialogue (this agreement, or desire to agree, which gathers those present together) does, indeed, determine the development and orientation of the discussion. But, again, the necessity here at work can hardly be brought to coincide with necessity in the strictly logical sense, understood according to contemporary parlance.

One could perhaps speak here of dia-logical necessity, of a necessitating force operating in the space of dialogue, characterizing the results (if results there be) of dialogue and sustaining its unfolding.[28] In this sense, no claim put forth in this space, in any singular dialogical scene, may present itself as logically necessary. It could even be said that such a category is not pertinent in this context (and, if not in this, one wonders in what other context such category would be pertinent). For the λόγος of δια-λόγος, by its very occurrence, calls into question the distinction between logically sound, universal claims and claims dictated by contingent necessity, as well as, more broadly, the separation between the domain of λόγος and that of contingency. Dialogical necessity will have manifested itself in and as an operation, in and as ἀναγκάζειν—a force, so to speak, which compels.

Similar remarks may be put forth with regard to the later announcement by the Muses. In light of its compelling character, this kind of statement cannot be dismissed as having a merely contingent value. Yet, in what sense, in what way, if otherwise than universally, does the Muses' statement express a necessity? One would wish to think the order of necessity here glimpsed at in terms of life, in terms of the necessity of the living, maybe as living necessity—spoken by the Muses through Socrates. Beyond the logic defined by the polarity of contingency and universality (the logic made possible by a certain isolation of and purification from contingency), such order of necessity would involve the acknowledgment of and coming to terms with a set of delimiting factors *experienced* as ineludible. It involves extending and generalizing such acknowledgment only tentatively and never quite abstractly. The experience of the human limit concerning sight extinguishes neither the desire nor the quest for a vaster, more discerning vision.

Of Justice without Idea

Thus, what was brought into being following the way of the Muses, what, in its development, found its cohesion and direction by reference to the Muses, will become "more unmusical" and gradually wither. Because of a certain inability of humans to track the Muses and abide in their presence, to grasp their whispering and master the mathematics of the living, the musical city, precisely in its claim to divine ancestry and endless duration, is reminded of its mortality. What was given by the Muses, the Muses will have taken back. Thus operate the Muses—that is, the law of becoming, the order of its unfolding, the justice of coming into being and passing away. (In this connection, let it be recalled, laws in the sense of νόμοι can be comprehended as songs sung to the music of justice.)

What, then, of JUSTICE? What of the possibility of understanding it, of finding out about it in itself? If justice cannot be thought apart from the horizon of γένεσις; if, as was shown, the detour through the theater of the just city is essential to the investigation of justice; if, indeed, justice originally gives itself in written letters only to be magnified; if, that is, justice cannot be thought as separate and as such; or, again, if thought is not strictly and exclusively *of* εἶδος—then justice must be thought anew.[29] It *demands* to be thought anew. If the discourse of the eidetic is infused with change (mutability and lie . . . myth), then justice must be thought in the light of the impossibility of its purely eidetic identity—in the light of the problematization of identity tout court. But thinking anew in the light of the loss of eidetic purity means thinking over and over again, never having thought a question through to the end, being bound to thinking—to the recurrence of thinking, to its returns and repetitions.

Justice seems to give itself to THINKING as that which cannot be thought once and for all. For essential reasons, justice appears as that which does not let itself be brought to a last (final) determination. No shape given to it, no shape through and as which it presents itself, appears simply to endure intact. Nor does justice allow itself to be captured in terms of the synthetic aggregation (i.e., of the simultaneously integrative and superseding collection or recollection) of all its partial moments. For the recurrence of thought demanded by justice does not appear to find a rest and a completion, especially not the rest and completion constituting the reward of the dialectical labor. Rather, the demand *of* justice discloses thinking, in its emergence, as structurally intertwined with and implicated in the structures of becoming—indeed, as that which the structures of becoming indeterminately call for and in(de)finitely provoke. Thinking occurs as re-thinking, then—in its addictive, intoxicating structure and dynamic character. Thus, repetition is revealed at the heart of thinking and as vital to thinking.

It is in this way that thinking comes to respond and correspond to justice. In giving itself to thinking as the yet-to-be-thought in its recurrence, justice sets thinking in motion, demands that it unfold and become. It lays a claim on thinking, as if calling it into question, contesting each of its shapes. Thinking gives itself in and as response to such claim, to this extent revealing the claim itself. The provocation soliciting thinking is articulated in the movement of thinking itself. In this sense justice would not be brought to light, uncovered *by* thought, let alone thereby determined. Justice would come to light *through and as* the thinking articulation. It would inform, simultaneously call for and give itself as, thinking.

But if, indeed, thinking moves according to the provocation of justice (as though both pursued and eluded by it); if justice is that which moves thinking, the movement of thinking itself, then, in its movement (in its errant pursuit of justice), thinking pursues, that is to say, interrogates itself. The movement of thinking is crucially an interrogation of its own order, that is, of the structures of the DISCOURSE as which it presents itself. The dialogue on the πολιτεία and on the δίκαιος, through which and as which thinking unfolds, is incessantly provoked by the question of justice and articulates (itself as) such provocation. Compelled by this question, the dialogue does not come to a resolution, to rest absolved from the relational bonds constitutive of it. What the dialogue shows is not the unfolding of thinking according to the fixed determination of its proper order—of thinking as autonomous, free from involvement. Rather, it exposes thinking in its giving itself through the impulsion to come to terms with what provokes it, unfolding at one with such *vocatio* (or, which is the same, ordering itself through its unresolved impulsion to divine its own most proper possibilities). In this further sense, justice presents itself through and as thinking in its self-interrogation, in its movement of self-discovery, in its quest for the ordering and way of articulation most proper to it.

The dialogue on the πολιτεία articulates the question and mystery of LIFE. Since Socrates' initial confrontation with the doxastic crystallizations of life, it is clear that the investigation concerning the essence of justice will revolve around the question of generation, of γένεσις, of becoming—around the freeing of further possibilities for gathering and giving shape to becoming, around the desedimentation of ossified practices and assumptions which curb life, around the healing of the πόλις which is out of joint, so that it may come back to life and life may flow through it again. But, intimated by numerous provisos disseminated throughout the dialogue, and eventually heralded by the Muses in Book VIII, the limits of the Socratic attempt irrepressibly shine forth. Such consistent marking of limits accompanies the discourse in its unfolding, in its coming into being and drawing to a conclusion. It points to the passing character of the dialogue even in its genuinely constructive moments, even as the dialogue itself is growing.

As pointed out above, Socrates' interruptive response to the doxastic violation or stiffening of life presents, in a few of its moments, a violence analogous to that which it seeks to interrupt. The Socratic response is to an extent bound to repeat certain features of that against which it moves. This is paradigmatically evident in the construction of the just city grounded on the dream (or nightmare) of the calculation of life. But this violent response is also, in its turn, recognized as such and interrupted. In this sense are the limits of the discourse marked. Even the supposedly incorruptible claims to and of transcendence, even the attempt at bringing the instability of becoming under an order other than the order of becoming, even the vision of the capitulation and final illumination of mystery has its time and must fade away. The philosophical discourse is specifically that articulation which does not dissimulate its violent character and which, eventually, admits its own violation. And the interruption it undergoes is not a mise-en-scène, the theatrical simulation which it will have predicted, calculated, and projected for itself.[30] This discourse unfolds as the undoing of another and does not conceal the undoing to which it itself is exposed. Not only is the interruption undergone not masterfully simulated, but also not dissimulated, not denied, not covered over in its occurrence. What comes to appear in and through the undoing *of* this discourse (the undoing perpetrated and undergone), what this discourse lets transpire and is haunted by is the play, unexplained but insuppressible, of γένεσις—of coming to be *and* passing away. In the dialogue on the πολιτεία and on the δίκαιος, then, the mystery of life is unfolded as such. Pervading and shaping the dialogue, life appears in its cycles, repetitions, and returns. This discourse is, literally, *of life*—more precisely, *of life returning.*

In an exchange previously mentioned, the unity of justice, thinking, discourse, and life is decisively exposed. At 432d–e, Socrates points out that justice was in play since the beginning of their inquiry, but in the mode of λήθη. Because of this, it escaped their attention (their sight is not that sharp after all). He continues: "It seems to me that we have been saying (λέγοντες) it and hearing (ἀκούοντες) it all along (πάλαι) without learning from ourselves (μανθάνειν ἡμῶν) that we were in a way saying it (ἐλέγομεν)" (432e). For the sake of a still perplexed and eager Glaukon ("A long prelude," he observes, "for one who desires to hear [ἐπιθυμοῦντι ἀκοῦσαι]"), Socrates elucidates further:

> Listen whether after all I am making sense in speaking (ἄκουε, εἴ τι ἄρα λέγω). That rule we set down at the beginning (ὃ γὰρ ἐξ ἀρχῆς ἐθέμεθα) as to what must be done in everything when we were founding the city—this, or a certain form of it (τούτου τι εἶδος), is, in my opinion, justice (ἡ δικαιοσύνη). Surely we set down and often said (πολλάκις ἐλέγομεν), if you remember (εἰ μέμνησαι), that each one must practice one of the functions in the city, that one for which his nature made him naturally most fit. (433a)

The intimation is that justice has informed the inquiry of justice and shaped its discursive development from the outset and throughout. Justice appears to have latently ordered the λέγειν through and as which the inquiry developed. Conversely, however, it should be emphasized that justice is as such glimpsed thanks to the labor of λέγειν. For justice was set down, yet remained undiscovered. It took the verbal articulation to recognize it, a posteriori—to make it surface and project its operation backwards. It is to such an extent that the emergence of justice and the venture of thinking-speaking are intertwined.

In the remarks that follow this exchange, moreover, justice is crucially connected with generation as well as the sustenance of what has come into being. Indeed, not only is justice said to be the source, the δύναμις engendering the other virtues and preserving them in their becoming (433b), but it ends up being associated with the movement of γένεσις in a broader sense. Socrates' suggestion, shortly thereafter, should be recalled again, according to which justice is nothing other than the "power that produces out of itself (παρέχεται) such men and cities" as the just ones (443b). In this further sense, justice emerges as a cipher of the working of life. But, again, besides announcing the belonging together of justice and γένεσις, this remark adumbrates the convergence and coincidence (if not the identity) of justice, discourse, and thought in its envisioning. For those humans and their city were brought forth "in λόγος," the discursive articulation in and as which thought gathers itself.

It is in light of this manifold concurrence that above it was proposed that, on one hand, justice would give itself through and as the thinking articulation, while, on the other hand, thinking, in its movement and pursuit of justice, would interrogate, pursue itself. If the inquiry is informed by that concerning which it is an inquiry, then inquiry will never have been free from the task of self-examination—self-examination of the inquiry itself in its λέγειν, as well as of that being whose mode of being exquisitely makes itself manifest through inquiry. Thus, compellingly emerging in the midst of the living, the question of justice appears to be, in an important sense, a question concerning this being who, as inquiring and as living, is informed by justice.[31]

Notes

1. It should also be pointed out that, in order to bring forth a city called just, or even merely an icon of it, a working comprehension of justice (however preconceptual, even preconscious) is required. A pre-understanding of justice grounds (perhaps motivates as well) the founding through which justice is sought. The founding reveals such prior, if unthematic, grasp. In this sense the labor of founding and contemplating appears as the self-articulation of the inarticulate, as an ex-plicating, literally, an un-folding.

2. Notice here the theme of the foreignness of that which is near, the invisibility of it.

3. With respect to this point, see contrasting passages such as *Phaedo* 79a.

4. Here one sees an illustration of *inventio* in its twofold sense.

5. Proclus calls these kinds "forms of life" (*In Remp.* II:74 ff.).

6. Notice that, strictly speaking, qua founder Socrates belongs with the makers.

7. There is no term in the Platonic text to designate the concept of political or socioeconomic class. At times (e.g., at 434b) εἶδος is used, but more often γένος (the term used to designate the mythical "races," which are *by nature*).

8. See the discussion on the καιρός, the crucial moment, in Book II (370b f.). "I suppose," says Socrates at that point, "that if a man lets the crucial moment in any work (ἔργου καιρόν) pass, it is completely ruined (διόλλυται)." Thus, he concludes, "each thing becomes more plentiful, finer, and easier, when one man, exempt from other tasks (σχολὴν τῶν ἄλλων ἄγων), practices one thing according to nature and in the crucial moment (κατὰ φύσιν καὶ ἐν καιρῷ)." See also 374c.

9. It is worth noticing, then, that the resolution of the riddle of the human being would annihilate the human being *as such*.

10. See, e.g., 351a, 351d, 382b.

11. Notice the juxtaposition, on the one hand, of justice, production, wisdom, knowledge, and, on the other hand, of injustice, destruction, ignorance, opinion. Things are, however, more complex than this schema would suggest. Let it simply be mentioned here that λύσις (destructiveness in the sense of dissolution, but also letting loose, and hence resolution, releasing, even redemption) is associated with philosophical liberation as much as it is with injustice: "Now consider . . . what their release and healing (λύσιν τε καὶ ἴασιν) from bonds and folly would be like if something of this sort were by nature to happen to them. Take someone who is released (λυθείη) and suddenly (ἐξαίφνης) compelled to stand up, to turn his neck around, to walk and look up toward the light" (515c). The philosophical movement, too, demands a certain destructiveness—just as the movement of life demands a certain resistance and coming to linger always already harbors a falling apart.

12. It is true that in this passage the language of (re)production is conspicuously used. And, yet, such language is only equivocally employed in connection with nature or the divine and, thus, comes to designate something quite different from human making.

13. In a rigorously Platonic fashion, poetry and myth are understood here as synonyms. See *Phaedo* 61b, where Socrates says that, "after the god," he considered that "a poet, if he is really to be a poet [maker] (ποιητὲς εἶναι), must compose [make] myths (ποιεῖν μύθους) and not speeches."

14. Myth (that is, on Socrates' own terms, injustice, delusion, instability) is, then, at the heart of the just city. Movement and mutability, the motility of δύναμις . . . *this* pervades the just city.

15. This, of course, is what Socrates himself does, in bringing forth the city in speech.

16. In this regard, it should be noticed that the just city does not seem to enjoy good health; it seems to be recovering from severe malaise and to need vigorous treatment in order to heal and preserve its well-being. Indeed, it will be necessary for its rulers "to use many drugs" (φαρμάκοις πολλοῖς). To this extent, such a city is contrasted to "bodies not needing drugs" (φαρμάκων), but willing to respond to a prescribed course of life" (459c). However just, the πόλις brought forth bears the trace of its origin out of the corrupted, even the "feverish" city (372e). In order to treat a similar case, Socrates points out that "the most courageous physician" is needed (459c). For the sake of the ailing city, the skilled political doctor, lacking adequate knowledge but not audacity, will administer lies—tell stories, sing songs, make music.

17. What follows is, properly, the discourse of the Muses speaking through Socrates, the inspired poet. Earlier in Book III, by failing to mention the invocation to the goddess with which the *Iliad* begins, Socrates had denied the Homeric saying its divine origin (392e f.).

18. See the comments above on the connection between the language of λύσις and injustice.

19. Generation and corruption are understood in terms of the ability and inability to bring forth (φέρειν) fruits, in terms of φορά (γονή) and ἀφορία (ἀγονία). The theme and language of sterility, of barrenness, of the interference interrupting γίγνομαι will be considered again later, in the context of the discussion of war. But the connection be-

tween lack of harmony, decay, inability to generate (or to generate properly), and conflict is quite explicit even at the end of this discourse (547a).

20. The divine, too, is inscribed within the circle of becoming.

21. Socrates had earlier imagined addressing such most excellent humans in this way: "So you must go down (καταβατέον), each in his turn, into the common dwelling of the others (τὴν τῶν ἄλλων ξυνοίκησιν) and get habituated along with them (ξυνεθιστέον) to seeing the dark things (τὰ σκοτεινὰ θεάσασθαι). And, in getting habituated (ξυνεθιζόμενοι) to it, you will see (ὄψεσθε) ten thousand times better than those there, and you'll know (γνώσεσθε) what each of the phantoms (εἴδωλα) is, and of what it is a phantom, because you have seen (ἑωρακέναι) the truth (τἀληθῆ) about beautiful, just, and good things. And thus, our city will be governed by you in a state of waking (ὕπαρ), not in a dream (ὄναρ) as the many cities nowadays are governed by men who fight over the shadows (σκιαμαχούντων) with one another" (520c–d). Yet, as it turns out, these rulers (however clear-sighted and awake) will not simply have prevailed over the shadows of entanglement, sleep, forgetfulness.

22. The passage on the nuptial number is one of the most obscure moments of the dialogue. For a list of interpretive attempts, see Adam, *The* Republic *of Plato*, p. xlviii ff.

23. The Muses were in play since the very beginning, after all.

24. Socrates' concern with the possibility of the just city is pervasive in the central Books of the dialogue, especially Book V. It should be said, however, that even at that stage the heuristic character of the discourse is not fully covered over. Says Socrates: "It was, therefore, for the sake of a pattern (παραδείγματος) . . . that we were seeking both for what justice by itself is like, and for the perfectly just man. . . . We were not seeking them for the sake of proving (ἀποδείξωμεν) that it's possible (δυνατὰ) for these things to come into being (γίγνεσθαι)" (472c–d).

25. On λύειν, again, see 443e–444a.

26. In his remarkable *Contemplation et vie contemplative selon Platon* (Paris: Vrin, 1950), André Jean Festugière calls this distance of the just city from itself (that is to say, this self-differing manifesting itself in the midst of the just city, this impossibility of simply leaving behind the realm of γένεσις in order to attain the pure contemplation of justice in its eternal, unchangeable essence) the tragedy of the just city—indeed, "le tragique de la *Republique*" (p. 401). The inescapable character of becoming is disclosed as tragic within the framework of a striving, of a passion for θεωρεῖν. See also *Laws* 803b–c.

27. For life does not come back only in its irrepressibly disruptive and deteriorating power, but simultaneously as the opening up of possibilities, as bringing forth of further, unimaginable fruits. As will be shown in detail later, the circulation of life appears to involve death.

28. In the context of dialogue, the pursuit of truth is never dissociated from the dimension of agreement, which entails both a coming to rest together and a movement to further determinations. Agreement may indeed be seen as that coming to rest which grants the openness and unfolding of the inquiry. As Socrates says in Book I, dialogue is that engagement whereby there is no need "of some sorts of judges who will decide (διακρινούντων)" and evaluate competing speeches. Instead, "if we consider just as we did a moment ago, coming to agreement (ἀνομολογούμενοι) with one another, we will ourselves be both judges and pleaders (δικασταὶ καὶ ῥήτορες) at once" (348b).

29. The view of the belonging of justice in γένεσις finds ulterior corroboration in two passages, in which justice (just as injustice) is said to be something that becomes

(γίγνομαι) (369a) and grows in the way in which things of nature grow (ἐμφύω) (372e). To the extent that the city provides the observatory, soil, and stage for the contemplation of justice, this seems indeed inevitable.

30. According to an understanding of the theatrical as exceeding the dimension of instrumental utilization, this sentence could alternatively read: And the interruption it undergoes is a mise-en-scène, but nonetheless not that which it will have predicted, calculated, and projected for itself.

31. Ultimately, then, the dialogue on the πολιτεία and on the δίκαιος may be seen as a transposition of the quest expounded in the *Apology*—the quest for self-knowledge elicited by the Delphic provocation.

PART TWO.
"A TALE WAS SAVED AND NOT LOST" (621 b): VISION AT THE END OF THE VISIBLE

Things await humans when they die which they neither expect nor imagine. (Her. 22 B 27)

There is no doubt that the Greeks sought to explain to themselves the ultimate mysteries "of the destiny of the soul" and everything they knew concerning education and purification, above all concerning the immovable order of rank and inequality of value from human being to human being, from their Dionysian experiences: here is the great depth, the great silence, for everything Greek—one does not know the Greeks as long as here the concealed subterranean entrance lies blocked.

. . . .

To wait and to prepare oneself; to await the springing of new sources, to prepare oneself in solitude for strange faces and voices; to wash one's soul ever cleaner from the fair dust and noise of this age; to overcome everything Christian through something over-Christian, and not only to remove it from oneself—for the Christian doctrine was the counterdoctrine against the Dionysian —; to discover again the South in oneself and to spread out above oneself a luminous, glittering, mysterious Southern sky; to conquer again for oneself Southern health and concealed powerfulness of soul; step by step to become more comprehensive, more over-national, more European, more over-European, more Eastern [morgenländischer], finally more Greek—for the Greek was the first great gathering and synthesis of everything Eastern and thus the inception of the European soul, the discovery of our "new world": —whoever lives under such imperatives, who knows what he may encounter one day? Perhaps even—a new day!

(Nietzsche, Fragment 41 [7], August–September 1885)

III. Preliminary Remarks in a Rhapsodic Form

By reference to the Socratic meditation on poetry, the present chapter undertakes to delineate Socrates' own μυθολογεῖν in its singular traits. Heterogeneous reflections, occasioned by the final myth as well as Socrates' statements on poetic matters, converge here, bringing together the theme of myth as restitution and recollection, the question of imitation in its ethical valence, the problematization of the thought of subjectivity in light of the experience of the poet. However preliminarily, such a multifarious strategy undertakes to respond to the difficulty of the mythical material and to solicit (if not encircle) it in its manifold suggestiveness.

Following the Socratic characterization of narrative-poetic modes, it becomes evident that no poetic utterance, indeed, no mode of discourse, may simply be free from the obscuring operation of μίμησις. Consequently, far from being distinguishable on the basis of a theoretical distinction between imitative and nonimitative enunciation, a poetic mode crucially differs from others in its *manner* of imitation, that is, according to *how* it is imitative, *how* it reckons with what cannot be eluded. Since, then, the uniqueness of a poetic saying is primarily a matter of comportment, comparative myth analysis proves to be particularly illuminating in the attempt to understand the way of Socratic μυθολογεῖν. In this preparatory and multifarious investigation, Socrates' ἀπόλογος is juxtaposed to Homer's epico-tragic singing, to Hesiodic poetry, and to the *Bhagavad Gita*. The turn to these texts, let this be said explicitly, is ventured so that, in their proximity, the Socratic saying may emerge in its irreducible characteristics. By no means does this juxtaposition undertake to develop detailed analyses of the other works.

The somewhat unusual reference to the *Gita* is occasioned quite simply by certain thematic parallels between the Hindu poem and the myth of Er—especially by the fundamental connection with the battlefield which is crucial in both cases. At any rate, there may be more reasons warranting a connection of the story of Er with Levantine mytho-philosophical districts than reasons grounding, for instance, the assimilation of the Platonic texts to the language and framework of Christianity—an assimilation systematically carried out, generation after generation, by Western philosophers no less than by classicists. At the same time, however, when in later chapters the myth of Er will be considered more closely and the issue of the circulation of the souls (from life to death and back to life) will be discussed, the parallel with the *Gita* will no longer be followed. It is precisely in this connection that classical scholarship traditionally turns to various Eastern sources and refers the "doctrine" exposed in the Platonic myth to Orphic and Pythagorean, but especially Indian, "theories" of the transmigration of the souls. Thoughtful (that is to say, philosophically discerning) research in this direction is a much needed task. But broaching such a theme just in passing, in the midst of a work otherwise oriented, would make the peril of superficiality practically inescapable. In order to avoid facile pronouncements on the exceedingly difficult question of the relation between Socrates' myth and the immense, immensely heterogeneous, Asian literature on metempsychosis, after this chapter consideration of the *Gita* will almost completely recede into the background.

At the beginning of Book X Socrates confronts poetry yet another time. The myth following this last confrontation and concluding the dialogue reflects and in a way repeats the arguments constituting the body of the dialogue. But this repetition is also a transfiguration. The crucially imaginal, metaphorical character of the discourse of life surfaces in its magnificence. The overpowering movement, the moving order, of life is brought into an outline but not captured, imaged but neither resisted nor calculated. This gathering moment, this coming together of the dialogue as a whole, is the place of the self-disclosure of life. More precisely, the gathering of the dialogue discloses the "daimonic place" (614c) of the circulation of the ψυχαί, that is, of the living.[1] The iconic discourse of μῦθος occurs as the self-disclosure of the ψυχή, as the discourse through which, as which the ψυχή gives and e/affects itself. But the circular motion of the souls, the field of their restless motility, is a moving figure of life. Indeed, the circling and transiting of the souls, their passing through thresholds between incommensurable dimensions, their crossing narrow openings and open expanses, their journeying across disintegrating emptiness and walls of forgetfulness images the circle of life in its fathomless discontinuity—the unfolding of life which enfolds death, the embrace from which life emerges as "death bearing" (617d).

Giving Back

The dialogue on the πολιτεία concludes with a myth. With the narration of the myth Socrates intends to celebrate justice, to do justice to the just and give back to them "in full" (τελέως) what the λόγος, in its insufficiency, still owes them. Socrates, that is, undertakes to *speak of* justice in such a way as to *do* justice, hence to bring about justice.[2] Socrates sets out to bring justice forth, to let it shine through his speaking, to let it transpire as that which at once calls for, structures, and orders his speaking.[3] This narration will properly have brought the dialogue to an end. It is already late.

This speaking will have had to gather the foregoing arguments and to repeat them. But, at the same time, such gathering and repetition will have occurred in a strange voice, in a way somewhat foreign to that which is gathered and repeated, as excessive and irreducible to the logic of summation and summary—of the *summa* tout court. This gathering, far from disguising itself, making itself invisible, and disappearing into the transparency of recapitulation, gives itself in its iconic thickness. In its spectacular conspicuousness, it presents the twofold character of originary disclosure *and* repetition, of creation *and* recollection—it presents, as is clear already, a problematic duplicity.

The story Socrates sets out to recount is an ἀπόλογος—an apologue, a fable, but also an apology (614b). For, indeed, its saying and the giving back occurring through it will not have been calculably adequate to and commensurate with what the λόγος still owes. Or perhaps, that which the λόγος still owes, which exceeds and escapes the grasp of the λόγος and to which the λόγος for essential reasons cannot respond—in brief, that which leaves the λόγος radically indebted, would precisely have to be thought as the immeasurable, the incommensurable, the incalculable. If this were the case, the restitution occurring through the fable would, in its very inadequacy, in its tentative character and fundamental lack, paradoxically appear to be most appropriate. The fable supplements and completes the λόγος—but not according to the logic and aspirations of the λόγος. The supplementation and completion the ἀπόλογος provides, rather, will have reflected the radical indeterminacy that pervades the λόγος in its exposure to an indeterminate claim—the indeterminacy belonging to λόγος while, indeed, marking its limits and exceeding it.[4]

But how to indicate, if not grasp, that which the λόγος still owes—that which keeps the λόγος indebted and will have demanded an ἀπόλογος? After enumerating "the prizes, wages, and gifts (ἆθλά τε καὶ μισθοὶ καὶ δῶρα) coming to the just man while alive from gods and human beings, in addition to those good things (τοῖς ἀγαθοῖς) that justice itself provided (αὐτὴ παρείχετο ἡ δικαιοσύνη)," Socrates points to the further task of recalling those rewards that "await each when dead" (613e–614a). "And these things should be heard," he proposes, "so that in hearing them each of these men will have gotten back (ἀπειλήφῃ) the full measure of what the argument owed (τὰ ὑπὸ τοῦ λόγου ὀφειλόμενα)" (614a). It is, then, in order to elaborate on justice in its broadest ramifications, in order to glimpse at its operation in the domain of living and dying, that the ἀπόλογος is necessary. Λόγος will not, indeed, have sufficed to carry out this task—and this for fundamental reasons, reasons grounding or, better, un-grounding the λόγος. Indeed, it is not that μῦθος becomes indispensable when moving beyond the domain of the mortal sojourn, while λόγος would be adequate to account for justice within this domain. For even the account of the prizes enjoyed by the just in this life will have been highly tentative, marked by reiterated qualifications and signs of caution.[5] Nor, furthermore, is it possible to draw a clear distinction between life (this life) and death, for the concern with justice shows precisely their unity and interpenetration.[6] The problem is more serious, profound, and regards λόγος as a whole, as it has unfolded since the beginning.

In the remarks leading to the μῦθος of Er which will conclude the conversation, the radical indebtedness of λόγος is revealed. Socrates returns to collect a credit that initially had to be granted to his interlocutors: "Then, will you give back to me what you borrowed in the argument (ἐν τῷ λόγῳ)?" he asks Glaukon (612c). What was given earlier was the possibility of dissociation between the being and the seeming of justice, so that it would be possible for someone unjust to seem just, and vice versa. The discourses of Glaukon and Adeimantos in Book II maintained precisely this, and, in undertaking to respond to them, Socrates had to concede such a premise. This dissociation, Socrates now points out, "had to be granted for the sake of the λόγος (τοῦ λόγου ἕνεκα)" so that the argument could at all take place (612c). At this point, however, thanks to the λόγος, justice and injustice "have been judged" (κεκριμέναι). Hence, Socrates continues, "on justice's behalf, I ask back again the reputation (δόξης) it in fact has among gods and among human beings; and I ask us to agree (ὁμολογεῖν) that it does enjoy such a reputation, so that justice may also carry off the prizes that it gains from seeming and bestows on its possessors" (612d). What was accorded must be returned—not so much to Socrates, but to justice itself "and the rest of virtue" (612b–c). Socrates makes such a request so that it may be recognized that appearances and reputation may be at one with being and that through them, thanks to them, being (the being of justice, for example) may shine forth. This restitution entails the shared acknowledgment, the agreement that what was initially granted "for the sake of the argument" has been shown, in the course of the argument, to be untrue. The argument had to be made possible in order to show, through its own unfolding, the impossibility of its premises, of what was conceded for the sake of it. Hence, this giving back will require the withdrawal of the concession (for what was conceded turns out not to be the case) and the restitution of justice to itself, that is, the recomposition of the broken unity of its being and appearance. Justice is reclaimed in its being as well as in its manifestations, in its occurrence in thinking as well as in its phenomenality.

Thus, returning justice to itself (i.e., speaking in such a way as to give back to justice what is its own, to let justice manifest itself) and giving back to the just what the argument still owes them occur in one and the same movement. In its indebtedness, the λόγος (or even the δια-λόγος) strives to account for justice—that is to say, simultaneously, to account for what makes the just ones just, for the justice governing them, for the justice that they *are*. It is in such a striving to say justice and do justice that the λόγος will have become an ἀπόλογος. For the judgment, the κρίνειν carried out thanks to λόγος will always have been haunted by a radical inadequacy—will, in other words, have been grounded on a borrowed premise now to be given back, unmasked, recognized as questionable. What this un-grounding movement shows, among other things, is that doing justice will never have coincided with judging.[7]

It should be observed, incidentally, that this dynamic of restitution whereby the λόγος turns against itself resembles the radical questioning of hypotheses which was said to distinguish dialectic. Indeed, as was pointed out in Book VI during the discussion of the divided line, the singular feature of dialectic would precisely be the problematization of premises, which leads to their withdrawal qua unquestioned beginnings, and hence to a certain emancipation from them. As Socrates puts it,

> By the other segment of the intelligible I mean that which λόγος itself grasps with the power of dialectic (τοῦ διαλέγεσθαι δυνάμει), making the hypotheses not beginnings (ἀρχάς) but really hypotheses—that is, stepping stones (ἐπιβάσεις) and springboards (ὁρμάς)—in order to reach what is free from hypotheses (ἀνυποθέτου) at the beginning of the whole. When it has grasped this, argument now depends on that which depends on this beginning and in such fashion goes again down to a completion (ἐπὶ τελευτὴν καταβαίνῃ); making no use of anything sensed in any way, but using εἴδη themselves, going through them to them, it ends (τελευτᾷ) in εἴδη too. (511b–c)

The resemblance between the suspension of beginnings outlined here and that taking place toward the end of the dialogue is so striking that one wonders whether the latter discussion, in which Socrates withdraws what was initially conceded, asks back the appearance or reputation of justice, and proceeds to tell a fable, might perhaps be envisioned as a kind of dialectical exercise. For what would dialectic itself be, if not that which occurs in and as διαλέγεσθαι, the power of disclosing insight through the unfolding of dialogue? And is the ἀπόλογος, the concluding story, not made possible by the discussion heretofore articulated—is it not necessitated precisely through what the διάλογος has come to show? In other words, does it not take the development of the entire dialogue in order to cast light on the dubious character of its premises? In drawing to a close, the dialogue points beyond itself, suspends its own assumptions, announces a decisive shift away from the analyses, judgments, and assessments so far formulated. It is, of course, of the utmost importance that, in this "dialectical enactment," the twisting free of λόγος from hypotheses as well as from itself coincides with its turning into μῦθος.[8]

If the structure of such twisting and turning were indeed to be acknowledged as inherently dialectical, as the proper unfolding of dialectic, the "going down again to a conclusion" through and toward εἴδη, this κατάβασις barely indicated at the heart of the dialogue would have to be understood by reference to the journey of Er through and toward layers of images, or even by reference to Socrates' initial κατάβασις mirrored in the final myth.[9] After all, the difficulty involved in drawing an ultimate distinction between the journey from εἴδη to εἴδη and a movement through orders of images is suggested by Socrates himself when, in the course of his elaboration on the line, he associates the eidetic to the visible and speaks of "visible (ὁρωμένοις) εἴδεσι" (510d). Er's voyage, then, would appear to be the moving image of dialectic, or even dialectic itself, the psychological venture opening up through dialogue, suddenly lighting up out of the dialogical engagement and flashing in its midst.

The turning of the λόγος into ἀπόλογος does not bespeak the emendation of the former's inadequacy: it only makes such inadequacy perspicuous. Thus, the giving that occurs through and as the narration of the story will never have adequately rendered back the full and exact measure of what is owed—it will have neither completely done justice to the just nor appropriately accounted for justice. The giving of such a narration will never properly have come to rest. Or, more precisely, rest will follow. The last word, at least for that night, will in fact be said. But this will not have been so for reasons internal to the conversation and final narration. Indeed, it will have been so for reasons which even call into question the possibility of any purely internal, purely discursive (i.e., logical) logic. It will have been so because of reasons having to do with time and place. It will have been late—late in the day and in the conversation. And the order of day and night, the rhythm of the living, will have imposed itself with the force of necessity—of a necessity other than and even prior to logical necessity. Such is the necessity, indeed, the propriety of the ἀπόλογος.[10] The ἀπόλογος displays an inevitability and a compelling force that exceed the bounds of the contingent context. Yet it does not speak in the mode of universality.

Socrates' ἀπόλογος will have been a story of war and death, of death in war, and of life returning. It will have celebrated vision—the vision that prevails even over the darkening of death and blossoms in the midst of its imageless plain. But it will also have honored the suspension of vision—the momentary lapse of illumination, of enlightenment, even, involved in the bringing forth of life, the moment of blindness in coming to see the light, the mystery and blackout of birth (the secret, withdrawal, and concealment of unconcealment). It will, therefore, have been a story of death and life in their many turns—of death overflowing, teeming with oneiric images like a starry sky, dreaming of the return of life. And of life's insuppressible but discontinuous triumph, of its flashing, of its vessel bearing the mark of death, forgetfulness, unconsciousness.

The story Socrates recounts opens on a battlefield. Like that other narration constituting the *Bhagavad Gita* (the narration of Samjaya, the minister and poet, to Dhrtarastra, his blind king), Socrates' recounting evokes a vision for the blind. It awakens those who are blind to the layers of images beyond the visible (for there are still images beyond the visible) and lights up previously unseen landscapes for them. It discloses to the blind what surrounds them, opens up the place and dynamics of their existence—the movements they engage in, the broad configurations enfolding their lives.[11] Like that other narration, Socrates' narration tells of a warrior, of a warrior impelled to wander and to witness. Just like Arjuna, Er is called to a fantastic envisioning which, in its hallucinatory precision, discloses the laws of life—the figures, that is, the images of those laws which, behind the many veils of appearances, behind even the blackness of death, underlie and govern the endless spinning of becoming. No less than Arjuna by Krishna his charioteer, Er is driven away from and simultaneously deeper into his mortal course.

But a few crucial distinctions should be observed. This will require taking a series of detours, in order to reflect (at least in a preparatory fashion) on poetic comportment in connection with the practice of imitation; on the interrelated questions of recollection, narration, and justice; and on the disclosure of the being of the poet. Only after these diversions will the discussion of war as the element of Socrates' myth be resumed.

Of Poets and Distance

At the outset of the *Bhagavad Gita*, Dhrtarastra addresses Samjaya the poet-minister as follows: "When in the field of *dharma* . . . assembled together, desiring to fight, what did my army and that of the sons of Pandu do, Samjaya?" (I.1).[12] In response to the blind king's request, Samjaya's narration begins to unfold. It presents the preparation to and development of warfare "in the field of *dharma*" and is a saying whose simultaneity with the gestures taking place on the battlefield seems literally to bring forth, guide, and sustain the unfolding of the events, and not simply to accompany them and give them the rhythm of a song. Indeed, even if such narration unfolds in the past tense, it unmistakably reveals a profound intimacy between the poet and the unfolding of events on the battlefield. The poet is a seer who follows every deed and hears, in their articulate development, nearly imperceptible dialogues. His transcendent character ensures his ubiquitous presence on the scene of the action presented and intimates the demiurgic power of his presentation. To such an extent does he display mastery over the becoming of the story, as his name also suggests. Moreover, the merging of Samjaya's singing with the actions it sings is, in turn, enveloped within the merging of the unknown poet with the character of Samjaya, that is, within the poet's projection of himself as Samjaya. It is, thus, the complex structure of a twofold immediacy that characterizes the narration of the *Gita*.

Socrates' narration, on the other hand, occurs at a remove from the action. His recounting is indefinitely mediated. It is the telling of a story told by Er the warrior when he came back from his strange wandering, when he woke up from his dream—when, that is, he was born again. The root from which Socrates' recitation springs is not the enraptured immediacy of poet and heroes or deeds which distinguishes the *Gita*. The root of Socrates' narration is not the absorption of the poetic saying in the action it unravels, the lack of distance between them and their pure coincidence. Socrates' saying acknowledges an interval, a discontinuity, a remoteness, and does not present itself as the simple coming forth of what it names. It does, indeed, have the power of bringing forth what it names—the power of evoking the dynamic unfolding of events through the event of its own dynamic unfolding, the power of calling forth the developments in deed which its own discursive development mirrors. It does, in its δύναμις ποιητική, cast spells and call moving images into being. But Socrates' thaumaturgy is oblique and indirect—like his discourse. The discussion of narrative modes taking place in Book III is enlightening in this respect.

The lack of distance essential, for example, to the Hindu poem is recognized by Socrates as a constitutive element of most kinds of poetry (poetic genres) known to him. Curiously enough, it is precisely such a con-fusion that, at this juncture, Socrates names imitation (μίμησις). The logic of imitation, in his view, essentially informs the kinds of poetry recognized and legitimized within the πόλις—dramatic composition as well as epic. Socrates articulates this point by turning to the exemplary case of Homeric ἔπος. A distinction is drawn between the opening lines of the *Iliad*, in which "the poet himself speaks," and the segments following this inception, in which the poet speaks "as though someone other than he were speaking" (393a). In these later moments, Socrates observes, the poet "speaks as though he himself were Khruses and tries as hard as he can to make it seem to us that it's not Homer speaking, but the priest, an old man. And in this way he made pretty nearly all the rest of the narrative about the events in Ilium as well as about those in Ithaca and the whole Odyssey" (393a–b). It is this coinciding of the poet and the character, their speaking in one voice, that Socrates proceeds to call mimetic. For "isn't likening himself (ὁμοιοῦν ἑαυτὸν) to someone else, either in voice or in looks (σχῆμα), the same as imitating (μιμεῖσθαί) the man he likens himself to?" It seems, then, that "he and the other poets make the narrative through imitation (διὰ μιμήσεως τὴν διήγησιν ποιοῦνται)" (393c).

This logic of poetic elocution is based on deception, on a seductive delusion, on an occultation which, moreover, appears to be deliberate, unnecessary, and dispensable. Socrates observes that "if the poet nowhere hid (ἀποκρύπτοιτο) himself, his poetic work and narrative as a whole would have taken place without imitation" (393c–d). An illustration of such "simple narrative" (ἁπλῆ διήγησις), of a saying free from the cryptic contamination of μίμησις, follows. "I'll speak without meter (ἄνευ μέτρου); for I'm not poetic (οὐ γάρ εἰμι ποιητικός)," Socrates warns. Then, returning to the *Iliad*, he proceeds to show how the poem might have been composed, had Homer spoken "as Homer" and not "as though he had become Khruses" (393d). This paraphrase turns the polyphonic and poly-logic texture of the Homeric song into a consistently indirect speech—just as in the inception of the poem. Such would be the discursive comportment worthy of being embraced.

It should not go unnoticed that at this juncture Socrates neglects the invocation opening the *Iliad*—whereby the Muse is called to sing through the poet. In this light, what Socrates calls the speaking of the poet himself, as it were, reveals itself rather in terms of divine in-spiration, indeed, possession—that is, in terms of the self-dispossession characterizing the experience of ἐνθουσιασμός. What Socrates is truly implying, while carefully avoiding saying it, is that one would most properly be oneself and speak in one's own voice precisely when undergoing the experience of the Muse speaking through one, that is, when becoming the place of the resonance and momentary dwelling of the divine. Socrates' omission of the Homeric invocation of the Muse allows him to cover over this problem, to speak unproblematically of the "poet's own" voice. A similar complication should be underlined with respect to dithyrambic verse, which, in the same context, is said to stem from the poet himself and to exhibit no mimetic corruption. This is a rather curious result of the elaboration of the question of μίμησις by reference to poetic genres. "Of poetry and tale-telling" (τῆς ποιήσεώς τε καὶ μυθολογίας), Socrates says, "one kind proceeds wholly by imitation—as you say, tragedy and comedy; another by the poet's own report (ἀπαγγελίας)—this, of course, you would find especially in dithyrambs; and still another by both—this is found in epic poetry and many other places too, if you understand me" (394b–c). The dramatic and epic texts, whether exclusively or preeminently dominated by the logic of μίμησις, are sharply distinguished from lyric poetry—particularly the singing to and of Dionysus, the dithyrambic utterance of the poet himself, in which the imitative element appears to be altogether lacking. It is, then, to the Dionysian dithyramb that the narration of the one who is "beautiful and good" would be akin. The example of "simple narrative" by which Socrates illustrates the speaking of the poet who does not conceal himself, the indirect λόγος prefiguring the narration of the myth of Er would be attuned to the primordial poetic saying dedicated and belonging to Dionysus. But such singing occurs as the self-disclosure of the singer only in a highly qualified way: as the disclosure of the singer as ἄγγελος (the one who reports, messenger), through whose singing the god is disclosed. But this line of thinking introduces a further difficulty. By situating within poetry the contrast between imitative and nonimitative poetic modes, Socrates is making it impossible simply to attribute the mimetic function to poetry in general and to identify the contrast of imitative and nonimitative discourses with the contrast of poetry and philosophy.

This discussion, of course, casts the question of imitation in quite perplexing terms. Μίμησις, indeed, comes to emerge both in its coinciding with *ek-static* absorption (the immediacy brought about in the fading of boundaries) and in its being antithetical to it. On the one hand, the delusional and concealing character, the lie of μίμησις, would have to be understood in terms of an excessive proximity, of a proximity which would veil, assimilate, and confuse instead of exposing and disclosing. In such merging into one, not only would delimitations vanish, but also all distance would be annihilated, all gaps covered. It is, then, the pure coinciding characteristic of μίμησις which dazzles, covers over, hides—which, thus, lies. On the other hand, though, in the *ek-static* transgression of boundaries (as, for instance, in dithyrambic inspiration) a comportment other than imitative, an antidote to imitation, would be found. Such is the rather paradoxical suggestion harbored in this passage.[13]

Imitation, thus, would have to do with a lack of distance, with an excessive, compromising intimacy with that which is in the process of coming forth— with too direct, hence blinding, an exposure to what emerges. Through this erasure of distance, the voices and deeds evoked emerge in their brilliance and directness. The self-subtraction of the poet, in this sense, is for the sake of a more vivid bringing forth. As the poet recedes and disappears toward the background, those he sings of acquire their own voice, as it were, and seem in fact to sing themselves, of their own accord. Yet the clarity of this way of poetic elocution enfolds an obscuring moment. Such clarity is dazzling to the one who performs it. One no longer accompanies, as a witness, that which is taking shape, merely making contours more vivid, putting details into relief, giving rhythm to the action: one *becomes* that which is taking shape. One loses oneself in this singing. Moreover, one does so indiscriminately, readily identifying with whatever, whomever happens to be brought forth by means of imitation. However, this extreme plasticity conceals the truth of human finitude, dissimulates the limits of human power. Indeed, it projects the dream of infinite extendibility, that is, of human omnipotence. It is in this sense that a lie lies at the heart of μίμησις, and it is because of this that Socrates warns against such practice. As he tells Adeimantos, "the nature of humans looks to me to be minted in even smaller coins . . . than this, so that it is unable either to make a fine imitation of many things or to do (πράττειν) the things themselves of which the imitations are in fact only likenesses" (395b).

And yet, at this point one can hardly avoid noticing the pervasiveness of the imitative strategy in the dialogue on the πολιτεία as a whole. After all, this dialogue in its entirety is narrated by Socrates. And it is preeminently by resorting to direct speech, to the mimetic evocation of other voices, that Socrates recalls the conversation which, one is told, took place the day before. In other words, it is crucially by resorting to μίμησις that Socrates renders the alleged conversation—in spite of the reservations against μίμησις that he articulates in the course of that conversation. Socrates' reservations against μίμησις may even make his mimetic evocation more forceful, more convincing. Indeed, against the backdrop of such general hostility toward imitation, the interlocutors evoked appear all the more vividly defined, all the more independent from Socrates' voice. The movement, within μίμησις, against mimetic presentation evidently displays a genuine poietic effectiveness.

And what to say about that other narrator behind Socrates, that other one who makes Socrates remember and narrate, even write? What to say of this one, who writes dialogues but himself never speaks, who never says anything in his own voice, and rather writes "as though he had become" someone else, indeed, many others? If the dialogues of this narrator behind Socrates are, in general, the locus of the hiding of their maker, the dialogue on the πολιτεία unfolds thanks to a double gesture of self-dissimulation—that of Socrates, through whose voice the interlocutors are enacted, and that of Plato, as always completely disappearing behind the scene. Here Plato's disappearance is itself a μίμησις of Socrates' μίμησις.

But Socrates' reflection on imitation is more complex than has heretofore transpired. The impossibility of simply excluding imitation and its danger is decisively acknowledged in the course of the argument. Time and again one is reminded that even the diction of those who are "beautiful and good" may have to be imitative to some degree or other. Socrates withdraws his earlier assertion that indirect speech would simply be free from imitation and introduces important qualifications. Indeed, he distinguishes "two forms of style" (εἴδη τῆς λέξεως) (397b), "a certain form of style and narrative in which the gentleman (καλὸς κἀγαθός) narrates whenever he must say (λέγειν) something" and another in which the common man speaks (396b–c). While the diction of the latter "will be based on imitation of voice and looks (διὰ μιμήσεως φωναῖς τε καὶ σχήμασιν), or else include only a bit of narrative" (397a–b), that of the former "will participate (μετέχουσα) in both imitation and the other kind of narrative, but there will be a little bit of imitation in a great deal of speech (ἐν πολλῷ λόγῳ)" (396e). Imitation, then, seems, albeit in varying degrees, to be a constitutive element of λέγειν—even of the simplest narrative, even of a speaking rigorously bound to the rule of indirect speech (which, per se, would be neither unimaginable nor impossible).

It appears that speaking, however much "in one's own voice," by its very occurrence echoes (even without directly quoting) something else, something preceding—an other prior speaking, other voices. In order to speak, one will have had to hear, to listen. (Accordingly, speaking will have been, above all and to begin with, a responding. How can one begin to appropriate this?) In speaking one will always inevitably have overstepped one's own boundaries, challenged them (that is, found oneself challenged). One will have had, in a way, to become another, to enter that space of gathering and sharing which demands a certain transgression of one's self-enclosure. Speaking will always have implied repeating, quoting (whether explicitly or not), in fact, being spoken: it will have arisen out of the intertwinement of voices conversing or indeterminately interfering, from plays of signification and concomitant doxic commitments not originating in the speaker, but rather speaking through the speaker and disputing all claims to propriety, property, and autonomy of intentional structures. It is in this way that speaking will have occurred, will have been recognized as such. As Socrates concludes, "all the poets and the men *who say anything* (οἵ τι λέγοντες) fall into one of these patterns of style (τύπῳ τῆς λέξεως) or the other, or make some mixture of them both" (397c; emphasis added). Such are the conditions for speaking—if, in fact, one "must say (λέγειν) something" at all. Having forcibly to imitate, the "sensible man" (μέτριος ἀνήρ) will imitate those like himself, while being "ashamed" of imitating those unworthy—unless it be "brief" and "done in play" (396c–e).[14] This is his only distinctive feature, and an elusive one.

The naked and "simple" narrative of the "beautiful and good" (the "gentlemen"), this plain, indirect λόγος through which the poet would let himself surface to manifestness, importantly foreshadows the narrative mode in which the story of Er will be recounted. But in the λόγος of the μῦθος of Er there will have been a few exceptions (rather unexceptional exceptions, to be sure, if, as intimated above, the contamination of imitation is invariably at work). Indeed, in telling the myth of Er the warrior, Socrates will have broken the rule of indirect speech quite a few times. It is in order to report speeches heard by Er that direct speech is utilized—most notably in the presentation of the discourse of "a certain spokesman" (προφήτην ... τινὰ) who delivers Lákhesis's statement (617d–e), but also in recalling certain stories told by souls about their vicissitudes while journeying, fragments of dialogues that Er happened to witness. In these moments one discerns less a gesture of self-subtraction, a deliberate hiding on Socrates' part, than a sign of recognition, as it were—a recognition compelling Socrates to imitate both the spokesman (as if himself drawn to Lakhesis, to speak on her behalf, maybe desiring to let her directly speak) and the souls sharing what they endured (as if affirmatively being at one with this strange crowd).

One last observation should be put forth concerning the reflection on poetic modes taking place in Book III. The contrast between the narrative comportment of the noble poet and the ordinary man is stark. Socrates' rendition of the latter is unmistakably a caricature:

> As for the man who's not of this sort, the more common he is, the more he'll narrate everything and think nothing unworthy of himself; hence he'll undertake seriously to imitate in the presence of many everything we were just mentioning—thunder, the noises of winds, hailstorms, axles and pulleys, the voices of trumpets, flutes, and all the instruments, and even the sound of dogs, sheep, and birds. (396e–397a)

What Socrates seems to be pointing to in the case of the ordinary human being is a certain indifferent, indiscriminate readiness to (re)produce everything and anything—to consider "nothing unworthy," and hence to undertake to imitate, without any reservation, "horses neighing, bulls lowing, the roaring of rivers, the crashing of the sea, thunder, and everything of the sort" (396b). This is what children do in their plays (plays which disclose the world to them and, through the imitative play of repetition and response, open them up to learning the ways and correspondences of the world . . .). Here, however, the formative role of imitation is not emphasized. Or, rather, in one and the same movement Socrates acknowledges the radically informing power of imitation and underlines its dangers, hence the necessity of delimiting it. "Haven't you observed," he asks, "that imitations, if they are practiced continually from youth onwards, become established (καθίστανται) as habits and nature (ἔθη τε καὶ φύσιν), in body (κατὰ σῶμα) and in sounds (φωνὰς) and in thought (διάνοιαν)?" (395d). The exquisitely ethical dimension of Socrates' discourse begins to shine through the concern with truth-obscuring μίμησις. Imitation, its inevitable darkening, emerges as an issue inviting caution and discernment. The further implications of this problem will be considered in the last section of the present chapter.

The ghost of imitation, the shadow of a cryptic receding from pure and full manifestation, will, thus, have haunted any discourse, even this one. The second treatment of μίμησις, in Book X, further clarifies why such inevitability must be acknowledged, despite the fact that in principle the disciplined practice of indirect speech would not be implausible. Whereas the early analysis of imitation rests on the distinction between discursive strategies, the examination of this theme in Book X is developed mainly by reference to the visual arts and to the deception involved in the production of images of originals—although, to be sure, this treatment is meant to include and account for poetry proper too. The elaboration in Book III concerns the reproduction of sound, of particular voices and characters, and particularly the development of stories. Such an approach emphasizes the temporal dimension of imitation, imitation as a certain reproduction of time through the unfolding of events. In Book X Socrates seems instead to address specifically the power of bringing forth images, whether through the plastic arts or by evoking them discursively (e.g., the image of a cave, of a ship, or even of a city). It should also be noticed that, besides highlighting different facets of the subject matter, the discussion of μίμησις in terms of dramatico-epic elocution and that of μίμησις in terms of imaginal reproduction are structurally discrepant. The identification of the mimetic lie with the poet's use of direct speech emphasizes the deceptiveness of immediacy, while the description of imitation as a copying twice removed from the truth of the original emphasizes the deceptiveness of the remoteness from the source. Whereas the discourse in Book III problematizes the imitative pretense of the poet who speaks as if he were someone else (the imitator as too close to the imitated), according to the argument in Book X the imitator is a liar because he is "at the third generation from nature," and "this will also apply to the maker of tragedy, if he is an imitator." Indeed, "he is naturally third from a king and the truth, as are all the other imitators" (597e).

Discourse (just like the plastic arts) is imitative when it brings forth or conjures up that which it is not, that which is far and may not be seen accurately—that is, to a degree or another, *always*. Whatever its discursive modality (its style or diction), it is qua imaginal, evocative of images that λέγειν is imitative. Socrates' reminders pointing to the essentially imitative, image-bound character of the λέγειν in which he finds himself involved could hardly be more pervasive in the dialogue. Especially frequent are the analogies between the dialogical conduct and the way of proceeding of the painter or visual artist. Socrates compares the course of inquiry he and his interlocutors are following to "paint-ing statues" (420c–d). The philosophical pursuit is described by reference to the art of painting (472c–d). Analogously to the practice of the painter, philosophy would be a matter of looking off (ἀποβλέπειν) to the subject matter, concen-trating one's attention on it. More important still, just like painting, philosophy may be unable to prove that the beauty it has come to envision, however ade-quately (ἱκανῶς) rendered, is also possible. In other words, it is unable to assert itself apodictically and ultimately to distinguish itself from purely visionary, imaginative work.

In the same passage, Socrates also makes perspicuous the convergence of the visual (or pictorial) and the scriptural by exploiting the semantic ambiva-lence of the terms γράφειν and γράμμα, designating both figurative presenta-tion and symbolic notation. The intersection, even confusion, of the imaginal and the generally discursive orders is provocatively underlined by Socrates with the invitation to *watch* what comes to be in speaking (369a) and the call to *lis-ten to* what is imaged (488a). It is said, finally, that through the dialogical labor the figure, the σχῆμα of the πολιτεία, is outlined in speech (548d). The paral-lel between painting and the work of philosophy is reiterated further (484c–d, 500e, 501c). The philosopher appears as a "painter of regimes" (πολιτειῶν ζωγράφος) (501c), whose task is focusing on the "divine paradigm" (500e), "looking off (ἀποβλέποντες), as painters (γραφεῖς) do, toward what is truest (ἀληθέστατον), and ever referring to it and contemplating (θεώμενοι) it as pre-cisely as possible" (484c–d). As will be seen more closely below, the myth of Er presents itself as yet a further exercise in such "looking off toward" the noblest subject, in an attempt at grasping it (in however visionary a fashion), attending to it, drawing its outline. As Socrates says, thanks to the vision attained through the myth, one "will be able to draw a conclusion and choose—in looking off toward (ἀποβλέποντα) the nature of the soul—between the worse and the bet-ter life" (618d).

It is by developing the question of the imitative lie by reference to the bring-ing forth of images, then, that the second argument on imitation complements and completes the first, albeit without subsuming it.[15] It is in this further sense that, finally, the dialogue as a whole is made manifest as thoroughly imitative in its unfolding, and not only because of the prevalence of direct speech in it or be-cause of its political (re)production and other particular image-making spells. The text in its entirety is revealed, inescapably though not exclusively, as phan-tasmagoria.

But, after all, Socrates intimated this since the beginning, when inviting Adeimantos and Glaukon to follow him in a λέγειν presenting itself at once as διαλέγεσθαι and μυθολογεῖν—in a λέγειν of μῦθος enfolded within μῦθος: "Come then, like men telling tales in a tale (ἐν μύθῳ μυθολογοῦντές) and at their leisure, let's educate the men in speech (λόγῳ)" (376d). And later Socrates will have underscored again the doubly mythical structure of image-making (itself having a mythical character and being enfolded by myth) as well as the interpenetration of myth and λέγειν. At this juncture, the city brought forth in the likeness of justice, or as the image of justice, is referred to as "the regime about which we tell tales in speech (ἣν μυθολογοῦμεν λόγῳ)" (501e).

From the point of view of its implication in imitation and, hence, of its relation to truth, the whole dialogue can hardly be distinguished from epico-dramatic poetry—and from the work of the anonymous poet narrating in the name of Samjaya, the minister of the king. Also, analogously to these works, what the Socratic discourse ardently pursues is a vision of human possibility (a vision of what humans can be or become) by "taking hints from exactly that phenomenon in human beings which Homer too called godlike (θεοειδές) and the image of god (θεοείκελον)" (501b).

The myth concluding the dialogue, however, is prevalently enunciated according to the formula of indirect speech. Although allowing for no privileged claims to truth and illumination, this feature of Socrates' storytelling sets his myth at a distance from the lack of distance essential to the dramatic texts and significantly characterizing the singing of ἔπος. It is also (if not only) for this reason that, as Socrates points out before beginning to recount, his narrative will not be "a story of Alkinoos" (614b). It will not be like the story narrated in Odysseus's own voice, as if by Odysseus himself, about his skilled action, his descent to the underworld, his successful utilization of the experience down below. In this narration set in the halls of king Alkinoos, occupying Book IX through Book XII of the *Odyssey,* the con-fusion of poet and hero is complete. Their voices merge and present themselves, indiscernibly, as one. But the Socratic myth does not seem to spring from this source.

Speaking from a distance and by indirection, the myth of Er marks a significant shift from the mostly direct speech through which the dialogue is recalled. In the myth, simultaneously, the dialogue is brought together and its logic subverted. A remoteness is inscribed within the immediacy and absorption made possible by the imitative expedient of direct speech. Such remoteness does not simply haunt the dialogical illusion but, more precisely, crowns it, constitutes its highest achievement and culmination. Sourceless voices, which not even Socrates will simply have appropriated, transpire through and beyond the staged interplay of identifiable characters. Letting an irrecoverable distance from the source, an indeterminate mediation be manifest as such—this seems to be a distinctive feature of the concluding μῦθος.

Healing from Oblivion

Socrates' narration stems from a root other than the immediacy that he detects in the main forms of μυθολογεῖν. Rather, it comes to be through the compulsion to recount a saying in its distance, in its strangeness and elusive character—to retain the saying in its withdrawal, to remember it in its passing. It comes to be through the compulsion to *save* a saying—to preserve it from destruction (ἀπώλεια) and simultaneously to give it shape without confining it, to let it come forth without owning it. In this way the mythical saying may release its power to inform, to save those who saved it. Socrates suggests this when, at the conclusion of his tale, he prepares to take his leave from the stage of the dialogue: "And thus, Glaukon, a tale was saved (μῦθος ἐσώθη) and was not lost (ἀπώλετο); and it could save (ἂν σώσειεν) us, if we were persuaded by it, and we shall make a good crossing (εὖ διαβησόμεθα) of the river Lethe and not defile our soul" (621b–c). It will be opportune to return to these words at a later moment. Here only the following remarks are in order. Given the relatively original character of the myth of Er, that is, given its status as an exquisitely Socratic (Platonic) *inventio* (in its double meaning, both a finding and a bringing forth), saving here cannot simply mean conserving and cannot merely be a matter of antiquarian passion. The semantic range of the verb σώζω is twofold. On the one hand, the term signifies saving, keeping (keeping in mind, keeping secret), retaining, preserving, and in this sense even making secure, strengthening, confirming, empowering, substantiating. On the other hand, the term should be considered in its fundamental connection with σεύω, in turn related to the Sanskrit *cyávati*, meaning to set in motion, and hence to give life, to animate, even to let fall.[16] In this connection σώζω indicates saving in the sense of keeping alive, protecting against death and destruction, even healing or promoting recovery from a malady, and hence regenerating. Just like the related adjective σάος, σῶς (meaning safe and sound, alive and well, whole, undiminished, but also sure, certain) σώζω crucially evokes safety, reassurance, firmness as well as life in its pervasive movement, dynamic growth, trans-formation. (Socrates' name itself is evidently not unrelated to these related terms from the root σο- or σα.) Mnemonic retention and the protection of the living seem to stem from a common source.

In the Platonic texts σώζω is consistently associated with the power of ἀνάμνησις. This term denotes the resurfacing (ἀνά) of mnemic traces, the recalling, the calling to mind again of what is retained. But ἀνάμνησις means (is) also the negation (αν-) of the negation (-α-) of μνήμη and μνῆστις—remembrance, recollection, memory. Ἀν-ά-μνησις, thus, names the recovery of the soul from the impairment called ἀ-μνησία, ἀ-μνηστία, or, which is the same, λήθη. The operation of ἀν-άμνησις and the unfolding of ἀ-λήθεια, thus, should be understood in their essential unity. Ἀνάμνησις: the power to recover the power of the soul, the power of the soul to recover its own power—to rescue the originally lost power called μνήμη, the mindfulness designated by the verb μνάομαι, from the disempowering hold of forgetfulness. The double, even negative, privation called ἀνάμνησις lifts the shroud of oblivion from the soul and un-covers μνήμη (notice, however, that this term indicates memory as a power of the soul but, like μνήμα, also signifies a tomb, the place of commemoration). In this way the soul, out of joint and in disarray under the disintegrating sway of forgetfulness, regains its own.

But the privation of a privation, the double privation occurring as ἀνάμνησις, involves at once the countermovement to the malady of mnemic loss and the original realization of this malady as such. That is to say, ἀνάμνησις is of ἀμνησία at least as much as it is of μνήμη—and this in spite of all the attempts to reduce the complex and manifold relation between forgetfulness and remembrance to a schematic opposition. This reveals the anamnestic surfacing in its obscure, elusive character, particularly as regards its origin and status.

Indeed, the dimness of the phenomenon of ἀνάμνησις, and hence the difficulties involved in its analysis, should be traced back both to its implication in λήθη and to its *dynamic* connection with μνήμη. On the one hand, precisely as the recovery of what was lost and had receded into latency, ἀνάμνησις belongs to λήθη. That which was buried, covered over, forgotten is shaken, as if out of a slumber. Such belonging to oblivion should be understood in its profound (indeed, nearly unfathomable) implications. It indicates an envelopment in and a development from out of λήθη, a taking shape originating in formlessness, a coming forth from utter receding. In giving itself, ἀνάμνησις, the event of articulation secreted out of withdrawal, signals the radically problematic character of its provenance and operation. It appropriates the lost out of loss.

On the other hand, in its belonging to μνήμη, ἀνάμνησις presents itself as the articulation, even the actualization, *of a power.* It occurs as the stirring up of the δύναμις of mindful preservation. It summons what is not manifest into manifestation. But, again, such activation of possibility, such conversion of power into actuality, presents problems analogous to those just observed. For in this respect, too, ἀνάμνησις gives itself in its recessive character (comes forth, as it were, as receding). It emerges as the translation of the undifferentiated, as a journey through the nonmanifest, as a determining operation pervaded by indeterminate force. For, indeed, how even to begin speaking of δύναμις aside from and prior to (its) actualization? And does such actualization not take place through the anamnestic emergence, indeed, *as such upsurge?* Subsequently, how to construe δύναμις as measure and ground? To be sure, one might insist (as has been done time and again) that ἀνάμνησις is the bringing back of what was once mindfully contemplated and kept safe—that is, that recollection is not merely a matter of activating potentiality, but the recovery of prior actuality, even of hyperuranian essences. But does this position not stem from an eminently noteworthy, that is, questionable forgetfulness of forgetfulness? Does such a stance not trivialize, in order ultimately to bypass, the immense problem of ever-intervening loss? How can one forget this forgetfulness that makes the forgotten indifferently inaccessible—this oblivion which is no banal game to be downplayed, but which sweeps away, makes occult, dissipates, leaving behind only traces that may neither be simply intelligible nor allow for authoritative reconstructions? It is with such force that ἀνάμνησις is always already contending.[17]

In belonging both to λήθη and to δύναμις, ἀνάμνησις surfaces as an articulation that can hardly be traced back to a determinate origin, secured to a genealogical derivation, evaluated as a more or less appropriate (reliable, accurate), more or less worthy representative (heir) of a given source. For such a source (how to say this?) would not simply appear as withdrawn but, precisely in eluding all appearing, would have to be intuited as the withdrawing itself. In this way, ἀνάμνησις hardly delineates itself in its surfacing. It gives itself as liminal surfacing, indeed, as the *limen* of what surfaces—in and of itself (almost) nothing.

In a sustained and consistent way, a strand of the Socratic reflection seeks to establish a sharp distinction between, on the one hand, the power of preserving and keeping with oneself (the saving of retention and recollection) and, on the other hand, the powerlessness of incontinence (the loss, dilapidation, sheer expenditure of forgetfulness). But such sharp distinction is possible only if recollection is understood as the simple unveiling of what was covered over—as if the covering over would occur as an inessential accident, and as if that which is thus concealed would subsist, intact, beneath the veil. In other words: it is an understanding of recollection as the surfacing of the self-subsisting soul (recovered in its structures and originary visions) that makes such distinction possible. Beneath the operations of revelation as well as occultation, as their common ground, the psychological substratum would grant the measure and measurability of both and would, thus, determine them as opposites. Remembering and forgetting would be a matter of bringing to light and obscuring the same.

But what if, conversely, one were to wonder about what it is that is remembered? What if one were to remain unconvinced of the identity of the forgotten and the recollected, of what is lost and what is found? What if one were unable to overcome in that way the difficulty concerning the loss of what is lost? What if, in other words, one were compelled to comprehend recollection in terms of the *dynamic* (δύναμις-related) play of the soul in its becoming, in its enactment, in its enfoldment in the veils and folds of oblivion? Indeed, to the extent that remembering is understood as the play of the emergence of the soul, as the indeterminate and interminable play of the unfolding of the soul, and as the exploration of the soul's powers (possibility, potentiality), memory cannot not be intimately related to, even defined in terms of, the forgetfulness with which it wrestles. A brief digression may be opportune to let this issue emerge (if all too concisely) in its main traits.

Retention, as a power of the ψυχή, is involved in discovery in a twofold sense. On the one hand, retention may name the bearing of essential traits of which there may well not be any awareness, and which would merely have to be dis-covered in the sense of un-veiled, wrested from latency and brought to mind. Retention (the retained in its delimitation and structure) would in this case present a certain priority with respect to discovery. Discovery would have to be understood as a recovery, retrieval, and healing of the soul, a coming of the soul into its own, into what it is to be and already is. In other words, discovery (even in the sense of education or learning) would appear as a mere breaking through the opacity of oblivion and freeing the soul from the thick veil separating it from itself, from the vision to which it was originally exposed (the vision that it itself is). And the soul, even its powers, would be posited in their full, un-problematic actuality. In this sense, discovery or recovery would be a matter of *returning* to the retained—to that which is most fundamentally, most intimately known.

On the other hand, discovery may name the movement of apprehension roused through experience, that is, through worldly exposure. (The question, of course, would still remain concerning how experience would rouse such movement, that is to say, how learning comes to pass. For does such stirring not occur in response to, and thanks to, a kind of recognition, however indistinct? Does this motion, through which things are apprehended, not resemble an echo? But—of what?) In this context, retention may be construed as the keeping safe of that which was first discovered through the experiential exposure and as involved, once awakened and called forth through experience, in the possibility of further discovery and further learning. In this case retention would appear to be *of* experience, to be activated through experience. It would present a relatively secondary status with respect to the experience of discovery (whose subsequent developments it would nevertheless sustain) and involve an understanding of education as an original shaping of souls. Accordingly, the ψυχή would appear to be caught in the game of concealment involved in any disclosure, in the revealing play of learning which, in its determinate bringing to light, in its uncovering that determines, also indeterminately covers over, renders inaccessible, annihilates. The ψυχή would appear as such play, as this only partially determinable structure, as the torso (or an even less recognizable fragment) of this structure—never to be fully remembered and completed, indeterminately blending with forgetfulness, with λήθη, with possibility. This is unavoidably the case if the recovery and discovery of the truth of the soul is in fact to happen within the horizon of becoming.[18] Remembrance (the discovery that remembrance is), again, shows itself as a journey—not, however, as the return to what is one's own and most essentially known. Rather, it appears as a journey in the course of which something emerges whose provenance, whether or not from the past, from any kind of primordiality, temporal or otherwise, is elusively shrouded—a journey in which the dimension of recovery and the surfacing of what presents itself for the first time are not, in the final analysis, distinct. In this sense, memory would seem to be (also) of the unknown, that is, of the new. It would be a matter of a discovery accompanied both by recognition and by wonder, by the element of repetition and by surprise before what is perceived as unprecedented. One could speak here of repetition of the unknown, or, what is the same, of memory of the new.

Even the virtually most straightforward moments of the dialogue on the πολιτεία present a tremendous ambivalence, an indecisiveness with respect to this double option concerning the construing of the ψυχή. Even when the anamnestic process is explicitly presented as the uncovering of psychological structures in their naked simplicity and unproblematic self-subsistence, such a presentation quite provocatively lends itself to questioning. In the previous chapter this difficulty was already encountered, specifically in Socrates' attempt to sever the psychological formation from the work of education.

A further passage exemplary in this respect is to be found in Book V, in the course of the argument meant to demonstrate the aptitude of women, as women, for all the activities customarily practiced by men, most notably for politico-philosophical functions. "That the female (θῆλυ) bears (τίκτειν) and the male (ἄρρεν) mounts (ὀχεύειν)," Socrates maintains in unusually explicit terms, is not a difference on whose ground one may contest the law that "our guardians and their women must practice (ἐπιτηδεύειν) the same things" (454d–e). Rather, he points out, it is differences in the configuration of the ψυχή that account for a human being's suitability for one task or the other. Thus, it is reasserted that "a man and a woman whose soul (ψυχὴν) is suited for the doctor's art have the same nature (τὴν αὐτὴν φύσιν ἔχειν)," while "a man doctor (ἰατρικὸν) and a man carpenter (τεκτονικὸν) have different ones (ἄλλην)" (454d). In order better to elucidate such "sameness" in nature and, conversely, such nonsexual difference, Socrates asks:

Did you distinguish between the man who has a good nature (εὐφυῆ) for a thing and another who has no nature (ἀφυῆ) for it on these grounds: the one learns something connected with that thing easily, the other with difficulty;

the one, starting from slight learning, is able to carry discovery far forward (πολὺ εὑρετικὸς) in the field he has learned, while the other, having chanced on a lot of learning and practice (μελέτης), can't even preserve (σώζοιτο) what he learned; and the bodily things (τὰ τοῦ σώματος) give adequate service (ὑπηρετοῖ) to the thought (διανοίᾳ) of the man with the good nature while they oppose the thought of the other man? (455b)

Socrates decisively casts the psychological question in terms of φύσις—nature itself, whether comparatively better or worse at a given task. On the one hand, he suggests, it is one's psychological inclination, one's nature, that determines one's response to a certain course of studies and, hence, the degree of one's ability in a certain activity. On the other hand, in proceeding to consider the dynamics of apprehension and discovery, Socrates emphasizes the formative role of the learning experience in the arising and definition of one or another psychic structure. Ultimately no clear position is taken on this subject. Both the priority of psychological structures in their natural, that is, transcendent determinacy and the shaping power of experience are implied in such a discourse on the soul. In fact, they appear to be interdependent. For, if it is the case that different psychological configurations respond in dramatically different ways to the exposure that occurs through and as learning, it is also the case that, conversely, only thanks to such responses (always and necessarily singular, unique, contingent) is the recognition of the different types at all possible and do the psychological types originally emerge.

The ambiguity of passages such as this lies in positing a clear separation between retention and forgetfulness, while, at the same time, deferring an adequate determination of the ψυχή. Indeed, here as well as in other places, "being able to preserve what one learns" (μάθοι σώζειν δύναιτο) is sharply distinguished from "being full of forgetfulness" (λήθης ὢν πλέως) (486c). And yet, to the extent that a stance is not taken with regard to the question of the soul, such a distinction cannot properly be made. As long as one is not prepared unambiguously to grant to the soul, whether behind or before the veil of oblivion, the status of autonomous actuality, remembering and forgetting (unveiling and veiling) cannot in principle be discerned from one another. In the end the distinction between ἀνάμνησις and ἀμνησία or λήθη seems to be possible only in a highly qualified way and in specific respects, only in terms of the living, in terms of *praxis* and *ethos*, in terms of the unfolding of becoming in which the ψυχή is inevitably implicated—at least in this life, essentially in this life.

It should then be noticed that the question of the ψυχή, even at later stages of the dialogue, is not adequately taken up. Even as the discourse on the immortality of the soul draws to an end, immediately before the introduction of the myth of Er, no elucidation concerning the being of the ψυχή is offered—indeed, this question is as such never explicitly posed. A formidable caution surrounds the λέγειν around the ψυχή.[19] Every disclosive gesture is followed by the repositioning of a veil, as is paradigmatically the case in these last remarks on the issue, with reference to the figure of Glaukos:

> Well then, that the soul is immortal both the recent argument and the others would compel us to accept. But it must be seen (θεάσασθαι) such as it is in truth, not maimed by community with body and other evils, as we now see (θεώμεθα) it. But what it is like when it has become pure (καθαρὸν) must be examined (διαθεατέον) sufficiently by calculation (λογισμῷ). And one will find it far fairer and discern (διόψεται) justice and injustice and everything we have now gone through more distinctly. Now, we were telling the truth about it as it looks at present (ἐν τῷ παρόντι φαίνεται). However, that is based on the condition (διακείμενον) in which we saw it (τεθεάμεθα). Just as those who catch sight of (ὁρῶντες) the sea Glaukos would no longer easily see (ἴδοιεν) his original nature (ἀρχαίαν φύσιν) because some of the old parts (παλαιὰ) of his body have been broken off and the others have been ground down and thoroughly maimed by the waves at the same time as other things have grown (προσπεφυκέναι) on him—shells, seaweed, and rocks—so that he resembles any beast rather than what he was by nature (φύσει), so, too, we see (θεώμεθα) the soul (ψυχὴν) in such a condition because of countless evils. (611b–d)

It would take the vision of calculation alone in order to grasp the soul freed from compromising associations—as if calculation, λογισμός, could operate alone, without the aid of sensation.[20] The appearances presently besieging the interlocutors must be transcended, if one is to catch sight of the soul as it is, in its pure, unmixed state. Yet it is again by resorting to appearances, to the suggestiveness of images, that the vision of the soul in its being is analogically induced. Then Socrates adds: "But now, I suppose, we have fairly (ἐπιεικῶς) gone through its affections (πάθη) and forms (εἴδη) in its human life," and "its true nature (ἀληθῆ φύσιν)—whether it is many-formed (πολυειδὴς) or single-formed (μονοειδὴς), or in what way it is and how" remains inaccessible (612a). Even the argument concerning the immortality of ψυχή, its unlimited resilience, does not disclose the psychological configuration—*what it is* that lives and endures for ever.

Shortly thereafter the μῦθος will provide a clue for understanding such prodigious difficulty. The function of the tale would appear to be to indicate what was not said (perhaps could not be said) of the soul in the course of the previous discussions. As Socrates observes while recounting, the myth in the process of being brought forth is a way of "looking off toward the nature of the soul." Thanks to such insight one may become capable of discerning the better from the worse life, and of choosing accordingly (618d). The myth would seem, however elliptically, to yield an understanding of the soul analogous to that attained through λογισμός (if, of course, this were attainable, that is to say, if λογισμός could operate unimpeded). It would disclose the spectacle of the soul moved by love of wisdom, "akin (ξυγγενὴς) to the divine and immortal and what is always" (611e). Through the imaginal discourse of the myth one would, as it were, come to envision the soul's power and possibility, "what it would become like if it were to give itself entirely to this longing and were brought by this impulse out of the deep ocean in which it now is" (611e).

Yet the matter at stake is far more complex than this. Not even a myth will possibly have dispelled the mystery of the (human) ψυχή. The myth will not have been an expedient allowing Socrates to say, though in a qualified fashion, what could otherwise not be demonstrated. Not only will such a saying not have provided an account of the soul, but, in addition to this, it will have failed to perform a much more circumscribed task. It will have failed unambiguously to confirm Socrates' expectation, even that most moving, volatile image of the soul projected by Socrates' own desiring soul, namely, the image of the soul caught in its involvement with desire, longing, and lack—a soul akin to the divine not so much in virtue of the wisdom it would possess, but because of the love making it vibrant. Indeed, among the crowd of souls conjured up by the myth, many are said to be blindly driven, wandering in torment, striving for treasures clearly other than wisdom. The reason for this is that the passion for wisdom, recovery, and discovery, albeit an essential trait of the soul, seems to present itself along with innumerable other impulses and appetites, to lose itself in their midst or, minimally, to undergo confusing interferences. There appears to be no priority of such divine striving over the rest, no preexisting structure securing the relative integrity of the soul as it navigates through a life. It is said that, "due to necessity," a soul becomes "different according to the life it chooses." One discerns no order (τάξις) of the soul other than the order acquired through living, with all the perils and uncertainties ensuing (618b). This means that the souls do not live through the cycles of their lives as if merely wearing the ephemeral clothes and masks of various individuals. Death is not for the soul a process of undressing, leaving the soul, for a time, in its naked integrity. The soul bears the marks of lives lived, not as external layers but as integral and informing elements. Hence, according to how a soul will have lived, it might look at times as though all trace of the fierce and divine, yet fragile, love of wisdom had been erased, as though only the turmoil of inconsequent passions would determine the soul— as though nothing could be saved anymore.

It is in light of these problems that the discussions of ἀνάμνησις in the dialogue should be understood, in spite of the doctrinal, thematic claims concerning recollection as the simple resurfacing of the ever-present. In this way ἀνάμνησις appears as radically, constitutively intertwined with λήθη and even rooted in the loss named in the naming of λήθη—like a play of disclosure and withdrawal, of illumination and obscuration taking place on a receding ground, in the dark.

As was pointed out above, then, remembering, just like narration, is a saving—or, even, that saving within which the saving of narration is inscribed. Under the heading of preservation, of saving from sheer disappearance, the power of the ψυχή and the λόγος of μῦθος are brought together. After all, as Socrates recalls in the *Theaetetus,* Mnemosúne (remembrance, memory, mindfulness) is the mother of the Muses (191d).

What is remembered in this passage is the Hesiodic saying concerning the coupling of Zeus and Mnemosúne, the daughter of Gaia and Ouranós—and the generation following this conjunction. (It should be noticed, parenthetically, that according to Hesiod's divine genealogy Mnemosúne belongs to an earlier generation than that of the Olympians. She is among the "youngest-born" of Earth and Sky, older even than her brother, the Titan Kronos [133 ff.]. And yet, Memory, the older sister of Time, is disclosed *only* later, *after* the beginning of Time, as it were—in the temporalization of the singing of her daughters. As will be considered, the myth of Er culminates with the vision of a mother surrounded by daughters who sing of what has been, of what is, of what will be.) Briefly turning to the Hesiodic poem may shed further light on the interconnected issues of preservation, recollection, and narration; on the character of the poet's self-manifestation in the singing that proceeds "by the poet's own report"; and, again, on the ineliminable shadow pervading even the saying which strives to avoid hiding and to achieve pure disclosure.

The Poet and Other Voices

In the *Theogony,* Zeus and Mnemosúne's coupling and its fruit are evoked twice. It is the Muses who dictate to the singer the truth of their own begetting. Under such dictation, the singer tells of the birth of those whose singing for the first time illuminates the immeasurable succession of past and future births. The singer sings this birth of all births, this birth before which there is no singing, this birth before which are silence and darkness, and after which the luminosity of singing projects itself back, populating the nocturnal expanse with images, bringing to appearance the depths of time in the form of endless galleries of portrayals. To this birth of births the singer, in his singing, gives birth. The first narration of the birth of the Muses takes place near the beginning of the poem:

> In Pieria, after lying with the Kronian father, Mnemosúne bore (τέκε) them,
> the lady ruling over (μεδέουσα) the high grounds of Eleútheros,
> forgetfulness of evils and rest from cares (λησμοσύνην τε κακῶν ἄμπαυμά
> τε μερμηράων). (53 ff.)[21]

The poet sings the origin of these goddesses once again near the end of the poem:

> Again, he [Zeus] loved Mnemosúne beautiful-haired,
> from her were born to him the Muses with a golden ribbon on their
>   foreheads (χρυσάμπυκες),
> nine, pleased by luxurious feasting (θαλίαι) and the joy of singing (ἀοιδῆς).
> (915 ff.)

In this way the birth of the Muses, which in turn will disclose the spinning of numberless other divine and human generations, is given birth—indeed, a double birth. In this way, that is, their birth is brought forth—twice. As if once were not enough. As if the immensity, the momentous character of this eminently memorable event would demand repetition in order to be remembered as is fit.

From the Muses and through the Muses the poem finds its inception. It is these goddesses "ready of words" (ἀρτιέπειαι) (29), whose ἔπος is ἄρτιος, who "once taught Hesiod the beautiful singing (ἀοιδήν)" (22). Hesiod recounts:

> They handed me a staff (σκῆπτρον), a luxuriant bay-tree (δάφνης
>   ἐριθηλέος) shoot
> they broke off, admirable; they breathed into me a singing (ἐνέπνευσαν δέ
>   μοι αὐδὴν)
> divine (θέσπιν [θεός, ἔσπον = εἶπον]), that I could celebrate things future
>   and those being before (τά τ' ἐσσόμενα πρό τ' ἐόντα).
> they urged me to sing hymns (ὑμνεῖν) to the race (γένος) of the blessed ones
>   who always are (αἰὲν ἐόντων),
> themselves at first and at last always to sing (πρῶτόν τε καὶ ὕστατον αἰὲν
>   ἀείδειν). (30 ff.)

It is according to this exhortation, then, that the poet sings of the birth of the Muses twice—near the beginning and near the end. But the remembrance of the Muses marking the threshold of the *Theogony* is itself redoubled. The poem opens with this invitation:

> from the Helikonian Muses let us begin to sing (ἀρχώμεθ' ἀείδειν)
> who possess the great and sacred (ζάθεόν) mountain of Helikon
> and dance by the purple spring (περὶ κρήνην ἰοειδέα) on soft feet
> and by the altar of the very mighty son of Kronos;
> and wash their tender skin in the Permessos
> or in the spring of the Horse or in sacred (ζαθέοιο) Olmeios,
> and on highest Helikon created round dances (χοροὺσ ἐνεποιήσαντο)
> beautiful and charming; they move nimbly with their feet.
> From there they started, covered with much mist,
> they walked in the night, sending forth a very beautiful voice
> singing hymns to aegis-bearing Zeus . . .
> and the sacred race (ἱερὸν γένος) of the other immortals who always are.
> (1 ff.)

A few lines down, the opening address is echoed, as if it were necessary to recall it, to remind the listeners of its invocation and injunction:

> You, let us begin (ἀρχώμεθα) from the Muses, who of Zeus the father
> the great mind within the Olympos delight by singing hymns,
> by telling of things which are, which are to be, which are before (τά τ' ἐόντα
>   τά τ' ἐσσόμενα πρό τ' ἐόντα)
> agreeing with the voice (φωνῇ); their tireless sound (αὐδὴ) flows
> sweet from their mouths (στομάτων); and rejoices the house of the father
> Zeus loud-thundering at the voice (ὀπὶ) like lily of the goddesses
> that scatters, and the head (κάρη) of snowy Olympos echoes
> and the house of the immortals (ἀθανάτων). They sending forth an
>   immortal voice (ἄμβροτον ὄσσαν)
> first the venerable race of the gods celebrate with song
> from the beginning. (36 ff.)

In singing of the Muses' birth twice, once near the beginning and once again near the end of the poem, the poet follows the prescription and dictation of the Muses. He sings what and how the Muses told him. But not only that. The narration of the origin of the goddesses, the moments of their remembrance, the words offered to them and to their memory proliferate in the course of the poetic saying—almost excessively, as if out of wonder and astonishment, remarkably exceeding the requirement imposed on the poet. Breathing in and breathing out, expiring the inspiration instilled into him, according to the rhythm of breath and the beat of dancing feet, the poet's saying unfolds pulsating, occurring, recurring. The poetic saying (the event, advent, and bringing forth of memory) repeats itself. In doing so, it keeps evoking the fundamental repetition in which it originates—the repetition rooted in listening, repeating that which is heard in the listening. The iterative quality of such speaking, thus, calls attention to the intrinsically mnemonic character of saying, whatever its thematic focus and subject matter. Also, the recollective movement configured here is clearly not a self-enclosed system of repetition but, rather, an open play with an other.

In the interplay between the Muses manifesting themselves through the poet and the poet bearing and honoring such manifestation, the poem comes forth—like a child. For the poet is not simply, not only the locus of the Muses' sounding. He is also the one who, out of a posture of receptivity, gives back. He is the one who echoes the goddesses' sounding and resounding, who repeats their inspiration and, in doing so, brings it into an outline. In the poet's repetition of the Muses' sounds, in his weaving the echoes and reverberations of the Muses' singing like strands, in his repeated beginnings and cyclical returns, the poem is born and comes forth, originally and essentially iterative in its singing. Such a dynamic of iteration variously informing the poet's saying seems to be most appropriate to the singing *of* those who are double essentially and in many ways. Already at the outset of the poem, Hesiod recalls the perplexing ambiguity of the Muses' first address. "This is the word (μῦθον) the goddesses at first spoke (ἔειπον) to me," he reports (notice, this time, the use of direct speech) (24 ff.):

> You shepherds dwelling in the fields, base reproaches (κάκ' ἐλέγχεα), mere bellies (γαστέρες),
> we know (ἴδμεν) how to say many false things similar to the true (ψεύδεα πολλὰ λέγειν ἐτύμοισιν ὁμοῖα),
> and we know, when we wish to, how to speak true ones (ἀληθέα γηρύσασθαι). (26 ff.)

Thus speak those who, in one breath, bring the relief of forgetfulness (λησμοσύνη, λήθη) and inspire poetic disclosure, disclosure (ἀλήθεια) tout court. And the contrast between disclosure and oblivion should not be reduced to that between simple uncovering and covering, exposure and occultation. Rather, such contrast appears to be internal to the logic of the veil. For the Muses, the mistresses of words (29) proceeding from out of night (10), are essentially the veiled ones, "wrapped up in mist" (9). And yet, their forehead shines "of gold" (916). The ladies of the words, then, are both impenetrably opaque and gleaming, concealing and illuminating. It is through the unveiling veil of words that they bring at once vision and delusion, that they withhold as they give. Thus speak those who infuse vision into the soul—especially into the soul of the one who is out in the wilderness, close to nothing.

From the point of view of the mode of elocution, the poet of the *Theogony*, the "shepherd dwelling in the fields," does not speak in a strictly imitative fashion. Like Socrates in his narration of the story of Er, the poet and shepherd does not hide himself in his telling of the divine genealogies. Rather, he speaks in his own voice as he recollects, repeats, and thus preserves the strange saying he has come to hear.[22] Saving (telling, remembering) the myth, then, means harboring a shape, letting it come into itself while letting it come to pass, granting it stability (if in passing), protecting it from pure dissipation—according to the laws of life, that is, of becoming. It means making room for the strangeness of a saying which, in its movement, cannot fully be grasped, even as one thinks one is lending one's voice to it. In fact, one's voice will not have been lent by one but irresistibly claimed—as if one would have owed it, as if one would have had to breath out the inspiration that came of its own accord, to let it go, to let it return. Saving means, in a certain sense, giving back—taking up and giving out.[23]

Above all, saving means keeping safe that strangeness that eludes and strains one, whose provenance one does not know, even as (especially as) that strangeness is *one's own*. (The myth of Er the warrior is not, or not simply, a piece of popular wisdom or a traditional saying found and quoted. In an important, if mysterious, sense, it is *Socrates' own.*) Saving, then, comes to mean finding oneself saying surprising things, being the vessel of a saying unknown to one and wondrous, which one could not predict or expect. Indeed, even when briefly switching to the mode of direct speech, immediately releasing the words of the Muses as if he had become the goddesses themselves, the poet does not vanish, let alone dissimulate himself. Rather, in reporting how the Muses address(ed) him, the poet brings himself forth in his utter alienation from himself—in his own remarkable, even shocking strangeness. Thus, saving a saying involves connecting with that remote, always receding, inaccessible, and foreign source of wonder *in one*—letting it speak as such, in the midst of oneself, as it were, in its uncanny voice, letting it spring forth, come over one, overcome one.[24]

Saying as saving would in this way distinguish itself from the pure passing away inherent in the mimetic practice of direct speech, from the pure loss of boundaries which allows for the indifferent, indiscriminate emergence of all voices, all sounds, and all shapes in their vividness, while denying their unbridgeable distance, the gap of their peculiarity. The denial of such distance is precisely what constitutes the mimetic lie. At the same time, though, this saying which saves is not in its essence a harnessing, let alone an immobilizing. It lets emerge, brings into a shape, *and* lets go. It does not hold in its power that which it brings forth. Analogously to the structures and operations of mnemonic retention, which it mirrors, it is not a pure storing of information or a preservation without loss. It is, rather, a dynamic arranging. Its saving occurs through a manifold play of veils, revelations, disappearances, gleams in the dark. It is a battle waged in *and* against the devouring field of oblivion, the ravenous, the all-swallowing. (How is one to think the belonging of the battle in that against which the battle is waged is precisely the issue.)

Apología: *The* Êthos *of* Poíesis

A certain ineluctability of μίμησις was shown above to result from the Socratic reflection begun already in Book III. In reconsidering the subject at later junctures, however, Socrates displays a reluctance to draw the consequences of his own findings rigorously. Only in the very last segment of the dialogue, after considerable denial, is Socrates' recognition of this allowed to surface and explicitly articulated. The extent of Socrates' ambivalence toward the truth of μίμησις, the depth and gravity of the conflict between philosophical discourse and poetry, and the manner of the Socratic acknowledgment late in the dialogue deserve closer scrutiny. Among other things, reviewing these matters will help shed further light on the singular features of Socrates' own mythical narration.

In what follows, the previous examination of the issue of imitation is taken up again and expanded, particularly in light of the remarks occasioned by Hesiodic singing.

In Book III Socrates develops the distinction between "two forms of diction" (τὰ δύο εἴδη τῆς λέξεως) (397b), both of which, to differing degrees, display imitative traits. In fact, they differ from one another according to the extent of their employment of imitation. That is why Socrates reformulates in the following way Adeimantos's assertion that, of the different kinds of poets, they should admit into the city "the unmixed imitator of the decent" (τὸν τοῦ ἐπιεικοῦς μιμητὴν ἄκρατον) (397d): "We ourselves would use a more austere and less pleasing poet and teller of tales (ποιητῇ . . . καὶ μυθολόγῳ) for the sake of benefit, one who would imitate the diction of the seemly one (ἐπιεικοῦς λέξιν μιμοῖτο) and would say what he says in those models that we set down as laws at the beginning, when we undertook to educate the soldiers" (398a–b). That way of speaking is to be favored which, however imitatively, according to the established modalities adheres to the parameters of decency. The assumption that it may be possible to avoid imitation altogether already at this juncture appears not to be viable. As was pointed out above, this realization presents implications of considerable importance.

Yet, as if oblivious of such conclusion, later (indeed, very late in the dialogue, in Book X) Socrates restates the early charge of imitative deceptiveness against poetry. As he says, "only so much of poetry as hymns to gods or praises (ἐγκώμια) of those who are good should be admitted into a city" (607a), while "any part in it that is imitative" (595a) should in principle be excluded. Despite the fact that the Homeric saying, too, may at times happen not to lie and even justly to prescribe to honor those who are good (468c–d), the imponderable danger of its lie makes the rejection of it necessary. In order to acknowledge such necessity, Socrates must overcome a deeply rooted respect for the Homeric song. As he concedes at the beginning of Book X, "a certain friendship for Homer, and a sense of awe (αἰδὼς) before him, which has possessed me since childhood, prevents me from speaking. . . . Still and all, a man must not be honored before the truth, but, as I say, it must be told" (595b–c). The force of this reverence for the proto-tragic singing of Homer cannot be underestimated.[25] Socrates repeatedly points out, not without a certain sarcasm, "the inborn love (τὸν ἐγγεγονότα μὲν ἔρωτα) of such poetry" due to "the rearing in these fine regimes (τῶν καλῶν πολιτειῶν)" (607e–608a) and the extent to which "we ourselves are charmed (κηλουμένοις)" by this singing (607c). For these reasons, Socrates insists on the necessity of responding to the charm of imitative poetry with the antidote of another way of speaking. In order to do so, he says, "we'll chant (ἐπᾴδοντες) this argument (λόγον) to ourselves as a countercharm (ἐπῳδήν), taking care against falling back again into the love (εἰς τὸν ... ἔρωτα) which is childish and belongs to the many" (608a).[26]

The myth of Er should be viewed in the context of the Socratic pronouncements against (proto-)tragic verse and the logic of mimetic absorption, that is, μίμησις-without-distance. Socrates' myth would be the speaking through and as which a certain illumination of the poet (of the one who tells the story) occurs. But, as became apparent through the brief reflection on the *Theogony*, such illumination of (the experience of) the poet presents itself as no less excessive, no less obscured than the tragic poet's loss of boundaries and fusion with his heroes, with the gods, or with the elements. In other words, the disclosure occurring in what Socrates calls the narration of "the one who is beautiful and good" appears to be, although in its own unique way, no less pervaded by shadow than the lie of imitative immediacy. It is, to be sure, a speaking in which the poet does not hide himself—but not in the sense of an utterance through which the poet, programmatically and in possession of himself, would bring about his full self-disclosure. Rather, in such narration the poet's singing should be understood as the exposure without shelter to that over which one has no power. It should be understood as the defenseless speaking of the poet inhaling an alien breath, pervaded by its sound, letting this invasion sing itself through him, at once irresistibly and incomprehensibly.[27] This is what the Socratic saying would share with the dithyramb and with that other singing which is neither epic nor tragic—the Hesiodic saying that unfolds as the poet's experience of the divine and as an offering to the divine. This is also what the Socratic saying shares with the opening lines of the *Iliad* and those other rare moments in the Homeric songs in which "the poet himself speaks."

Socrates' narration would, in this sense, be the locus within which the exposure to and emergence of strange voices becomes perspicuous, manifests itself *as such*, instead of disappearing into the lie, into the pretense of the sameness of these voices and the poet. Such narration would unfold out of another kind of absorption, an absorption without fusion, without oneness or absolute proximity. An absorption resembling the undergoing of what comes to one, of what wells up from within one, of a provocation dictating involvement—perhaps. The saying of the poet not hiding, not protecting himself, far from involving the pure and simple illumination of the poet, that is to say, the self-showing of the self-possessed poet, stems again from a certain being-possessed and even dispossessed. Indeed, it stems from a possession and dispossession, from an incursion that is unfathomable in its imperfection. For something remains hidden both concerning the voices pervading the poet and concerning the poet. Something remains hidden in the *speaking of the poet* through whom the Muses speak and in the *speaking of the Muses* to whom the poet gives birth and voice. Neither the disclosure of the Muses' truth nor the disclosure of the poet's truth is fully achieved. The voice of the Muses, resounding but also filtered through the poetic saying, will not have been purely presented. In turn, the poet, *himself speaking* and *not hiding himself,* will have disclosed himself through an alien voice *in* himself.

This saying, haunted by a numinous nebulosity, unveils the emergence of alterity and its veils in the midst of the one who recounts—an emergence revealing one as an other, the same as differing from itself. It is the upsurge of a strange voice, wondrous and elusive, through the one who speaks, which paradoxically discloses the speaker as such and calls forth such speaking. Whereas the logic of μίμησις involves a disruption of boundaries and the fusion of the poet with that which is other than and to him, the logic of Socrates' saying intimates the upsurge of that which is foreign, as such, within oneself. Such an intimation, in turn, reveals an understanding of oneself as constitutively empty, dynamically determined through a play one does not determine—as the resounding hollowness of the fool, of the vessel, of the belly.

It is in this way that the Socratic myth seems to occur as a response to and avoidance of the lie of mimetic con-fusion. And yet, in spite of distance, indirection, and indirect speech, even Socrates' counterspell cannot be free from the flaw of μίμησις. Even the Socratic myth is accompanied by a shadow. The saying to which the Socratic saying aspires will not have been a pure preservation, a pure coming to the light and remaining in light. As was observed already, this is so for reasons having to do with language itself, whose operation was above associated with a certain transgression (for the work of language always covers distances and crosses boundaries) and, most decisively, with imaginal evocation.

If imitation is not simply eludible, and if its fundamental flaw presents itself even in that poetic comportment which strives to diverge from the logic of μίμησις, then the basic distinction between the Homeric-tragic saying and Socrates' own is unstable, unclear, and appears to be irreducible to the contrast between imitative and nonimitative speaking, lie and full disclosure, shadow and illumination. It is at the level of ἦθος, however, that the distinction between the Homeric and the Socratic manner of elocution decisively emerges. The exquisitely Socratic cipher of the ending myth appears to be an awareness of the limits marking its own unfolding, of the shadows accompanying it, and a readiness to let these limits and shadows as such appear. It is in this way that, in the end, Socrates' λέγειν becomes ἀπολογία. But this requires further elucidation.

Reference to the discursive mode of apology occurs at various stages in the dialogue, before the telling of the ἀπόλογος of Er. In fact, the dialogue as a whole may be seen as a transmuted version of the trial undergone by Socrates, recalling the accusations brought against him and his self-defense or, more precisely, his defense of philosophy. At crucial points the discussion seems to hinge on the dynamic tension between κατηγορία and ἀπολογία, to receive its impulse from such a confrontation. In virtually all cases, it is the philosopher who undergoes accusations and is called to respond defensively.[28] There is, however, a critical exception to this pattern. In Book X, after the second argument on imitation and in the course of the anti-Homeric invective considered above, the philosopher acknowledges himself as the accuser—as the one who, throughout the dialogue, has pressed charges against poetry. He avows the friction emerged in the previous discussions between the philosophical discourse and poetry. More specifically, the sustained attack brought against poetry is recognized in its both polemical and openly condemnatory character.

At this stage, in keeping with the forensic tenor of such confrontation, Socrates concedes that poetry may be admitted back into the city—if only it will make its apology. Even though it may be informed by the logic of pleasure and of imitation, poetry will be received again into the city if it, along with its lovers, will show that the city thrives on its ground and will not be impaired by its deception—that "it's not only pleasant (ἡδεῖα) but also beneficial (ὠφελίμη) to regimes and human life (τὰς πολιτείας καὶ τὸν βίον τὸν ἀνθρώπινόν)" (607d). Such is the apology requested. That poetry should show itself in this way means that it should comport itself truthfully, without deception, even toward its own untruthfulness and deceptiveness—that it should come to terms with the impossibility of simple disclosure, openly exposing the undisclosed that accompanies any bringing forth. It means that poetry should allow itself inadequately to acknowledge its own inadequacy, the lie it harbors, the residue of darkness. In this way poetry would give up its pretense, the falsity of mimetic immediacy, and renounce the delusional power that the mimetic logic always makes available. While such power would not be surrendered (for it cannot be; it is bound to remain a possibility pertaining to all saying), *its operation would no longer continue in secret.* Thus, paradoxically, would poetry genuinely disclose itself. And in this way it would show that it belongs in the city—or that the city may acknowledge its own belonging to it. The ποιεῖν of poetry would become that particular mode of bringing forth that is not blinding, not all-absorbing, not obscure about its obscurity, occult about its occultation—a making that shows itself as such, lets itself appear in its conspicuousness, instead of disappearing as the neutral, transparent field in which what is made (sung) takes shape, comes into an outline, as though of its own accord.

As Socrates says, then, "if poetry directed to pleasure and imitation have any argument to give showing that they should be in the city with good laws, we should be delighted to receive them back from exile." But, he warns, "it isn't holy to betray what seems to be the truth" (607c). It is in order to honor "what seems to be the truth" that the apology should be made. Those who "aren't poets but lovers of poetry" will have the chance to "speak an argument without meter" on behalf of poetry. As far as poetry itself is concerned, however, it is "just for it to come back in this way—when it has made an apology in lyrics or some other meter"—when, that is, it will have presented *itself as* an apology (607d). Such is the poetic ἦθος that would be accepted in the just city—which would, indeed, be vital to an envisioning of justice. What is crucial to the Socratic discourse, then, is the showing of poetry, of this fundamental ποιεῖν, in terms of comportment.

It is in such a circumstance that poetry is brought to the point of turning into apology. It would seem, however, that it is because of its subjection to the relentless philosophical attack that poetry must defend itself. Indeed, it would seem as though the logic operative here were still that of indictment, on the one hand, and of defensive, self-legitimizing reaction, on the other hand.

Yet it should be noticed that this Socratic reprise of the imputations against poetry is not itself simply in the register of accusation. Indeed, the acknowledgment of the accusatory character of the previous arguments, far from repeating them, is already in and of itself apologetic. That the Socratic argument against poetry should at some point undergo such a shift rigorously follows from the treatment of μίμησις and the recognition of its inevitability. In accord with such treatment, it must finally be acknowledged that it was not primarily because of its mimetic structure, not because of the lie that poetry carries within itself, that poetry was initially expelled. In fact, these flaws (whether the confusion discussed in Book III or the impairing distance considered in Book X) may not be avoidable, even as one departs from certain formal features associated with such flaws. For their shadows reemerge in the midst of disclosure in varied and apparently ineludible guises. Λόγος never seems simply to position itself at the appropriate distance from the truth (i.e., neither too close to it nor too far from it). Hence, it must be made clear that, properly speaking, the problem was never the lie of μίμησις, but the comportment toward it—the ἦθος toward the irrepressible and inassimilable remainder of darkness harbored within saying, any saying, and constantly threatening to resurface with its unrest and disquiet. In this way it becomes evident that, in accusing poetry on the ground of its mimetic character, Socrates has let himself be carried away and determined by those concerns which now appear to have been merely strategic, even sophistical. The charge of mimetic obscurity brought against poetry appears to be im-pertinent, even irrelevant, for in no way does the contamination of μίμησις concern poetry alone. Hence the necessity of the apology—the apology of the accuser, first of all:

> Since we brought up the subject of poetry again (ἀναμνησθεῖσι περὶ ποιήσεως), let it be our apology that it was then fitting for us to send it away from the city on account of its character. The argument overpowered (ᾕρει) us. Let

us further say to it, lest it convict us for a certain harshness and rusticity, that there is an old quarrel (παλαιὰ . . . διαφορὰ) between philosophy and poetry (ποιητικῇ). For that "yelping bitch shrieking at her master," and "great in the empty eloquence of fools," "the mob of overwise men holding sway," and "the refined thinkers who are really poor" and countless others are signs of this old opposition (παλαιᾶς ἐναντιώσεως). (607b–c)

It was philosophy, then, that had to defend itself against the ludicrous characterizations of it devised by poets and, in reacting to such accusations, ended up becoming itself accusatory, that is, reiterating the gesture of those against whom it thought it would take a stance. Socrates allows his own argument against imitative poetry to appear in its one-sidedness and vulgarity—to appear in its error and purely contentious character (i.e., in its injustice). The differing of poetry and philosophy with respect to one another is irreducible to opposition, however old the institution of this formula may be. That the polemic of διαφορά cannot be brought to coincide with simple antagonism entails a suspension, even a discrediting, of conflict in its rudimentary forms and calls for a thoughtful engagement (a confrontation, even) with διαφέρειν in its complexity.

The Socratic accusation tends in this way to lose its accusatory force and, in fact, to become something altogether other than an accusation. Subsequently the apology required of poetry is not so much a matter of a philosophico-forensic prosecution, to which poetry should reply apologetically, in self-defense. What is thus required, rather, is a self-manifestation of poetry *and* its shadow. But the Socratic discourse does not limit itself to requiring. After turning from accusation into apology, Socrates' λέγειν itself turns into poetry, that is, μυθολογεῖν—in other words, it proceeds to perform and to become poetry in its apologetic self-manifestation, poetry no longer hiding its hiding, showing itself in its hiding. Such is the transition from the apology for a certain "harshness and rusticity" to the mythical narration. The ἀπόλογος of Er would be the enactment of a further apology—the apology enacted by the Socratic λέγειν itself and not merely prescribed to poetry, the development of a λέγειν first *proffering* its apology and, then, *becoming* apology.

Thus, it is in the recognition of its own constitutive insufficiency, in the compulsion to acknowledge its inadequacy, that is, in its envisioning the need for an apology, that the Socratic narration shows its own distinctive features. But the Socratic discourse cannot provide an adequate acknowledgment of its inadequacy. The apology carried out by this discourse, then, is neither a polite excuse nor a defense strategically set forth for the sake of self-justification. Such an apology is not a legitimizing device, which would leave the discourse intact and, indeed, make it more irresistible, even more effective in its seduction. Rather, Socrates' saying gives itself in its inability to reappropriate and appropriately acknowledge its inability. It gives itself as the contemplation of a necessity before which it is structurally inadequate. Unable aptly to apologize, Socrates' saying presents *itself as* apology—as the apology it cannot represent.

What the narration shows in showing itself as apology is its radical, irredeemable insufficiency. Socratic storytelling, then, does not simply apologize for the foregoing λόγοι, but especially for itself, for its own λέγειν. This is the λέγειν of μῦθος, the kind of poetic discourse that would be admitted into the city—a discourse not without shadows but letting these shadows show.

One final observation is in order before turning to the λέγειν of the μῦθος, that is, to the ἀπόλογος proper. As was shown above, Socrates' "dithyrambic saying" (animated by the aspiration to overcome μίμησις, and yet obscured in its aspiration) is a saving, a remembering. But saving, on Socrates' own terms, is in this context another name for and of justice. Once again, one might recall the paradigmatic passage in Book IV, in which justice is associated with the coming into being of the other manifestations of the good (virtues)[29] as well as with their preservation and in which, by the same token, injustice is connected with destruction and dissolution (433b–434b). But the double function of justice, connected with both generation and preservation, is fairly consistently confirmed throughout the dialogue. Justice, indeed, names the δύναμις by which σοφία (or, e.g., at 433b, σωφροσύνη), ἀνδρεία, and φρόνησις can come to be (ἐγγίγνομαι) as well as the saving and holding together, the σωτηρία of that which has come into being. Pervasive in an analogous way is, on the other hand, the association of injustice and destruction, war, division, dissolution—ὄλεθρος and κακουργία (434b–c), μάχη and μῖσος (351d), λύειν (444a).[30]

It is worth, however, extensively quoting the following passage concluding Book III, in which the broad spectrum of implications pertaining to the relation between justice and injustice is remarkably exposed. In this passage, indeed, the contrast between justice and injustice, between saving and disintegration, is developed by reference to the golden and silver kinds and is presented in its simultaneously political and psychological significance. This statement, furthermore, calls attention to the question of the relation of δικαιοσύνη to τὸ ὅσιον, that is to say, to the question of justice in its relation to the other-than-human. Or, one could even say, this statement calls attention to justice as essentially and fundamentally grounded in the other-than-human, in the nonhuman—grounded in that radical *mise en question* of the human as such which the pervasiveness of the nonhuman brings about. Says Socrates:

> We'll tell them that gold and silver of a divine sort from the gods they have in their soul always and have no further need of the mortal sort; nor is it holy (ὅσια) to pollute the possession (κτῆσιν) of the former sort by mixing it with the possession (κτήσει) of the mortal sort, because many unholy things (ἀνόσια) have been done for the sake of the currency (νόμισμα) of the many,

while theirs is untainted. But for them alone of those in the city it is not lawful (οὐ θέμις) to handle and to touch gold and silver, nor to go under the same roof with it, nor to hang it from their persons, nor to drink from silver or gold. And thus they would save themselves as well as save the city (σώζοιντό τ' ἂν καὶ σώζοιεν τὴν πόλιν). Whenever they'll possess private land, houses, and currency (ἰδίαν καὶ οἰκίας καὶ νομίσματα κτήσονται), they'll be householders and farmers instead of guardians, and they'll become masters and enemies instead of allies (δεσπόται δ' ἐχθροὶ ἀντὶ ξυμμάχων) of the other citizens; hating and being hated (μισοῦντες δὲ δὴ καὶ μισούμενοι), plotting and being plotted against (ἐπιβουλεύοντες καὶ ἐπιβουλευόμενοι), they'll lead their whole lives (πάντα τὸν βίον) far more afraid of the enemies within than those without (τοὺς ἔνδον ἢ τοὺς ἔξωθεν πολεμίους). Then they themselves as well as the rest of the city are already rushing toward a destruction (ὀλέθρου) that is very near. (416e–417b)

This overflowing (because already masterfully concise) passage is later concentrated, brought to a further degree of simplicity (that is to say, of overflowing complexity). It receives a reformulation involving a polishing, purification, and reduction to its minimal terms. The minimalist precipitate of this passage is to be found in Book X, where Socrates plainly, that is to say, boldly, affirms that "what destroys and corrupts everything is the bad, and what saves and benefits is the good" (τὸ μὲν ἀπολλύον καὶ διαφθεῖρον πᾶν τὸ κακὸν εἶναι, τὸ δὲ σῷζον καὶ ὠφελοῦν τὸ ἀγαθόν) (608e).

And yet, what should be noticed with regard to the previous passage on the justice and injustice in and of rulers and guardians is a strange tension—a tension between, on the one hand, the attribution of all destruction and destructiveness to injustice and, on the other hand, the characterization of the rulers and guardians as ξύμμαχοι. The justice of the rulers and guardians is to be allies, companions in war, to fight (μάχομαι) along with the other citizens or even for them, on their behalf—for the sake of the preservation of the city. Μάχη is, then, essential to the saving of the city. There is war (division, disintegration, dissipation) at the heart of justice. There is strife at the heart of the striving for preservation.

Notes

1. Living (ζῆν) is said to be the assignment (ἔργον) of the soul at 353d. Later the soul is alluded to as "that very thing by which we live (ζῶμεν)" (445a).

2. Shortly before the introduction of the ἀπόλογος of Er, Socrates already exhibits a certain compulsion to speak (specifically, about the endurance and immortality of the ψυχή) in order "not to do an injustice" (μὴ ἀδικῶ) (608d). In the same discussion, doing justice is also associated with recollection: "I should indeed be doing an injustice" (ἀδικοίην μέντ' ἄν), says Glaukon, "if I didn't [remember]" (612d).

3. It should be noticed that, at this stage in the conversation, Glaukon's interjections repeatedly suggest that Socrates' speaking *says* the just (δίκαια . . . αἰτεῖ, 612d–e; δικαια . . . λέγεις, 613e).

4. The conclusion of the dialogue is foreshadowed at a much earlier stage, in Book VI. Here Socrates, preparing to present the allegory of the city-ship, tells Adeimantos: "listen (ἄκουε) to the image (εἰκόνος) so you may see (ἴδῃς) still more how greedy I am for images (ὡς γλίσχρως εἰκάζω). So hard is the condition (χαλεπὸν τὸ πάθος) suffered by the most decent men with respect to the city that there is no single other condition like it, but I must make my *image and apology* (εἰκάζοντα καὶ ἀπολογούμενον) on their behalf by bringing it together (ξυναγαγεῖν) from many sources (ἐκ πολλῶν)—as the painters paint goatstags and such things by making mixtures" (487e–488a; emphasis added). There appears, indeed, to be a crucial connection between the order of the mythical-imaginal (in its essential character of ἀπόλογος and ἀπολογία) and the question of (quest for) justice.

5. As late as in the last few exchanges before the myth of Er, Glaukon still qualifies what is being said as "likely" (εἰκός), as something which is the case "at least in my opinion" (613b). Socrates, too, does not surmise the truth of what has been said, but returns to the theme of dialogical agreement and asks Glaukon whether he will "stand (up) (ἀνέξει) for" the result of their inquiry (613e).

6. See, for instance, Socrates' remark according to which everything that happens to the just man, "insofar as it comes from the gods, is the best possible, except for any necessary evil that was due to him for former mistakes (προτέρας ἁμαρτίας ὑπῆρχεν)" (612e–613a). To this Socrates adds: "it must be surmised in the case of the just man that, if he falls into poverty, diseases, or any other of the things that seem bad, for him it will end in some good, either in life or even in death (ἀγαθόν τι τελευτήσει ζῶντι ἢ καὶ ἀποθανόντι)" (613a).

7. It should not go unobserved that the language of debt and repayment echoes the definition of justice provided by Kephalos at the outset. The theme of indebtedness is at once preserved and transmuted in the dialogue. By the end, obligation no longer bespeaks giving back what is owed (money to humans, sacrifices to gods). Rather, in light of a shift inconspicuously announced already in Book I (332c), from giving back what was taken to giving back what is fitting (προσῆκον: what is the case, hence appropriate), obligation has come to indicate the task of giving back to the just ones a discourse, a λόγος, of justice—the task, that is, of honoring the just ones as such by making manifest in λόγος (which will have become a μῦθος) that which sustains and informs them. Incidentally, it should be observed that giving back the discourse of justice means returning it to those who are just *already* and that, consequently, allegorico-edifying interpretations of such discourse are ruled out.

8. In the context of the progression leading to the "enactment of dialectic" (to the dialectical journey away from hypotheses), μῦθος seems to acquire a somewhat necessary character, to occur in light of a certain necessitating movement.

9. It is remarkable that, at the culmination of the ascent along the line, dialectic should resolve into a descent. The "divided line" comes to resemble rather a "repeated circle," joining end and beginning.

10. In beginning to relate Er's story, Socrates warns: "Now, to go through the many things (πολλά) would take a long time (πολλοῦ χρόνου), Glaukon. But the sum (κεφάλαιον), he said, was this" (615a). The rule of the rhythm of day and night is formu-

lated in the Homeric song: "Night (νὺξ) is upon us (τελέθει); and it is good (ἀγαθὸν) to be compelled by night" (*Il.* VII.282).

11. The *Gita* suggests a connection between absorption in action and a certain blindness. It is the poet who gives to the blind king (to the king blindly participating in the deeds of warfare) the sight of (and insight into) himself and his belonging in the vast upheaval (I.8). Aside from the reflective space disclosed through the poetic utterance, as Nietzsche will have said, "our consciousness (*Bewusstsein*) of our own meaning (*Bedeutung*) is hardly other than that which soldiers painted on canvas have of the battle presented on it" (*The Birth of Tragedy*, § 5).

12. Here and for the rest of the work, the translation of the Sanskrit text is based on the English versions by Winthrop Sargeant (Albany: SUNY Press, 1984) and Sri Aurobindo (Bhagavad Gita *and Its Message* [Twin Lakes, Wis.: Lotus Light, 1995]).

13. This kind of statement, in the end, may tempt one to take up the Nietzschean reflection on the Dionysian and on the Socratic or Platonic relation to it. Socrates' distinction between dithyrambic singing and dramatic composition seems to problematize what in Nietzsche's texts (paradigmatically, but not exclusively, in *The Birth of Tragedy*) is thought under the heading of the Dionysian. Socrates' allusion to the somewhat dithyrambic character of his narrative, furthermore, seems to call into question Nietzsche's rendition of the Socratic voice as utterly anti-Dionysian, the non-Dionysian par excellence.

14. Notice a certain preference accorded to the specifically comedic mode of imitation—or to the epico-tragic as well, to the extent that it is not taken "seriously" (396d).

15. The account in Book X, in its discussion of all forms of mimetic techniques, is often treated as more complete, inclusive of the earlier one (see, e.g., S. Halliwell's *Plato: Republic 10* [Warminster: Aris & Phillips, 1988], pp. 3–16). However, while the later discussion does in fact address a broader range of imitative practices, it does not necessarily represent a subsumption, a deepening, let alone a radicalization of the argument in Book III. In fact, it is not evident how the problematization of μίμησις in terms of insufficient distance (Book III) could be assimilated to the problematization of μίμησις in terms of excessive distance (Book X). To this extent, the earlier argument, in its unique traits, deserves close and separate consideration. Ultimately the two elaborations should be understood in their unity and complementarity—but as irreducible to one. On imitation in its twofold typology, see Rémi Brague, *Du temps chez Platon et Aristote* (Paris: PUF, 1982), p. 60. See also Jean-Luc Nancy, *Le Partage des voix* (Paris: Galilée, 1982), especially p. 71 ff.

16. *Cyávati* and the related noun *cyavas* (motion) pertain to the living, to that which comes to be and perishes. The participle *acyuta* (with privative prefix *a-*) appears at times as an epithet of Krishna (the unmoved, unshaken, imperishable one, the one who has not fallen; e.g., *Bhagavad Gita* XI.42).

17. Even the *Phaedrus* is not oblivious of such a difficulty. As this text shows, the actuality of what was originally witnessed, the fact itself of an originary witnessing, can only be recalled through myth and brought forth as a myth.

18. In the dialogue, the discussion of the just city-soul in Book IV illustrates this manner of discovery. It shows the necessity of going through the dialogical toil in order to obtain an insight that then (and *only then*) is said to transcend such toil and, indeed, to precede it (albeit in the mode of λήθη). See 432d–e.

19. In the *Phaedrus* and in the *Symposium* one finds statements concerning the ψυχή analogously circumspect and, at the same time, magnificently paradoxical. In the former,

Socrates, undertaking to determine the "truth" of the "nature of the soul" (ψυχῆς φύ-σεως), speaks of the ψυχή as immortal (ἀθάνατον) *and* ever-changing (ἀεικίνητον)—source of motion *and* itself always moving (245c ff.). Following this remark is the presentation of the soul through the image of the winged horses and charioteer. In the latter dialogue, however, Diotima speaks of the ψυχή as undergoing the same processes of loss and renewal pertaining to everything that comes to be and passes away. As she points out, "one is always undergoing renewal (νέος ἀεὶ γιγνόμενος) while losing (ἀπολλύς) some element of one's hair, flesh, bones, blood, and all parts of the body generally. *This is so not only with regard to one's body, but also with regard to one's soul* (κατὰ τὴν ψυχὴν)—one's habits, character traits, opinions, desires, pleasures, pains, fears (οἱ τρόποι, τὰ ἤθη, δόξαι, ἐπιθυμίαι, ἡδοναί, λῦπαι, φόβοι), none of these ever stays the same (τὰ αὐτὰ πάρεστιν) in anybody; some are coming into being (γίγνεται), while others are passing away (ἀπόλλυται). Yet even more strange (ἀτοπώτερον) than these points is the fact that not only do bits of knowledge (αἱ ἐπιστῆμαι) come into being and pass away for us (we are never the same even in terms of our knowledge [οὐδέποτε οἱ αὐτοί ἐσμεν οὐδὲ κατὰ τὰς ἐπιστήμας]), but each single bit of knowledge also undergoes the same experience (ταὐτὸν πάσχει). What is called studying (μελετᾶν) takes place because knowledge departs (ἐξιούσης). Forgetting is the departure of knowledge (λήθη γὰρ ἐπιστήμης ἔξοδος), and study saves the knowledge (σῴζει τὴν ἐπιστήμην) by pro-ducing (ἐμποιοῦσα) a new memory (μνήμην) in place of what has gone away (ἀπιού-σης), so that it seems to be (δοκεῖν εἶναι) the same knowledge. *Everything that is mortal* is saved (σῴζεται) in this way, not by being the same in every way forever (παντάπασι τὸ αὐτὸ ἀεὶ εἶναι), like what is divine, but by having what is old and departing leave behind (ἐγκαταλείπειν) another like itself that is new. Through this device (μηχανῇ), Socrates . . . a *mortal* thing participates in immortality, both in terms of its body and in *all other regards* (θνητὸν ἀθανασίας μετέχει, καὶ σῶμα καὶ τἆλλα πάντα)" (207d–208b; emphases added). The development of the analogy between σῶμα and ψυχή in re-spect to mortality and participation in immortality could hardly be more thorough. It could perhaps be argued that Diotima here is speaking of the "constitutive elements" of the soul, and not of the soul "itself," as undergoing constant renewal. However, this would hold for what is said of the body as well: Diotima would be speaking of the bod-ily parts and not of the body itself. But just as it is arduous even to imagine the subsis-tence of body aside from its "parts" (flesh, hair, blood, etc.), so one wonders what it would mean to speak of the abiding of the soul "itself" in light of the passing away of its ele-ments and actual structures. Like the body (or, rather, *a* body, *this* body), in its utter par-ticularity the soul (*a* soul) withdraws from eidetic determination. However, what is one to say of the soul or, for that matter, of the body in the lack of individuation, of actual-ized dispositions and configurations? In the passing away of its "parts" and, ultimately, in dying, the body is not annihilated in an unqualified sense, yet its radical transformation defies the attempts at providing further, proper accounts of it—indeed, defies the very idea of propriety itself. The question concerning the ψυχή presents the same difficulties. There remains, to be sure, what is said of the soul and its continuity in the *Phaedo*. But, without even pretending to broach a discussion of this dialogue in the present context, it should be recalled that, in the final analysis, everything that is put forth there (the so-called "doctrine of the immortality of the soul" above all) is put forth in a crucially quali-fied way. Socrates' λόγοι unfold as a kind of μυθολογεῖν (61e), as charms offered to dis-pel the "child's fearing" before death, as the singing of an ἐπῳδός (77d–78a).

20. Even in the most excellent human beings, λογισμός is "aided by sensation," the Muses intimated in the beginning of Book VIII.

21. Although Richmond Lattimore's version (Hesiod, *The Works and Days. Theogony. The Shield of Herakles* [Ann Arbor: University of Michigan Press, 1991]) was consulted, the translation of this and the following quotations significantly diverges from it. Guidance for the formulation of the present rendition was found in Cesare Pavese's word-for-word translation into Italian (*La* Teogonia *di Esiodo e tre inni omerici* [Torino: Einaudi, 1981]).

22. In this sense the Hesiodic saying is more consistently in agreement with the Socratic directions expounded in Book III than the stylistically heterogeneous Homeric elocution. In "The Ideas and the Criticism of Poetry in Plato's *Republic,* Book 10," *Journal of the History of Philosophy* 19, no. 2 (1981), pp. 135–50, C. Griswold observes that Homer, rather than Hesiod, is the primary target of Socrates' critique of poetry.

23. With reference to the reflections on giving back proposed above, it is now possible to note that the plexus of saving (preservation), narration, and remembrance bears a crucial relation to justice. The preservation which does not occur as self-preservation, but rather as a mode of giving back, appears as an enactment of justice, a doing justice.

24. The overflowing, unmasterable character of Music(al) alterity is suggested, among other things, by the terminological proliferation conspicuous there where the poet is attempting to signify the Muses' voices, the sound coming from that source. The poet tries a multiplicity of terms, as if struggling with certain limits of language, straining language in an attempt to expand its range. See, e.g., lines 39–44.

25. In this context Socrates treats Homer as a precursor of the tragic poet. This is perfectly consistent with the previous juxtaposition of tragedy, comedy, and epic as imitative poetic forms and turns the category of the tragic into a comprehensive heading not simply designating a genre but a poetic mode, mood, and comportment. Homer, Socrates says, "seems to have been the first teacher and leader of all these fine tragic things" (ἔοικε μὲν γὰρ τῶν καλῶν ἁπάντων τούτων τῶν τραγικῶν πρῶτος διδάσκαλός τε καὶ ἡγεμὼν γενέσθαι) (595c). Again, later Socrates exhorts Glaukon to acknowledge Homer as "the most poetic and first of the tragic poets" (ποιητικώτατον . . . καὶ πρῶτον τῶν τραγῳδοποιῶν) (607a).

26. For the language of ἐπᾴδειν, see *Phaedo* 77e and 114d, in which the way of the philosopher is shown in its spellbinding power.

27. In a way, Hesiod the poet and shepherd "dwelling in the fields" is defenseless and has no shelter. The lack of shelter is not, however, absolute. It is, indeed, on a certain inevitability of shelter, of outline (as diaphanous and transient as it may be) that the disclosure of the breath as alien rests.

28. In the opening of Book IV, Adeimantos interrupts the conversation, accuses Socrates of being responsible for the unhappiness of the guardian class, and asks that he provide an adequate defense of his position (419a–420b). In the early stages of Book V, another accusation forces Socrates to defend the thesis that men and women sharing the same nature must practice the same things (453c–e). More remarkably still, at the beginning of Book VI Adeimantos again forces Socrates to offer a defense. This time the accusation has to do with the alleged uselessness, even viciousness, of philosophers in the city. It is in response to such a charge, not utterly dissimilar to the charges confronted in the *Apology,* that Socrates brings forth the analogy of the city-ship (487b–489a; see n. 4 above). It should also be remembered that the dialogue opens with the motif of the ar-

rest of the philosopher and his submission to the court (328b). This motif is reiterated in Book V, marking in a way a new beginning (449a–450b).

29. The virtues can be seen as an articulation of the good. Indeed, concerning the "perfectly good" (τελέως ἀγαθὴν) city Socrates says that "clearly . . . it is wise (σοφή), courageous (ἀνδρεία), moderate (σώφρων), and just (δικαία)" (427e).

30. It was noticed already that λύσις and λύειν also indicate the generative, fecund, liberating dimension of dissolution, as Socrates' elaboration of the cave image shows (515c).

IV. War

I went down not long ago
to the Mad River, under the willows
I knelt and drank from that crumpled flow, call it
what madness you will, there's a sickness
worse than the risk of death and that's
forgetting what we should never forget.
Tecumseh lived here.
The wounds of the past
are ignored, but hang on
like the litter that snags among the yellow branches,
newspapers and plastic bags, after the rains.

(MARY OLIVER, from "Tecumseh")

After the foregoing remarks, and with these in mind, it is opportune to return to the beginning of the telling of the story of Er—to return, that is, to *the
discourse of justice.*

Like the *Bhagavad Gita* and the proto-tragic Homeric ἔπος, Socrates' narration is in a crucial way connected with the disclosure and unfolding of war.[1]
But, as was observed above, Socrates' saying, unlike those other narrations, is
not simultaneous with the action it narrates. Rather, it occurs at a certain remove
from action and allows for the manifestation of the remoteness of what is
brought forth in the saying. This gap is not the distance and separation which
would allow for a crystalline, fully illuminated representation of the presented.
In virtue of this gap Socrates' recitation distances itself from what he views as
the pretense of con-fusion, coincidence, oneness (the pretense involved in the
purely poietic aspiration of singing). A matter neither of shedding light and totally dispelling all shadow nor of a fully mimetic bringing forth, Socrates' narration presents itself in its mixed character, at once as the presentation of that
with which it does not coincide and as a wondrous and unaccountable moment
of ποίησις. Such is the thaumaturgic character of Socrates' speaking. Through
this speaking shines the Greek understanding of the demiurgic moment as less
than purely founding and fundamental, as less than radically creative, as delimited by a residue which it cannot assimilate and whose irreducible priority it
must undergo. Through this speaking shines the understanding of creation as
nonoriginary, already as re-creation.

However, even the saying of Samjaya in the *Gita* is simultaneous with action only in a highly qualified sense. Indeed, while his narration begins by evok-

ing the phase preparatory to action (in fact, the deployment of forces on the battlefield, before the war), its unfolding constitutes precisely the suspension and deferral of the action announced. Strictly speaking, the body of the poem consists of Samjaya's articulation of the dialogue between Arjuna and Krishna his charioteer—a dialogue taking place on the battlefield and indeterminately delaying the operations of warfare proper. Samjaya, the immortal, ubiquitous poet and seer presenting himself in the guise of Dhrtarastra's minister, the one who sees everything without being anywhere, untouched by weapons and fatigue alike, relates a dialogue.[2] Such relating, indeed, is the dialogue. It is, then, to the dialogue between the warrior and the charioteer that the poet is present. It is with such dialogue that the poetic utterance is simultaneous and coincides. Rather than merely bringing forth the unfolding of action without any further qualification, the poetic saying brings to the fore action in the form of a dialogue-yielding vision.[3] What is thus emphasized is the unfolding of action in a multiplicity of registers and modes. Most importantly, this saying effects the interpolation of the peculiar deed of dialogue (of that peculiar deed which dialogue is) into the fabric of the deeds pertaining to war. In this sense Samjaya's singing possesses a fissuring, interruptive character with respect to action—at least, that particular action that war is. His singing occurs in and as a breach in the time of that action. It occurs in and as a momentary hesitation before action as war, in and as the timelessness (or the other temporality) of that moment. It does not speak, therefore, of valiant warriors and noble feats.

In this specific respect, the Hindu song is closer to Socrates' narration than Homeric tragedy is. The proto-tragic celebration of bravery, the love for the commotion of the battlefield, the enraptured depiction of the hero surrounded by the splendid aura of glory are, in fact, not to be found in the Socratic story. Already in the preceding conversation Socrates' attitude toward the manly ἦθος celebrated in epic poetry is typically ambivalent. On the one hand, he inherits the repository of heroic values and acknowledges their centrality in the philosophical undertaking. This is particularly evident in the references to courage (ἀνδρεία) ubiquitous in the dialogue on the πολιτεία. Given the crucial function of virility in a city ruled by warriors, not surprisingly one of Socrates' main concerns in his assessment of poetry is the promotion of citizens "fearless (ἀδεῆ) in the face of death," who choose "death in battles (ἐν ταῖς μάχαις) above defeat and slavery" (386b). To this end, poetry should refrain from instilling fearsome images of the realm of the dead. Hence, Socrates adds, "concerning these tales (μύθων) too, it seems we must supervise (ἐπιστατεῖν) those who undertake to tell them and ask them not simply to disparage Hades' domain in this way but rather to praise it, because what they say is neither true nor beneficial (ὠφέλιμα) for men who are going to be fighters (μέλλουσι μαχίμοις)" (386b–

c). This pronouncement parallels the reflections on death put forth in the end of the *Apology*, which reveal the philosopher in his unmoved posture, in his readiness, even willingness, to die (40c ff.). Later, conversing with the spirited Glaukon, Socrates surmises that courage, specifically "political (πολιτικήν) courage," is linked to preservation, to the ability to abide by what one has lawfully learned, whatever the cost may be: "This kind of power and preservation (δύναμιν καὶ σωτηρίαν), through everything, of the right and lawful opinion about what is terrible (δεινῶν) and what not, I call courage (ἀνδρείαν); and so I set it down, unless you say something else" (430a–c). However, in statements of this kind it is clear that courage is simultaneously praised and metamorphosed, imperceptibly but unmistakably subtracted from the literally warlike dimension of the epic song. In this sense the philosophical pursuit rests on the cultivation of the warrior's ability to endure, to stay constant and, simultaneously, entails the transmutation of the entire warlike framework. Socrates reiterates the point later: "I suppose we call a single man courageous (ἀνδρεῖον) because of that part—when his spirited part preserves (θυμοειδὲς διασῴζη), through pains and pleasures, what has been proclaimed (παραγγελθὲν) by the speeches about that which is terrible (δεινόν) and that which is not" (442b–c). It is in being a warrior that he, finally, "becomes his own friend" (443d). The philosophical way entails risks (κινδύνευμα, κινδυνεύειν, κίνδυνος) requiring that one be as bold as a warrior on the battlefield (451a–b, 467b–c, 618b). Thus, the analogy between the philosopher and the epic hero is maintained, precisely as the alienation from the archaic framework is gradually deepened.

On the other hand, the Socratic reflection also displays a more unambiguous reluctance to sanction, in however transposed a fashion, the quintessentially Greek fondness for glorious deeds in war, brilliant reputation in war-related matters, and above all death on a campaign, at a young age. Numberless statements in epic song as well as in the various forms of lyric poetry reflect such fondness. Even Heraclitus is reported to have said, in exquisitely Homeric parlance: "Gods and humans honor those slain in war" (killed by Ares, Ἀρηιφάτοῦ) (22 B 24), and "Greater deaths (μόροι) obtain greater fates (μοίρας)" (22 B 25). But in Book V, after having made provisions for the burial and worship of those "daimonic and divine" beings who died on the battlefield, Socrates adds: "And we'll make the same conventions for any of those who have been judged exceptionally good in life when dying of old age (γήρᾳ) or in some other way" (469a–b). In this assertion one discerns a more explicit divergence from the male-heroic ἦθος, a resistance to the archaic-classic outlook associating a sense of shame or embarrassment with death in old age, in a time of peace.

Socrates' narration of Er's death, descent, and vision is significantly foreign to the logic of heroic ἦθος in general and in particular to that self-celebration in which Homer alias Odysseus recounts his own descent to the underworld. For the narration of the descent of the poet-hero into obscurity is still thoroughly informed by the comportment of the unvanquished warrior who, in the triumph of his permanent victory, knows only how to shine.

The Homeric-heroic descent into the realm of the shades, this darkest moment in the hero's journey and most extreme challenge to the hero's integrity, is narrated as if nothing could disturb the serenity, dazzling luminosity, and unshakable self-confidence of the protagonist. Within the Homeric-heroic framework, the ritual summoning of the dead (νέκυια) is still primarily the deed of the living warrior. The νέκυια is still a matter of warfare—indeed, a matter of victory over and utilization of the dead. For the Homeric warrior knows only how to conquer and plunder.

The rhetoric of (trust in) heroic valor placidly persists in the face of the most disruptive threats posed to it. Socrates' narration of Er's κατάβασις, then, is a polemic (if also apologetic) response to the story narrated in Alkinoos's halls by Odysseus under the nom de plume of Homer (or by Homer under the nom de guerre of Odysseus). It is a response questioning the story of the hero's triumphant travel down below and of his return, victorious and intact—as well as an apology for such an outrageously bold and indestructible naïveté.

Analogously to the Socratic saying, the Hindu poem presents itself as a suspension, a challenging and problematization of the rhetoric of heroic valor and value. And yet, although occurring as a moment of crisis in which the action of war is suspended, although saying nothing of glorious acts on the battlefield, the *Gita* begins with the preparations for warfare. The poem opens with the intimation and the promise of the war to come—of a war that, even if suspended and delayed, even if at the limits of the poem proper, will nevertheless have taken place within the broader epic framework of the *Mahabharata*. War (a war within the family, rending the community from within) is marked by inevitability—as if already there, impending. Samjaya's speaking, prompted by the request of the blind Dhrtarastra, opens with the disclosure of the armies arrayed on the battlefield—on the open field of *dharma*. Socrates' narration, instead, begins with the disclosure of what remains of the armies, on the open field, after the war.

Socrates' ἀπόλογος opens on a battlefield. It evokes the battlefield after the war is over and even the lamentations have faded, leaving room only for the mute remains. Socrates' saying, then, begins with a silence—not a dialogue. It begins with a pause, with the desolation following the end of the war—not the suspension or deferral of the war. Socrates' saying begins by conjuring up an expanse covered with cadavers and unfolds in the midst of it. The field which was the theater of war, the place in which the armies took a stand against one another and crossed arms, is now a place where no stand is taken any longer and life has disappeared, the place of the retreat and fleeing of life, the expanse disseminated with dead bodies—like seeds scattered on the barren ground.

The story opening in this way and in this place is not "an ἀπόλογος of Alkinoos (Ἀλκίνου)," but of "a strong man, Er, son of Armenios, by race a Pamphylian" (ἀλκίμου μὲν ἀνδρός, Ἡρὸς τοῦ Ἀρμενίου, τὸ γένος Παμφύλου) (614b).[4] The ἀπόλογος begins:

> Once upon a time he died in war (ἐν πολέμῳ τελευτήσας); and on the tenth day, when the corpses already decayed (τῶν νεκρῶν ἤδη διεφθαρμένων) were taken up (ἀναιρεθέντων), he was taken up in a good state of preservation (ὑγιὴς μὲν ἀνηρέθη). Having been brought home, he was about to be buried (θάπτεσθαι) on the twelfth day; as he was lying on the pyre he came back to life (ἐπὶ τῇ πυρᾷ κείμενος ἀνεβίω) and, come back to life (ἀναβιοὺς), he told what he saw in the other place (ἔλεγεν ἃ ἐκεῖ ἴδοι). (614b)

Er, the strong son of Armenios and valiant warrior, is said to have met his destiny in war. On the battlefield his life found its completion and came to an end (τελευτάω). The story begins with that which will never simply have been a matter of human deeds. Er's remains were found lying there, when the battle was over and all was lost. After this brief introduction, the indirect narration of Er's own visionary report properly begins. However, a few remarks are in order concerning this threshold, these words leading into the myth proper.

Passing Places

The theme of warfare resurfaces at crucial junctures throughout the dialogue on the πολιτεία and on the δίκαιος. The figure of war should be understood in the context of the general motility pervading and informing the dialogue as such and as a whole. For this dialogue occurs as the articulation of movements of ascent and descent, of submersion and reemergence from the depths, of circulation, turning, and cyclical recurrence. Such pervasive dynamism uniquely marks the dialogue—its inception, its heart, and its end (the gathering ἀπόλογος). Inscribed within the movement of the dialogue, within this dialogue in movement, warfare presents itself as the most extreme, most remarkable figure of motion. It is the figure of motion brought to its dramatic, traumatic extreme and reverting (in the moment of its completion, even if only for that moment) into the rigor of death and withdrawal of all movement, into the quiet immobility of lifeless bodies on the battlefield.

In a crucial sense, then, the question of war belongs in the broader question of dynamism informing and framing the text on the πολιτεία. This dialogue, let it be recalled once again, finds its beginning down at the port, at the threshold of the city, in that place of passage, transit, and exchange. The stage of the dialogue is the space within which the trajectories of vastly imponderable and certainly incommensurable journeys cross one another, within which travelers from many places mingle with one another—as travelers, that is to say, in passing. This is the space of the dialogue, the setting disclosed through such a beginning, a place of crossing and mingling, that is, a place harboring and simultaneously belonging to such crossing and mingling. The place of the dialogue at once gathers and consists of, embraces and is traversed by, the intertwined unfolding of invisible courses.

The initial image of the port, which opens up the space and possibility of the dialogue, is magnified and reelaborated in Er's vision of the daimonic place which concludes the dialogue. As is appropriate for a narration bringing the whole dialogue to an end, the final ἀπόλογος recalls the features of the initial setting—simultaneously repeating, amplifying, and transfiguring them.[5] It may be opportune to mention, by way of anticipation, a few moments of the structural and thematic parallelism between the inception and the conclusion of the dialogue. Just as the port is that frontier, that stretch of land, in between the high citadel and the sea, the daimonic expanse of Er's vision stretches out in between what is below and what is above, earth and sky, γῆ and οὐρανός (614c). Just as Piraeus is the place of transit to which Socrates descends and from which he strives to ascend (the repeated efforts of such striving, indeed, constitute the form and unfolding of the dialogue as such), the daimonic place is the theater of the restless ascents and descents, of the interminable circling and migrations of the ψυχαί, of the psychic movements seizing even Er's ψυχή. In the setting down at Piraeus, as the conversation develops, the commitment (the assignment) to which the philosopher is bound makes itself manifest. It manifests itself as a sustained ascensional striving whose accomplishment is severely limited by the returns and descents necessitated throughout the dialogue by an apparently irresistible geotropism. Analogously, through Er's envisioning of the δαιμόνιος τόπος, something comes to manifestation concerning the task of the philosopher. Shining through the narration of Er's gazing, the philosophical task shows itself as a compulsion to capture, illuminate, and thus dispel the mystery of life—that mystery within whose embrace the answer to the question of justice is harbored, that mystery whose unfolding is governed by justice and within which justice is enfolded. But, as will be shown later, the possibility of such compulsive capturing and illuminating is crucially limited by structural visual deficiencies.[6] This compulsion whose end is not fully achievable, then, tends to become a gesturing toward, a contemplation preserving the mystery of life as such, a magnification of life in its uncapturable, incessant, and somewhat inscrutable movement.

Through the transposing repetition of the beginning effected by the concluding ἀπόλογος, the dynamic character of the dialogue is reconfirmed and sealed—is allowed to emerge in its magnificent operativity and present itself in its splendor. The play of mirrors, reflections, and refractions between the beginning and the end of the dialogical event, between the movement of crowds at Piraeus and the psychic currents in the daimonic place, indeed, celebrates the dialogue in motion and of motion—the dialogue as a receptacle of motion, even *as* motion. Furthermore, as will become evident in a moment, the all-encompassing motility evoked by the parallelism between the outset and epilogue of the text and thoroughly pervading the progression of the dialogue sheds light on a set of quite remarkable features characterizing the figure of Socrates. Again, by way of anticipation, let it be simply mentioned here that understanding the figure of Socrates by reference to that of Er will necessarily entail finding the issue of motility, mobility, and motion at the very heart of the question concerning the philosopher—who the philosopher is, how the philosopher operates, that which the philosopher responds to and pursues. Viewing Er as yet an other image of the philosopher, as an other manifestation of the same striving, will involve thinking the love of σοφία in light of the call undergone by Er's ψυχή to wander—to travel, see, listen, and recount. It will involve thinking the philosophical πάθος in light of the errant, extravagant (in the Latin sense, *extra vagans*), essentially ek-static character of the messenger-warrior.

But for the moment it might be desirable to defer an appropriately detailed treatment of these issues. What matters at this point is to underline the belonging of the motif of war in the general question of dynamism, in the dynamic topography and conduct playing an essential, indeed, constitutive role in the dialogue on the πολιτεία and on the δίκαιος. And just to insist on this point, to demonstrate that it cannot be overemphasized in this case, and to deepen the insight into the relation of war and movement (into the nature of this *belonging* of the former in the latter), it might be helpful to turn to that other dialogue in which Books II–V of the text on the πολιτεία are said to be summarized. Turning to the *Timaeus*, in the course of which crucial remarks concerning war are uttered, may indeed, by contrast, help bring into relief even more vividly the function and place of the figure of war (this unique figure of motion) within the dialogue which presents itself as the moving discourse of justice.[7]

The Feast of War

In the *Timaeus* the issue of war is introduced, according to Socrates' invitation, in order to dynamize the static presentation of the city. This courteous, festive dialogue begins with a schematic recapitulation of the λόγος περὶ πολιτείας which Socrates apparently presented the day before (17c). The discourses that are to follow, then, will have taken place in response to and as prescribed by Socrates' preceding discussion.

The dialogical exchange develops in the context of a gathering of friends and receives its impulse from the unanimous acknowledgment of the law of hospitality, of the law prescribing the friendly entertainment of foreigners and the reciprocation of what has been kindly offered. In the exchange opening the dialogue both Socrates' invocation of friendship and Timaeus's repeated turning to the language of ξενία make it clear that the dialogue ensuing will have occurred (according to possibility and as is just) in the effort to entertain Socrates, who yesterday was the host entertaining his friends and now is their guest (17a–b). But it is not simply yesterday's presentation by Socrates which models today's conversation. Socrates prescribes the course and aim of the dialogue more directly, more explicitly when, after briefly recalling the features of the city he previously laid out, he adds:

> Next listen to how I happen to feel (πεπονθὼς) with regard to the city we went through in detail (περὶ τῆς πολιτείας ἣν διήλθομεν). I may compare (προσέοικε) my condition (πάθος) to something of this kind, to someone who has been looking (θεασάμενος) at some beautiful living beings (ζῷα καλά), whether drawings (γραφῆς εἰργασμένα) or truly alive (ζῶντα ἀληθινῶς) but motionless (ἡσυχίαν δὲ ἄγοντα), and is moved with desire (ἐπιθυμίαν ἀφίκοιτο) to look (θεάσασθαι) at them in motion (κινούμενά) and engage in contest (κατὰ τὴν ἀγωνίαν ἀθλοῦντα) as seems fitting (δοκούντων προσήκειν) to their bodies. This is how I feel (πέπονθα) with regard to the city we went through in detail (πρὸς τὴν πόλιν ἣν διήλθομεν): gladly would I listen to someone telling in words (του λόγῳ διεξιόντος) of the city engaging in the struggles (ἄθλους οὓς πόλις ἀθλεῖ) which cities carry out (ἀγωνιζομένην) against others, going to war (εἴς τε πόλεμον ἀφικομένην) in an appropriate manner, and yielding in its warring (ἐν τῷ πολεμεῖν) what is fitting to its education and rearing (παιδείᾳ καὶ τροφῇ), whether in feats of arms (ἐν τοῖς ἔργοις πράξεις) or in negotiations (ἐν τοῖς λόγοις διερμηνεύσεις) with every single city. (19b–c)

Then, after explaining that his hosts are more entitled to take up such an assignment than the poets, the sophists, and himself, Socrates concludes:

> So, with this in my mind (διανοούμενος), when you requested yesterday to go through that which concerns the city (τὰ περὶ τῆς πολιτείας διελθεῖν), I readily gratified you, for I knew that nobody could give back (ἀποδοῖεν) more appropriately than you the next discussion (τὸν ἑξῆς λόγον), if you would want to; you alone, of those who now are, could render back (ἀποδοῖτ' ἄν) the city engaged in a suitable war and lay down all the features belonging to it. So, having spoken that which had been prescribed, I in turn prescribed for you the task which I am now explaining. In conferring together among yourselves you agreed to give me back in turn (ἀνταποδώσειν) the feast of discourses (τὰ τῶν

λόγων ξένια) today. So here I am in full dress for the entertainment that I am the most eager of all to receive. (20b–c)

This is the address calling forth the discourses constituting the dialogue. The *Timaeus,* the Platonic dialogue concerning φύσις and the cosmologico-cosmogonic framing of such a question, appears to be, first of all, a dialogue on war.

Before Timaeus's response proper, Socrates' injunction receives a quite literal interpretation. The "celebration of discourses" (τὴν τῶν λόγων ἑστίασιν) (27b) opens with Kritias's narration of a λόγος strange (placeless, ἄτοπος) and true (ἀληθής) (20d). This is the λόγος of Athens's multiple and repeatedly forgotten origins, of the Greeks beginning over and over again, always forgetful and young (νέοι) (23a–b), in a condition of eternal childhood.[8] It is the λόγος delineating an identity of Athens in primeval times, an identity mostly unknown, especially to the Greeks themselves. It is an account, a knowledge of Greek origins jealously preserved by a foreign people, the Egyptians, and offered by one of its priests as a gift of hospitality to traveling Solon—allegedly, that is, and in an already distant past.

The central aim of Kritias's story is to show, according to Socrates' demand, "the great and admirable exploits performed by our own city long ago" (20e). It is through the recollection of ancestral Athens's glorious deeds in war that the city described by Socrates the day before is set in motion. For the arrangement of the Socratic city, "by some daimonic chance" (δαιμονίως ἔκ τινος τύχης) (25e), happens to bear a striking resemblance to that of Athens in its forgotten past. In virtue of this turn, Socrates' founding effort the day before seems to assume a purely recollective character, the feature of a bringing back in virtue of which the same is reborn, unearthed, extracted again from the depths of time, wrested from the past and from oblivion. What is disclosed by the intellectual gaze and what is historically documented are brought to coincide. Kritias's discourse grounds Socrates' abstract exercise and validates it by granting it the force, limpidity, and appropriateness of a historical recovery. It is only in the context of this λόγος bringing back the lost story and history of Athens that Socrates' invention becomes plausible.

And yet, let this be noticed all too briefly, Kritias's account is far from having the status of historical narrative which, alone, would ground Socrates' invention in the truth of a remote but conclusively authenticated age. Or, which amounts to the same, such an account, in virtue of its traits, shows historiographic procedures as well as historicist aspirations in their radically questionable character and, thus, casts a strange light on history itself—on the very category of the historical, on its authority and possibility. Kritias's contribution to the feast purports to be an account of "the Athenians of those times, of whose disappearance (ἀφανεῖς) we are informed by the saying of the sacred writings (ἱερῶν γραμμάτων φήμη)" of the Egyptians (27b). Yet it should be noticed that, in the first place, the outline of the story (the full account is never given in the *Timaeus*) results from a long series of narrations and repetitions. It has been transmitted from generation to generation, by Solon to Dropides (Kritias's great-grandfather), who in turn told it to Kritias (Kritias's homonymous grand-father), who in his old age told it to his grandson Kritias, then a child (20e–21b). Also, Kritias himself, as he now says, needed to refresh his memory before re-ferring the tale to Socrates—he thus had to repeat the story to himself (going through it the previous night), and then to the other friends, before convening for the feast of speeches (26a–c).[9] Secondly, it should not be forgotten that the story, as is said, was originally preserved as a written record—a record kept safe in hallowed archives, written in a language other than Greek (23a–c, 27b). The telling of such a story, then, requires a manifold operation of translation, which involves traversing time (surviving its destructiveness, undergoing its maiming and deforming work), reaching other shores, passing from written letters to oral narration and from one idiom to another (not to mention the unique difficulties inherent in the transposition of the speaking of writings said to be sacred). Third, it should be recalled that, even when the story was first told to Solon, it was neither read from the record nor shared in its integrity. Rather, the old priest is said to have recounted it from memory and to have limited himself, quite de-liberately, to a fragmentary version of the tale: "the account about everything in precise order we shall go through again at our leisure, taking the writings" (23e–24a). The uncertainty of this originary moment could hardly be more profound.

Kritias's contribution, then, relates wondrous stories kept safe in the secret receptacles of a foreign culture and adventurously facing the incalculable diffi-culties of mediation, transmission, translation. Again, the problem is not so much that Kritias's account would lack the general features of a historical ac-count in the strict sense of the term. Rather, and much more disquietingly, what emerges from his report is a certain evanescence of the historical "in the strict sense," a certain not so strict, indeed evasive tendency of "the historical" to re-cede, even dissipate, upon closer scrutiny.[10] This discourse that Socrates ac-knowledges as a "true discourse" (ἀληθινὸν λόγον), as a λόγος before which his own speculation concerning the just city is but an "invented tale (μῦθον)" (26e), thus, is true in a quite extravagant sense. Be it as it may, however, thanks to this strangely true discourse the city at first accounted for in its immobile abstract-ness is brought to life.

The community schematically delineated by Socrates is given flesh and blood, is made alive and set in motion by the narration of Athens's ancient glory in matters of war. It takes an athletico-agonistic rendition of the city to bring it to life. It takes the recollection of unheard-of struggles, of spectacular conflicts, of tremendous enemies courageously and victoriously confronted in order to begin to envision the city in its proper potential, in the unfolding of what is worthy of it, in its fullest manifestation. In brief, it takes the vision of the warring movement in order to gain a deeper, more complete understanding of the city, of what the city is, of what it can (be). So much, at least, is expressed by Socrates' desire and demand. This is what Socrates desires to see and hear—how he wishes to be entertained. After concluding the synoptic narration of the Egyptian-Solonic story and promising a version of it in full detail to be delivered later, Kritias restates its purpose. Thanks to this account, he says,

> We will transfer the citizens and city you described yesterday as if in a myth (ὡς ἐν μύθῳ) from hither into the domain of the true (μετενεγκόντες ἐπὶ τἀληθὲς δεῦρο); we will take the city to be that ancient city of ours and say that the citizens conceived of (διενοοῦ) are those true ancestors (ἀληθινοὺς . . . προγόνους) of ours, whom the priest spoke of. (26c–d)

The preoccupation with the truth of the tale (that is, with the historical character of the story) and the emphasis on truth as a matter of historical embodiment (that is, of becoming) could hardly be more consistently conspicuous. But what should be underlined above all in this context is, again, the fact that the forgotten (hi)story of primal Athens revolves around the outstanding excellence demonstrated on the battlefield. After all, this city, as well as Saïs, its Egyptian counterpart, was founded by the goddess "lover both of war and of wisdom" (φιλοπόλεμός τε καὶ φιλόσοφος) (24d). It was the goddess (whether Neïth or Athena) who bestowed upon the city its laws and institutions, who instructed its citizens in matters of wisdom as well as in the several arts, and, especially, who made the city "preeminent above all others in valor and in the arts of war" (πάντων γὰρ προστᾶσα εὐψυχίᾳ καὶ τέχναις ὅσαι κατὰ πόλεμον) (25b–c). Incidentally, here the question of the relation between philosophy and war should be noticed. This relation is not simply shown as intimate but rather in its essential, founding, and originary character. More will be said about this later, especially in conjunction with a reflection on the figure of the philosopher-warrior and on the meaning of such condensation.

In the *Timaeus*, thus, Socrates' prescription involving the equation of war and motion, of the polemic and the kinetic, is taken up and responded to in a relatively unproblematic, literal fashion. It is also remarkable that Timaeus's account of the origin and structure of the κόσμος, at least according to the intended plan for the entertainment of Socrates, would merely have the function of introducing Kritias's narration of the Egyptian story in its integrity (which actually does not take place in the dialogue). Timaeus's λόγοι, accounting for the becoming of the world, would quite intuitively have to precede Kritias's account of the enterprises of the best of men. Both accounts concern a genetic horizon. Timaeus's discourses on the coming into being and becoming of the world would provide the appropriate framework within which the exquisitely historical discourse by Kritias would take place and position itself. But, moreover, an essential continuity is suggested between the two accounts. After Timaeus, who "will begin with the birth of the world (τῆς τοῦ κόσμου γενέσεως) and end with the nature of mankind (ἀνθρώπων φύσιν)," Kritias tells Socrates, "I am to follow, taking over from him mankind, which came into being through his speech, and from you a select few especially well trained (πεπαιδευμένους διαφερόντως)" (27a–b).

After the account of the whole of φύσις, whose essence is movement and mutability, would have to follow, in full detail, the account of the ancient people of Athens, of these superlatively educated and most remarkable of all humans, whose essence (again, quite intuitively) is belligerence. This much it would take to set in motion the just city which, according to the abbreviated description recalled at the beginning of the dialogue, was presented the day before by Socrates in its still, lifeless purity.

The *Timaeus*, this dialogue whose setting is a festive convening of friends in the respect for the law of hospitality, begins with the immobile picture of the just city. The true discourses of motion, that is to say of war, are invoked in order to bring life into the picture, to bring the picture to life, to make it *move* and make it *true*.

In this context war is to humankind what motion and change are to φύσις. War appears to be a kind of imitation, by humans, of nature in its agitation and, more precisely, in its blind destructiveness. For it should be remembered that the *Timaeus*, at least in its opening stages and most notably in the contribution of Kritias, provides an image of φύσις as utterly ravaging. According to the words of the Egyptian priest, natural disasters periodically sweep away entire civilizations, reconfiguring the surface of the earth and the entire cosmos. "There have been and there will be," he says, "many destructions of mankind (πολλὰ φθοραὶ . . . ἀνθρώπων), the greatest by water and fire, the lesser by numberless other means." Nature appears as the unending cycle of ruination caused by shifts in the orbits of celestial bodies and the purifying initiative of the gods (22c–e). Such violent upheavals exceed the φθορά that essentially belongs in the unfolding of becoming, the decay inherent in coming into being, the mortality marking the living. Such less traumatic, apparently more integrated, rhythmic manifestation of natural destruction is recalled at the very outset of the dialogue, as Socrates and the others reckon with the absence of one of them who was there the day before. Some kind of sickness, of ἀσθένεια, is preventing him from being there (17a). Not being there: this is always a possibility for the living—

whether because of death, illness, and other incapacitating changes, or because, never subsisting unmoved, always becoming other, the living may seldom, if at all, fully be what it is, let alone be there. This mode of destruction inheres in that which is alive. Yet even the extraordinary or not so ordinary manifestations of natural devastation do not seem to result in pure annihilation, but to effect change and rearrangement in the geobiological domain. In noticing, then, that war appears to be the human imitation of natural ruination, a number of concomitant questions arise. In general, how is one to understand motion, change, and the phenomenon of genuine destruction in their unity and difference? More specifically, would not the belonging of natural destruction in the movement of generative upsurge, alone, interrupt the analogy between natural destruction and human war? Indeed, in what exquisitely human generation would war belong? Also, what would an exquisitely human generation be? Is it not to the extent that they are *not* exquisitely human but *of* φύσις that humans generate— that they engender, procreate (reproduce), even create (produce)? Conversely, are not all forms of construction and reconstruction exquisitely human, in fact, so human as often to lack—life? How would, then, human destruction and construction, war and reconstruction be related?

Through the figure of war something essentially defining civilization comes to be visible, a feature exclusively pertaining to humankind, indeed, to humankind at its best. Warfare is but the counterpart, in the realm of human and tribal interaction, of movement in the realm of nature.[11] Warfare is but the educated, cultivated translation of movement and, as such, perfectly in agreement with nature. Warfare is the mode of being (of moving) characteristic of the ἄνθρωπος, the movement and animation of the ἄνθρωπος as such, the being of the ἄνθρωπος according to nature. It is the time, the pulse of humankind gathered in the πόλις, that without which the πόλις would remain an inert schema, that is, the purely formal caprice of an architect or an artisan in λόγοι—just as unthinkable as the κόσμος without its revolutions. But issues do not quite stand in this way in the dialogue on the πολιτεία and on the δίκαιος.

Moving Dialogue

First of all, the dialogue on the πολιτεία and on the δίκαιος does not begin with the formal, immobile presentation of the just city. Rather, it begins with a κατάβασις to Piraeus. It begins with a movement down to a place of movement. In its very inception, this dialogue is already (in) motion. It begins with motion, its beginning is motion, its occurrence is inscribed within motion, *already*. This dialogue does, indeed, strive to articulate and account for the just city. The discussion of the just city does receive a most sustained, conspicuous, and consistent elaboration in the course of this conversation (to the point, in fact, of appearing to be its theme). A nuanced account of the just city does gradually take shape as the evening dies away and night supervenes, of which the synopsis inaugurating the feast of that other dialogue, the *Timaeus,* may even be considered an accurate recapitulation. But this account begins, follows its turns, and progresses already seized within movement, enfolded within a dynamism that it cannot transcend. Hence, nowhere can this account unfold in a shorthand, abbreviated mode—achieve the quietness of formality. Nowhere in the dialogue on the πολιτεία does schematism (its purity, its simplicity, its timeless staticity) characterize the discursive laying out of the just city. In fact, it seems to be precisely the passage from this detailed discourse (flowing slowly and painstakingly, encountering every sort of complication and obstacle on its way, just as the ascent Socrates strives for) to the relatively unproblematic mode of the summary presented in the *Timaeus* which makes all the difference.

It is this transition from the discourse caught in its opening up, in its springing forth and taking shape, to the summary re-presentation of a discourse previously presented but presently only recalled and not pronounced, experienced, that is, not thought through anew—it is this transition, inconspicuous as it may seem, which involves the most momentous shift. For in the schematic representation all temporal and dynamic indexicality has disappeared, as if it were dispensable and inessential. But, on the contrary, all the cautious provisos and problematizations interspersed throughout the γένεσις of the just city in speech, all the concessions to mythical elements and to imaginative-phenomenal suppositions, and especially the admission of change and decay at the very heart of an account whose aspiration is the fixity of determination— these are not secondary features accidentally and somewhat extrinsically attached to the discourse. These are not details ornamenting an autonomously self-subsisting discourse. Rather, they constitute the very ground on which the discussion rests, that which fundamentally makes the discussion possible, that which allows the discussion to take off and to overcome the impasses it encounters in its several stages and turns. In this dialogue the discursive fabric of the just city is woven out of the fantastic strands of temporal spinning, of cyclical revolutions, of fabulous flights spanning bottomless and otherwise unbridgeable clefts. That is also why in this dialogue the discourse of the just city does not occur alone, let alone separately and autonomously. Occurring in the midst of becoming, the erection of the just city is accompanied by its downfall— and the construction of the city is not simply *followed* by the moment of decomposition, according to the way in which events follow one another within the frame of linear temporality. Instead, the moments of instability are in play since the beginning, indissolubly turning and twisting along with the movements of the founding effort—always already announced, in their simultaneously dissolving and delimiting, endangering and engendering power.

After all, this dialogue evolves into the elaboration of the just city only thanks to a number of astonishing stipulations which, traversed one by one like a succession of thresholds, lead to the discourse that in the *Timaeus* is synoptically rendered, that is, arbitrarily abstracted from its environment, deracinated, purified. In this dialogue that is itself born out of the womb of becoming, Socrates explicitly inaugurates the series of efforts aiming at clarifying the essence of justice by pointing out the manifoldly adventurous, tentative, and aporetic character of the enterprise he and his interlocutors are setting out to undertake. In Book II, just a moment before his assertion that "first we tell tales to children (πρῶτον τοῖς παιδίοις μύθους λέγομεν), and surely they are, as a whole, false (ψεῦδος)" and his remark on beginning (ἀρχή) as "the most important part of every work" (παντὸς ἔργου μέγιστον) (377a), Socrates addresses the sons of Ariston with an invitation quoted earlier, which is worth recalling: "Come then, like men telling tales in a tale (ὥσπερ ἐν μύθῳ μυθολογοῦντές) and at their leisure, let's educate (παιδεύωμεν) men in speech (λόγῳ)" (376d).

Such is the laborious and perilous beginning of the founding effort, of the discourse concerning the just city. Unlike the *Timaeus*, the dialogue on the πολιτεία does not begin with the safe clarity of a lifeless outline.

Secondly, the dialogue on the πολιτεία and on the δίκαιος does not take place as a conversation among friends exchanging the gifts of hospitality according to the law. Nor does it take place in the overall festive atmosphere of entertainment through discourses. Even the fact that both dialogues occur in the shadow of a female deity does not mitigate the profound difference in their respective moods.

Athena-Neïth is the goddess repeatedly invoked in the initial phases of the *Timaeus*, the goddess whose two names significantly mark the entrance into the dialogue proper. Whether or not this is the same goddess whose festival is being held as the conversation unfolds (26e) is, after all, secondary. What is remarkable is the crucial role of this motherless goddess in the coming into being of the forgotten, primeval city. This is "the goddess who obtained for her portion (ἔλαχεν), nurtured (ἔθρεψεν), and educated both your city and this here" (23d–e), the Egyptian priest would have said to Solon—the goddess who established the Greek as well as the Egyptian city, chose for them an appropriate place, gave them their law and arrangement so that they might grow in accord with the order of the κόσμος, taught their people the several arts (crucially, the art of war) in an orderly and systematic fashion, and infused them with love of learning and understanding (24a–d).

This is the founder and protector of the ancestral city of Athens (Saïs), the deity thanks to which the ancestral city, or at least the memory of it, is preserved—for it is in order to honor and gratify the goddess that the Egyptian priest apparently told the (hi)story of it to Solon (23d). But the economy of the whole dialogue rests on and revolves around this (hi)story and, thus, around the tutelary goddess to which the narrative is offered. For the city brought forth in λόγος by Socrates strangely resembles that which the deity is said to have brought forth, and, indeed, Kritias's (hi)story has the function of setting in motion Socrates' schematic account. And, since setting in motion the Socratic scheme is the task taken up by the convening friends, that which compels and motivates the conversation, the dialogue as a whole bears the mark of the goddess Athena-Neïth, is crucially signed by and takes place in her name(s). The *Timaeus* as a whole, then, takes place in the sphere of influence of the goddess who loves war and wisdom alike—the deity of clarity who brings the gift of shields and spears (24b).

The dialogue on the πολιτεία also takes place in conjunction with the festivities dedicated to a female divinity. Indeed, Socrates descends to Piraeus in order "to pray to the goddess" and to "observe how they would put on the festival" (327a). But this is not an autochthonous deity and, therefore, has no established function in matters of political or cultural founding. Bendis is the name of the lunar goddess worshipped in Thracia and now celebrated in Athens for the first time.[12] It is this foreign deity, this Thracian Artemis-Hecate recently imported into the city, who marks the inception of the dialogue. A sign of the changing times, of innovation and openness to exotic customs, the new cult is established at the outskirts of the city, along its mobile and permeable boundaries. This event is hardly the welcoming of an alien custom respectfully and reverently hosted as such, in its foreignness. Neither should it be seen as an assimilative gesture on the part of the dominating community with respect to the world it is incorporating. Rather, in the nocturnal setting, in the place underneath where the dark goddess is being celebrated, a vivid demarcation between the native and the alien seems to be lacking. Both a sharply defined sense of communal identity and the correspondingly sharp perception of what is extraneous to it seem to be fading in the increasing confusion of the inferophantasmatic place.

In spite of the fact that the dialogue begins with a reference to the festival (or, perhaps, precisely because of the nature of the festival), its atmosphere is far from being festive. Even aside from the specificity of the public celebration, the gathering at Polemarkhos's place is essentially different in character from the reunion of the *Timaeus*. Far from occurring within the framework of courteous entertainment and of the rigorously lawful exchange of discursive gifts, far from representing the joyous convening of friends, the dialogue on the πολιτεία is marked by a certain heaviness; it already begins as a challenge, even a trial. Socrates, who has undertaken his κατάβασις (literally an *avatara*, a going [*tara*] down [*ava*], a passage or entrance to another place, a sudden appearing there) out of a wish to pray and, at the same time (ἅμα), to contemplate the organization of the festival, ends up having to face unforeseen tribulations. The initial moments of the action narrated by Socrates should be recalled again:

> After we had prayed and looked on, we went off toward town (πρὸς τὸ ἄστυ). Catching sight of us from afar as we were pressing homewards (οἴκαδε), Polemarkhos, son of Kephalos, ordered (ἐκέλευσε) his slave boy to run after us and order (κελεῦσαι) us to wait (περιμεῖναι) for him. The boy took hold of my cloak from behind (ὄπισθεν) and said, "Polemarkhos orders (κελεύει) you to wait (περιμεῖναι)." And I turned around and asked him where his master was. "He is coming up behind (ὄπισθεν)," he said, "just wait (περιμένετε)." "Of course we'll wait (περιμενοῦμεν)," said Glaukon. (327b)

Socrates' insistence on the language of imposition is noteworthy. The force of Polemarkhos's order, indeed, ineluctably interrupts Socrates and Glaukon's ascent to town and announces a confinement which, for the moment at least, cannot be eluded. This order interferes with the upward walk back from the port, slows it down, deflects its trajectory, forces Socrates and Glaukon to wait. A force, from behind and below, is holding Socrates back. And Glaukon complies with it. Socrates is alone, isolated. Speaking, sustaining a conversation, presents itself, in this case, both as that to which he is compelled (unwillingly bound) and as that through which he can attempt to resume the journey, to break free of the bonds. It presents itself both as his confinement and as his way out of it. Socrates sees this immediately. To Polemarkhos's crude affirmation ("Well, then . . . you must either prove stronger [κρείττους γένεσθε] than these men or stay here" [327c]), he replies, already, by asking a question: "So then, isn't there still one other possibility . . . our persuading you that you must (χρὴ) let us go?" (327c).[13] The unfolding of the dialogue, then, will have been Socrates' way of freeing himself, of persuading the young man and his friends to set him and Glaukon free. It will have been his way, in the long run, of proving stronger, of prevailing over the violence of brute self-assertion. The dialogical involvement will have been Socrates' fight.

But this will have been no small task. Especially because, let this be said in passing, Socrates' imprisonment seems to be due neither to an unfortunate chance encounter nor merely to the caprices of a young and volitive man overly eager to exert his power and to fathom the extent of his resources. There seems to be, rather, the unmistakable element of necessity in play in this development of events. The encounter of the ascending couple with Polemarkhos's group and the consequences of this crossing of paths seem to be the result of a careful calculation or design. This much becomes apparent when considering the words with which Kephalos salutes Socrates' arrival. "Socrates," he says,

> You don't frequent us in coming down to the Piraeus; yet you ought to (χρῆν μέντοι). Now, if I still had the power (δυνάμει) to make the trip to town (πρὸς τὸ ἄστυ) easily, there would be no need (ἔδει) for you to come here; rather we would come to you. As it is, however, you must (χρὴ) come here more often. . . . Now, don't do anything else: be with these young men, but come here regularly to us as to friends and your very own kin (οἰκείους). (328c–d)

The capture of Socrates, then, far from being a random occurrence, seems to respond and correspond to deep (if not fully accessible) exigencies. There *must* be an encounter between the two worlds, between those who dwell above and those who dwell below, and given that those below cannot go up (they lack the power to do so), those from above must go down. Or, as in this case, if those dwelling in the citadel above descend to the port and try to go back up without having appropriately paid a visit to the dwellers of that place, they are detained and forced to pay their due. Indeed, those who cannot (anymore) go up toward town impede the journey of those who can and who are in fact already on their way. The former even go so far in their audacity as to invite those whom they hold captive, those whom they are preventing from going home (οἴκαδε), to consider themselves at home in that place, and to frequent the people there as members of the same kin (οἰκεῖος). It is in this way that Kephalos, the voice of ancestral authority, ratifies Socrates' arrest, thus revealing it as such—as somehow necessary and unavoidable.

Not only, then, is Socrates not the guest to be entertained in this dialogue, but the task he must carry out is not primarily that of entertainment. Rather, caught within an inscrutable plot characterized by a fierce necessitating vigor, Socrates must speak in order to defend himself, in order to survive the strange predicament and to move away from the place of captivity. He must also speak to serve whatever function, whatever purpose may be assigned to him by circumstances. In other words, he must not draw back from the situation in which he has come to find himself and, rather, has to work his way through it. Indeed, he may have unique contributions to make in that context (after all, as Kephalos clearly states, the dwellers down below long for the arrival of someone like Socrates from above; they need this visit—eagerly await).[14] Conversely, his prolonged engagement with and exposure to the world below may yield precious resources and unique, perhaps even revolutionizing, insights to be brought back to the city above.[15] The exchange and circulation between worlds, besides appearing to be somewhat necessary, seems to be crucial to the life (that is to say, to the cycles of growth, decay, and regeneration) of each world in its distinctness.

But it is the question of survival which imposes itself with its undeniable priority, and, in this sense, speaking is Socrates' way of guarding against the dangers inherent in the situation. For he encounters numerous obstacles, resistances, and threats as he attempts to move on along his path—the first of which is the somewhat virulent attack of Thrasumakhos, who, like a "wild beast (ὥσπερ θηρίον)," is ready to fling himself against Socrates "as if to tear" him apart (336b). Utterly removed from the friendliness and politeness of the interaction in the *Timaeus*, the unfolding of this dialogue is accompanied by a certain harshness. Sustaining the interaction imposed on Socrates requires the courage and impassibility necessary on the battlefield—for it involves the challenge of a life-and-death combat. Survival and the possibility of transformation (that is, of a certain death): this much is at stake in the dialogical involvement and conduct.

Again, it should be recalled in passing that the *Apology* offers a similar warrior-like image of Socrates. The philosopher must confront difficulties simultaneously pressing and shadowy—in fact, all the more urgent precisely because elusive. He has to "fight with shadows (σκιαμαχεῖν)," ghosts from the past, a doxic heritage unreflectively formed and fixated (18d). Later in the defense, Socrates describes his condition by reference to the heroic paradigm, specifically to Achilles' readiness to act as he believes he must without considering "death and risk" (θανάτου καὶ κινδύνου) (28d). Then, recalling his past services as a hoplite, he maintains that, just as in that circumstance he remained where he had been stationed by his commander, so he must remain there where the god has stationed him in this world (28d–29a). In this life the god stationed Socrates as a philosopher (so at least Socrates has understood), as someone whose assignment is inquiry, examination of himself as well as others. Analogously to the military task, the philosophical work requires that one "remain and run risks" (μένοντα κινδυνεύειν), enduring in the midst of danger (28d). Socrates proceeds then to anticipate the argument that he will further articulate to conclude his discourse, according to which not fearing death is a most eminently philosophical posture: "For to fear death, men, is nothing else than to suppose oneself wise when one is not; for it is to suppose one knows what one does not know (δοκεῖν γὰρ εἰδέναι ἐστὶν ἃ οὐκ οἶδεν)" (29a). The philosopher's steadiness before death no longer amounts to the defiant resistance or persistence in the face of death distinguishing the military ἦθος, but rather indicates a preparedness to give oneself up, always already to be swept away, to be undone—to change one's mind, to die to a dream, a conviction, a delusion in order to encounter what is there. Such supple steadiness, openness to dying as a mode of living, curiosity toward the mystery of death, should also be considered by reference to Alkibiades' portrait of Socrates in the *Symposium* and to the sustained meditation on dying constituting the *Phaedo*. In the latter dialogue, again, the frequentation of death is treated as central in genuine philosophical pursuit. Indeed, "genuine (ὀρθῶς) philosophers practice dying (ἀποθνῄσκειν), and death is least terrible to them of all human beings" (67e). Philosophy essentially means to practice (μελετάω, to study, apply oneself to, focus on, care for, learn) "dying" (τεθνάναι). Indeed, as Socrates asks, is philosophy not "the practice of death" (μελέτη θανάτου) (80e–81a)? The sense of wonder before death, the realization of not having knowledge "of the things in Hades" (περὶ τῶν ἐν Ἅιδου, *Apology* 29b) echo the Heraclitean pronouncement on the unimaginable, unforeseeable character of what befalls human beings when dying (22 B 27).

The moving dialogue on the πολιτεία, then, is of war, not of friendship. It is of war in a way other than that of the friendly conversation in the *Timaeus*. It is not, or not only, a discussion concerning war, leisurely carried out in order to revitalize an account too formal to be alive and in movement. It is especially not an envisioning of war as the luminous field of virility rewarded with immortal, dazzling glory. It is of war in the sense that in its development war is *enacted,* in the sense that it happens in the midst of war as such, to which it belongs. It is of war because it harbors the experience of war, exposes the sense of urgency and gravity inherent in this experience, interrogates the difficult connection between philosophical engagement and the battle for (of) life. Performatively, if not thematically, this dialogue confronts the question of the discursive ἀγών at a most fundamental level, by showing the struggle of persuasion as other than a rhetorical game, and instead as a mode of living. Not simply as a way of preserving (one's) life, but rather as a way of letting life flow in its manifold openness, in the blossoming of its possibilities. Not simply as a way of surviving, but in fact as a way of opening up, grasping at, glimpsing the possibilities of the living. One finds it difficult, in this respect, not to marvel at the systematically trivializing appropriations of Platonic dialectic as a matter of argumentative contention conducted for its own sake and involving winners and losers. For, indeed, even if winning and losing were recognizably an issue, it seems clear that the battle carried out at the level of discourse is never simply kept within the logico-discursive bounds and that the stake is not reducible to the reward for rhetorical skill. Here what seems to be at stake is a struggle whose end, if there is such a thing, is other than victory, or a wholly other kind of victory . . .

Socrates' Third Way

In this dialogue, then, war is enacted, not only discussed. The agonistic and antagonistic tenor of the interaction is clear from the very first segments of the text, as the analysis of Book I presented above also showed. In this context the relational mode of struggle and war constitutes an outstanding element in the overall discursive conduct and perhaps the most conspicuous manifestation of the movement of life and the living. In its performative stratum, that is to say, at the level of its enactment, the dialogue proposes the experience of war, its violence and pain, its severity and ineluctability. In fact, the whole dialogue can be seen as a movement from one battle to the next, as a *moving through* the several stages of war, through the whole campaign in its many aspects, and out— from the initial challenge Socrates must confront in Book I, to the battle mentioned at the beginning of Book VII, for which the one must be ready who has ascended from the cave and now prepares to go back down, finally to the silence after the war with which the myth in Book X begins (a silence which is a prelude to the vision disclosed in and through the end of the war).

But, in spite of such pervasiveness of war in its various figures, it would be arduous to assert, in connection with the dialogue on the πολιτεία, what was suggested in the case of the *Timaeus*. In the latter dialogue, a splendid example of education and civility, the figure of war is resorted to in order to dynamize the schematic rigor of speech. The basic presuppositions on which this emendation of discursive immobility (i.e., lifelessness) rests are, firstly, a radical distinction between motion and immobility (war and speech), and, secondly, the totalization of motion as war, that is to say, the unproblematic treatment of war as coextensive with motion, indeed, as the moving of humans.

The dialogue on the πολιτεία, as was pointed out above, finds its inception in movement (a descent). The successive battles marking its development are disclosed by and within such dynamism. There is no preexisting and separately subsisting schematism to be revitalized. In fact, the discourse of the just city, far from occurring schematically and subsisting apart from (prior to) motion, begins to form through movement and through movement is trans-formed, de-formed, undone. The λόγος of the just city is alive and in motion. It comes into the stability of a certain shape while already moving away from it, beyond it. It keeps taking shape. That is also why it announces the necessity of decay—of the city as well as its own. There is no drastic opposition of movement and immobility, then. In fact, the very category of immobility appears to be dubious and can nowhere be clearly discerned. The distinction between war and speech is internal to motion, should be understood in modal terms, and can in no way be reduced to the distinction between motion and stillness. War is not indifferently named as a synonym of motion but as one of its modes. Motion manifests itself in its modal manifoldness.

In the dialogue on the πολιτεία, thus, war emerges as a mode of motion. Discourse itself, opening up in its temporality, belongs to motion. This is eminently, though not exclusively, true of the discourse in and through which war is enacted. Such a discourse is, as was said above, of war—that is to say, it is a mode of war, a mode of that unique mode of motion which is war. As such, it is informed by the unique movement that warfare involves. It is indeed, as was intimated, a way of fighting. And yet this particular way of fighting should be appreciated in its specificity with respect to other modes of polemic confrontation. Of course, this specificity should not be reduced to a virtuality which would at best amount to the harmless and safe mimicking of war in its full and pure embodiment. This would in fact mean to neutralize the discourse of war as such, to deny its performative character and to bring it back to the ἦθος of representational discursivity, to a discourse contemplating war from out of a distance, remaining tranquilly unaffected. The mode in which warfare is conducted is not and cannot be a matter of indifference.

This is clear also from Socrates' response (in the form of a question) to Polemarkhos's defiant invitation either to gain the freedom to ascend by physically prevailing over him and his comrades or to acknowledge their predominance and surrender. Socrates suggests that there may be yet another possibility besides this basic alternative, a *third way*. This is not proposed simply because the sheer numerical superiority of the men associated with Polemarkhos would make a physical confrontation vain, even unthinkable. Indeed, in this specific circumstance it might seem that Socrates has no choice other than to surrender. But it soon becomes evident that the way followed by Socrates, which obviously is not that of physical struggle, is not that of surrender either, let alone of flight. Socrates undertakes to combat by turning his opponents into interlocutors. And this working through issues, fighting one's battles, moving through the stages of a war in the mode of discourse is definitely not a form of avoidance, a comportment to which one resorts when no other option is available, a way of fleeing in the face of what one cannot confront. It is in Book III that what is implied in Socrates' initial interaction with the lord and instigator (ἄρχων) of war (πόλεμος) receives a thematic treatment. Here, in the course of the discussion of education (more specifically, concerning the balance of spiritedness and gentleness achieved through an education in which gymnastic and music are appropriately blended), Socrates takes into consideration the man who "labors a great deal at gymnastic and feasts himself really well but never touches music (μουσικῆς) and philosophy" (411c). About this man he observes:

> But what about when he does nothing else and never communes with a Muse (μηδὲ κοινωνῇ Μούσης μηδαμῇ)? Even if there was some love of learning in his soul (φιλομαθὲς ἐν τῇ ψυχῇ), because it never tastes of any kind of learning (μαθήματος) or investigation (ζητήματος) nor partakes in speech (λόγου μετίσχον) or the rest of music (τῆς ἄλλης μουσικῆς), doesn't it become weak (ἀσθενές), deaf (κωφὸν), and blind (τυφλὸν) because it isn't awakened

(ἐγειρόμενον) or trained (τρεφόμενον) and its perceptions aren't purified (οὐ-δὲ διακαθαιρομένων τῶν αἰσθήσεων)? . . . Then, I suppose, such a man becomes a misologist (μισόλογος) and unmusical (ἄμουσος). He no longer makes any use of persuasion (πειθοῖ) by means of speech (διὰ λόγων) but goes about everything with force (βίᾳ) and savageness (ἀγριότητι), like a wild beast (ὥσπερ θηρίον); and he lives (ζῇ) ignorantly (ἐν ἀμαθίᾳ) and awkwardly (σκαιότητι) without rhythm or grace (μετὰ ἀρρυθμίας τε καὶ ἀχαριστίας). (411d–e)

The soul, the man, described here evidently corresponds to the man encountered by Socrates on his way up, the man impeding his upward walk—although, after this first encounter, Thrasumakhos, who also is said to resemble a "wild beast," will turn up on the scene as a much more vivid instantiation of the psychological profile described. And it is equally evident that the emphasis on persuasion as a way of moving through the several circumstances that may propose themselves, as a way of living and of fighting, reflects Socrates' comportment in the opening scene.

This is a way of fighting through, thanks to, and for the sake of, understanding. It is a fighting set in motion by a lack of understanding and unfolding in (as) the opening up of the understanding striven for—a fighting which does not require frontal clashes and traumatic opposition, but rather prescribes a movement in the direction of those confronted, along with them, so that their logic and their drives may be com-prehended (literally, taken with oneself), engaged, and only on this ground deactivated. It is a way of being in war which is informed by rhythm, by that harmonious composure which, while allowing for the articulation of conflict in its complexity, tensions, and frictions, aims at the transformation rather than at the simple suppression of what (whom) is confronted. For it involves undoing and disallowing but not in the sense of pure destruction. Such peculiar warfare, Socrates' third way, is a problematization, a suspension of (and, hence, a response to) war in its utterly shattering, disruptive movement.

It is important to underline that such warfare does not diverge from the sheer destructiveness of war simply because the combat involved is not physical—that is, because it occurs at the level of λόγος. In a sense, precisely on the ground of Socrates' insistence on the indissoluble bind between corporeal conduct and psychological structure, the ἀγών of persuasion, too, involves the body, even if in oblique ways. Furthermore, such a struggle not oriented to the destruction of the opponent is not the exclusive prerogative of logical combat. There may be, indeed, there are, modes of physical confrontation analogously informed by the lack of and the striving for understanding rather than by the purpose of bringing (giving) death. And, on the contrary, one can definitely conceive of modes of psychological dueling leaving only devastation, psychological wastelands, behind. What is crucial is that the Socratic mode of confrontation, whatever the level at which it is carried out, is not driven by the passion for disintegration. It does not aim at annihilation, certainly not of the body and not of the ψυχή—*especially not* of the ψυχη—however one is to understand such an underdetermined indication of that which lives. It is a way of accompanying the enemies to their own destruction, to the disempowerment occurring out of them and *according to* them. The Socratic warfare makes manifest (or makes itself manifest as) the impulsion to re-generation, notably to psychological regeneration—to transformation, that is, to that other death, that death which is other than termination. Moreover, since such warfare develops otherwise than as opposition, the transformation it announces (and is) concerns one as much as one's opponent. It concerns, indeed, both in their belonging together.

It is, however, the case that Socrates' combat prevalently, if not in a determinably exclusive way, unfolds in λόγος.[16] And it is the case that the ἀγών in λόγος, acknowledged above as a way of living and definitely not a game, as no less a deed than the deeds of warriors and soldiers on the battlefield, still differs quite importantly from hand-to-hand combat. In some respects they are even incompatible with one another. For the carrying out of a war on the battlefield (the falling of bodies, the spilling of blood) does not admit of the development of war in speech, let alone of speech tout court.[17] And, conversely, as long as war is in speech, as long as there is a dialogue belonging to war, a dialogue held in motion and even torn apart in its being (the theater of) war, in other words, a dialogue exposing the impossibility, the delusion of transparent communication and making manifest the risks and dangers of exchange—war proper is postponed.[18] War as a fully embodied phenomenon and as the drive to extinction happens in the ceasing of dialogue. Also, war in the strict sense always presupposes a certain naive self-confidence, the capacity for a relatively unproblematic self-assertion, the belief in the unity, inner agreement, and simple identity of the parties involved. But what the dialogue of war reveals and calls attention to, rather, is the ongoing war in the ψυχή itself, the ψυχή itself as a battlefield—the complexity of the psychological landscape, its partial unreadability, the nonsimple, composite character even of its harmony. It is this invisible war which, as long as it remains unattended (that is, unconscious), projects itself outwardly and, automatically and with utmost precision, reproduces itself in the world, fueling conflicts within the community or between communities. The dialogue of war interrupts such unrecognized automatism. In this way, too, the dialogue of war suspends war proper. Such are the implications of Socrates' third way, the way of war in (the mode of) discourse and of discourse in (the mode of) war.

Socrates contra Socratem

The intimation that war literally understood as warfare is not indifferently interchangeable with motion (that it is not the unproblematic extension of the natural into the historico-political domain) and, furthermore, the enactment of the question of war in its irreducible manifoldness constitute a most noteworthy moment of departure of the dialogue on the πολιτεία from the *Timaeus*. But, in that dialogue, the thematic discussions of war, too, make evident the extent to which the issue of war is and, indeed, remains a problem. These more or less sustained, more or less direct approaches to the question of war show in no uncertain terms that war persists as a question and that almost nothing regarding it is a matter of course. The theme of war, traversing the whole dialogue as one of its leitmotifs and receiving disparate elaborations in the course of the conversation, presents itself in its aporetic openness. It is broached in various and not always consequential (if not altogether contradictory) ways. It explodes in a manifold of radically heterogeneous aspects. It is this deflagration which the dialogue, in its development, simultaneously captures, undergoes, follows, and becomes. No discursive reconciliation, no reunion of the mutually conflicting insights into the question of war is attained in the dialogue. Many ends are left loose, many tensions unresolved—in a way that is, somewhat paradoxically, quite felicitous. In the dialogue there is an open conflict (a conflict openly displayed and left open) concerning conflict.

The several discussions of war in this dialogue would, in and of themselves, constitute a worthy subject for an extensive analysis. Here only a few of their relevant features should be recalled. War, whether taking place in the world or intrapsychically (and the distinction between these two fields of war is fleeting), since the beginning is associated with disorder, division, faction, dissolution—in brief, with injustice. In Book I, after having momentarily conceded to Polemarkhos that the "work" of the just man is "to help friends and harm enemies," and that it is "in making war and being an ally in battle" (ἐν τῷ προσπολεμεῖν καὶ ἐν τῷ ξυμμαχεῖν) that the just man accomplishes this (332e), Socrates already formulates the position to which he will return time and again in the course of the dialogue. The passage is paradigmatic and must be considered carefully:

> Then it is not the work (ἔργον) of the just man to harm either a friend or anyone else, Polemarkhos, but of his opposite, the unjust man. . . . Then, if someone asserts that it's just to give what is owed (τὰ ὀφειλόμενα . . . ἀποδιδόναι) to each man—and he understands (νοεῖ) by this that harm is owed to enemies (ἐχθροῖς) by the just man and help to friends (φίλοις ὠφέλειαν)—the man who said it was not wise. For he wasn't telling the truth (οὐ γὰρ ἀληθῆ

ἔλεγεν). For it has become apparent (ἐφάνη) to us that it is never (οὐδαμοῦ) just to harm anyone (οὐδένα). (335d–e)

Socrates' claim is peremptory: justice must be understood totally apart from the logic of punishment or revenge. Causing harm, in other words, can never be undertaken in the name of justice, let alone of a just cause. What is already foreshadowed here, moreover, is the understanding of justice beyond the concern with reward and retribution, especially outside the framework of calculability. The argument, again, is based on the identity of the good and the just. For "the just man is good," and it is as good that this man does not (cannot) harm anyone. Harming, in fact, is not "the work of the good but of its opposite" (335d).

And yet, almost immediately (just the time for Polemarkhos to assent), Socrates adds: "We shall do battle (μαχούμεθα) jointly (κοινῇ), then, you and I . . . if someone asserts that Simonides, or Bias, or Pittacus or any other wise and blessed man said it" (335e). Here, first of all, the defense of the "wise and blessed" men, two of the legendary seven and Simonides the poet, should be noticed. Because of the evident falsity of the claim concerning the justice of harming enemies, no wise man can have uttered it. In fact, the attribution of such a claim to one of the ancestral wise men represents that against which Socrates and his ally wage war. Secondly, the aporetic structure of Socrates' stance against the association of justice and war should be emphasized. Socrates, indeed, for the love of justice and out of a desire to come to behold its essence, commits himself to refuting the assertion of the possibility of just war. But it is in a warlike fashion, through the language of war, that he articulates his position against the injustice of war. And although it could be observed, even on the ground of the foregoing remarks on the different modes of warring, that the battle Socrates sets out to undertake is not aimed at harming but rather at transforming, the intimation emerging from this passage is clear and perplexing: war will never have been fully, simply escapable. The structure, the logic, of warfare will have haunted, marked, left its trace upon and within the approach to the question of war, especially that approach turning into a movement against a certain unreflective legitimization of war. Of course, it is crucial to realize the difference between, on the one hand, war as the turmoil of difference, that is, as the acknowledgment of disagreement, and, on the other hand, war as the unreflective limitation, repression, or denial of difference, as a differing unable to sustain difference, a movement aiming at immobility. The dialogical unfolding as the place of the affirmation of incongruity, as the surfacing itself of motion and difference, as the letting be of the irreducible clearly calls into question the unquestioning exercise of warfare in its possibility, the very possibility of practicing or even just promising war unquestioningly.

This passage is exemplary in that it illustrates a pattern recurring throughout the dialogue and, hence, reveals one of the ciphers of the dialogue as a whole. What becomes clear already is the fact that Polemarkhos's initial conjecture regarding the justice of being allies of friends in war is never fully left behind and that, even more importantly, his stance seems to be perfectly consistent with Socrates'—at least with a quite substantial stratum of the Socratic discourse. And though, in the specific exchange with Polemarkhos, Socrates could be said to resort to the language of war merely in order to win the lord of war over to his side, in the discourse of the just city the figure of war is too ubiquitous, too outstanding to be explained by reference to Socrates' seductive strategy. As was pointed out above, Socrates himself later in the dialogue adopts the language first introduced by Polemarkhos and defines the best men in the just city, that is, the guardians and rulers, "allies in battle" (ξύμμαχοι). Thanks to the work of such "friends," destruction is perpetrated without while another kind of destruction (confusion, unrest, decomposition) is avoided within the just city (417a–b). In the course of the articulation of Socrates' position it becomes increasingly clear that the war he admits and whose justice he defends is that action necessary to the saving, to the preservation, of a certain interiority. Whether the inner unity to be protected be that of the ψυχή, of the city, or of a people considered in its unity, it involves the identity, the cohesiveness, of a given organism as opposed to what (whom) is foreign, extraneous to it—in one word, different. This strand of the Socratic reflection is evidently at odds (at war) with the basic resistance to war asserted in Book I with unmistakable vigor. In this sense the initial exchange with Polemarkhos begins to appear less as the confrontation with (and disempowerment of) the man responsible for Socrates' arrest than as a preliminary rehearsal of Socrates' inner conflict—of Socrates' oscillation between conflicting positions, which remains unresolved throughout the dialogue. Polemarkhos's surmise of the justice of assisting friends in battle, indeed, so accurately prefigures Socrates' intimations regarding the justice of defending what is one's own that Polemarkhos ends up appearing as nothing more than Socrates' projection. His voice and Socrates' are in this way no longer safely discernible.[19]

A later passage illustrates the essential, if polemical, unity of the voices of Polemarkhos and Socrates—that is, the nonsimple character of Socrates' ψυχή, even as he asserts the simplicity, unity, and integrity of interiority. The passage takes place in Book V, during the discussion of the guardians' ἦθος in matters of war. After having established a terminological distinction between two different types of hatred, "faction" (στάσις) and "war" (πόλεμος) ("the name faction is applied to the hatred [ἔχθρα] of one's own [τοῦ οἰκείου], war to the hatred of the alien [τοῦ ἀλλοτρίου]" [470b]), Socrates goes on to say:

> I assert that the Greek stock ('Ελληνικὸν γένος) is with respect to itself its own
> (οἰκεῖον) and akin (ξυγγενές), with respect to the barbaric (βαρβαρικῷ), for-
> eign (ὀθνεῖόν) and alien (ἀλλότριον). . . . Then when Greeks fight with bar-
> barians and barbarians with Greeks, we'll assert they are at war (πολεμεῖν) and
> are enemies by nature (πολεμίους φύσει), and this hatred (ἔχθραν) must be
> called war (πόλεμον); while when Greeks do any such thing to Greeks, we'll
> say that they are by nature friends (φύσει . . . φίλους), but in this case Greece
> is sick (νοσεῖν) and factious (στασιάζειν), and this kind of hatred (ἔχθραν)
> must be called faction (στάσιν). (470c–d)

This statement says even more than Polemarkhos initially ventured to say. For
in the early argument the proviso was added that "it is just to do good to the
friend, if he's good, and harm the enemy, if he's bad" (335a). Here, on the contrary, there is no such qualification involved. Socrates' point here can be refor-
mulated as follows: it is admissible (healthy, according to nature, and, in this
sense, just) to wage war only against the alien, the barbarian as such, whatever
status the opponent may have with respect to the categories of good and bad;
while it is sick (and presumably unjust) to fight against one's own kin, against
those who speak the same language and are familiar, whatever status they may
have with respect to the categories of good and bad.[20] (It should be underlined
that, however sick faction within a community may be, it is not against nature.
Sickness is no less by nature, φύσει, than health.) Thus, whether someone may
be considered a friend (an ally) or a foe does not depend on considerations pertaining to the good. Rather, it is *as alien* that an alien man, or people, is obviously, naturally an adversary. Likewise, it is *as akin* that the kinsmen are obviously, naturally friends. The contrast between what is foreign and what is one's
own is exacerbated by the fact that the two categories are presented in somewhat
static terms, as if the distinction between Greeks and barbarians were an essential one (sharply demarcating sameness, i.e., homogeneity, ξυγγένεια, and alterity, i.e., unlikeness, ἀλλοτριότης) and not a matter of the language spoken,
of the way in which a culture literally shapes and signs the body, in fact, φύσις
itself.[21]

The outcome of this simple dichotomy can ultimately be traced back to an
analogy established early in the dialogue, inaugurating the discourse on the
character and proper education of the best citizens, that is, those displaying both
a philosophical nature and an inclination to war. This most excellent, amphi-
bolous class is accounted for and shaped by reference to the nature of dogs. "By
nature (φύσει)," Socrates says, "the disposition (ἦθος) of noble dogs is to be as
gentle as can be with their familiars (συνήθεις) and people they know (γνωρί-
μους), and the opposite with those they don't know (ἀγνῶτας)" (375e). He then
explains further the philosophical element in the dog's behavior: "When it sees

someone it doesn't know (ἀγνῶτα), it's angry, although it never had any bad (κακὸν) experience with him. And when it sees someone it knows (γνώριμον), it greets him warmly, even if it never had a good (ἀγαθὸν) experience with him" (376a). *This* is "truly philosophic" (ἀληθῶς φιλόσοφον) in the nature of the beast—that

> it distinguishes (διακρίνει) friendly (φίλην) from hostile (ἐχθρὰν) looks by nothing other than by having learned (καταμαθεῖν) the one and being ignorant (ἀγνοῆσαι) of the other. . . . And so, how can it be anything other than a lover of learning (φιλομαθές), since it defines what's its own (οἰκεῖον) and what's alien (ἀλλότριον) by knowledge (συνέσει) and ignorance (ἀγνοίᾳ)?" (376a–b)

A human being, too, if he or she has to be both gentle with those known to him or her and hostile to the others must possess an analogously "philosophic" nature (376b–c). It should be said that this determination is truly "worthy of wonder" (376a). One is struck by its outrageous audacity. For does such a reduction of philosophy to self-preservation, to the defense of what is one's own, not amount to the denial and suppression of philosophy? How is one to avoid being, with Heraclitus, sardonic when considering that indeed "dogs do bark at those they do not know" (22 B 97)? How is one to consider this—philosophy? Would this canine version of philosophy, its predilection for what has been learned, not bespeak the betrayal of philosophy understood as love of learning? For does the love of learning not entail an attraction to the unknown, rather than a fondness for (contentment with) the known? Indeed, does the very process and experience of learning not always imply a departure from the known and, thanks both to the known and to the departing from it, call for an openness to that which is as yet unknown, other than known? Does learning not always involve this transition and risk? Does this not happen to dogs too, after all? Do they not, at some point, *somehow,* come to know someone or something and stop barking? Why is it, when is it that things change, that a turning takes place, such that, out of the known, one makes oneself available to (the claim of) the unknown? How is one to account for this astonishing leap taken every time learning is involved? How is one to account for the wonder of this journey and transformation? It is above all worth noticing that it is out of the dialogue itself that these questions impose themselves on one. They are *dictated* by the dialogue. The Socratic discourse raises and asks itself such questions. Most notably, Socratic pedagogy in its entirety (the movement meant to turn the soul toward the unknown, to make the unknown not simply the object of hostility, to overcome such resistance) represents a fundamental questioning of the logic of the guardian-watchdog.

However, the reduction of difference (whether between the same and the differing, the familiar and the unfamiliar, or the known and the unknown) to an essential, natural, warlike contraposition constitutes a significant strand of the Socratic discourse. It is not clear, at this point, whether such contraposition should be understood as intra- and interpolitical or as extra-political—whether, that is to say, it should be viewed as internal to the domain recognized qua political (as a contraposition of one πόλις to another) or as constitutive of the political itself (disclosing the political precisely through the opposition of it to its other, to the other-than-political). Moreover, the issue is further complicated by the nonunivocal character of the term "political." For in the dialogue on the πολιτεία, at stake is not so much the founding of the political without any further qualification, of *the* πόλις, but rather of the *just* πόλις—which clearly neither coincides with the πόλις tout court nor exhausts the horizon of the political.[22] At any rate, such a reduction of difference reminds one of another early segment of the dialogue, namely, Socrates' story of the generation of the three main human kinds corresponding to the metals. In this narration, too, the naturalization of cultural and political identity goes hand in hand with the relatively unproblematic (self-evident, as it were) intimation of the necessity of war against what lies outside the familiar surroundings, that is, one's own.

The passage has already been quoted. It describes the nonhuman ποίησις of the human—the human beings being fashioned in the womb of the earth (of nature) by a divine hand. Within this only metaphorically poietico-dynamic horizon (for the all too human language of ποίησις can be utilized only equivocally to refer to divine undertakings), human essence is secured to a transcendent fixity, determined outside of the fluctuations of γένεσις. "When the job had been completely finished," the story goes, "then the earth (γῆ), which is their mother (μήτηρ), sent them up (ἀνῆκε)" (414e). An operation divine in character, a sparkle, a movement taking place within the hidden recesses of the earth, engenders humans. To be even more precise, it originates the citizens of the just city, just citizens. Indeed, in their belonging to various types, the human beings emanating from the earth are already and essentially citizens. For it is thanks to such typological differences that they can serve their specific purpose within the communal organism.

This much was already noted in the previous discussion of this passage. What was not taken into consideration at that point, however, is Socrates' remark immediately following the image of the birth of the citizens from the womb of the earth. Socrates adds: "and, now, as though the land they are in (τῆς χώρας ἐν ᾗ εἰσὶ) were a mother (μητρὸς) and a nurse (τροφοῦ), they must plan for (βουλεύεσθαί) and defend (ἀμύνειν) it, if anyone attacks (ἐπ' αὐτὴν ἴῃ), and they must think (διανοεῖσθαι) of the other citizens (ἄλλων πολιτῶν) as brothers (ἀδελφῶν) and born of the earth (γηγενῶν)" (414e). It is, then, in virtue of being born of the earth, in virtue of the quite portentous circumstances marking their birth, that these human beings are instantly citizens and brothers, that is, naturally belong together, flow into a unitary whole, constitute a community. Political constitution is accounted for in terms of nature and/or divine action. More specifically, what makes these human beings citizens and brothers is their origin out of a unique place (χώρα), out of an utterly singular earthly receptacle, and not just out of any place or of what one might be tempted to call "the earth in general." It is their birth from that particular womb (χώρα, that is, δελφύς) and their belonging in that particular place which make them brothers (ἀδελφοί)—which at once endow them with a unique identity and distinguish them from those coming from elsewhere. The (natural) necessity of war, of defending the motherland against those belonging in another place and lineage, of preserving the (natural) community of brothers against those who (by nature) have little or nothing in common with that family is already quite clearly suggested here.[23]

According to Socrates, then, and in spite of Socrates (that is, according to Polemarkhos-Socrates and against an other Socrates), war between the mutually alien is by nature unavoidable, in fact, a quite unproblematic phenomenon. This natural hatred (ἔχθρα) called war, aimed at the preservation of what is one's own in its integrity against the threat of the uncanny, is a sign of health. It is, on the contrary, faction inside, within the walls gathering those who belong together, which is condemned as execrable and, in the symptomatological vein of Socrates' remark, sick.

But war against the alien (more generally, the anticipation of it, the attitude toward it, and the preparation for it) does not simply have the function of defending the city. The alarm surrounding the encounter with the alien, the construction and projection of such an encounter in its ominous character, and the subsequent being-ready or having-to-be-ready for war, for the ever-possible war, rather, seem to be involved in the very possibility and in the coming into being of the just city qua just. War, or its impending possibility, in other words, seems to play a determining role in the emergence of the order and structure of the just city. For such a city is essentially, if not exclusively, a city of warriors, a city whose best citizens are warriors—if also lovers of wisdom. The guardians are not brought forth after the founding of the city, for the sake of the preservation of what is already completely there. They do not serve a purely conservative purpose. On the contrary, since the beginning of the dialogue, it is around the formation and education of the class of the guardians and rulers that the development of the just city in speech revolves. The concern with war, therefore, far from being a derivative aspect of the founding effort, is one of its radical, that is, primary and fundamental, elements.

It should be noticed, subsequently, that the distinction proposed by Socrates between the natural hatred called war and the division called faction (still natural, albeit in the mode of sickness) is less stable, less clear than it seems at first. Such evaluation of the two forms of conflict appears to be somewhat arbitrary, especially in light of the fact that they are necessitated and informed by the same logic. The same class of citizens is in charge for the waging of war as well as the avoidance of faction, that is, the preservation of harmony. In both cases, the task is that of defense, whether against the enemy outside (such is the assignment of the warriors in general) or against the enemy inside (such is the assignment of the best of warriors, those who must rule).[24] In both cases the issue at stake is the protection of an established identity. As long as the auxiliary guardians and the ruling guardians function as they are meant to, extraneous elements will be warded off and interiority preserved in its self-sameness. There seems to be a deep unity, a relation of mutual implication, between the readiness for war outside and the avoidance of faction inside. The relation between outside and inside, therefore, also appears as otherwise than simple. In fact, the harmony, peace, and self-sameness of the inside seem to be possible, that is, imaginable and thinkable, only at the price of the exclusion of the outside—the very constitution of the inside as such seems to rest on the resistance to any unpredictable element and on the construction of the unpredictable as foreign and dangerous (465a). The preservation of the city in agreement with itself, the defense of its peaceful self-reproduction against any destabilizing accidents, that is, its resistance to becoming, requires vigilance, even war against the outside. A constitutive allergy, literally, a concern with the operation of the other, is at work *in* the establishment of interiority as identity.

Socrates "himself," interestingly enough, despite his insistence on the necessity of distinguishing war from faction (470b, 471a), seems to become confused and easily to lose sight of this distinction. Thus, just a few moments after having first expressed the desirability of such terminological precision, he resorts to the language of war in connection with the recomposition of quarrels inside the city. In these cases, he says, it would be opportune to be moderate and "to have the frame of mind of men who will be reconciled and not always be at war (οὐκ ἀεὶ πολεμησόντων)" (470d–e). This happens again at a later juncture, in that delicate passage in which Socrates provides the conclusive evidence for his claim that those are fit to rule who do not desire to do so: "when ruling (ἄρχειν) becomes a thing fought over (περιμάχητον), such a war (πόλεμος)— a domestic war, one within the family (οἰκεῖος ὢν καὶ ἔνδον)—destroys (ἀπόλλυσι) these people themselves and the rest of the city as well" (521a). This utilization of the language of war with respect to dynamics internal to the city opens the possibility of understanding conflict as quite healthy and according to nature, even when taking place within the city—or, conversely, of understanding war against the alien, too, as sick. Of course, this discursive comportment also problematizes the distinction between inside and outside in subtle ways.

The contrast, *internal* to φύσις, between the health of war and the sickness of faction turns out to be elusive, to say the least, indeed, perplexing—as Socrates himself shows in calling for a meticulous discernment between them while, at the same time, blurring the distinction and falling short with respect to his own requirement.[25] Socrates, however, makes clear the extent to which the constitution and preservation of the just city rest on the logic of war against the other. Like a peaceful island in the midst of a roaring ocean, the just city finds itself surrounded, even besieged, by a world essentially foreign to it. More precisely still, it establishes itself through such an account of the outside world. What is elaborated in this stratum of the Socratic discourse is something like a narrow, limiting concept of justice. Justice, initially connected with the prescription of not harming anyone, here is articulated as the exclusive prerogative of the just city. The initial prescription is replaced by a version of it which is restricted in scope, namely, the injunction not to harm the fellow citizens. In turn, the possibility and subsistence of the just city, where "men live in peace (εἰρήνην) with one another" (465b), rests on the injustice of harming the alien.

Thus, it is to the extent that the πόλις is defined or founded (defines itself or arises) as unitary, self-same, and self-enclosed that it is fundamentally at war with its other. War is the counterpart of political institution and identification, the price to be paid when the truth of dynamism, of movement, is forgotten, covered over. War occurs in the turning of preservation (saving) into resistance to becoming.

But the city is at war with itself at the same time, precisely in asserting itself as self-same. For such self-assertion, in its denial of difference, is as violating as war against the outside. In both cases, at stake is the destruction of the other. This city results from a dream of φύσις (of a natural ground) without sickness, of justice untouched by injustice and other changes, of eternal health and peace.[26] Yet at the heart of this dream is the vision, however exorcised and projected as far outside the city walls as possible, of horror and destruction, of difference so unsustainable as to require enmity, of a peace so exiguous that it must be fiercely fenced in, for it cannot be shared. And in the repression and projection of such deep disquietudes for the sake of order and stillness lies the disorder, the utter injustice, of this dream—therefore, a nightmare.

War and Greatness

The unresolved ambiguity outlined here accompanies the development of Socrates' treatment of and approach to the question of war throughout the dialogue. Such ambivalence may even be seen as a conflict within which Socrates is irremediably caught. After all, war presents itself as an ineluctability to which Socrates must bend very early on during the founding effort, given the direction taken by the conversation under Glaukon's impetus. Indeed, it is the transition forced by Glaukon from the "healthy (ὑγιής) city" to the "luxurious," "feverish (φλεγμαίνουσαν) city" (372e) which makes the conflictual relation of the city to its outside inevitable. In yielding, however reluctantly, to Glaukon's thrust, Socrates acknowledges and introduces a new element into the dialogue. After rapidly pointing out in succession all the precious superfluities and the additional needs of the overproliferating luxurious city (the city will now need "all the hunters and imitators," new servants, swineherds, and more doctors to care for the precarious health of the citizens [373b–d]), he prepares to announce a new necessity, unknown to the previous city. Socrates recalls the slow progression leading to this announcement:

> "And the land (ἡ χώρα), of course, which was then sufficient for feeding the men who were then, will now be small although it was sufficient. Or how should we say it?"
>
> "Like that" he said.
>
> "Then must we cut off a piece of our neighbor's land (τῆς τῶν πλησίον χώρας), if we are going to have sufficient for pasture and tillage, and they in turn from ours, if they let themselves go to the unlimited acquisition of money, overstepping the boundary of the necessary?"
>
> "Quite necessarily, Socrates," he said.
>
> "After that won't we go to war (πολεμήσομεν) as a consequence, Glaukon? Or how will it be?"
>
> "Like that," he said.
>
> "And let's not yet say whether war works evil or good (μήτ' εἴ τι κακὸν μήτ' εἰ ἀγαθὸν ὁ πόλεμος ἐργάζεται)," I said, "but only this much, that we in its turn found the origin of war (πολέμου . . . γένεσιν)—in those things whose coming into being in cities most of all brings into being evils (κακὰ) both private and public."
>
> "Most certainly."
>
> "Now, my friend, the city must be still bigger (μείζονος), and not by a small number but by a whole army (στρατοπέδῳ), which will go out and do battle with invaders for all the wealth (οὐσίας) and all the things we were just now talking about." (373d–374a)

War is introduced into the discussion and its origin uncovered. Simultaneously the just city in all its main features is born. It is the city that will be developed and scrutinized for the rest of the dialogue. It is for *this* city, then, that war is indispensable and constitutive. It is *this* city that, in its very inception and possibility, is sustained by the need to defend (ἀμύνειν) its own—whether from "other families" (from people who are not "brothers," not born of the same μήτηρ) or, broadly speaking from the non-Greek. However, that the logic of political identification (and its counterpart, war/defensiveness against otherness) may be constitutive of/for the "just" city means neither that it is constitutive of the πόλις, of the political without any further specification nor, subsequently, that war would be the fundamental mode of acknowledgment or construction of alterity. Indeed, war seems far from being originary in this sense. The text lets transpire, however fleetingly, suggestions to the effect that alterity may be acknowledged otherwise than through the invention of the other concomitant with the founding of sameness/identity.

One of these suggestions can be heard precisely in that segment of the dialogue quoted above, in which Socrates establishes the distinction between Greeks and barbarians. This move may, in fact, also be read as an attempt to broaden the scope of domestic harmony and extend peaceful coexistence beyond the just πόλις—an attempt, that is, to move beyond the construction of the just city carried out so far. In order to do so, Socrates stretches the understanding of brotherhood to include all the Greeks. In this way interiority no longer designates what lies within the borders of the city, but the entire Greek world. But such an expansion of the notion of identity already heralds its destruction, for it opens the way for an understanding of difference as *internal to* the Greek people, that is, as pertaining to interiority and sameness. Socrates suggests this when he asserts that, "as Greeks" (i.e., qua same),

> they won't ravage Greece or burn houses, nor will they agree that in any city all are their enemies (πάντας ἐχθροὺς)—men, women, and children—but that there are always a few enemies (ὀλίγους ἀεὶ ἐχθροὺς) who are responsible for the disagreement (τῆς διαφορᾶς). And, on all these grounds, they won't be willing to ravage the earth (τὴν γῆν) or tear down houses, since the many are friends (φίλων); and they'll keep up the quarrel (διαφοράν) until those who are responsible are compelled to make amends (δοῦναι δίκην) by those who are not responsible and who are suffering (ἀλγούντων). (471a–b)

Here Socrates, besides reframing the question of identity in terms that exceed the horizon of the "just" πόλις, that is, in terms that exceed an understanding of the political narrowly based on *this* city, also mitigates the rigor of the distinction between the proper and the other. A certain operation of difference is recognized within the same—an operation disseminating disquietude, discordance, and unrest which, however, need not degenerate into self-annihilation. It is also noteworthy that Glaukon interrupts Socrates in this progression (which he perceives as a diversion) and calls him back to the main topic: "Let it be given," he says. "And this and what went before are fine. But, Socrates, I think that if one were to allow you to speak about this sort of thing, you would never remember what you previously set aside in order to say all this" (471c). The contextual-dialogical delimitation of the philosopher's range of action (πρᾶξις and λέξις) is particularly prominent here.

An even more explicit, if inconspicuous, suggestion in the direction of a mode of founding which would not entail the logic of identity/war should be noticed at an earlier stage, in the brief discussion of the first city. Let it simply be mentioned that such a city, far from being naively unconscious of the world outside, entertains systematic exchanges with other cities, by land and by sea (370e–371b). In fact, in conjunction with this city the scene of harmonious political interdependence is envisioned. The city will need "imports" from "another city" (ἄλλης πόλεως), and thus the citizens "must produce at home not only enough for themselves but also the sort of thing and in the quantity needed by these others of whom they have need (δέωνται)" (371a).²⁷ The city necessitated by need, taking shape as an enactment of solidarity in response to need (369b), understands itself and other cities otherwise than on the ground of strict identification and a priori hostility. Such a ground is, thus, disclosed as non-originary.²⁸

At any rate, for the feverish city in constant expansion, for the city that has lost the sense of its own measure and limits, war is quite simply a matter of survival.²⁹ It is because of its originary having overstepped "the boundary of the necessary," because of its projecting itself according to the madness and voracity of "limitless acquisition," that this city can never have enough. Nothing can ever suffice for it. Hence, its constant overflowing, its discharging itself outside, in order to conquer more resources, more vital space. Parenthetically, the paradoxical nature of this outward assimilative movement should be noticed: in its struggle for survival and self-assertion, the city, in fact, lives in the utter mobility of its boundaries, that is, in the restless reformulation of its shape and identity.³⁰

But for Socrates only the previous one is the "true city" (ἀληθινὴ πόλις) (372e), the city where life is said to be simple and austere, where the citizens "feast themselves" with "noble loaves of barley and wheat" (372b). After gratifying themselves in this way, Socrates says, "they will drink wine and, crowned with wreaths, sing of the gods. So they will have sweet intercourse with one another, and not produce children (ποιούμενοι τοὺς παῖδας) beyond their means (οὐσίαν), keeping an eye out against poverty and war (πενίαν ἢ πόλεμον)" (372b). There is, however, no going back to this place—especially because this place is unknown. Such a place where humans would keep themselves purely within the limits of the necessary, therefore, will always already have been left behind. The philosopher, in his attempt at understanding the situation within which he finds himself, at encountering the interlocutors, at moving along with them without resisting their indications, must acknowledge Glaukon's desire, assent to it, and move on to the city of excesses, that is, to the only city Glaukon knows, to the city as the interlocutors know it. This is, indeed, a momentous concession, for, once set in motion within the city, the whirlwind of increasing needs and further forms of sophistication cannot be brought to a halt. On the contrary, the irresistible, necessitating force it displays will drive the early city away from itself, without return. The philosopher, then, is caught between the necessity to yield to the general request of the passion encountered in the world and his vision that is not always of this world. That is why, while envisioning a community whose moderate lifestyle would involve neither division inside nor hostility toward the outside, Socrates has to found a city whose inner peace crucially rests on an aggressive relation to the outside, indeed, on the very positing of its own interiority and of exteriority as such, and whose overall functioning owes much to the class of "solid, lean dogs" ready to fight for it (422d). That is also why, while asserting that war is the business of the wolf-tyrant, for it is the tyrant who "is always setting some war in motion (πολέμους τινὰς ἀεὶ κινεῖ), so that the people will be in need of a leader" (566e–567a), Socrates has to bring forth a city whose best children are to be "men skilled in war" (ἄνδρας πολεμικοὺς) and must consequently be brought to the battlefield as "spectators of war" (θεωροὺς πολέμου) (466e–467c), even "be led up near and taste blood (γευστέον αἵματος), like the puppies" (537a).

Thus, it is war that the philosopher himself *experiences*, in the sense of πάσχειν. This why his discourse, besides presenting itself as a quite torn and conflictual thematization of war, also enacts war, takes place in the midst of it, has to move through the dangers and threats of the battlefield, to undergo death and be deflected—that is, has to move according to the indications and directions received in the encounter with the interlocutor and cannot ever transcend them. This dynamic to which the philosopher is bound and which delimits his comportment and discourse belongs, indeed, to the essence of dialogue. Dialogue is impossible without such binding. At the very same time, the attempt at overcoming captivity is impossible without dialogue. The circumstance and the company surrounding one cannot be transcended—or else they would never be reached, understood, persuaded, that is, won. It is, then, of the essence of the philosopher to do *what she can*—not what she wants.

War, on whose logic the just city rests, is ordered, and lives, is a cipher of the intertwinement (of the unity-without-identity) of justice and injustice, of order and disorder, of death and life. Internal to the death-bearing movement of war runs the distinction between death as transformation and death as annihilation, between the suppleness of metamorphosis and the rigor of destruction, between the yes-saying to passing away and a resistance to passing away which is nevertheless bound to be (indeed, calls for being) overpowered, even slain, all the more violently the more fiercely it resists. For, indeed, as was suggested above, many are the modalities of combat, of bearing and giving death, of dying—and in various ways that which is of death may belong in life. To keep alive means also to let die—for that which is alive is always also dying. "Death-bringing cycle" (περιόδου θνητοῦ)—thus will mortal coming into being be called (617d). This much is revealed by Socrates' performative as well as thematic involvement in the question of war.

Through the foregoing remarks the intimate relation between thought and war has gradually begun to emerge in its complexity. Down at Piraeus, in the cave, in the daimonic place at the end, and in speech throughout the dialogue, the philosopher (especially the philosopher-king) is also and eminently a warrior. Whether envisioned as a port setting, as a recess within the earth, as the barren field from which Er's journey starts, or opening up through and as the dialogue itself, the place of philosophy is essentially a battlefield. This is so precisely because of the engagement of philosophy with life. It is precisely because he is *not* in the position to transcend the indications coming from his own setting that Socrates not only must acknowledge, though ambivalently, a certain ineluctability of war, but also *finds himself* at war already. Through the consideration of Socrates' comportment, however, the multiplicity of modes of warfare also became apparent—so much so that yielding, following, understanding were revealed as ways of fighting, alongside the forms of physical violation ranging from duel to genocide. In fact, resoluteness joined to suppleness, sharpness joined to docility, appeared to be the characteristics of Socrates' comportment in battle.

Er the warrior who once died in war is now more fully uncovered as Socrates, as the philosopher returning in yet another guise—and his story as the recapitulation of Socrates' deeds and discourses, of the dialogue as a whole. One of Socrates' features that can be inferred from the very beginning of the action is his literally "cosmopolitan" equanimity, his situating himself above and beyond ethnico-cultural identification and, therefore, his ability equally to appreciate "the procession of the native inhabitants" and "the one the Thracians conducted" (327a). Er, on the other hand, is "by race a Pamphylian" (τὸ γένος Παμφύλου) (614b). Literally, he is, by race, of mingled tribes or races. Er is all-races, every-kind—utterly singular and, at the same time, not further identified, un-differentiated in his uniqueness.[31] And yet both Er and Socrates participate in that warlike dynamic crucially resulting from the establishment and fixation of identity. In fact, their being warriors is not an accidental attribute of theirs, but rather grounds and informs them in their being. Being a warrior is called forth, even necessitated, by circumstances. Again, in spite of himself and of what he sees, the philosopher cannot simply move beyond the environment surrounding him. On the contrary, he must respond to it, is bound to it, even though, in his inability to identify himself with it, he cannot find himself at peace there. The philosopher is called to war and is at war with respect to such a call. Such is the philosopher's agonistic and agonizing predicament. And in such a way the warrior's ἦθος will have been both evoked and transcended. For one will not have waged war. One will, rather, *have become war,* the battlefield itself. One will have become the field of (the contemplation of) a certain revolution, the field, itself changing, of change and transformation—not even of a willingness to die, but of a certain openness to dying.

Er is said to have died in war. And, though his body was saved, he met death—as radical trans-formation. He is said to have gone under, traveled to the other side. Then he is said to have come back to the rippled surface of life, as a messenger (614d), to narrate what he saw in the midst of, beyond, on the other side of darkness. Socrates, analogously, comes back to narrate what he saw and what happened down below—to narrate, that is, the dialogue on the πολι-τεία. Such, then, is the task, the daimonic existence of the philosopher (warrior, traveler, and messenger): circulating back and forth, up and down, spanning worlds and unspeakable gaps, speaking nevertheless.[32]

Notes

1. Leon H. Craig's work *The War Lover: A Study of Plato's* Republic (Toronto: University of Toronto Press, 1994) was a provocative point of reference in the elaboration of the present chapter.

2. See Mahadev Desai, *The Gospel of Selfless Action, or: The* Gita *According to Gandhi* (Ahmedabad: Navajivan, 1946), p. 10 f.

3. "Thus," says Samjaya in the end, "I have heard from the son of Vasudeva / and the son of Prtha, whose self is great, / this wondrous dialogue / causing the hair to stand on end. / Through the grace of Vyasa I am the one who has heard / this supreme secret yoga / which Krishna, the lord of yoga, has divulged, / before the eyes, speaking himself. / O king, recollecting, recollecting / this wondrous and pure dialogue / of the handsome haired one and Arjuna, / I rejoice over and over again. / And recollecting, recollecting / that more than marvelous form of Hari / my amazement is great, o king, / and I rejoice again and again" (XVIII.74 ff.).

4. Notice the word play of Ἀλκίνου and ἀλκίμου. As Bloom points out, "if one were to translate the root words of the name, the sentence would read: ' . . . an ἀπόλογος of a man not strong of mind, but strong . . .'" (*The* Republic *of Plato*, p. 471, n. 13). Concerning the origin of the name of Er, see S. Halliwell's *Plato: Republic 10*, p. 170. For an early discussion of the identification of Er and Zoroaster, see Proclus, *In Remp.* II:109. For a general evaluation of the Greek fascination with Near and Middle Eastern narratives of transcendence, see Arnaldo Momigliano's *Alien Wisdom: The Limits of Hellenization* (Cambridge: Cambridge University Press, 1975), especially pp. 142–48. In order to examine the possibility of an indirect influence of Zoroastrianism on Plato through the pre-Socratics, see Mary Boyce's *A History of Zoroastrianism* (Leiden: Brill, 1975), pp. 153–63. See also Joseph Bidez and Franz Cumont's *Les Mages hellénisés: Zoroastre, Ostanès et Hystaspe d'après la tradition grecque* (Paris: Belles-Lettres, 1938).

5. As already mentioned, Kahn points out that "Book 1 is the formal counterpart of

Book 10" ("Proleptic Composition in the *Republic*," p. 136). For interpretations high-lighting more generally the symmetrical (concentric) structure of the dialogue and the revolving of the dialogue around the center of the cave image, see Eva Brann's "The Music of the *Republic*," *St. John's Review* 39, nos. 1–2 (1989–90), pp. 1–103, and R. Brumbaugh's "A New Interpretation of Plato's *Republic*," *Journal of Philosophy* 64 (1967), pp. 661–70.

6. In this way the final myth will have repeated and confirmed the diagnosis put forth in Book II, concerning those "who don't see (βλέπουσιν) very sharply," who are not "terrible" (δεινοί) enough (368 d). See Chapter II above.

7. On the connection between the two dialogues, however, see Brann's remarks in "The Music of the *Republic*," p. 23 ff. On the question concerning the sequence *Republic-Timaeus*, see A. E. Taylor's *Commentary on Plato's* Timaeus (Oxford: Clarendon, 1928), p. 15 f., and F. M. Cornford's opposite view in *Plato's Cosmology: The* Timaeus *of Plato* (London: K. Paul, 1937), p. 4 f.

8. "Ἕλληνες ἀεὶ παῖδές ἐστε," the Saïtic priest is said to have said to Solon (22b).

9. Kritias himself repeatedly underlines the precariousness of his own recollection and gives the listeners reasons to meditate on the possibility (indeed, the inevitability) of mmemonic lacunae. The day before he was quite aware of his need to recover a more organic recollection, for "through time" (διὰ χρόνου) his memory had lost its vividness—hence the exercise of multiple repetitions, both solitary and shared with friends (26a). But after such an exertion, he assures us, the story is indelibly stamped in his mind and he is ready to tell it—now as old a man as his grandfather was when he told it to him (26b–c). However, his narration of the story in outline proves that the reliability of his report is (for reasons that may not be merely contingent) less than above all suspicion. Kritias, for instance, mentions the line of transmission of the story twice, in discrepant ways. The second time he forgets to name Dropides altogether, thus simplifying the account of mediations intervened (20e, 25d).

10. Thucydides, too, in the opening remarks of the *Peloponnesian War* lets transpire his doubts concerning the ultimate reliability and veridicality of the historical account. On numerous occasions, however cautiously, he refers to the authority of poets, especially Homer, warning that a pure and simple emancipation from the poetic accounts may not be plausible (1.II.2–3, 1.IX.3–4, 1.X.3–5, 1.XII.5). In his "search for the truth" (ζήτησις τῆς ἀληθείας) the historian must watch against the "adorned," fantastic versions of poets and logographers alike, yet it is clear than he will not simply have spoken from a source absolutely other than those (1.XX.3–XXI.1). But the methodological problems the historian has to confront are even more severe, as Thucydides points out by reference to the report of speeches. It is "difficult" (χαλεπὸν) to repeat them with precision, he observes, even when one heard them firsthand (1.XXII.1). Then he concludes with a startling remark on a certain blindness, a certain absence marking the presence of the witnesses. In the case both of occurrences the historian himself witnessed and of those witnessed by others, the fundamental difficulty arises from the fact that "those present at the several events would not say the same about the same things" (οἱ παρόντες τοῖς ἔργοις ἑκάστοις οὐ ταὐτὰ περὶ τῶν αὐτῶν ἔλεγον), but would give their report according to their "favorable inclination" (εὐνοίας) to one side or according to their "memory" (μνήμης) (1.XXII.2–4). After having thus qualified the historical discourse, Thucydides resolves that he will be appeased if the reader will want to judge his work "beneficial" (ὠφέλιμα) (1.XXII.4).

11. In the *Peloponnesian War* the language of motility in conjunction with the qualification of greatness is pervasively employed to indicate warlike operations. At the very outset of the work, Thucydides calls the πόλεμος he is going to document "the greatest movement" (κίνησις . . . μεγίστη) ever stirring the Greeks (1.I.1–2).

12. Pauly-Wissowa, *Realencyclopädie*, 24 vols. (Stuttgart: Metzler, 1894–1963), vol. 3, pp. 269–71.

13. Thrasumakhos's definition of justice, associating force and justice (338c), is here performatively anticipated, even proleptically corroborated. For it is by sheer force that Socrates is kept in that place, to begin with. It is force, in its abusive and violent manifestation, which to an extent engenders and determines the dialogue and its order.

14. The necessity of doing and practicing that of which one is capable (that for which one has the δύναμις) is emphasized in various respects throughout the dialogue. Ultimately, even the pivotal prescription, in Book VII, that those who have ascended come back to rule is predicated upon their "being more able" (μᾶλλον δυνατοὺς) to live both above and below (520c). In this connection, one of Xenophon's memories comes to mind. He reports that once Socrates, with a remark analogously joining δύναμις and ἀνάγκη, urged Kharmides to take up political obligations. "I believe," Socrates is said to have told him, "that you shrink from involvement in tasks (ὀκνεῖν ἐπιμελεῖσθαι) of which you are capable (δυνατὸν), in which it is necessary (ἀνάγκη) for you, as a citizen, to participate (μετέχειν)" (*Memorabilia* III.vii.2).

15. In the *Phaedrus* the figure of κατάβασις is disclosed not so much in terms of detention and confinement, but rather as a descent to the source of inspiration, as a going down to the roots of speaking, to a certain listening. "You go and tell Lusias," Socrates tells Phaedrus toward the end of the dialogue, "that we two went down (καταβάντε) to the spring of the Nymphs and the shrine of the Muses and listened to speeches (ἠκούσαμεν λόγων) that enjoined us to say (ἐπέστελλον λέγειν) [what follows] to Lusias and to anyone else who composes speeches (λόγους), and also to Homer and anyone else who has composed poetry (ποίησιν) without musical accompaniment or to be sung, and thirdly to Solon and whoever has written political speeches, calling them laws (ἐν πολιτικοῖς λόγοις νόμους ὀνομάζων συγγράμματα ἔγραψεν)" (278b–c).

16. On philosophy as occurring at the intersection of λόγος and struggle (μάχη), and developing as their unity, the following passage from Book VII is illuminating: "Unless someone is able to separate out the idea of the good from all other things and distinguish it in the argument (τῷ λόγῳ), and, going through every test, as it were in battle (ἐν μάχῃ)—eager (προθυμούμενος) to meet the test of being rather than that of opinion—he comes through all this with the argument still on its feet; you will deny that such a man knows the good itself, or any other good" (534b–c). It should be noticed that it is ardent courage (θυμός) that binds together the discursive and warlike elements, sustaining the dynamic challenge that follows.

17. This is literally the case in phalanx warfare, the mode of warring prevalent in the Greek world from the seventh century B.C. and arguably Greece's military legacy to the West. See John Keegan's account in *A History of Warfare* (New York: Knopf, 1993), especially pp. 244–54.

18. The dialogue here at stake is evidently not the exchange between equally constituted subjects mirroring one another, that is, the conversation structuring intersubjectivity as the field of rationality. Kant envisions such dialogue among rational subjects (and, by extension, among nations) as the solution, on a planetary level, to the problem

of conflict (*Perpetual Peace*). Analogously, contemporary authors as diverse as J. Habermas (e.g., *Communication and the Evolution of Society*, trans. Thomas McCarthy [Boston: Beacon, 1979], especially ch. 1, "What Is Universal Pragmatics?") and H.-G. Gadamer (e.g., *Dialogue and Dialectic: Eight Hermeneutical Studies on Plato*, trans. P. Christopher Smith [New Haven: Yale University Press, 1980]) tend to understand dialogue and its ethical valence in terms of the primacy of rationality, even of "universal communication," that is, as more fundamental than the moment of conflict and difference. Irreducible to dialogue thus construed, in connection with which Blanchot speaks of "dialectical optimism," the exchange in which Socrates is engaged bespeaks a certain contestation of the "ideal" of "unity" and of purely rational (i.e., logical) intercourse. This means, to borrow again Blanchot's words, "ceasing to think only with a view to unity," hence "not fearing to affirm interruption and rupture in order to come to the point of proposing and expressing—an infinite task—a truly plural speech" (*The Infinite Conversation*, trans. Susan Hanson [Minneapolis: University of Minnesota Press, 1993], pp. 80–82).

19. This is in accord with what was noticed above concerning Socrates' imitative narration and its direct evocation of the several interlocutors. In *Socrates' Second Sailing: On Plato's* Republic (Chicago: University of Chicago Press, 1989), Seth Benardete observes that in this text "Socrates is himself and plays all other parts" (p. 9).

20. Notice that the Greek word for faction, στάσις, suggests that sedition is a matter of taking a stand, of a position that comes to be rigidly, statically maintained. Faction, thus, constitutes a block in the moving order of the πόλις, an obstruction of the movement of gravitation around the πόλος. (On the etymologico-speculative connection between πόλος and πόλις, see Martin Heidegger, *Parmenides*, trans. A. Schuwer and R. Rojcewicz [Bloomington: Indiana University Press, 1992], p. 89 f.) Socrates uses the word στάσις also to indicate division, disorder, and conflict within the ψυχή, which are analogously associated with injustice (see, e.g., 351d–352a, 440b, 444b).

21. It is essential to notice how, in the passage quoted, the profound difficulty of the distinction between same and other is at once announced and covered over. Socrates does not attribute to the Ἑλληνικὸν γένος the qualities of οἰκειότης and ξυγγένεια, while defining τὸ βαρβαρικόν (οἱ βάρβαροι, not even a γένος, just an indefinite, disparate multitude) as ὀθνεῖον and ἀλλότριον. Rather, it is the Greek γένος that is οἰκεῖον and ξυγγενές (in relation to itself) but, *at the same time*, also ὀθνεῖον and ἀλλότριον (in relation to the barbarians). Rigorously speaking, then, it is the Greek kind that is *both* the same and different, familiar and foreign—in different respects. The difference between the same and the different appears to be internal to the same. This is not, however, what Socrates emphasizes at this point.

22. This quasi-Schmittian problematic (Schmitt's speculative scheme, precisely in the Platonic tenor of its argumentation, is in Plato's text both exceeded and eluded) will be briefly addressed later.

23. As was surmised in Chapters I and II, Socrates' attempt to deactivate the automatisms of tribal belonging and to envision the political in its fundamental alliance with nature has as its counterpart a paradigmatically violent and instrumental appropriation of nature, a desire to calculate it, to force it to work in the service of the political program.

24. The following remark regarding "marriages (γάμοις) and procreations (παιδοποιίαις)" clearly conveys the extent of the delicacy of the rulers' task. After having spoken of intercourse between the best men and women as well as between ordinary

people, Socrates adds that "the offspring of the former must be reared but not that of the others, if the flock is going to be of the most eminent quality. And all this must come to pass without being noticed (γιγνόμενα λανθάνειν) by anyone except the rulers themselves if the guardians' herd is to be as free as possible from faction (ἀστασίαστος)" (459d–e).

25. If, as Nicole Loraux also points out, the rigorous distinction between war and faction is indeed of fundamental importance in matters of political "invention," the Platonic-Socratic gesture of equivocation, although generally unrecognized, cannot not undermine by its very nature the ideological program and narrative of political unity. See Nicole Loraux, *The Invention of Athens: The Funeral Oration in the Classical City*, trans. Alan Sheridan (Cambridge, Mass.: Harvard University Press, 1986), pp. 198–202, 331, and passim.

26. "Then that dream of ours (ἡμῖν τὸ ἐνύπνιον) has reached its perfect fulfillment" (443b).

27. The hypothesis that the "healthy" city should ultimately not be seen as impossible, let alone as a rhetorical provocation disingenuously utilized and readily abandoned by Socrates, is corroborated by salient moments in the *Laws*. In this dialogue the determination of the parameters according to which the city should grow (or, rather, maintain its proper size, not expanding beyond its means) and the development of measured intercourse with the outside are pervasive concerns. See, for instance, the considerations concerning the ratio between land and population (737c ff.) and the regulation of imports and exports (847b ff.).

28. It is in light of similar considerations that the Platonic text appears profoundly remote with respect to Carl Schmitt's theorization of the constitution of the political, and that Schmitt's own appropriation of Platonic language in order to sustain his position is clearly problematic (*The Concept of the Political*, trans. G. Schwab [New Brunswick, N.J.: Rutgers University Press, 1976], p. 26 ff.). This needs to be emphasized, for the Schmittian interpretation-assimilation of Platonic argumentation, far from representing an idiosyncratic episode, inherits the inveterate structures, schematisms, and categories of a scholarly-humanistic tradition that has made of selective, reductive reading one of its traits. (Its comportment toward Plato and, more broadly, Greek antiquity is more than paradigmatic. It is founding.) On this and related matters, see also Derrida's reflection in *Politics of Friendship*, trans. G. Collins (London: Verso, 1997), especially chapters 4–7. Even Derrida, however, speaks of "the axioms, the conceptual veins, the oppositions and associations which structure not only dominant Greek discourse but, *on the other hand, elsewhere*, Plato's least ironic political discourse, in the most numerous places of the platonic 'corpus,' especially in the *Republic*, with regard, precisely, to the political enemy *qua* πόλεμος or στάσις" (p. 103).

29. Glaukon's readiness for war on account of his fascination with greatness cannot be sidestepped as an accidental or idiosyncratic feature. Thucydides' *Peloponnesian War* illuminates the degree to which, on the contrary, it is exemplary. In this text greatness is variously associated with war. In the first place, the event of war itself is proudly said to bear the mark of greatness. The author devotes many introductory pages to the comparative evaluation of the greatness of wars that had occurred in the past and more recently, in order to substantiate his view that no previous war compares to the one which has shaken the Peloponnesus. This has been, he states in the opening lines, "the greatest" (μεγίστη) upheaval (see also, e.g., 1.XXIII.1–2). Secondly, as is ubiquitously observed

in the historical account, the enterprise of war bespeaks a certain greatness—reputation, even fame, is related to it. Finally, war is caused by and rooted in the greatness (in the sense of hypertrophic growth) of the city. As is well known, according to Thucydides, the genuine cause of the Peloponnesian war was not the political unrest in the city of Epidamnos. Rather, the underlying reasons eventually leading to the conflict were, he "believed" (ἡγοῦμαι), "the growth of the Athenians to greatness" (τοὺς Ἀθηναίους . . . μεγάλους γιγνομένους) and the "fear" (φόβον) this provoked at Sparta (1.XXIII.6).

30. Among other things, the logic of expansion entails an overcoming of the perception of the land (χώρα) in terms of motherland, that is, as a unique, utterly singular place. Indeed, the process of conquest of the neighbor's land rests on a progressive generalization and abstraction of the understanding of place (χώρα, even τόπος). In appropriating neighboring land one no longer perceives it as inassimilable receptacle, but rather thinks of it as *more land* being annexed, as the readily measurable addition of a homogeneous quantity. This already announces the concept (nowhere to be found in the ancient Greek insight) of space.

31. Curiously enough, in the *Politicus* 291a–b, with the phrase "a certain Pamphylian race" (Πάμφυλόν τι γένος) the Stranger indicates the sophists. Here the sophists (this "race of all tribes") are described as beasts of several kinds, from lions to centaurs, but especially as satyrs and chameleons, polytropic beasts (beasts of many turns) which can assume each other's "shapes (ἰδέας) and power (δύναμιν)" with great rapidity. The souls in the daimonic place, as Er envisions them, follow the movement of migration from one embodiment to the other, across discontinuities and forgetfulness, across abysmally differing lives, forms of life, bodies even other than human.

32. "Be bold and speak" (ἀλλὰ θαρρήσας λέγε), urges Glaukon (451b).

V. Vision

> Yes. Sometimes I write Necessity with a capital N. That is to say it
> is a singular necessity, not simply the law, but Necessity, the other
> which I cannot escape. And, in the present case, affirmation, such
> affirmation means Necessity. You cannot but have already traced
> the trace, and this has to do with a singular experience, with
> Anánke, a singular situation, whose singularity is Necessity.
>
> JACQUES DERRIDA

The myth of Er begins with the barrenness (ἀγονία) of a battlefield after
the struggle (ἀγών) and agony (ἀγωνία) of war. It begins with a momentary arrest of becoming (ἀγονία: privation of γονή and γονεία, of γενέσθαι), with a
lapse, an interruption of movement, with that moment of silence and emptiness
which marks the consummation of the undertaking of war (the ἄγειν and
ἀγωγή of ἀγών), when all life seems to have fled. On the battlefield everything
is now at rest. This theater of movement is now an empty space marked by a
withdrawal.

And yet this moment of utter suspension is but the promise and incubation
of an other movement. Harbored (carried) within the motionless landscape,
protected by the desolate screen of what appears after the war, invisibly, movement is already beginning to unfold anew. This seems to be so, at least, according to the words that Er reportedly said when he came back up to life—when,
that is, after ten days, he was brought away from the battlefield and resurged.
For, apparently, on the twelfth day, "as he was lying on the pyre, he came back
to life (ἀνεβίω) and, come back to life (ἀναβιοὺς), he told what he saw in the
other place (ἔλεγεν ἃ ἐκεῖ ἴδοι)" (614b).

While dead to his world, Er traveled to another world—to a world other
than the one in which he fought, albeit not necessarily else*where*. The movement of this journey unfolded in the shadow of his corpse, sheltered from the
glowing of images that light up in this world and can be shared. Er went away,
unseen, while remaining as a dead body. He went away, invisible—especially to
those who came and picked up his remains. Only an unreadable trace was left
behind: the body still intact, healthy (ὑγιής), as it were.[1]

The story Er apparently narrated, then, would be the recollection of a journey to an other place, indeed, to a most foreign place. His story is an attempt at carrying that place over, at translating that place into this place, after coming back or, even, *in* coming back. It is an attempt at preserving and articulating an uncanny vision, at bringing the uncanny back *from* that other place, in fact, *as* that place itself (which, let this be repeatedly emphasized, can only equivocally be called a place). Indeed, such a vision disclosed itself to him as he was wandering through a place incommensurable with the place to which he returns—a place radically discontinuous with, although inseparable from, the place of his reawakening (that of the funeral pyre and, more broadly, of his people gathered to mourn and perform the rites of burial). Er's translation, the transposition of that place into this place, gestures toward the uncanny that accompanies, pervades, belongs to, and simultaneously disrupts the everyday. It is, furthermore, the translation of someone who is himself being translated, of someone who crosses the threshold of death and comes back through it again—who, in journeying far away and returning, in moving back and forth through the only seemingly diaphanous membranes between worlds, across the quiet, dark night and the many rifts of disappearance and oblivion, simultaneously covers and undergoes the disintegrating impact of radical discontinuity.

The translation Er offered of his journey, when he came back, is the translation *of* the one who was not, or not simply, present to his own traversing, not self-same throughout his passage—the speaking *of* the one who was seized by a movement not of his own and who lost (sight of) himself. In a certain sense, offering such narration, translating such passing through another world into the words of this world, translating that other place for those of this world, translating one's own being-translated (that is to say, transiting, being-in-transition) is a way of reconstituting oneself again, after the excesses of such moving, sinking, and disappearing, after the disruption and loss of oneself. However, in another sense, such offering (the offering of yet another translation) confirms the excessive character of the narration, of the experience narrated, and of the narrator as well. Like a continuation of the journey, the narration exposes the one who has come back, who now speaks, as someone other than the one who left. It calls attention to a return that is out of joint with respect to the departure. Not only, then, does such a traveler-narrator move to and from worlds incommensurable with one another, but he himself is incommensurable with himself. For, throughout his wanderings, he does not subsist intact, ready to effect measurements. The narration-translation calls attention to the condition of the one who hovers between worlds, who bears and holds worlds together—worlds which belong together, and yet cannot simply be conjoined. It discreetly indicates that one will never simply have been somewhere or someone, let alone one.

Beyond the Gateway

At least according to the words attributed to Er, thus, for the warrior the battlefield is the gateway to other-worldly places—to the topological disclosure of an other world, or to places otherwise than worldly. The barren land after the war secretly bears life returning. In the midst of the stillness of the scattered remains an other movement, a journey, is initiated. The scene of the battlefield, then, is that of a beginning, of an initiation, even. From the battlefield, the warrior is translated to the places (indeed, in the plural) of rebirth.

It should be noticed that, through this journey enveloped within and taking place beyond the images of this world, through this journey across the imageless domain of death and the blindness of the dead, through this crossing itself invisible and protected from the vision shared in this world, more images are disclosed. After the brilliance of this world has faded out, absorbed by the dissolving obscurity of death, still other images arise. The departure from this world does not involve a transcendence of imaginal shining, but rather the celebration of it. It is said that, upon his return, Er recounted what he "had seen" (ἴδοι) beyond the gateway.[2]

Socrates continues with his indirect narration of the story of Er, evoking it from a distance, as it were, in its remoteness and mediated character. It reports the spectacle of the manifold movement of life contemplated by a ψυχή (by that which lives). This is the first station on the course of Er's soul:

> He said that when his soul departed (ἐκβῆναι τὴν ψυχήν), it made a journey in the company of many (πορεύεσθαι μετὰ πολλῶν), and they came (ἀφικνεῖσθαι) to a certain demonic place (τόπον τινὰ δαιμόνιον), where there were two chasms (χάσματα) in the earth (γῆς) next to one another, and, again, two in the heaven (οὐρανοῦ), above and opposite the others. Between them sat judges (δικαστὰς) who, when they had passed judgment, ordered the just to continue the journey (κελεύειν πορεύεσθαι) to the right and upward, through the heaven (τὴν εἰς δεξιάν τε καὶ ἄνω διὰ τοῦ οὐρανοῦ); and they attached signs of the judgments in front of them (σημεῖα . . . τῶν δεδικασμένων ἐν τῷ πρόσθεν). The unjust they told to continue the journey to the left and down (τὴν εἰς ἀριστεράν τε καὶ κάτω), and they had behind them signs of everything they had done (ἐν τῷ ὄπισθεν σημεῖα πάντων ὧν ἔπραξαν). And when he himself came forward, they said that he had to become a messenger to human beings (ἄγγελον ἀνθρώποις γενέσθαι) of the things in that place (τῶν ἐκεῖ), and they exhorted (διακελεύοιντό) him to listen and to look at (ἀκούειν τε καὶ θεᾶσθαι) everything in the place (ἐν τῷ τόπῳ). He saw (ὁρᾶν) there, at one of the chasms of both heaven and earth, the souls going away (ἀπιούσας) when judgment had been passed on them. As to the other two chasms, souls out of the earth, full of dirt and dust (ἐκ τῆς γῆς μεστὰς αὐχμοῦ τε καὶ κόνεως), came up (ἀνιέναι) from one of them;

and from the other came down (καταβαίνειν) other souls, pure from heaven (ἐκ τοῦ οὐρανοῦ καθαράς). And the souls that were ever arriving (ἀεὶ ἀφι-κνουμένας) looked as though they had come from a long journey (ὥσπερ ἐκ πολλῆς πορείας φαίνεσθαι ἥκειν): and they went away (ἀπιούσας) with delight to the meadow, and set up camp (κατασκηνᾶσθαι) there as at a public festival (ἐν πανηγύρει). (614c–d)

This preparatory passage leading into the story proper calls for a number of remarks. In the first place, the exhortative, indeed, authoritative mood of the judges' addresses should be noticed. The judges admonish, compel, order (κελεύω, διακελεύομαι). It is in such fashion that they address the souls to be judged as well as Er's. Socrates had resorted to this same terminology at the outset of the dialogue, when recalling the way in which he and Glaukon were prevented from going up to town and brought back down. At that time Polemark-hos, transmitting his order to wait through his slave boy, quite effectively managed to reach the two friends and block their ascent. Analogously, in the daimonic place Er's soul is sorted out, denied the continuation of its journey, and assigned an other task. Instead of moving further into that other world, Er's soul must return to this world and tell what it has heard (ἀκούω) and seen (θεωρέω) in the place beyond. The order to become a messenger (ἄγγελος) for the other human beings means just this. In the light of this later analogy between Socrates' predicament and the unusual destiny of Er's soul, the hypothesis put forth above (concerning the necessity, indeed, ineluctability of Socrates' descent, detention, and visit with those down below) imposes itself retrospectively with an even greater force.

Despite Socrates' systematic avoidance of facile identifications with the voices he echoes in his narration, the convergence of the figure of the philosopher and that of Er can hardly be dismissed and, in fact, presents itself with increasing definition. The tension between, on the one hand, the Socratic distance from the mythical material recalled and, on the other hand, the undeniable, if not fully readable, analogy holding Socrates' and Er's ventures together just makes the juxtaposition of the two characters more provocative. The mirror play between the two stories, indeed, reveals a common eidopoietic ground—which may not be represented as the purely formal and calculable principle structuring, informing, underlying the elaboration of the two figures in action but, at the same time, *is not nothing.*

Just like Er, then, the philosopher must be a messenger, hovering between worlds and weaving them together in their irreducibility. He must always come back and speak, recount, relate what he has observed, that is, undergone.[3] In this respect it might be opportune to point out the ubiquity, in the Platonic dialogues, of the characterization of the philosopher as a messenger. It might, in fact, be appropriate to mention a few passages elucidating such proximity (even identity) of, on the one hand, the love of wisdom and, on the other, the gathering of worlds which the messenger effects.[4] Even marginally doing justice to the exceedingly difficult passages quoted below, selected from dialogues other than that on the πολιτεία, will be impossible—just as it will be impossible, through the brief mention of these fragments abstracted from their backdrop, to evoke the broader context of each discussion and the slight shifts, the significant discontinuities between different dialogues. Citing a few exemplary moments of the discussions of the philosopher-messenger from otherwise heterogeneous sources, however, is a risk that must be taken in the attempt to cast light on the pervasiveness of such theme and on its many ramifications.

Metaxú

In the *Theaetetus*, Socrates draws an essential connection between philosophy and wonder and, somewhat unexpectedly, ends up identifying philosophy with the figure of Iris, the rainbow and messenger of the gods. In his words, "wonder (τὸ θαυμάζειν) is the condition (πάθος) of the philosopher. Philosophy indeed has no other origin (ἀρχὴ), and he didn't make a bad genealogy (οὐ κακῶς γενεαλογεῖν) who fittingly said that Iris is the child of Thaumas (Θαύμαντος ἔκγονον)" (155d). The reference is to the genealogist Hesiod, who, in the *Theogony*, tells of the generation of "swift (ὠκεῖαν) Iris" from Thaumas and Elektra, "the daughter of deep-flowing Okeanos (Ὠκεανοῖο)" (265 f.). "Swift-footed (πόδας ὠκέα) Iris, daughter of Thaumas," is mentioned again later in the poem as the one who "comes and goes (πωλεῖται, goes back and forth) over the wide ridges of the sea bringing a message (ἀγγελίην)" (780 f.). Just like Iris, then, the philosopher (besides being marked, signed, indeed, engendered by wonder) is disclosed as "swift-footed," as the one whose being is (in) motion and who, in (as) such motion, connects, transmits, weaves paths, and bridges holding together what is apart.

In the *Cratylus*, by juxtaposing Iris and Hermes both in terms of their function and in terms of the etymology of their respective names, Socrates adds another facet to the figure of the messenger. In this case the operation of the messenger is emphatically juxtaposed to that of the interpreter, of the thief, and of those who master speech in cunning and deceptive ways. For, indeed, speech always allows for that, always lends itself to being utilized in like manner—such is the power of speech and simultaneously its defenselessness. The passing along, handing over, and sending forth which constitute the task of the messenger, then, are situated within the problematic framework of linguistic dynamics—even more exactly, of linguistic comportment. Says Socrates:

Well then, Hermes seems to have to do with speech (περὶ λόγον τι εἶναι), to be an interpreter (ἑρμηνέα) and a messenger (ἄγγελον) and a thief and wily in speech (ἐν λόγοις) and a bargainer (ἀγοραστικόν); all this activity (πραγ-ματεία) has to do with the power of speech (περὶ λόγου δύναμίν ἐστιν). Now, as I said before, εἴρειν means the use of speech (λόγου χρεία ἐστί), and the word ἐμήσατό, which Homer often utters (λέγει), means to contrive (μη-χανήσασθαί ἐστιν). From both these words, then, the lawgiver imposes on us the name of the god who contrived (μησάμενον) speaking (τὸ λέγειν) and speech (τὸν λόγον)—for λέγειν means εἴρειν. O human beings, he who con-trived speaking (τὸ εἴρειν ἐμήσατο) should justly be called Εἰρέμης by you. We beautified the name, as we think, and call him Hermes. Iris also seems to have been called from εἴρειν, because she was a messenger (ἄγγελος).[5] (407e–408b)

Shortly after this statement, Socrates proceeds to explicate the irreducibly twofold character of speech by identifying it with Pan, the "double-natured (διφυῆ) son of Hermes" (408b). Speech is once again shown in its essential dynamism—as the tense gathering of opposites vertically arranged, indeed, as their improbable conjunction:

You know that speech indicates all things and always makes them circulate and move about (Οἶσθα ὅτι ὁ λόγος τὸ πᾶν σημαίνει καὶ κυκλεῖ καὶ πολεῖ ἀεί), and is twofold (διπλοῦς), true (ἀληθής) and false (ψευδής). . . . Well, the true part is smooth and divine (λεῖον καὶ θεῖον) and dwells above among the gods, but falsehood dwells below among the multitude of human beings, is rough and goatlike (τραχὺ καὶ τραγικόν); for tales (οἱ μῦθοί) and falsehoods (τὰ ψεύδη) are mostly there, around the goatlike life (περὶ τὸν τραγικὸν βίον). . . . Then Pan, who discloses (μηνύων) and always moves (ἀεὶ πολῶν) all (πᾶν), is rightly called goatherd (αἰπόλος), being the double-natured (διφυὴς) son of Hermes, smooth in his upper parts (ἄνωθεν), rough and like a goat (τραγοειδής) in his lower parts (κάτωθεν). And Pan, if he is the son of Hermes, is either speech (λόγος) or the brother of speech (λόγου ἀδελφὸς), and that brother resembles (ἐοικέναι) brother is not surprising (θαυμαστόν). But, as I said, O blessed man, let us move away from the gods. (408c–e)

In the *Phaedrus*, too, Socrates names "Pan the son of Hermes," along with "the Nymphs daughters of Akheloïos," as the source of inspiration of his own speak-ing (263d). It is within the framework of essentially bifurcated λόγος, the son of cunning Hermes and brother of two-natured Pan, or even identical with Pan "himself," that the task of the philosopher-courier should be situated.[6] It is in the context of such doubleness and motility that the philosophical πάθος begins to emerge in its many aspects. The philosopher does not simply move across gaps that cannot be recomposed, from one world to another, and back. Rather, the philosopher's own composure and oneness are radically lost in this movement, as is the possibility for an adequate, unambiguous account of the movement undertaken and undergone. The philosopher undergoes the rifts he traverses, is *himself* crossed and fissured, bears the marks and traces of a radical loss of simplicity. The bringing together of worlds involves, or perhaps simply *unveils*, a fundamental duplicity, a lack of unity and univocity. The philosopher is a literally amphibious being whose speaking can, in turn, only be amphibological.

The philosopher who hovers between worlds, holds worlds together in their strangeness and irreducibility, gathers the mutually alien *as such* and bears it in *himself* is also otherwise called with the name of Eros. Eros is acknowledged by Socrates as his "despot" in the *Phaedrus* (265d). But it is in the *Symposium* that the convergence of philosophical passion and erotic desire, and hence the inscription of the philosophical πάθος within the domain of daimonic compulsion, come to light. The lovers of wisdom (φιλοσοφοῦντες) are in an intermediate position (μεταξύ) between wisdom and ignorance, and Eros is one of them (204a–b). The love of wisdom and the love of the beautiful appear, then, as belonging in one and the same movement, in one and the same striving.

The philosopher-messenger shares with daimonic Eros his essentially medial and dynamic nature. For Eros, according to what Socrates says Diotima told him, is a "great daimon" (δαίμων μέγας), and "the whole of the daimonic is between divine and mortal" (πᾶν τὸ δαιμόνιον μεταξύ ἐστι θεοῦ τε καὶ θνητοῦ) (202e). Asked by Socrates about this daimon's power (δύναμις) and tasks, Diotima is said to have replied:

> Interpreting (Ἑρμηνεῦον) and carrying across (διαπορθμεῦον) to the gods what pertains to humans and to humans what pertains to the gods; entreaties and sacrifices from humans, and injunctions and requitals from the gods: being in the middle (ἐν μέσῳ) between the two it fills (συμπληροῖ), so that the whole is united with itself (συνδεδέσθαι). Through it come all divination and the priestly arts concerning sacrifice and initiations and incantations, and all divination and sorcery. The god does not mingle with the human being: but through the daimonic is all communion and discourse (διάλεκτος) from human beings to gods and from gods to human beings, whether waking or asleep; and whoever is wise (σοφὸς) in these matters is a daimonic man (δαιμόνιος ἀνήρ); being wise in other matters, as in arts (τέχνας) and crafts (χειρουργίας), is for the mechanical. Many and multifarious are these δαίμονες, and one of them is Eros. (202e–203a)

This characterization of Eros, Socrates' daimonic ruler, illuminates yet an other facet of the philosophical nature. The philosopher is disclosed as medium—not simply as one whose task is crossing the boundary between worlds and translating, transposing the one into the other, but also and primarily as one who *dwells* in between mutually extraneous regions and whose gathering operation rests precisely on such an intermediate position, on such hovering midway and pervading (filling) the gap between worlds. In this sense the philosopher is revealed as one who is, properly speaking, not at home in either world—as one who does not dwell anywhere or whose dwelling should be understood in a quite peculiar sense, as the inhabiting of a place that is no ordinary place, as the inhabiting of the limit and of the frontier. The philosopher is the being who dwells in that place of passage and transit—who, in the most pregnant sense of the phrase, dwells in passing.

Finally, it should be at least briefly mentioned that, according to the specific nature of the daimon Eros, the philosopher is in an important sense connected with generation—with the constant metamorphosis and the self-perpetuation of the realm of becoming. Diotima, in fact, apparently said that the comportment (τρόπος), practice (πρᾶξις), or work (ἔργον) to be termed erotic, that for which the lover uniquely strives, is nothing other than "giving birth (τόκος) in the beautiful (ἐν καλῷ) both in relation to the body (κατὰ τὸ σῶμα) and in relation to the soul (κατὰ τὴν ψυχήν)" (206b). The foreigner from Mantinea is said to have explained her statement to Socrates as follows:

> All human beings are pregnant (κυοῦσι), Socrates, in relation to both body and soul, and when reaching a certain age (ἡλικίᾳ) our nature desires to give birth (τίκτειν ἐπιθυμεῖ ἡμῶν ἡ φύσις). It cannot give birth in the ugly but in the beautiful. The conjunction (συνουσία) of man and woman is giving birth (τόκος). It is a divine deed (πρᾶγμα), and in the mortal creature (ζῴῳ) there is this which is immortal, conception (κύησις) and engendering (γέννησις); and it cannot occur (ἀδύνατον γενέσθαι) in the discordant. The ugly is discordant (ἀνάρμοστον) with everything divine, whereas the beautiful is accordant (ἁρμόττον). Thus, Beauty (Καλλονή) is Fate (Μοῖρα) and Eileíthuia [the goddess who assists women in childbirth] for generation (γενέσει). When, therefore, the pregnant (κυοῦν) approaches the beautiful it becomes gracious, and, cheering up, it spreads and gives birth (τίκτει) and engenders (γεννᾷ); but when it approaches the ugly, then, sullen and distressed, it coils itself up and turns away and shrinks up and does not engender (γεννᾷ), but, holding fast that which is conceived (κύημα), bears it with difficulty. Therefore, in the one who is pregnant (κυοῦντί) and ripe an intense passion for the beautiful comes to be, for this can relieve the one who possesses it from the pains of travail. For love (ἔρως), Socrates, is not of the beautiful, as you think. . . . It is of engendering (γεννήσεως) and giving birth (τόκου) in the beautiful. (206c–e)

The erotic (and hence philosophical) task, then, is conceiving, bearing, and giving birth—making generation and regeneration possible, keeping the cycle of procreation in movement. Eros the philosopher is made manifest as a force, a striving involved in the self-renewal of life. The erotic and philosophical passion is, thus, linked to the mystery of the immortality of becoming, that is to say, of everything mortal.

The philosopher, then (this Erotico-Hermetic traveler, warrior and narrator, translator and interpreter, messenger and medium, pregnant lover and midwife), will have been a daimonic being. The lover of wisdom and of learning is the one who experiences and dwells in the daimonic. In the myth concluding the dialogue on the πολιτεία, let this be said by way of anticipation, the daimon, chosen by the ψυχή as "a guardian (φύλακα) of the life (βίου) and a fulfiller of what was chosen (ἀποπληρωτὴν τῶν αἱρεθέντων)," will lead (ἄγειν) the ψυχή away from the presence of Necessity and her daughters, into the new mortal cycle, and throughout the existence chosen (620d–e). The daimon is, therefore, presented as the governing principle, the driver, the charioteer, even, of the ψυχή as it makes the circuit. In brief, it is presented as *comportment*.[7]

But it is now time to return to the beginning of the story of Er—to the story of the philosopher-ἄγγελος coming to a daimonic place between heaven and earth.

Souls in a Meadow

Er's soul departs and proceeds "in the company of many." Despite the fact that such a journey is a moving away from this world of sharing and from what can be shared in this world, Er does not travel alone. This is no solitary trip away from the multitude and from the community of the many. The being-together essentially characterizing the condition of humans in this world is not contrasted to an enterprise undertaken without companions, in ascetic isolation. Rather, away from the world of involvement and entanglement, Er's soul is still on its way with many, still sharing its way with them. The transition seems to be from one way of sharing to an other and reveals the irreducibility of sharing to commonality, to having in common. This transition, then, does not point to something other than being-together, but rather to an other (way of) being-together.

In the daimonic place, however, Er must, according to the order of the judges, part from the souls in the company of which he arrived there. These, after being judged, continue their travel either through the sky or through the earth, but Er is ordered to remain and observe everything there. He, then, finds himself in the company of those who, passing through the chasms in the sky and in the earth, arrive from their long journey and go "with delight to the meadow (λειμῶνα), as at a public festival (πανηγύρει)," in order to "set up camp there" (κατασκηνᾶσθαι) (614e). These are the souls which, having completed their journey in those places, are preparing themselves to be reborn. They, Socrates says in recalling Er's words,

> told stories to one another (διηγεῖσθαι δὲ ἀλλήλαις), the ones lamenting and crying, remembering (ἀναμιμνησκομένας) how much and what sort of things they had suffered and seen (πάθοιεν καὶ ἴδοιεν) in the journey under the

> earth . . . and those from heaven, in their turn, told (διηγεῖσθαι) of the in-conceivable beauty (ἀμηχάνους τὸ κάλλος) of the experiences (εὐπαθείας) and the sights (θέας) there. (614e–615a)

Like refugees, the souls gather and share the stories of their passages. Again, it should briefly be pointed out that these discourses are for the most part reported by Socrates indirectly. However, for the narration of the monstrous punishment reserved to Ardiaeus and certain other tyrants, Socrates resorts to direct speech, as though after the fashion of Er himself:

> For he said (ἔφη) he was there (παραγενέσθαι) when a man was asked by an-other, "Where is Ardiaeus the Great?" This Ardiaeus had been a tyrant in a certain city of Pamphylia just a thousand years before that time; he had, as was said (ὡς ἐλέγετο), killed his own father and elder brother and done many other unholy deeds. Now, Er said (ἔφη), the man asked responded (εἰπεῖν), "He hasn't come. Nor will he come here," he asserted (φάναι). "For this, too, of course, was one of the terrible sights we saw. When we were near the mouth about to go up (μέλλοντες ἀνιέναι) and had suffered (πεπονθότες) every-thing else, we suddenly (ἐξαίφνης) saw him and others. Just about all of them were tyrants, but there were also some private men, of those who had com-mitted great faults. They supposed they were ready to go up (ἀναβήσεσθαι), but the mouth did not admit them; it roared when one of those whose bad-ness is incurable or who had not paid a sufficient penalty attempted to go up (ἀνιέναι)." (615c–e)

But this rather exceptional passage is punctuated with indications of the medi-ated and indirect character of Socrates' narration. Socrates insistently empha-sizes the citatory nature of his own saying by bringing it back to what Er appar-ently "said" (ἔφη . . . ἔλεγεν . . . διηγεῖτο) (615a–616a). He also underlines the fact that Er himself did not directly witness the occurrences related by those who traveled down below, but simply "was there" (παραγενέσθαι) when the souls recounted them (615c). Such subtle and consistent marking of the dis-tance from the material narrated counteracts the con-fusion and identification of the mimetic lie—although, let this be noticed in passing, the insistence on the speaker in the third person occasionally makes Er's voice and that of the soul he happened to hear indiscernible. Socrates never fully disappears behind that which he recounts, never fully becomes (speaks in unison with) the one(s) of whom he recounts. Attention is constantly called to a fundamental lack of syn-chronicity between the elements of discourse—to storytelling as repetition, as a saying not purely originary and originating, never purely uttered for the first time.

But what is above all crucial to underline here is the cause necessitating the souls' experiences in the underground or through the sky. The souls articulate an account of the journeys assigned to them in terms of the logic of retribution and reward. It is the kind of life they lived which determines in what direction they must continue their journey, whether through underground tunnels and receptacles or on heavenly paths. It is according to the life they lived that the nature of their stay, whether beneath or above, is established along with the kind of experiences and visions which will present themselves in the course of the sojourn. The souls must pay penalty (δίκην διδωκέναι) "ten times over" for anything unjust they did while living—the more extreme the injustice committed, all the more severe the conditions of the underground travel and nightmarish the experiences involved (615a–d). And although the souls' journey is said normally to last a thousand years, those who have not paid "a sufficient penalty" or whose "badness" (πονηρία) is incurable cannot "go up" (615e). Just like Socrates in the opening of the dialogue, the souls who suppose they are ready to ascend, but are not, are detained—they cannot pass through the opening which, like a roaring mouth, sends them back.

"Such," concludes Socrates, "were the penalties (δίκας) and punishments (τιμωρίας); and, on the other hand, the bounties (εὐεργεσίας) were the antistrophes of these" (616a). Nothing specific is said about the passage of the just souls across the sky. Socrates simply suggests that it should be understood as a specular reversal of the passage through the earth. Thus, one can conjecture that, whereas for the souls traveling in the underworld the prolongation of their stay must be a punishment, for those traveling above and experiencing inconceivable delight the prolongation of their stay should be a reward. Again, for the souls in the underground, not being admitted back up, not being allowed to come back to life, is certainly a curse—for it entails remaining in that place of utter gloom. To the souls moving above, conversely, not being called back down, not having to return to life again, might appear to be the highest recompense. It is not clear, from Socrates' repetition of Er's story, whether there are souls which, because of their superlative wickedness or goodness, completely escape the law of circulation, the circular movement between worlds, the endless returns to this life—and indefinitely dwell beneath or above.[8] What is nevertheless quite evident is that the logic of reward and retribution does not so much, or not exclusively, have to do with what awaits the soul after death. Rather, to the administration of punishment and recompense, to the principle governing such apportionment, are linked the possibility of living again in this world and the modality of the next life. (More will need to be said on this.)

A related remark should be introduced at this point, which will require further consideration. The courses which the souls must follow are determined through the evaluation of the justice and injustice informing the life each soul led. This is to say that the overall circulation of the ψυχαί is ordered according to justice—or, even, that the order of their movement *is* justice. In this way, justice is disclosed as the order of life.[9] The attempt at gaining an insight into the essence of justice, then, would be a striving to unveil the truth of life—the truth of its immortal returning and, more precisely, of the order and modality of these returns. The investigation of justice, in brief, would seem to yield elements essential to the understanding of how and why the souls come back.

At this juncture, however, it is necessary to proceed very cautiously, perhaps to pause, or even to go back and start anew—to repeat and start once again from the beginning, namely, from the circumstances of the journey of the ψυχαί.

In the characterization of the daimonic scene it is possible to discern, as if against the light, the traits of the place down by the sea, the main features of the environment at the harbor where the dialogue began. In the rendition of the daimonic place between earth and sky (indeed, on the surface of the earth) one sees the port transfigured—its crowd in movement, those arriving and those departing, those coming and those going, ascending and descending, the fatigue and sweat of the journey, the encounters, the settling down for a pause, as if for a public assembly in honor of some deity. All this, unmistakably, reminds one of the opening lines in Book I. In fact, one is even struck by the altogether mundane tenor of the description of what is supposed to be a psychological journeying and, instead, turns out to involve efforts comparable to those of miners in the bowels of the earth, the setting up of tents for rest and refreshment, the bearing of conventional signs, whether in front or behind, and other such details. One is struck, that is, not only by the spatio-temporal structure of the daimonic place, which quite consistently redoubles that of the world left behind, but also and especially by all those narrative elements (the indication of gender, the phenomenological tenor of the accounts of psychological vicissitudes, the sense of transience and tentativeness) which evidently suggest an understanding of the ψυχαί as embodied and, hence, as virtually indiscernible from the ἄνθρωποι and, more broadly, from the living. Eventually, one also wonders whether the place and unfolding of this journey could at all be rendered otherwise than according to the structures of experience in and of this world—whether, in other words, the spatiality and materiality of this world disclosed through experience could simply be expunged from language, or whether, on the contrary, they might turn out to be an ineliminable element both of experience here and of its discursive articulation.

The Image of the Law

Analogously to the opening scene, then, the daimonic place is disclosed as the intersection of various courses and trajectories to and from other worlds. And yet the story of Er, this repetition, transfiguration, and translation of the dialogical articulation, presents a genuinely novel feature with respect to the previous discussions. The myth of Er completes the dialogue, bringing to it an element without which it could not properly find a rest, namely, the elucidation (or, more precisely, the imagination, envisioning, figuration) of the logic underlying and sustaining motion.

Thus, the concluding ἀπόλογος does not merely reenact the movement of a preceding moment of the dialogue, or even of the dialogue as a whole. It does not merely present a transposition of the journeying previously discussed or performed. Rather, it also shows what governs, what presides over movement. It *shows the law* of movement. In the myth, indeed, not only is the all-encompassing movement of the ψυχαί and of the κόσμος itself depicted, within whose frame alone each singular motion can be properly situated, not only is such comprehensive dynamism presented as unfolding in a rhythmic, orderly fashion—but, furthermore, the source and bestowal of order are revealed. This is the exquisitely original contribution of the final narration and what makes its function unique. The flow of crowds (human and otherwise) is made manifest in its regularity and in its belonging in a general mobility harmoniously composed. Far from occurring randomly, the various modes of motion are shown in their belonging in a broader (in fact, the broadest) polyphony. They are brought back to a profound unity of pitch, pulse, and rhythm. Here, already, one is caught at the intersection of two simultaneously concomitant and diverging questions. On the one hand, one wonders how that which would paradigmatically defy showing, imaging, let alone imitation—how that which seems utterly discontinuous and excessive with respect to the imaginal-imaginative domain can be shown. On the other hand, one wonders whether such law, and the unity it grants, could be said otherwise than mythically, that is to say, otherwise than imaginally or indicatively—whether such law could be said at all and not, at most, shown or sung.

In disclosing the circular motions of the souls (moving back and forth from life to death and back to life), the μῦθος articulates the order (justice, law) at once governing the psychic migration (i.e., informing the ἦθος of the souls in death and life) and presiding over the becoming of the cosmos. This vision inscribes ethical necessity within the sphere of cosmic (natural) necessity, thus showing them in their essential conjunction. Necessity itself is brought to the fore, as it were—exposed in its all-encompassing centrality. By supplementing the previous discussions in this way, the concluding ἀπόλογος crowns the dialogue.

The μῦθος of Er intimates the harmonious, that is, at once complex and unitary articulation of movement already in its initial stage, through the figure of the judges. It is they who regulate the circulation of souls and prescribe the kind of trajectories to be followed. The source and principle of the ordering operation of judgment is not revealed, yet, but its servants and representatives are shown at work already—judging, assigning, directing, conducting. The reason operative behind it all, of which the judges are but the executors and pale reflection, will be elaborated (that is to say, depicted) shortly thereafter, through the contemplation of the κόσμος. According to Er's narration, the souls, after a sojourn of seven days in the daimonic place of judgment and four days of travel, come to see (καθοράω) "a straight light, like a column, stretched from above through all of heaven and earth, most of all resembling the rainbow (μάλιστα τῇ ἴριδι προσφερῆ), but brighter (λαμπρότερον) and purer (καθαρώτερον)" (616b). They travel one more day and draw closer to the dazzling, ἶρις-like pillar. Here, "at the middle of the light," they see (εἴδω, ὁράω) "the extremities of its bonds (τὰ ἄκρα αὐτοῦ τῶν δεσμῶν) stretched from heaven; for this light is that which binds heaven (ξύνδεσμον τοῦ οὐρανοῦ), like the undergirders (ὑποζώματα) of a trireme, thus holding the entire revolution together (πᾶσαν ξυνέχον τὴν περιφοράν)" (616c).[10] It is in the proximity of the stream of light that the souls are admitted to behold the spindle of Necessity and, more precisely, the system of eight concentric whorls and the intricate pattern of their relations according to dimension, color, direction, and swiftness of rotation.

At the center of this vision sits Necessity, immobile and silent. It should be recalled that in Book II, in moving away from the first "healthy" city to the "feverish" one, Socrates and his interlocutors seemed to have left behind the order of "the necessary" (τὰ ἀναγκαῖα) (373a), undertaking to explore human community in its irreducibility to (even freedom from) necessity and its bonds. It is quite noteworthy, then, that the discourse crowning the dialogue should reorient itself to necessity—that it should culminate with a presentation of necessity, however profoundly metamorphosed into Necessity. But, of course, as pointed out above, a certain claim of necessity (in fact, a claim demanding a most profound rethinking of the question of necessity) was already foreshadowed, indeed, prescribed, by the necessitating discourse of the Muses in Book VIII.[11] There seems to be an essential bond between that which pertains to the Muses (Music) and necessity. In this sense not only will the dialogue have had to culminate with a discourse around necessity, but, at the same time, the conclusion in the musical-mythical form will have been necessary. Hence, the paradoxical appropriateness of the ending μῦθος of Ἀνάγκη.

All movement rippling the surface of images, sustaining the life of the soul, and pervading the entire universe originates here, somewhere *in the proximity of* this female figure of whom nothing more is said in the myth and who, in this myth, says nothing. Socrates recalls Er's testimony as follows:

> The spindle turned in the lap (ἐν τοῖς . . . γόνασιν) of Necessity (Ἀνάγκῃ).
> Above, on each of its circles (ἐπὶ δὲ τῶν κύκλων), stood a Siren, accompany-

ing its revolution (συμπεριφερομένην), uttering one sound (φωνὴν μίαν), one note (ἕνα τόνον); from all eight is produced the accord of a single harmony (μίαν ἁρμονίαν ξυμφωνεῖν). Three others are seated (καθημένας) round about at equal distances (δι' ἴσου), each on a throne. Daughters of Necessity, Fates (Μοίρας)—Lákhesis, Klothó, and Átropos—clad in white (λευχειμο-νούσας) with wreaths on their heads, they sing hymns (ὑμνεῖν) to the Sirens' harmony (ἁρμονίαν), Lákhesis of what has been (τὰ γεγονότα), Klothó of what is (τὰ ὄντα), Átropos of what is going to be (τὰ μέλλοντα). And Klothó puts her right hand to the outer revolution (περιφοράν) of the spindle and joins in turning it, ceasing from time to time (διαλείπουσαν χρόνον); and Átropos with her left hand does the same to the inner ones; but Lákhesis puts one hand to one and the other hand to the other, each in turn. (617b–c)

Unlike the errant, wandering necessity discussed in the *Timaeus*, Necessity is here presented as motionless[12]—outlined as the unmoved origin and center of all movement, as the timeless, impassible source of time and becoming. Quite fittingly, one would want to say, especially after Aristotle. But perhaps this appropriateness is only apparent—or, in fact, all too apparent. Perhaps such necessity, in its immobility, may be as disorienting and straying as the necessity elsewhere said to be wandering. The wandering of necessity and her enigmatic stillness may both be figures of the same illegibility. For it is not the fixity of necessity as a logical principle that this μῦθος-λόγος thematizes—not the motionlessness of a law apprehended in its purity, separate from the bodies and visions it governs.[13] Rather, it is the immobility of a seated woman, of the *appearance* of necessity, of Necessity always already personified, enacted, embodied—or, at least, imagined. It is the immobility of a phantasy and phantasm of necessity—Necessity evoked in her proper name and brought onto the stage, always already a phenomenon, the phenomenal appearing of origin, origin in its *physical* (φύσις-bound) incumbency.

This, of course, raises a number of questions. What does it mean that the all-encompassing order of necessity is strictly presented in images, in a language irreducibly ciphered and opaque? For such discourse of necessity, indeed, remains caught within the imaginal and imaginative, within the domain of imagination, without ever twisting free of its implications. Why would it be necessary or unavoidable to present necessity allegorically, literally to allude to necessity while speaking of something else (ἄλλο ἀγορεύω), indeed, of *someone* else—whose proper name is Necessity? Why this oblique discourse (in fact, a myth), which indicates necessity by indirection, by putting on stage a persona, a personification of necessity—by imaging necessity, transposing it into a female body? Why this theatrical detour of the proper name through image and body? Why the need of an actress (*if* she is an actress)? Can necessity be presented in no other guise? Can it not be presented on its own terms, *as itself, in no guise at all,* that is to say, *logically?* And what is the significance of the presentation of Necessity as a woman—a woman surrounded by her daughters? For, indeed, not only is necessity transposed into images and even (however imaginatively) embodied as an ἄνθρωπος, but the human being thus envisioned, the one bearing the proper name of Necessity, is a female.

One wonders whether this would be the imaginal transposition of what would autonomously subsist beyond and prior to the transposing, or whether such transposition may be grounding and originary with respect to that which is transposed and made visible. One wonders, in other words, whether necessity may be, to begin with and above all, a matter of sensibility. For, as imaginal and imagined, necessity would belong in the order of that which comes forth in effulgent glory and recedes, withdrawing from view, essentially unintelligible in its passing, that is, never self-same. Necessity would, in this sense, have to be thought *as* this coming forth and receding. But then, again, what would be shown in the myth would not be the constancy of necessity, the immutable presiding of necessity over the revolving life of the cosmos, over the journeys and choices of souls. What would thus be imaged would be the occurrence of all this—necessity as such occurring, recurring, becoming.[14]

Sphinx-like Necessity sits surrounded by her daughters. The three Moirai, remarkable offspring of unmoved Necessity, move the whorls—that is to say, originate movement and the opening up of time. It is opportune to point out, at least in passing, that in Hesiod's *Theogony* the three Moirai are said to be the offspring of Night, who generated them by herself, "having lain with no one" (213). This would suggest a rather noteworthy convergence of "baneful Night" and Necessity, the origin and principle of what is.[15] In this connection one can hardly avoid recalling that other solitary (mono-parental) generation discussed earlier in the dialogue, namely, that of the sun by the good. One will readily recall the celebrated passage in Book VI, where Socrates defines the sun as "the offspring of the good" (τὸν τοῦ ἀγαθοῦ ἔκγονον), that is, "an offspring the good begot in a proportion with itself (τἀγαθὸν ἐγέννησεν ἀνάλογον ἑαυτῷ)" (508c). Just as that other emanation from the good is the source of "generation, growth, and nourishment" (γένεσιν καὶ αὔξην καὶ τροφήν) (509b), so the daughters of Necessity are involved in the coming into being and passing away of that which is—in the bringing forth (unfolding, explicating) of what comes to be and in the withdrawing (enfolding, implicating) of what, having come into being, is always already passing away. Lákhesis, she who holds the lots for what has to come, sings of the past and, in so doing, presides over it. Klothó, who spins the thread of life (destiny), sings of the present. Átropos, the unbending, irreversibly sings (of) the future and rules over it. Together, they turn the revolutions of Anánke's spindle.

In the course of the dialogical unfolding, then, the issue of filiation and of descent undergoes a profound transformation—indeed, a shift in gender, from the patrilinear logic of the discourse concerning the good to the matrilinear imagery brought forth in the ending myth. This dialogue so critically organized around a most extraordinary paternity (that of the good) or, even, around the issue of paternity in general ends with the displacement of it. If in Book I Socrates may be seen challenging the institution of paternal authority, in later books his efforts to situate the question of justice (the order of the city as well as of the soul) under the aegis of the good may be understood as attempts at disclosing paternity (the father-son relation) in its perfection—at overcoming the conventional enactments of paternity and interrupting the automatisms of tribal belonging. In other words, such efforts may be seen as attempts at grounding paternity more primordially—*if*, that is, the hypereidetic status of the good could constitute a ground. And yet, or perhaps precisely because of the excessive character of the good with respect to being, at the end of this dialogue crucially revolving around the axis of the father-son relation and leading to the apotheosis of the good's sublime paternity, one finds a mother again—as if the dialogue would have drifted away from its center, or as if its center itself were drifting. One will have found a mother—and not a mother in principle, not an invisible, disembodied principle of maternity, but Anánke herself—as if the ascent were unthinkable, which would leave behind embodiment, the shining of phenomena, and the imagination that finds its life there.[16]

Thus, Necessity appears at the end of the dialogue that has wandered astray, away from the sublimation of paternity culminating in the good. She sits still, enigmatically silent, unreadable. Like judges, the Moirai are seated on their thrones, disposed in orderly fashion around their mother.[17] Solemnly dressed in white (λευχειμονούσας), they sing of "what is, what is to be, what was before" in the manner of the Hesiodic Muses, those who also taught Hesiod to celebrate "things future and those being before" (*Theogony* 38, 32). Once again, the invitation presents itself to think together the singing of the Muses, the bringing forth (the making present) which occurs through and as poetic saying or singing (ὑμνέω), the spinning of singular threads (lives, destinies, narrative trajectories) and their interlacing.[18] Order, the law of movement, would accordingly have to be understood as the rhythm of singing and spinning. Even more precisely, order would have to be understood as the holding together of the manifold rhythms, directions, tempos—of the melodic and harmonic, but also lexical and chromatic values variously intertwined. The law of movement would have to be understood as such a weaving, as *orditum*.[19]

Such is the source of all movement, that which grants the unity and harmony of all movement—of humans, of the living, and of what remains through and after death. Held together by a stream of light as if by undergirders, the vessel of the κόσμος, the vibrating totality it encompasses and is, moves according to the harmony of the Sirens and the turning, spinning, singing of the offspring of Necessity, under Necessity's quiet glance.[20]

It is in this light, then, that justice, the order of the living, should be understood—in its intimate connection with the moving ὑμνεῖν of Necessity's daughters, with the harmony of the Sirens accompanying the circular movement of Necessity's spindle, with the vibrant images of the scansion of living and dying. Justice is glimpsed through the complex image envisioned at the center of the κόσμος, through the vision of the κόσμος in its glowing and resonant unfolding. In this way justice is quite literally revealed, that is, shown according to the double logic of *re-velare*, which entails at once the pulling back and replacing of the *velum*. This central image reveals justice both essentially and enigmatically—exposes it, allows one to catch a glimpse of it, while already withdrawing and enveloping it within its thick veils.

The Choice of the Daimon

It is said that at this second stage of the journey, in the luminous vicinity of Necessity, the scene of a singular choice unfolds. Each soul is called to choose a mortal course into which to be born again, that is, it *must freely* choose that to which it will necessarily have been bound.[21] At this crucial juncture, the souls are led forth and deployed before Lákhesis. From the lap of the one who sings of the past, "a certain interpreter" (προφήτην . . . τινὰ) takes "the lots (κλήρους) and the patterns of lives (βίων παραδείγματα)" (617d).[22] Then the interpreter-spokesman breaks the silence reigning over that place and delivers a speech (λόγος) on behalf of Lákhesis, the daughter of Anánke.

It should be granted, incidentally, that in this context one speaks of silence in a somewhat paradoxical way. For, after all, this is the place of the resounding of hymns chanted by the Moirai to the harmonics of the Sirens. But this harmonization accompanying the revolutions (συμπεριφέρω) is the sound, the very voice of the cosmos, of φύσις itself in its movement, the rhythm (indeed, the time) of its emergence. In this sense such a symphony (literally, an accord of voices [617b]) is the element, the field of resonance of all voices, sounds, noises. Thus understood, the music of cosmic circling suddenly takes on a certain ineffable, even inaudible, character, to the point of sounding closer than ever to silence. At the heart of the κόσμος and of the myth, near the center from which movement propagates, the interpreter utters these words:

> This is the speech (λόγος) of Anánke's maiden daughter, Lákhesis. Souls that live a day (ψυχαὶ ἐφήμεροι), this is the beginning (ἀρχὴ) of another death-bringing cycle (περιόδου . . . θανατηφόρου) for the mortal race (θνητοῦ γέ-νους). A daimon will not select (λήξεται) you, but you will choose (αἱρήσ-

ἐσθε) a daimon. Let him who gets the first lot (πρῶτος δ' ὁ λαχὼν) make the first choice of a life (αἱρείσθω βίον) to which he will be bound by necessity (συνέσται ἐξ ἀνάγκης). Virtue is without a master (ἀδέσποτον); in honoring or dishonoring her, each will have more or less of her. The blame (αἰτία) is of the one who chooses (ἑλομένου); god is blameless (ἀναίτιος). (617d–e)

Once again, Socrates reports a discourse without mediation, in direct speech. This is the discourse of a prophet, of one who interprets and lets the message of a god pass through, who translates the message from a divine source and brings it into words. But these are also the traits of the philosophical task—hence, in a sense, the appropriateness of the direct quotation.

And yet the prophetic-interpretive discourse thus appropriated, reported without mediation, is itself essentially mediated already. The prophet-herald speaks for (delivers the message of) Lákhesis, who, in turn, speaks in the shadow and under the auspices of speechless, undecipherable Necessity. The discourse taken up and enacted by Socrates comes from afar, after countless perilous and inscrutable passages. It comes from afar, whether from a remote time and place or from the unfathomable and a-topic depth inhabiting one, whether inherited and repeated or occurring all of a sudden, out of no place. It comes, furthermore, as the pale echo of its no longer resounding (in fact, perfectly silent) origin, and, therefore, as a solitary, wandering echo. This is so not only for Socrates, who, after all, speaks of the whole venture of the souls on the ground of hearsay, but even for the spokesman of Lákhesis himself. Even this interpreter speaks (λέγει), can only speak in the distance from and of the source, that is, in its radical emptiness. The procession from the stillness and silence of Necessity, to the in-forming singing and motion of her daughters, to the discourse (the translating and interpreting) of the prophet is far from a linear, continuous, that is, quantifiable progression indeed. To such an extent is the origin of λόγος shrouded.

It is, then, in a highly qualified way that, in appropriating the words of Lákhesis's spokesman, Socrates embraces the imitative ἦθος involving the erasure of distance. For not only does Socrates identify himself with the one through whom an other speaks, that is, with some one essentially not self-identical (such is the essence of a medium or passageway), not only is the discourse immediately uttered by Socrates in itself utterly mediated, but, most importantly, the discourse has no recognizably legitimate origin. It presents itself as coming from a certain source, and yet it occurs in the silence of that source. It even discloses its own source as silent, that is, as withdrawing—imperceptible and illegible. This is so not because such a source would have spoken or written imperceptibly and illegibly, but because it will have said and written nothing. Necessity will have spoken only through a literally infinite work of recovery. Or, perhaps, she will have moved in circles and sung—indirectly, through engendering.

Whether or not Necessity has a voice of her own, even a λόγος, one is not told. What is said is that she does not say anything in her own voice. *If* she does have λόγος, it remains encrypted, hidden. Not only, then, is Anánke (Bendis, Night) illuminated in a critically circumscribed sense (she is shown by the pure glow of the column of light), but, even in this imaginal, mythical discourse, she cannot be brought (let alone forced) simply to speak, to speak simply, to declare who, what she is, the law she imparts. The mythical presentation of necessity as Necessity does not diminish, not even mythically, the difficulties inherent in the λόγος περὶ τῆς ἀνάγκης, but rather shows them as such.

But what is thus allowed to surface is not simply a certain aphasia, a stuttering of discourse. Indeed, by disclosing its origin as silent, the discourse ultimately discloses itself (the very gesture of disclosure) in terms of betrayal. For not only is Necessity not brought to speak, but the silence of Necessity is as such covered over and irrecoverably lost. The μῦθος, then, shows itself as a λόγος literally περὶ τῆς ἀνάγκης—as a λόγος surrounding Necessity, *as if* transpiring from her, yet articulating itself in a movement of immeasurable distancing and loss. Necessity is indeed said to sit surrounded by a singing and gesturing to which she is related (as a mother to her offspring) and from which, in turn, a λόγος unfolds proclaiming to translate the song of one of the daughters. She is, indeed, said to be surrounded by that which can be heard as her echo, as the echo of silence. Yet, at the same time, through the echoing saying, she is not as such (as silent) heard.

Socrates' direct recitation of this discourse, rather than dissimulating unbridgeable distances, ends up making clear that Socrates' own saving (repeating, transmitting) the echoes from an other world occurs at a dramatic remove from that world (just as the discourse of Lákhesis's spokesman occurs at a dramatic remove from its source) and in the impossibility of making unambiguous claims to adequacy or authority. In other words, not even the philosopher-messenger, this paradigmatically medial being who moves and dwells between worlds, who holds worlds together by bringing them into one another, speaks out of a direct exposure to the divine. Far from involving direct access to both worlds, the frequentation of the between comes to be disclosed as the dwelling in the midst of mediations and mediations of mediations—in the midst of never unequivocal signs. It comes to be disclosed as a lack of familiarity with these worlds—as the becoming strange of (and becoming a stranger to) these worlds, as a dwelling in wonder. The speaking (i.e., ordering, judging, and assigning) of the divine reaches this world in an indeterminately indirect, uncertain way—to say nothing of its music, and finally of its silence, which λόγος can only betray and of which λόγος may, if at all, bear the most volatile trace.[23] This, let it be briefly observed, among other things points to a certain impossibility of imitation, to a certain inimitable residue haunting imitation—precisely there where the conduct is unmistakably (in the manifold sense elucidated in Books III and X) imitative. The μῦθος does not, through the immediacy of fusion and the conjuring up of images, come to evoke that which cannot otherwise be said. Rather, in its imitative comportment the myth shows the limits of imitation, even of its lie. For there are "things" that cannot be imitated or copied, but at most recalled in their missing, in the delay of their presence—especially things unheard, unknown, perhaps unknowable.[24]

The souls, then, say the prophet, Er, and Socrates in one voice, are brought before the daughter of Anánke to begin another mortal cycle—a cycle which will not simply end in death, but bear (φέρω) death throughout. To the life chosen each soul will be bound by necessity: by the silent decree of necessity they will have to live. It is the choosing to which the souls are compelled, it is this decision, discernment, and exclusion which essentially determines the unfolding within and of becoming. It is the limitation, the privation inherent in choosing which shapes becoming and animates its movement. Choosing is the cause of the manner of coming into being and passing away of that which comes into being and passes away. That is why, whatever the course of life chosen will entail, whatever the direction in which becoming will evolve, "god is blameless," that is to say, not responsible, not the cause.[25] Those who choose (more precisely, those who must choose and have no other choice, who necessarily choose, whether prepared or not—and one will never simply have been prepared *for this*) do so at their own risk. For causing anything involves being radically exposed to blame, radically blameworthy. The spokesmen's pronouncement seems to suggest that realizing one's responsibility means to comprehend one's mortal course as something for some reason previously chosen and agreed upon, as a comedy, a play to enact. In this sense the responsibility spoken of here seems to imply bearing one's life in its turns and upheavals, *as if* knowing its plot and underlying reasons, without cursing or blaming "chance, demons, and anything" rather than oneself (619c). What the representatives seem to demand, ultimately, is the realization that this life is a task taken up—however much in the dark about its significance one might be.

The souls are bound to choose and will be bound to the choice made. They are bound to choose one of the "patterns of the lives (τὰ τῶν βίων παραδείγματα) on the ground before them" (618a). The messenger recalls having seen lives of every sort scattered around and exceeding in number the souls gathered there. There were, he says,

> lives of all sorts of animals (ζῴων . . . πάντων βίους) and, in particular, all the varieties of human lives. There were tyrannies among them, some lasting to

the end, others ruined midway, ending both in poverty and exile and in beg-gary. And there were lives of men of repute (δοκίμων ἀνδρῶν)—some for their forms (ἐπὶ εἴδεσιν) and beauty and for strength in general as well as capacity in contests (ἀγωνίαν); others for their birth and the virtues of their ances-tors—and there were some for men without repute in these things; and the same was the case for women, too. An ordering of the soul was not in them, due to the necessity that a soul become different according to the life it chooses (ψυχῆς δὲ τάξιν οὐκ ἐνεῖναι διὰ τὸ ἀναγκαίως ἔχειν ἄλλον ἑλομένην βίον ἀλλοίαν γίγνεσθαι). (618a–b)

What is crucial to emphasize here is the shaping, structuring, in brief, poietic force of the experience of this life, of life here, of experience (πάθος) tout court. Indeed, it is thanks to their repeated cycles of embodiment, thanks to this ex-quisitely unique mode of living, that the souls acquire an order at all, that they learn, that is, order themselves. At the same time, though, far from unequivo-cally subsisting as the substratum underlying the many returns to life and into a body, the order which comes to be delineated in a soul and which articulates a soul through one of its lives is said to vary, necessarily, from life to life. The or-der of the soul in one of its lives is inseparable from the singularity of that par-ticular life and its conformation. It disappears with the end of that life—and it is impossible to divine, beneath the simultaneous emergence of radically novel and incomparable appearances, the persistence of the same under an other guise. Or, perhaps, such persistence can only, and at most, be divined—in no way assumed and unproblematically demonstrated.

The question at stake, evidently, concerns the assumption of psychic struc-tures subsisting separately from the utter singularity of a unique life and em-bodiment, remaining intact and unaffected by the modes and moods that a specific life (even just one of its days) entails, continuing throughout differing lives in spite of their dramatically different character, tone, and timbre. Whether and how such psychic order, in any of its aspects, would survive the end of that particular life; whether or not, that is, the order that came to be constituted in one lifetime may accompany the soul in its further ventures and, in fact, even determine the subsequent choices the soul will be called to make and directions the soul will take—this presents itself as an enigma which cannot properly be resolved, that is to say, as a question that can be approached and answered only in a radically qualified way. Indeed, this question is silently and surreptitiously answered already in the moment it is posed in these terms: for, to the extent that the issue is set up in terms of order accompanying (or not accompanying) the soul in its further ventures, a decision is already in place regarding the subsis-tence of the soul—a presupposition that, despite its inconspicuous character (indeed, its tendency to disappear), is far from being warranted.

In the myth recounted here, on the one hand, the souls are said repeatedly to undergo and move through cycles involving embodiment. The mere speaking of souls passing from life to death to life over and over again involves the presupposition of that which is designated as ψυχαί. In this sense the question is already, if improperly, settled. On the other hand, though, the metaphorical thickness, the imaginal-oneiric quality of the mythical saying, which calls attention to the imaginal-oneiric quality of saying in general, allows for the assumption (of something like a soul) only as a gesture, as an indication. In other words, in this context the designation of souls does not function as a conceptual determination and does not carry its force. Furthermore, and most importantly, in the course of the myth itself one finds the remark concerning the mutable character of the souls as they live different lives, concerning the utter structural mobility and the most thorough metamorphoses involved in the souls' wanderings. In this myth, then, the continuing and unaffected persistence of the soul is at once named (suggested or inevitably imposed by the strictures of naming) and undermined. The unity and continuity of the soul in its moving through lives, through worlds, and through moods is delineated and undone, said and unsaid at the same time—it is said under erasure. Indeed, the mythical discourse at once names the soul as such and, in accounting for its wanderings, cannot adequately distinguish the soul from the human being or other animal that allegedly would be but one of the soul's transient guises (the soul's latest mask). What is revealed through this discourse is the ψυχή as nothing other than the shining emergence of the worlds it virtually crosses, nothing other than the moods and atmospheres it undergoes—as *the place of worlds and moods*.[26] The linguistic exiguity allowing only for an always insufficient account of psychic vicissitudes also, at the same time, lets what exceeds such account transpire, however obliquely.

The passage just quoted, then, presents astonishing implications concerning the problem of recollection and of the essence of the ψυχή. For it indicates in no uncertain terms the dynamic and wandering character of the soul as it returns, over and over, life after life. It indicates the continuing "becoming other" (ἀλλοίαν γίγνεσθαι) of the soul, the restless movement of the soul always already away from itself, passing from world to world, through lives and bodies not even of the same kind, that is, not even necessarily human. In suggesting the lack of any structural permanence, it indicates the psychic returns as a straying—from the path once beaten as well as from identity and from eidetic constancy tout court. In this way such a statement contributes to an understanding of ἀνάμνησις as the surprising and open-ended play of discovery occurring through living (experiencing, learning) and contests the construction of it as the predictable uncovering of the present, as that recovery having a calculable culmination and completion. It also challenges the vision of the succession of lives as a progression leading, in a linear and hence inexorable fashion, to an obvious outcome—as a sequence of vicissitudes whose cumulative effects would give the measure of psychological growth or achievement. Indeed, the dissipation and the discontinuities involved in the abysmal circling of the souls make the direction and destination (if any) of this movement less than readable in any current sense of the term.

And yet to a certain extent the experiences constituting a lifetime are not purely lost in the translation from that life (condition, mood) to another. To be sure, because of the "becoming other" of the soul according to the life chosen, they may not be purely retained and give themselves as a consistent sequence organically unfolding from life to life. But it is nevertheless the case that the choice of the next life is vastly influenced by the kind of life previously led—at least according to the story of Er, who apparently contemplated the scene of the choice from a distance, without being admitted to it. Not fully decipherable, but at the same time *not nothing,* a trace remains which marks the soul in some way. Socrates continues his narration of Er's vision:

> He said that this was a sight (θέαν) surely worth seeing (ἰδεῖν): how each of the several souls chose (ἡροῦντο) a life. For it was pitiable, laughable, and wonderful (θαυμασίαν) to see (ἰδεῖν). For the most part the choice was made (αἱρεῖσθαι) according to the habituation of their former life (κατὰ συνήθειαν γὰρ τοῦ προτέρου βίου). He said that he saw (ἰδεῖν) a soul that once belonged to Orpheus ('Ορφέως γενομένην) choosing (αἱρουμένην) a life of a swan out of hatred for womankind; due to his death at their hands, he wasn't willing to be born, generated in a woman (ἐν γυναικὶ γεννηθεῖσαν γενέσθαι). He saw (ἰδεῖν) Thamyras's soul choosing (ἑλομένην) the life of a nightingale. And he also saw (ἰδεῖν) a swan changing (μεταβάλλοντα) to the choice (αἵρεσιν) of a human life; other musical animals (ζῷα μουσικὰ) did the same thing. The soul that got the twentieth lot chose the life of a lion; it was the soul of Ajax, son of Telamon, who shunned becoming a human being, remembering (μεμνη-μένην) the judgment of the arms. . . . And from the other beasts (θηρίων), similarly some went into human lives and into one another—the unjust changing (μεταβάλλοντα) into savage ones (τὰ ἄγρια), the just into tame ones (τὰ ἥμερα), and there were all kinds of mixtures. (619e–620d)

For the most part, then, the choice of a life is in some way dictated by the traces the soul bears of previous lives, by reminiscences of other guises, impressions, and configurations. It is in light of such necessitating traces that freedom, the "freedom of the choice," would have to be originally thought. In fact, the choice of the next life even displays a somewhat affective, reactive quality. Paradigmatically, the choice made by the soul that had been Orpheus's is the result of a certain retention of his previous life, of a wound yet to be healed, in fact, of the loss and dismemberment suffered in that life.

But, besides responding in a somewhat compensatory fashion to the signs and memories they bear, more generally the souls seem to oscillate, cycle after cycle, between felicitous and poor choices. Souls which have lived justly, but somewhat obliviously, that is, unreflectively, seem for the most part to choose bad, that is, unhappy, lives—and vice versa. In this sense, then, the mnemic traces do indeed guide the choice of the course to come, but not in the sense that they lead the soul through stages of progressive maturation. Rather, as if blinded, caught within a compulsory circle of repetition and undiminished confusion, as if crazed and disoriented, the souls keep moving from one extreme to the other, unable to break through the spell of pure reiteration (of reiteration without metamorphosis) invisibly confining them. By alternating opposite choices, paradoxically, they find and maintain a kind of equilibrium.

Thus, many souls cannot even hear the words of the spokesman of Lákhesis, who advises them "not to be careless (ἀμελείτω)" in their choice (619b). This is especially evident in the comportment of the soul that Er saw come forth and initiate the sequence of the choices. However, many others appear to be held captive within the exiguous space defined by the logic of opposite choices succeeding one another and reverting into one another:

> He said that when the spokesman had said this the one who had drawn the first lot (τὸν πρῶτον λαχόντα) came forward and immediately (εὐθὺς) chose (ἑλέσθαι) the greatest tyranny, and, due to thoughtlessness (ὑπὸ ἀφροσύνης) and gluttony (λαιμαργίας), chose (ἑλέσθαι) without having considered everything adequately (ἱκανῶς ἀνασκεψάμενον); and it escaped his notice (λαθεῖν) that eating his own children and other evils were fated to be a part of that life. When he considered it at leisure (σχολὴν σκέψασθαι), he beat his breast and lamented the choice (αἵρεσιν), not abiding by the spokesman's forewarning. For he didn't blame (αἰτιᾶσθαι) himself for the evils but chance (τύχην), demons (δαίμονας), and anything rather than himself. He was one of those who had come from heaven, having lived in an orderly city (ἐν τεταγμένῃ πολιτείᾳ) in his former life, participating in virtue by habit, without philosophy (ἔθει ἄνευ φιλοσοφίας ἀρετῆς μετειληφότα). And, it may be said, not the least number of those who were caught in such circumstances came from heaven, because they were unpracticed in labors (πόνων ἀγυμνάστους). But most of those who came from the earth, because they themselves had labored and had seen the labor of others, weren't in a rush to make their choices (οὐκ ἐξ ἐπιδρομῆς τὰς αἱρέσεις ποιεῖσθαι). On just this account, and due to the chance of the lot (κλήρου τύχην), there was an exchange (μεταβολὴν . . . γίγνεσθαι) of evils and goods for most of the souls. (619b–d)

The soul, then, "becomes other" according to the life it chooses. But it chooses on the ground of the previous life. What it will become, then, depends on the life or lives it once chose and led, that is, on what it used to be, on what it was (or will have seemed to have been) before (to begin with, even). To the extent it lived unphilosophically, the soul is bound to go back and forth between extremes—to choose reactively, without any understanding of the previous experiences. Such is the condition of many, of all those who lived without insight and illumination, of all those who were just or unjust only by chance (because of circumstances, undiscerning obedience, and other merely extrinsic accidents), and for whom living justly or unjustly was, after all, a matter of indifference.

These ψυχαί lack the awareness (φρόνησις) which, alone, would allow them to break through their purely iterative pattern. They lack the ability to overcome carelessness (ἀμέλεια), the folly of the appetites, the frenzy which blinds and leads them to make instant decisions. As if sunk into a deep sleep, they choose the next life while forgetful of the implications of such choice. The truth of their decision eludes their attention (λανθάνω) and will later catch them unprepared. They are like leaves in the wind—their life governed by τύχη.

Having Loved Sophía

In the case of the few souls having moved through a philosophical life, however, it is said that a more genuine equilibrium may be attained—a certain stability, stabilization, and rest from the traumatic passages to one extreme or the other. Indeed, those who once lived loving wisdom seem to be most likely to choose a philosophical life once more. It takes having lived philosophically to live philosophically again. It takes having undergone and lived the philosophical striving once to continue on that journey of discovery. Whence the philosophical desire, whence the mood and reason guiding the initial choice of such a life, is not explained here. Socrates, with Er, simply observes:

> If a man, when he comes to the life here, always philosophizes in a healthy way (ὑγιῶς φιλοσοφοῖ) and the lot for his choice does not fall out among the last, it can be (κινδυνεύει), on the basis of what is reported from there (ἐκ τῶν ἐκεῖθεν ἀπαγγελλομένων), that he will not only be happy here but also that he will journey (πορεύεσθαι) from this world to the other and back again not by the underground rough road (πορείαν) but by the smooth one, through the heavens. (619d–e)

It should be noticed, however, that according to the passage previously quoted, it is precisely the souls coming "from the earth," from the underground journey, that are most likely to choose the best life—for, being used to labor, they know how to take their time and not act on mere impulse. The experience of the underground, then, seems to be intertwined in an essential way with the very possibility of choosing the life of a lover of learning. Indeed, as Socrates' venture in this dialogue itself shows, it belongs to the lover of learning to go down and undertake the toilsome passage through the world beneath. What is notewor-thy here is the suggestion that the philosophical life does not find its perfection and fulfillment in bringing the cycle of embodiments to an end. This way of liv-ing is not chosen primarily for the sake of transcending the repeated returns to this earth and leaving this world behind. Rather, the essential and distinctive work accomplished through the mortal course of a philosopher seems to be en-abling the soul to choose well into what life to be embodied next—admittedly, with the necessary assistance of chance.

However complicated and tortuous the way, then, order comes to be in the soul through living—is not there prior to or separately from the passage through this life here. And it is only in the unlikely but not impossible circumstance of the experience of philosophical passion that the just order (the orderly regime) *may* not only be established in the soul but also be preserved there in some fash-ion. In light of the desirous openness of the philosophical thrust, "just order" comes to be disclosed in terms of aliveness, as a searching attunement to and en-gagement in (the) living—an engaged attunement that endures, is kept alive, preserved precisely through its availability to becoming.

It is a delicate and risky enterprise (κίνδυνος) that the souls are called to face—an unguarded, defenseless journeying through lives and moods thanks to which, alone, the souls become structured, thanks to whose signing and consti-tutive action the souls become *at all*. They must set out to undertake a journey, expose themselves to collision, contusion, and dissipation, even before having a shape, before being shaped, before being in this or that way. On the other side of the battlefield on which Er's body was recovered, the field of an other battle, of the facing of other risks, is illumined—the field of a ψυχομαχία.

Entering and participating in the circuit of the "death-bearing" cycles of life, then, does not simply involve the beginning of a period of embodiment, the beginning of a life in this world, that is to say, the event of the birth of an earthly being. Rather, through coming into being and into a body the soul itself, as it were, is also born—as such and only thus. With every birth, the soul as such comes to light and begins to become what it was to be—what, that is, it will have chosen to be. The lack of transcendent guidelines governing the becoming and granting the continuity of the soul makes the philosophical life all the more crucial and desirable—for such a life would seem to guide more safely than oth-ers the soul through its disorienting courses.

Thus, the philosophical life would seem properly to interpret (divine) and correctly to actualize the power(s) of the soul, that which the soul *can* be. After the disquieting disclosure of the order of the soul as coming to be only through the ventures of embodiment, Socrates interpolates the following reflection into the narration. The passage, again, is worth quoting extensively:

> Now here, my dear Glaukon, is the whole risk (κίνδυνος) for a human being, as it seems. And on this account each of us must, to the neglect of other studies, above all see to it (ἐπιμελητέον) that he is a seeker (ζητητής) and a student (μαθητὴς) of that study (μαθήματος) by which he might be able to learn (μαθεῖν) and find out (ἐξευρεῖν) who will give him the capacity and the knowledge (τίς αὐτὸν ποιήσει δυνατὸν καὶ ἐπιστήμονα) to distinguish (διαγιγνώσκοντα) the good (χρηστὸν) and the bad (πονηρὸν) life, and so everywhere and always to choose (αἱρεῖσθαι) the better (βελτίω) from among those that are possible (ἐκ τῶν δυνατῶν). . . . From all this he will be able (δυνατὸν) to draw a conclusion (συλλογισάμενον) and choose (αἱρεῖσθαι)—in looking off (ἀποβλέποντα) toward the nature (φύσιν) of the soul—between the worse (χείρω) and the better (ἀμείνω) life, calling worse the one that leads it toward becoming more unjust (ἀδικωτέραν γίγνεσθαι), and better the one that leads it to become juster (δικαιοτέραν). He will let everything else go. For we have seen (ἑωράκαμεν) that this is the most important choice (κρατίστη αἵρεσις) for him in life (ζῶντί) and death (τελευτήσαντι). He must go to Hades adamantly holding to this opinion (δόξαν), so that he may be undaunted (ἀνέκπληκτος) by wealth and such evils there . . . but rather he will know (γνῷ) how always to choose (αἱρεῖσθαι) the life between (τὸν μέσον) such extremes and flee (φεύγειν) the excesses (ὑπερβάλλοντα) in either direction in this life (ἐν τῷδε τῷ βίῳ), so far as is possible (κατὰ τὸ δυνατὸν), and in all of the next life (ἐν παντὶ τῷ ἔπειτα οὕτω). For in this way a human being becomes happiest (εὐδαιμονέστατος γίγνεται ἄνθρωπος). (618b–619b)

Such is the reward promised by the philosophical life, the protection it offers to the soul in its dangerous circulation. It is in this way that the power of the soul, the power that the soul is, can be attuned and harmonized—that the soul (its mood, its force) is originally brought into an outline and preserved. The philosopher, this daimonic being par excellence, can now more fully be understood as the safest, most expert charioteer.[27] Thanks to such a guidance, the ψυχή-ἄνθρωπος can find the equilibrium of justice, that is, travel (live) well and happily.[28]

And yet, in drawing to a close it is imperative to notice a quite surprising turn taking place in the myth, namely, the wise choice of the next life attributed to the soul that once belonged to Odysseus. Indeed, it seems that Er saw Odysseus's soul (the soul whose latest guise was Odysseus) preparing to choose. Having "by chance" (κατὰ τύχην) drawn "the last lot of all," it proceeded in this way:

> From memory (μνήμη) of its former labors (προτέρων πόνων) it had recovered from love of honor; it went around (περιιοῦσαν) for a long time looking for (ζητεῖν) the life of a private man who minds his own business (ἀνδρὸς ἰδιώτου ἀπράγμονος); and with effort it found one lying somewhere, neglected (παρημελημένον) by the others. It said when it saw (ἰδοῦσαν) this life that it would have done the same even if it had drawn the first lot, and was delighted to choose it. (620c–d)

The soul of the Homeric hero is said to choose on the basis of remembrance and according to the prescriptions of Lákhesis's spokesman. It certainly does not proceed heedlessly in its choice, nor does it appear disheartened (ἀθυμέω) for having drawn the last lot (619b). Thanks to its efforts and recovery, it chooses the life of a just man, against all odds, as a soul which was trained philosophically would. Such is the life of the one who is ἀπράγμων—who, un-like the πολυπράγμων, knows how to live quietly, free from the noise and the frenzy which mark the turning of life within the πόλις into political chatter. The cunning, warlike hero of Homeric lineage is both acknowledged and su-perseded. Indeed, because of who he was and how he lived, the soul that was his is said to be able to choose the next life wisely. And yet the life chosen in-dicates a turning away from (if not the denial of) the previous one, its toils and heroic pursuits.

Again, in this coda of the myth the distinction between the properly philo-sophical striving and that brought forth by epic poetry, between wisdom and in-spiration, between the philosophical and the tragico-heroic life, appears to be quite mobile and perplexing. And the work of the proto-tragic poet will never have been simply reducible to its formulaic and derivative utilizations, to those appropriations whose trivial character Socrates incessantly denounces.

But a few more words are in order concerning the justice of the life chosen by the soul of Homeric descent. The pattern selected by the soul that lived as Odysseus would seem to coincide with the good and just life that the lover of wisdom would choose—the life informed by the practice of what is one's own (τὸ τὰ αὑτοῦ πράττειν). The ἀπράγμον and private human being seems to lead such a life, as distinct from, even opposed to the πολυπράγμον, who inter-feres in others' affairs and lives a life of distraction.[29] The association of ἀπραγ-μοσύνη as well as ἰδιωτεία with the philosophical stance, though not uncon-troversial, seems to be corroborated by earlier moments of the dialogue. At 434b Socrates links the attempt to do many things simultaneously (ἅμα), which he calls πολυπραγμοσύνη, to the destruction (ὄλεθρος) of the city. Πολυπραγμο-σύνη and ἀλλοτριοπραγμοσύνη are also connected with faction (στάσις) within the soul (444b). More decisive still, in this respect, is Socrates' descrip-tion of the predicament of the few "remaining to keep company with philoso-phy in a way that's worthy" (496b). While exposed to the "madness (μανίαν) of the many" (496c), he says,

> one would perish before having been of any use to city or friends and be of no profit (ἀνωφελὴς) to himself or others. Taking all this into the calculation, he keeps quiet (ἡσυχίαν ἔχων) and minds his own business (τὰ αὑτοῦ πράτ-των)—as someone in a storm, when dust and rain are blown about by the wind (πνεύματος), stands aside under a little wall (τειχίον). Seeing others filled full

of lawlessness, he is content if he himself can live this life here (ἐνθάδε βίον βιώσεται) pure of injustice (καθαρὸς ἀδικίας) and unholy deeds, and take his leave from it graciously and cheerfully with fair hope. (496d–e)

An analogous statement is to be found in the *Apology*, where it is said that "someone who genuinely fights for the just (μαχούμενον ὑπὲρ τοῦ δικαίου), if he is to save his life (σωθήσεσθαι) even for a short time (ὀλίγον χρόνον), necessarily has to be a private citizen (ἰδιωτεύειν), not a public figure (δημοσιεύειν)" (32a). The reference to Pythagoras should also be considered, who, otherwise than Homer, would have been "in private (ἰδίᾳ) a leader of education (ἡγεμὼν παιδείας)" and handed down "a way (ὁδόν, τρόπον) of life (τοῦ βίου)," making his followers seem "somehow outstanding (διαφανεῖς) among the others" (600a–b).

Conversely, however, it should be conceded that Socrates scarcely fits the description of the man who keeps quiet and lives privately.[30] The problem is that, in the case of philosophy, private life and the practice of one's own do not seem to coincide. Indeed, what would properly constitute the philosopher's own, that which he should practice and mind? Could the philosopher's practice of "his own" ever coincide with living privately? How would the philosophical practice be properly delimited? Indeed, how is one to think philosophical life within the bounds of privacy, propriety, and unity of action?

In the dialogue the problem ultimately remains unresolved concerning how the wise human being would get involved in political matters and accept the responsibility of ruling and ordering the communal organism. Glaukon calls attention to this question at the end of Book IX. Here, in reply to Socrates' latest portrayal of the just man (one who, "in private as well as in public" [ἰδίᾳ καὶ δημοσίᾳ], avoids those kinds of honor [τιμή] that "would overturn [λύσειν] his established habit [ἕξιν]"), he points out that, "if it's that he cares about, he won't be willing to mind the political things (τά γε πολιτικὰ ἐθελήσει πράττειν)." To this Socrates responds: "Yes, by the dog . . . he will in his own city (ἔν γε τῇ ἑαυτοῦ πόλει), very much so. However, perhaps he won't in his fatherland (ἔν γε τῇ πατρίδι) unless some divine chance coincidentally comes to pass (θεία τις ξυμβῇ τύχη)" (592a). The problem seems to be rooted in a certain priority accorded to the psychological order over the political.

The reluctance of the lover of philosophy to step onto the political stage is already pointed out quite explicitly in Book VII, where Socrates bases the very possibility of the coming to be of the just ("well-governed" [εὖ οἰκουμένη]) city on the discovery (ἐξευρίσκω) of a life better than ruling and on the necessity, for the one who discovers it, to abandon it and return to the πόλις as a ruler (520e–521a). How the philosophical natures can be driven to leave their contemplative life and get involved in the shaping of (political) becoming is a matter requiring a somewhat drastic resolution on the part of the founders of the city. Thus, in spite of Glaukon's protests, in Book VII Socrates insists that "our task (ἔργον) as founders (οἰκιστῶν) . . . is to compel (ἀναγκάσαι) the best natures (φύσεις) to go to the study which we were saying before is the greatest, to see (ἰδεῖν) the good and go up (ἀναβῆναι) that ascent (ἀνάβασιν); and, when they have gone up (ἀναβάντες) and seen (ἴδωσι) sufficiently, not to permit them what is now permitted," that is, not to permit them "to remain there (καταμένειν) and not be willing to go down (καταβαίνειν) again among those prisoners or participate in (μετέχειν) their labors (πόνων) and honors (τιμῶν)" (519c–d).

The somehow wondrous and unaccountable character of such intervention, along with its compelling, indeed, necessitating force, reminds one of the strange shift in Book II where, thanks to an inspiration of unspecified origin, the two sons of Ariston, the "divine offspring" (θεῖον γένος), open themselves up to the enterprise of understanding, display the desire to learn characteristic of the philosopher, and thus give impulse to and make room for the dialogue that follows. It is, indeed, in response to their philosophical striving that Socrates undertakes the investigation of the essence of justice, the founding of the just city, and the parallel structuring-ordering of the soul. For, as he says, "you must have undergone something quite divine (πάνυ γὰρ θεῖον πεπόν-θατε)" (368a). Something "quite divine," quite strange and not fully presentable, seems to be involved in the lighting up of the philosophical vision as well as in the turn back to the world (the city, the community) in order to contribute to its unfolding.

Notes

1. The journey of the ψυχή is an essential feature of the cluster of practices and doctrines which goes under the all too vague heading of shamanism. For an account of the influence of shamanism on Greek culture, see E. R. Dodds's *The Greeks and the Irrational* (Berkeley: University of California Press, 1964). The issue is obscure and controversial. From the point of view of an understanding of their historical development, the various Orphic and Pythagorean lineages, and in general the teachings imparted in the context of mystery cults, pose nearly insurmountable problems. Compare the rather acritical acceptance of late ancient (especially neo-Platonic) data which characterizes nineteenth-century historiography (e.g., E. Rohde, *Psyche: The Cult of Souls and Belief in Immortality among the Greeks* [New York: Harper & Row, 1966]) to the more cautious exegetic stance of A. J. Festugière in "Les Mystères de Dionysos," *Revue Biblique* 44 (1935), pp. 192–211, 366–96. A somewhat intermediate position with respect to this issue is exemplified by Francesco Sarri's *Socrate e la genesi storica dell'idea occidentale di anima* (Rome: Abete, 1975). Concerning the journey of the soul after death, see Emily Vermeule's *Aspects of Death in Early Greek Art and Poetry* (Berkeley: University of California Press, 1979). Among recent contributions, Peter Kingsley's immensely learned work must be men-

tioned for its rigorous questioning of an eminently questionable assumption (originating in a certain Aristotelian-Theophrastian context and so deeply ingrained in the Western tradition as to rule, or at least to have ruled, unseen), namely, the assumption of a sharp distinction between the philosophical-scientific quest and the mythical, magical, even mystical dimensions of inquiry (see in particular *Ancient Philosophy, Mystery, and Magic: Empedocles and Pythagorean Tradition* [Oxford: Clarendon, 1996] and *In the Dark Places of Wisdom* [Inverness, Calif.: Golden Sufi Center, 1999]). Analogously subjected to methodical questioning in Kingsley's studies is the construction (or the fiction) of the Graeco-Roman world in its essential, already proto-European homogeneity, in contraposition to Eastern and Southern cultures. The separation of science from myth and the construction (identification) of the West as such are evidently correlative aspects belonging in one and the same movement. See also the classic study by Walter Burkert, *Lore and Science in Ancient Pythagoreanism* (Cambridge, Mass.: Harvard University Press, 1972), as well as, by the same author, "Itinerant Diviners and Magicians: A Neglected Element in Cultural Contacts" (in R. Hägg, ed., *The Greek Renaissance of the Eighth Century B.C.*, pp. 115–19 [Stockholm: Lund, 1983]) and *The Orientalizing Revolution: Near Eastern Influence on Greek Culture in the Early Archaic Age* (Cambridge, Mass.: Harvard University Press, 1992).

2. One will recall that, after Glaukon, in Book II Adeimantos had demanded that justice be praised not by reference to "reputations, honors, and gifts" (δόξας τε καὶ τιμὰς καὶ δωρεὰς), but to the operation of justice in the soul, to the way its "power" (δυνάμει) is at work "when it is in the soul of someone who possesses (ἔχοντος) it and is not noticed (λανθάνον) by gods and human beings" (366e). In other words, he asks Socrates to disclose justice in its invisible, non-sensible essence (however latent and neglected), lamenting that no one has ever undertaken to speak in this way. And yet, as will have become evident by the end of the dialogue, especially through the narration of Er's μῦθος, the discourse of justice (undertaking to expose the ineffable order of the soul) involves magnificent imaginal-phenomenal constructions. The sons of Ariston will have had to "give back" (i.e., to give up) the assumption of the separability of the visible and the invisible, of reputation and essence, world and psychological inwardness.

3. "You have been better and more perfectly (τελεώτερον) educated and are more able to participate in both lives (δυνατοὺς ἀμφοτέρων μετέχειν). So you must go down (καταβατέον)" (520b–c).

4. On this theme, see Joseph Souilhé's *La Notion platonicienne d'intermédiaire dans la philosophie des dialogues* (New York: Garland, 1987) and Stanley Rosen's "The Role of Eros in Plato's *Republic*," *Review of Metaphysics* 18, no. 3 (1965), pp. 452–75. On the atopic condition and Odyssey of the philosopher, see also Jean-François Mattéi's *L'Étranger et le simulacre* (Paris: PUF, 1983), especially part V ("Le Temps du retour"), pp. 413–559.

5. The authenticity of the last sentence has been disputed.

6. On Plato's unusually frequent and inventive use of the particle παν, see R. S. Hawtrey, "ΠΑΝ-Compounds in Plato," *Classical Quarterly* 77 (1983), pp. 56–65.

7. Ἦθος ἀνθρώπῳ δαίμων, Heraclitus is reported to have said (22 B 119). It is with the advent of a certain Christian or proto-modern positing of *liberum arbitrium,* of autonomy from nature or the universe (a positing which proclaims freedom in strict opposition to what will have been called determinism), that the figure of the δαίμων comes to be demoted from the role of cosmic guide to the undesirable reminder of a bond to na-

ture. The δαίμονες become demons, indeed—figures of a tormented acknowledgment of nature as bondage and persecution.

8. It is noteworthy that in the myth of Er the circulation between worlds, the circular movement enfolding life and death in their abysmal embrace, the cycle of life passing through death and returning from out of an unrecoverable dislocation is shown to be without direction, teleological orientation, beginning or end. In its discontinuous, ruptured character, the circle does not develop into a progression. The dialogue on the πολιτεία significantly differs, in this respect, from dialogues such as the *Phaedrus* and the *Phaedo*. In the former, first of all, the passage of the souls through this life is described as a falling (πίπτω) to this earth, into embodiment (248a–c). Secondly, the souls are said eventually to return to the place whence they came. The cycles of embodiment are not indeterminately repeated—they come to an end after the fixed amount of time has elapsed, which is necessary for the growth of the lost wings. This time can even be shorter in exceptional cases, such as those of the souls choosing to lead the philosophical life (248e–249d). The periods of embodied living, thus, are situated within a framework showing their purpose, resolution, and destination, that is, the final transcendence of this life. In the *Phaedo* one finds a similar, if unresolved, treatment of this issue. "Those who are found to have excelled in holy living (ὁσίως βιῶναι)," says Socrates, "are freed from these places within the earth and released as from prisons; they mount upward into their pure abode (καθαρὰν οἴκησιν) and dwell upon the earth (ἐπὶ γῆς). And of these, all who have sufficiently purified themselves (καθηράμενοι) by philosophy live (ζῶσι) henceforth altogether without bodies, and pass to still more beautiful abodes which it is not easy to make manifest, nor have we enough time at present" (114b–c). What is remarkable in this statement (and, thus, would deserve further inspection) is the affirmation of a bond between the living and the earth. It is still on this earth, indeed, that the "pure abode" (as far as can be made manifest) is located. At the same time, the view of a progression leading, through further degrees of purification, to "more beautiful" modes of living "without bodies" could hardly be more decisive. While, then, the soul is described in its distinctive longing to move on to that which is "akin to itself" (συγγενὲς) (84a–b), it is not clear whether or not the "path of purification" would ultimately demand and culminate in a transcendence of earth. Those who lived as philosophers are said to be allowed, after death, to reach the gods and commune with them (82b–c, 69c). Where, if anywhere at all, divine abiding would take place, one is not told. The question is thus left open concerning the topical or a-topic character of such abode and, more broadly, the relation of the a-topos (or "without body") to τόπος, body, and earth, indeed, to the body of the earth. (This relation may not be a simple opposition, let alone mutual exclusion.) Nor is it specified whether there is or must be a return from such a blessed dwelling. What should be underscored in this connection is Socrates' equation, by reference to the practices of initiation and purification in the Dionysian mysteries (τελεταί), of those who have truly philosophized with the Βάκχοι. Socrates then adds that in his life he has striven (προυθυμήομαι), in any way and with all his resources (κατά . . . τὸ δυνατὸν), to be one of them (69c–d).

9. The same conclusion was reached earlier, especially by reference to Book IV.

10. For an interpretation of this passage in light of the Pythagorean heritage, see Hilda Richardson's "The Myth of Er (Plato, *Republic* 616 B)," in *Classical Quarterly* 20 (1926), pp. 113–33.

11. This discourse made it clear that the rulers designated by Socrates and the other

interlocutors could by no means claim control over the unfolding of generation. The Muses' intimation of the ultimate finitude of humans (even the best among them) constitutes a prelude to the disclosure of Necessity in her magnificence, as the one who, sitting at the center of becoming, presides over its motion, that is, destiny.

12. In the *Timaeus* necessity is referred to as "the form of the wandering cause" (τὸ τῆς πλανωμένης εἶδος αἰτίας). However much "yielding to intelligent persuasion" (ἡττωμένης ὑπὸ πειθοῦς ἔμφρονος), such unstable and destabilizing figure of necessity cannot not announce a certain discursive instability, a drifting of discourse (48a).

13. Thus, it is simply not the case that the image concluding the dialogue on the πολιτεία presents a vision of the cosmos, of the all-embracing cosmic necessity, in its intelligibility. Or, if imaging is in a sense a way of making intelligible, then the very concept of intelligibility would have to be thoroughly reconsidered and brought, indeed, even beyond the conceptual framework.

14. Herein lies a certain iconoclastic character of the εἰκὼς λόγος that μῦθος is. For, to the extent that images present themselves in their transience and volatility, to the extent that the narration is not secured to structures of continuity and is therefore bound to repetition, the iconic discourse cannot not admit of incalculable shifts and mutations. As such, an image is always exposed to its own fading, its repetition is always also a dying, becoming other, making room for another.

15. It would, furthermore, suggest a connection between Necessity and the nocturnal goddess Bendis, celebrated with "a torch race on horseback" and "an all-night festival" (παννυχίδα) precisely as the dialogue is taking place (328a).

16. An indication of this shift is to be found at the end of Book VII. At that juncture Glaukon addresses Socrates as the heir of both his father and forefather's art (in the *Euthyphro* Socrates, the son of a statuary according to later sources, alleges his descent from Daidalos, the fantastic craftsman-sculptor [11c–e]). Says Glaukon: "Just like a sculptor (ἀνδριαντοποιὸς), Socrates, you have made (ἀπείργασαι) ruling men (ἄρχοντας) who are . . . wholly beautiful (παγκάλους)." Socrates, who already in the *Euthyphro* dismisses the hypothesis of an influence of his paternal ancestry on his own work, replies: "And ruling women (ἀρχούσας), too, Glaukon. . . . Don't suppose that what I have said applies any more to men than to women, all those who are born (ἐγγίγνωνται) among them with adequate natures (ἱκαναὶ τὰς φύσεις)" (540c). A son and rather perplexed heir of his ancestors' legacy, Socrates seem reluctant *simply* to embrace the role of father—especially of father of sons.

17. The phrase οἱ καθήμενοι, the sitting ones, in common parlance designates the judges, the court. In Aristophanes' *Clouds*, Strepsiades alludes to the "judges sitting" (δικαστὰς . . . καθημένους) in the courthouse as one of the distinctive features of the Athenian lifestyle (p. 208). Socrates, too, uses this expression in the *Apology:* "The judge (δικαστής)," he says, "is not seated (κάθηται) to give judgment by private interest, but to discern what is just" (35c).

18. Various hypotheses have been advanced concerning the etymology of ὕμνος and the related verb ὑμνέω. Some have related the Greek term to the Sanskrit *sumna*, meaning benevolence, grace, favor, but also devotion, prayer, and, indeed, hymn, song of praise. Others draw a connection between ὕμνος and ὑμήν (thin skin, membrane, ligament, hymen), which illuminates singing in its connective function. In accord with this insight, still others suggest a relation with the verb ὑφαίνω (I weave, scheme, create), thus disclosing hymn in terms of texture, as a woven fabric. Here one should recall Bakkhu-

lides' image "weaving hymns" (ὑφάνας ὕμνον) (Hymn V, 9 f.). The early understanding of song as a configuration of interwoven elements is echoed in expressions such as "hymn (made of) song" (ἀοιδῆς ὕμνον) (*Od.* VIII.429) and "sewing the song in new hymns" (ἐν νεαροῖς ὕμνοις ῥάψαντες ἀοιδήν) (Hesiod, fr. 357). Notice, furthermore, the connection between ῥάψις, ῥάπτω (sewing, stitching together) and ῥαψῳδέω, designating the recitation and "collation" of songs, the work of the rhapsode. On this issue, see Filippo Càssola, ed. and trans., *Inni Omerici* (Milan: Mondadori, 1994), p. ix ff.

19. The semantic range of the related Latin verbs *ordino* and *ordior* (which indicates ordering as ruling and instituting, as configuring, arranging and, moreover, as narrating, weaving, even initiating) clearly points to a certain convergence of singing, weaving, and ordering. "Lachesis plena orditur mano," writes Seneca (*Apocolocyntosis* 4), and Lactantius: "(Parca) hominis vitam orditur." On the cosmological as well as sociopolitical significance of the metaphor of weaving and of the gift of the woven fabric, see Bruce Rosenstock, "Athena's Cloak: Plato's Critique of the Democratic City in the *Republic*," *Political Theory* 22, no. 3 (1994), pp. 363–90.

20. The intuition of the organizing, formative, in-forming power of sound (hence the importance attributed to harmony as the gathering/attuning articulation of complexity in and as a chord) is of Pythagorean ancestry. Philolaos speaks of nature (φύσις ... καὶ ὅλος ὁ κόσμος καὶ τὰ ἐν αὐτῷ πάντα) as "harmonized (ἁρμόχθη) from the nonlimited and the limiting" (44 B 1). Relevant in this respect is also fragment 44 B 11. In this context number (understood in its essential relation to harmony, and subsequently to music) is said to be that which, through sense perception (αἴσθησις), harmonizes all things in the soul, fitting them together into a whole, into the whole that the soul is. Number/harmony, the giver of perceptual distinctness as well as body (σῶμα), that which apportions, divides, and assigns, is said to operate in daimonic and divine works as well as in human endeavors and words (λόγος), in crafsmanship (δημιουργία) and music alike.

21. Two Empedoclean sayings (31 B 115 and 117) convey in particularly vivid terms the insight of the return to further lives. Empedocles' vision of the overpowering journey through elemental exchanges is worth quoting: "There is an oracle of Necessity, ancient decree of the gods / eternal, sealed with broad oaths: / whenever one sins and pollutes one's own limbs with murder, / by one's own fault swears a false oath / —δαίμονες who have by lot (λελάχασι) long life— / one wanders away from the blessed for thrice ten thousand seasons (ὥρας), / growing to be through time all different forms of mortals (φυομένους παντοῖα διὰ χρόνου εἴδεα θνητῶν) / taking in exchange one troublesome path of life after another. / The force of the air (αἰθέριον) pursues them to the sea / and the sea spits them out onto the surface of the earth (χθονὸς), the earth (γαῖα) into the rays / of the blazing sun, and the sun casts them into the eddies of air (αἰθέρος ... δίναις). / One takes them from another, but all hate them. / Of them I am now one, a fugitive from the gods and a wanderer (ἀλήτης), / relying on raging Strife (Νείκεϊ μαινομένῳ)" (31 B 115). Again speaking in first person, as if out of a memory not dissipated, Empedocles also says: "For I have already been once a boy and a girl / a bush, a large bird (οἰωνός) and a leaping, journeying fish (ἔξαλος ἔμπορος ἰχθύς)" (31 B 117). Aristotle attributes the doctrine of rebirth and reincarnation to the "Pythagorean stories" (*De anima* 407b21 ff.). Geoffrey Theodore Garratt puts forth the hypothesis of the Indian ancestry of this Greek insight in *The Legacy of India* (Oxford: Clarendon, 1937), p. 5 f.

22. Notice how the theme of inheritance (the κληρονομεῖν first emerging as an is-

sue in Book I with the introduction of Polemarkhos, the κληρονόμος of his father's discourse [331e]) is at this point on the verge of a conclusive, most radical reformulation. As was repeatedly underscored, in the course of the dialogue the themes presented in the beginning are taken up and gradually, systematically transmuted. At this juncture, the extent of such transformation is made phenomenally perspicuous. The ending myth shows how far the consideration of one's lot (κλῆρος) in life has come from the unreflective appropriation of biological transmission, from conventional determinations of descent—from νόμος legalistically understood. It shows how, suffusing that which comes into being through the laws (order) of generation, something is born, which cannot be reduced to the prolongation or continuation of the parents in their offspring.

23. Concerning the in(de)finitely mediated and stratified character of the transmission of inspiration as well as divination, see Socrates' reference, in the *Phaedrus*, to the "prophets of the Muses" (τῶν Μουσῶν προφῆται) (the cicadas, in this case). It is they, and not the Muses themselves, who inspire and confuse us, who "sing above our heads" and breath through (πνέω) us (262d). See, furthermore, the distinction put forth in the *Timaeus* between diviners properly understood and the "race of prophets" (προφητῶν γένος), whose task is to interpret "the saying of obscure riddles (τῆς δι' αἰνιγμῶν . . . φήμης) and fantasy (φαντάσεως)" coming through the diviners (72a–b). Here again, what is conveyed is the relative remoteness of the divine source from the prophet and, consequently, the complex nature of mediation, which is carried out at multiple interconnected but distinct levels.

24. It is, thus, the nonfigural (in fact, unthinkable) figure of an abysmal *adaequatio* that comes to be established between that which cannot be (re)presented and the discourse exhibiting the singular impossibility of mimetic (re)presentation.

25. This statement should be read in connection with Socrates' earlier remarks concerning the good and the god. "The good," says Socrates in Book II, "is not the cause (αἴτιον) of everything; rather, it is the cause of the things that are in a good way (τῶν . . . εὖ ἐχόντων), while it is not the cause (ἀναίτιον) of the bad things. . . . Then . . . the god (ὁ θεός), since he's good, wouldn't be the cause (αἴτιος) of everything, as the many say, but the cause (αἴτιος) of a few things for the human beings and not responsible (ἀναίτιος) for many. For the things that are good for us are far fewer than those that are bad; and of the good things, no one else must be said to be the cause (αἰτιατέον); of the bad things, some other causes must be sought (ἄττα δεῖ ζητεῖν τὰ αἴτια) and not the god" (379b–c). Socrates returns to this issue shortly afterwards and insists: "the god is not the cause of all things, but of the good." Such is the "law," the νόμος following which "those who produce speeches will have to do their speaking (τοὺς λέγοντας λέγειν) and those who produce poems will have to do their making (τοὺς ποιοῦντας ποιεῖν)" (380c).

26. The awareness of a certain awkwardness inhering in discourse, of its somewhat cumbersome and coarse character, allows one to move beyond a narrowly literalistic approach and perceive subtler implications of the μῦθος of reincarnation. And rebirth begins to be disclosed in terms of the periodic renewal of life, as regeneration, as movement from πάθος to πάθος and through them, as the coming and going of moods. The succession of lives may be grasped as a motion through conditions of the soul—that is to say, in terms of *Befindlichkeit*, of the configurations, attunements, and modes in which one finds oneself there, *from moment to moment.*

27. The warrior, then, *is* the charioteer.

28. That is why, in Socrates' city-soul, the philosophers are remembered and hon-

ored as daimonic rulers and guardians: "always educating other like men and leaving them behind in their place as guardians (φύλακας) of the city, they go off to the isles of the blessed and dwell (εἰς μακάρων νήσους ἀπιόντας οἰκεῖν). The city makes (ποιεῖν) public memorials (μνημεῖα) and sacrifices (θυσίας) to them as to demons (δαίμοσιν), if the Pythia is in accord; if not, as to happy (εὐδαίμοσί) and divine (θείοις) beings" (540b–c). In the ending μῦθος the connection between the figure of the daimonic and the function of the guardian is restated. Each δαίμων is said to be chosen "as a guardian of the life and a fulfiller of what was chosen" (τοῦτον φύλακα ξυμπέμπειν τοῦ βίου καὶ ἀποπληρωτὴν τῶν αἱρεθέντων) (620e).

29. Incidentally it should be noticed that, at 565a, the quality of ἀπραγμοσύνη is attributed to the δῆμος.

30. In late antiquity Arrianus will have called Socrates πολυπράγμων (*Epicteti Dissertationes* 3.1.21).

VI. (Re)birth

I would have liked, yes, to give you everything that I did not give you, and this does not amount to the same. At least this is what you think, and doubtless you are right, there is in this Necessity.
I will ask myself what *to turn around* has signified from my birth on or thereabouts. I will speak to you again, and of you, you will not leave me but I will become very young and the distance incalculable.

JACQUES DERRIDA ("Envois," 30 August 1979)

It is in this way, then, that the souls are said to prepare themselves to travel back to the realm of γένεσις. Through Er's story a vision is shared, the contemplation of the souls' getting ready to return to that place where one is at war with oneself, fluctuating, oscillating, never of one mind—to the domain of conflict, of change, and of work as which time stretches out, gives itself, passes. (If, that is, the souls ever left behind these traits and modes which essentially define the articulation of becoming . . .) Each soul is assigned a daimon by Lákhesis, which will watch over and govern the execution of the soul's choice (for the daimon is "the guardian of the life and fulfiller of what was chosen"). Then, one by one, the souls are led to the other two Moirai, so that the thread of the life they have chosen on the ground of the past (before Lákhesis) may be spun (by Klothó, who turns the outer whorl in one direction) and made irreversible, that is to say, necessary (by Átropos, who turns the inner revolutions in the opposite direction). The souls' destiny in the next mortal course is, thus, established.

At this point the souls are driven away from the place at the center of the κόσμος where their momentous choice occurred. This is how they move on to the third and final station of their passage through that world—and how they reappear on the rippling surface of this world:

From there, without turning around (ἀμεταστρεπτὶ), they went (ἰέναι) under (ὑπὸ) Necessity's throne. And, having come out through it (δι᾿ ἐκείνου διεξελθόντα), when the others had also come through (διῆλθον), all made their way (πορεύεσθαι) through terrible stifling heat to the plain of Lethe. For it was barren (κενὸν) of trees and all that naturally grows on earth (ὅσα γῆ φύει). Then they made their camp (σκηνᾶσθαι), for evening was coming on, by the river of Carelessness (Ἀμέλητα ποταμόν), whose water no vessel (ἀγγεῖον) can contain. Now it was necessary (ἀναγκαῖον) for all to drink a certain measure (μέτρον) of the water, but those who were not saved by mindfulness (φρονήσει μὴ σῳζομένους) drank more than the measure (μέτρου). In drinking, each forgot everything (πάντων ἐπιλανθάνεσθαι). And when they had gone to sleep and it was midnight, there came thunder and an earthquake; and they were suddenly carried (φέρεσθαι) from there, each in a different way (ἄλλον ἄλλῃ), up to their birth (ἄνω εἰς τὴν γένεσιν), shooting like stars (ἀστέρας). But he himself was prevented (κωλυθῆναι) from drinking the water. However, in what way (ὅπῃ) and how (ὅπως) he came into his body he did not know (εἰς τὸ σῶμα ἀφίκοιτο, οὐκ εἰδέναι); but, all of a sudden (ἐξαίφνης), he recovered his sight and saw (ἀναβλέψας ἰδεῖν) that it was morning and he was lying (κείμενον) on the pyre. (620e–621b)

In this final segment of the myth, the images of passage could hardly be more vivid and pervasive. Indeed, this concluding section of the concluding ἀπόλογος discloses a number of most delicate transitions in a disconcertingly rapid sequence—perhaps quite appropriately so, since the occurrence of endings and beginnings appears to be essentially and exceedingly fast, abrupt, agitated. There is a suddenness, a sense of urgency to such passing.

First of all, the souls (all of them, one by one, as is emphatically specified) must "go under" and "through" the throne of Necessity. This traversal, this moving under Necessity, through the opening beneath her, evokes, as if it were the mediated (displaced) but still legible cipher of a passing through Necessity herself, a powerful image of birth. Once out of that passageway, the souls must continue through the plain of Lethe, the burning desert where nothing grows.

Like the barren battlefield after the war, the plain of Lethe is the place where all is lost—the place, indeed, where everything is forgotten. It is here that the souls, just as they did before in the daimonic place, set up camp (σκηνάω), thus establishing for themselves, again, a momentary dwelling in the course of their indefinitely long journey—an ephemeral stage, a backdrop against which they can appear. And here, after settling down, the souls forget—not out of any accidental deficiency or lack, but out of necessity. It is necessary, in fact, that each soul drink a certain amount of the water of Carelessness and that each forget everything. It is necessary that everything be lost for the soul, that the soul and whatever it retains be swept away in order to be born again. Those souls which "were not saved" by φρόνησις, which lack the insight and awareness paradigmatically yielded by a former philosophical existence, are said to drink more than the just measure. These are presumably the souls which, at the moment of the choice, could not remember their previous vicissitudes and chose in haste, without considering everything at leisure, negligently. It becomes apparent, once more, that it takes having been saved (specifically, by thoughtfulness) in order to be saved (preserved) again and to be able to save (that is, to be thoughtful, to remember, to retain and rediscover).

The souls which were saved and drank the liquid of oblivion only in the amount prescribed by necessity, too, are bound to forget. But apparently, as if not all mnemic traces were erased, as if the forgetfulness instilled into the soul would not simply and purely annihilate it, the soul illuminated by φρόνησις retains the ability to uncover and recover its order, the order it retained—that is, it retains the power to uncover and recover what it will have called the retained. It retains the power to bring itself forth and to project itself as the actualization of what it was to be.

Thus, for the most part, it takes mindfulness to breed mindfulness. It takes having seen to see again, to see through, and to be able to penetrate into the shining of what appears, image after image, layer after layer. However they may have been first saved, the souls who came in some way to see and to be ordered by such seeing are most likely to be preserved (to preserve themselves), to save this order, to choose and live according to it again. Whether through education (hence, always already with some delay) or through a sudden flash of recollective uncovering (hence, with the priority accorded to occurrences wondrous and divine), this disposition comes to be in the soul (this condition is undergone by the soul) in this life, here. *This* is the place of its actualization—whether this actualization be understood as brought about experientially out of the indeterminably vast domain of possibility or as the ever present but still indeterminable and unaccountable gift from some divine source, or, as may be the case, both. And yet, precisely in coming here, in coming into being, even the souls saved by φρόνησις are bound to take in the water of the river of Lethe—the water of Ameles, of carelessness, distraction, alienation, and oblivion. Even they, then, are not freed from the exposure to and legacy (propagation) of λήθη—if only in the fitting measure. A soul of this kind, too, which is to be the place of the lighting up of a certain mindfulness, is pervaded and accompanied by λήθη. It harbors λήθη, its contaminating water—if, that is, λήθη could be simply harbored and would not, rather, make any vessel an inconsistent shadow.

In the middle of the night, in the midst of their sleep, the souls are (or dream to be) carried away from that world, as the earth is shaking and thunder roaring. Up they go, "shooting like stars." Far from being a matter of falling or of descending, the transposition into embodiment is here rendered as an ascending, intermittent flashing in the dark, as vivid as fireworks. Up they go—each soul in a different way, into its life, into its body, here. How this happened, none of them will remember. Not even Er's soul, despite the fact that, again, it was not allowed to participate in the course of action ordained for the others and did not partake of the water of oblivion. In fact, it is with utter surprise that Er is said to have woken, to have opened his eyes and seen the morning light. Er, too, regains sight after a lapse of vision. Er, too, comes back into his body from out of utter darkness, reemerging, as it were, from blindness—from a blindness so radical that it cannot even be called his own. The traumatic rapidity of birth, this unexplainable leap, the blindness preceding and accompanying his coming to see the light are such that Er is filled with stupor and does not know "in what way and how he came into his body."

Er cannot tell how he came to the light, for he underwent a total blackout as he was on his way. This, first of all, presents crucial implications with regard to what he does tell. For what he is reported to have recounted is the *carrying over* of that which was seen on the other bank, beyond the river flowing through the plain of Lethe—the *carrying through* of that world on the other side into this world. Er's story is, then, a relic saved, preserved *after* the "crossing of the river of Lethe," in fact, after having repeatedly crossed (διαβαίνω) the disgregating, devouring, disarticulating flux of oblivion (621c). Under these conditions it is nearly impossible adequately to distinguish between invention and the preservation of what was taken with oneself during the crossing. For, indeed, the saving of the relic which comes to be made manifest through narration is at once a saving *in spite of* λήθη (a preserving through and beyond λήθη) and a saving *qualified by* λήθη, that is, out of λήθη and not intact, not untouched by its erosive operation.

Secondly, and most importantly, the utter ungraspability of birth, of the beginning and conditions of this life, discloses *this life* (to be sure, in its polymorphous and polytropic intertwinement with other modes of life and, even, with the utter discontinuities, the wounds, silent lacks, and fissures of death) as a mystery, as that through whose veils and folds one cannot fully penetrate. What this story, history, remembrance, and imagination makes visible is not only the return of life out of death, through the dark, the turning off of presence, the loss of horizon—but also death, this blackout, blindness, moment of withdrawal and pause, *remaining at work* in the midst of life ever returning. Simultaneously with the disclosure of the operation of death at the heart of the emergence of life, moreover, this imaginal and imaginative recovery shows the blossoming of life, its shooting and its brilliance, surrounded by sleep, by the dark night of forgetfulness occasionally populated by passing dreams.

It is life, the principle of life, then, which eludes even Er's attention. Even the one who did not have to drink the water obscuring one's presence cannot retain the memory of his own birth—let alone account for it. The one who was ordered to stay and observe everything in the daimonic district in order to return and recount this to the human beings; the messenger and interpreter whose narration (although marked by the rifts and barriers of that which cannot be articulated) accomplishes the most daring task of bringing forth the world beyond that of restless becoming; the warrior and lover who apparently had the audacity to disclose (albeit in a mythical voice) the domain of death; the one who, indeed, was brave enough to dare recount his journey and did so in the only way possible for someone in his condition, that is, by articulating the world beyond becoming as still becoming, the domain of death as the place of other modes of life (of life in latency, in λήθη, preparing its own return), the ψυχαί traveling and camping just like ἄνθρωποι, and motionless necessity as an image, specifically of a woman—the strong son of Armenios, "by race a Pamphylian," who apparently articulated death in terms of life, remains silent about life. He remains silent about his own birth—not out of reticence, but because of amnesia.

Concerning the coming into this body and the manner(s) in which this happens, Er has nothing to say and does not dare to say anything. Utterly surprised, perplexed, and overwhelmed by his sudden awakening, Er contemplates the light of a new day—for the day has already begun as he wakes up; he is already late. Wonder is the condition of the one who simply finds oneself there.

It is life, its beginning and center, then, which one will never have grasped. Wonder is the condition accompanying the realization of having always already missed something. The myth explains why this is so for all the souls Er saw: they had to take in oblivion. Why Er, for whom another destiny was ordained, cannot remember—this is not explained. The mystery of life, of its beginning, returns, and self-perpetuation, seems to be so ineffable as to elude even the most fantastic explication. Not even the myth can indicate the reason why Er does not remember his own birth—why, that is, birth is not remembered. As though apologetically and in awe, myth, *this myth*, inconspicuously, if out of necessity, refuses to account for (the beginning of) life.

Un-ending

Thus, "a tale was saved and was not lost." Why this is so is not said. No necessity is made apparent according to which the myth of Necessity would be saved, remembered, told. To save a myth is a matter of receptiveness and responsiveness to the unexplainable that comes, of availability to an advent that cannot be appropriated. So much so that, in the end, Socrates even lets go of the saving, relinquishes the effort of mnemonic retention ("But if we're persuaded by me . . . " [621c]).

The saving of a μῦθος concludes the dialogue, and in this way the dialogue is and is not concluded. On the one hand, in a formidable gesture of completion, the myth saved gathers the foregoing discussion of justice and situates it within a vision of the cosmos, even of the source of cosmic revolutions. Thanks to this contemplation of the whole, the dialogue would find rest. In virtue of such "comprehensive discourse of necessity," the concerns raised and the hypotheses offered in the course of the conversation would in the end properly position themselves.

On the other hand, the final discourse, precisely as myth, tends obliquely to elude the demands that only the logic of system will have fulfilled. For how could myth, in its imperviousness and volatility, properly gather the discursive manifold and bring it to a conclusion? What kind of closure would be achieved through a gathering vulnerable to mnemonic instability and even dissipation— with what legitimacy, force, indeed, self-enforcement? What decision, resolution, determinacy would thereby be reached? The ending myth will not possibly have overcome the difficulties of the inquiry, arranging and resolving them into a self-enclosed, all-inclusive unity. Rather, the ending myth will have illuminated a certain mythical quality of the end, its un-ending character. The openness to and of such an ending exposes the text thus ending in its defense-lessness or, more precisely, indefensibility.

Yet the compelling power, indeed, the necessity of the ending μῦθος can hardly be denied. In the first place, the turn to myth takes place so that the ob-ligation brought about through the unfolding of λόγος may be honored and what the λόγος still "owes" may be given back "in full." Discourse in the myth-ical mode appears as an altogether necessary supplement of λόγος, almost its antidote, which would emend and excuse, apologize for and justify (make just) the unjustifiable occurrence of λόγος. In addressing the problem of "logical" in-debtedness and the necessity of giving back the immeasurable, of giving back beyond measure and calculation, that is, beyond that for which λόγος can ac-count and of which an account may be given, the ἀπόλογος exposes the essen-tial limits of λόγος. This, among other things, calls attention to the intimate in-tertwinement and fundamental consistency of discursive modes (λέγειν, μυθολογεῖν). Indeed, beyond its shining articulation at the end of the dialogue, to different degrees μῦθος permeates the preceding δια-λόγος in its entirety. Uncontainable and unbound, μῦθος can by no means be confined to the con-cluding segment of the dialogue and regarded as the peculiar appendix of a self-contained λόγος. It is especially such lack of "logical" self-enclosure that the work presented here sought rigorously to pursue and illuminate in its conse-quences.

It is, indeed, the discussion in its overall development that calls for the mythical supplement—a supplement that will not have admitted of being set to work in the service of the logical program but, rather, will crucially have inter-rupted and transgressed it. In the course of the dialogue it becomes evident that the issues at stake cannot be adequately dealt with on a purely logical basis and that what is accomplished in λόγος must come to terms with an order of neces-sity that here was called extra-logical or dia-logical, pertaining to the living ("erotic," Glaukon suggests at 458d), ultimately associated with night—noc-turnal necessity. The founding myth of the autochthony of brothers in Book III or the disruptive disclosure of the Muses in Book VIII, for instance, as well as the gathering myth that concludes a remarkably lengthy nocturnal conversation all point to the sensible, embodied dimension of the philosophical engagement. In an exemplary fashion, they cast light on the impossibility of simply tran-scending sensibility—of overcoming the structures of δόξα by the unqualified appeal to an intelligible order, of calculating without the "aid of sensation," or of entertaining a conversation without tending to its physical (φύσις-bound) cir-cumstances. In its imaginal character μῦθος is never (cannot, constitutively, be) forgetful of the sensible, of the condition of souls living through their "death-bringing cycle."

The openness of myth and of a text closed by such openness reflects a dialogue significantly concerned with problems of delimitation and self-enclosure. The dramatic setting itself brings to the fore questions concerning geopolitical self-delimitation and the unstable distinction between belonging and not belonging, one's own and the alien. But these issues receive sustained thematic development and, in fact, prove to be remarkably intractable. For while, on the one hand, the city's doxastic self-identification is radically questioned, on the other hand, because of a certain impossibility of overcoming δόξα and its corollaries, the attempt at determining a communal organism on a purely intelligible basis remains unfulfilled. The discussion of the πόλις or ψυχή unfolds in the unavailability of ultimate conceptual determinations and directives. In this sense the dialogue is properly mirrored in the ending myth—mirrored both in the unending, indeed, opening operation of the myth and in the images it discloses.

A warrior so utterly singular as to be "of all tribes," souls coming to shine into unique bodies and proper names while remaining radically irreducible to such shining, indeed, obscure in their being excessive—thus is the problematic of delimitation, determination, self-enclosure imaged (gathered and transposed) in the mythical ending. Paradoxically, then, the ending myth brings together and concludes the dialogue most appropriately, for it brings forth the ἀπορία (the necessity and difficulty) of self-enclosure and self-identity which in-finitely provokes the dialogue in its development. It exacerbates such ἀπορία while disclosing it in its beauty and, at once, mystery.

From these considerations it follows that (1) myth demands to be thought in connection with necessity (and vice versa) and (2) the speaking of the dialogue on the πολιτεία is not political science. Averroes understands this very clearly when he programmatically concludes his commentary on this dialogue with a single paragraph dedicated to its last book. The paragraph, indeed, is meant to explain why it is irrelevant for him to comment on it. The content of this book is "not necessary" for the science of the political, Averroes says, which happens to be his concern and subject matter. To this end as well as in the enterprise of making humans just, the telling of stories is useless, if not dangerous. But perhaps Averroes is suggesting that it is at once unnecessary and impossible for the commentator appropriately to broach the question of myth. At the threshold of the mythical saying (as if such a saying could be so aptly delimited) the commentator must stop, the guide's task has come to an end, the teacher does not and cannot provide any further elucidation. The reader is left alone: "May God help you with that which you are presently undertaking; and, in his will and holiness, may He remove the obstacles." The inception of myth, then, would mark the ceasing of pedagogy but not the exhaustion of difficulties which, on the contrary, would become uniquely impervious.

Averroes's discourse delimits itself as scientific and pursues an edifying program rather than a visionary journey of discovery—that is, it does not so much strive to speak to and of the just so as to give them back what is owed to them, but rather undertakes to make humans just. For such a discourse to grow out of a text like that on the πολιτεία, the element of myth must be excised—not necessarily as irrelevant or even "messy" (this will have happened in its own time) but, in Averroes, as posing humanly insurmountable obstacles. The discourse establishing itself as scientific must, in order to go on at all, sidestep such obstacles and determine for itself a more circumscribed, protected field—even though from such a delimited domain it should end up making quite far-reaching, "universal" claims. This means that the ongoing intercourse between λόγος and μῦθος in the dialogue has to be denied and μῦθος in its magnificent final articulation ignored. It is in this way that the discourse of science (political, in this case) can properly unfold and conclude. In virtue of his dismissal, the commentator can say in the end, "The treatise is completed, and with its completion the explanation is completed. Praise be to God!" Such a statement would be unpronounceable, even unthinkable in light of the Platonic ending myth and myth of end—in light of a discourse that is comprehensive, but in the mode of undecidability, and discloses the κόσμος, but does not speak universally. The dialogue first opens up and in a sense, if one is to discern in the ventures of thought after Plato a certain degree of necessity, even prescribes the possibility of political science—yet cannot establish itself as political science.

Let this be said again: In the concluding pages of the dialogue on the πολιτεία a myth is told. More precisely, a myth is found in writing, which would have been recounted yesterday by Socrates, or so Socrates will have recollected tomorrow—according to Plato. In the recollection that Socrates is brought to recount by Plato, Er is brought to recollect and recount by Socrates. Both Socrates and Er are inside as well as outside the narration, both narrate while also crucially appearing in what is narrated: that is, both tell of vicissitudes they underwent, of things occurred to them. They tell of themselves—however such a pronoun should be understood here, and this is not a secondary question.

The myth of Er's journey to the "other place" mirrors Socrates' descent to Piraeus. It was suggested in this work that both journeys at once redouble and transfigure Odysseus's invocation and interrogation of the dead (νέκυια), just as both the figure of Er and that of Socrates transformatively respond to the heroic portraits found in epic poetry. In this sense the dialogue in its entirety may be seen as a reply to the Homeric founding words. But Er's and Socrates' wanderings in those other places mirror yet another νέκυια besides the ritual summoning of the dead saved in the Homeric song—namely, the νέκυια by which Socrates is interrogated and brought to speak after death, to recall and recount the dialogue on the πολιτεία. In the way in which Er is evoked and compelled to recount by Socrates, indeed, compelled to tell of himself and of his undergoing in a way that mirrors the one who made him speak and his own undergoing, is harbored the way in which Socrates is posthumously brought to speak by Plato, in fact, to speak in such a way as somehow to reveal Plato and his undergoing. Plato the inapparent writer is sheltered, but not simply hidden, in these figures and plays of mirrors, in the images such figures are brought to bring forth, in the visions occurring to them.

Unlike Odysseus, who calls the dead to his own living presence, in the myth Er undergoes death and because of this has a vision of the daimonic place. Er does not listen to the speaking of the dead, but himself dies, and it is out of this which can hardly be called "an experience" that he speaks. The hero and narrator is not the unaffected listener, but the one who has undergone. The dimension of πάθος is analogously dominant in Socrates' descent and sojourn below. How can this be brought to bear on Plato's νέκυια, on that evocation of Socrates which constitutes the genesis of the dialogue on the πολιτεία and, perhaps, of philosophical discourse tout court? What dying, what πάθος, what almost unspeakable rupture would compel this immeasurably fecund evocation and operate at its heart? How is one to understand one as the intersection of many voices, even lives—one as the simultaneous dispersion and retention of many? Or, again, how are Socrates and Plato one, and according to what hovering between life and death, to what law of elemental exchange, would such a one, barely a trace, speak? A meditation, however preliminary and exploratory, on the dialogue on the πολιτεία and on its mythical stratum leads one to begin to broach such questions.

The myth told by Er describes the setting and circumstances in which the souls' journey after death is fulfilled and their return to another life is prepared. As noticed already, this discourse represents the culmination of the dialogue, the moment in which the love of wisdom, that is, the ordering of the soul articulated through the unfolding of the conversation, or the philosophical comportment cultivated during a life, is shown to be what, alone, assists the soul as it chooses the life it will be bound to live next, the destiny that will inform "another death-bringing cycle." It is in virtue of how a life has been lived that another will be lived. What is at stake, then, is *this life here,* living well in order to "fare well" in the "thousand-year journey" and back here. It is hardly necessary to point out that the temporal structures that the myth offers to (be) thought are infinitely more worthy of being questioned than the syntax just adopted might suggest. For it is certainly not a matter, here, of thinking the issue merely in terms of the necessitating force of the past, of the determining hold of the past over the future—just as it is not a matter of deciphering the mythical saying as a sort of doctrine of reincarnation without further qualification, that is, of understanding death as that purely future event that would follow a life, put an end to a life, and even be translated as after-life. In the end it could in fact be said that the myth concerns neither the after-life, nor reincarnation, nor the immortality of the soul. Rather, it points to the intimations of death *in* life, to the involvement of death in regeneration and becoming, hence in giving birth and all manners of fecundity.

Death and the life interrupted by its punctuation could accordingly be thought in terms of forgetfulness and recollection, or even potency and actualization, in their protean mingling—a mingling that radically reveals the very character of the protean. Forgetfulness as the movement of dying away or losing oneself, as the fissuring accompaniment of continuity, as the pervasive bracketing of the unity of life which already calls attention to the plural character of one life, sheds a disquieting light on the institution of individuality, indivisibility, subjectivity, in brief, of personhood—on the intermittent and essentially self-differing resounding-through of the *persona*. In the cyclical recurrence of life, even the souls are ephemeral, utterly discontinuous. They live but a day. They drink and forget, some drink "more than the measure." But such mortality, vulnerability to oblivion, dreamlike evanescence, may not be reducible to the unqualified sway of the unconscious over consciousness simply construed as labile and fragmented. Indeed, questioning the privileging and self-enforcement of luminous consciousness over against unconscious privation can by no means amount to an inversion that would essentially preserve these terms in their distinctness and opposition. The openness to dying, to becoming other, indeed, may also indicate the irreducible resourcefulness of consciousness, its in-finite nuances and modes, its readiness and responsiveness to solicitations exceeding what it might have predicted or calculated in advance. It may indicate a certain power of consciousness to contemplate, if not own, itself even in its losses, even in the loss of itself—for instance, the power of bringing forth stories, if not accounts, of its own undergoings. Such stories would not appropriate the inappropriable, cast light on what is not seen, but point to the unseen as such, receding and concealed.

However wandering, consciousness may not simply be scattered or distracted. To be sure, it is attracted, drawn, that is to say, called forth, compelled to follow, to assent beyond its own understanding and determination. Thus drawn, provoked beyond itself, consciousness originally surfaces in and as a multiplicity of modes and moods. Its incalculable multitude betrays, in the broadest and most pregnant sense of the verb, the draw of and engagement with unconsciousness. Understood in terms of such overflowing, wandering richness, consciousness allows for the institution of subjectivity no more than the ravenous working of the unconscious. Indeed, it points to a certain passing character of structures of individuality and individuation. It articulates and outlines individuated configurations while, in its plasticity, intimating how individuation is suffused by what cannot be owned or brought back to one, especially not to oneself. The *individuum*, then, comes to be thinkable both in light of its divisibility and in terms of belonging together, interdependence, mutual implication—both as inherently, irreducibly multiple, other than itself, and as (at) one with other(s). In this sense, through the mutable shapes of consciousness no less than through the con-fusion of the undifferentiated, something like a trace of (the) one can—perhaps—be glimpsed. Something like this is brought to view in the myth, in the unity myth at once offers and withdraws.

Coming with or as a turn of consciousness, the next life will perhaps have been before tomorrow. Perhaps yesterday will not have emerged until its recollection. Perhaps even the bridging of the gaps of death and unconsciousness, even the cultivation of the awareness of them, will not be secured to an underlying constancy, especially not to the obstinacy, called immortality, of an "individual soul." The way in which the previous life will have determined the necessitating choice of the next, or this moment will have led to the next, across the abysmal fissures of oblivion as well as of decision, appears to be a subject matter of extraordinary difficulty.

Fragments from an unpublished correspondence found in Sarajevo, former Yugoslavia, in spring 1996:

Hi, my soul. Yes, it keeps snowing and I don't know what to think anymore. Uncertain snow, rain, and then snow.

War, you said, is around the corner, even here, always. And it is true, just so. For it is (in) us. We are (in) war, amongst ourselves, inside ourselves. This, too, is the soul——its landscape is this battlefield, too, this mystery, this longing for dissolution, this desolate expanse of shadows and bones. I do not know, . . . , whether this chilling landscape is still a part of the workshop of life, or whether it represents a malaise, a sickness of life and against life. Maybe both. Life returning, irresistible, insuppressible, will always already have prevailed over madness and havoc, wounds and attacks.

What I do know is that one cannot confront war without confronting oneself—each one of us, one by one, each according to the task assigned to him. War cannot be understood as a purely political phenomenon—or, better, the purely political aspect of war veils, makes occult and inaccessible what war inherently is . . . the war we are, the war inhabiting us, the war we carry through the world in our being in the world—conflicted, divided, angry. It is in this way that we find ourselves here, disoriented and unprepared, in this life.

Facing war, defeating war (not defeating an enemy, but war itself), means facing oneself, I believe. Acknowledging that one doesn't understand that much. Trying to understand more. Admitting that, even though all the commonplaces, unshakable convictions, and even the "bare facts" may demonstrate that we're alive, that we are already *in* life and living, we *do not know* how to live. We already live, but without understanding, without thinking, without realizing. The issue, in sum, may be admitting (against the most deeply rooted prejudices on this matter) that living is not merely a matter of having been born, of having been brought to the light of the world, but that, rather, it is a gift concerning which we will never have wondered enough, which we will never have fully understood, and which demands to be apprehended (to be taken in our hands, embraced, comprehended). One already lives, always. Yet one has always yet to learn how to live. Strange situation we're called to face. . . . It is still snowing. An embrace . . .

World as image of soul. Every motion, every death, every transformation taking place in the world have their counterpart in psychological ciphers and almost illegible traces. To be able to see this, to learn this, to catch a glimpse of such excess with respect to simply being born, put into the world. . . . This would mean to be able to be in the mood of wonder, to explore the *potentiality* of being what we are. It would mean to move simultaneously beyond our animal identity and beyond our human identity altogether. For, indeed, our human identity is based on the interpretation of excess and of potentiality as control, as a purely cognitive, conquering, colonizing adventure—on the interpretation of human excess as superiority, scientific maneuver, right to domination, as a form of subjection and plunder. But to be able to live in the mood of wonder, in the openness of learning, would mean *experiencing* excess in its uncontainable and unfathomable unfolding; undergoing excess, moving within it without possibly turning it into an instrument of mastery; undergoing excess without possibly reducing it to the remains of an already acquired, already accomplished knowledge of oneself and of things. . . . It would mean to embrace the world without strangling it. This is the potentiality, the possibility—not quite human to a higher degree, but signaling the fulfillment and overcoming of the human, without humanly saying it. . . . This is a possibility that is given to us—indeed, a possibility other than human.

A memory haunts us, which we won't recognize. . . . How are you? I haven't heard from you in days . . .

SELECTED BIBLIOGRAPHY

Adam, James, ed. *The* Republic *of Plato.* 2 vols. Cambridge: Cambridge University Press, 1963.

Adorno, Theodor W. *Notes to Literature.* Ed. Rolf Tiedemann. Trans. Shierry Weber Nicholsen. New York: Columbia University Press, 1991.

Allen, Michael J. B. *Nuptial Arithmetic: Marsilio Ficino's Commentary on the Fatal Number in Book VIII of Plato's* Republic. Berkeley: University of California Press, 1994.

Annas, Julia. *An Introduction to Plato's* Republic. Oxford: Clarendon, 1981.

Arendt, Hannah. *The Human Condition.* Chicago: University of Chicago Press, 1974.

―――. *On Violence.* New York: Harcourt, Brace & World, 1970.

Ast, Friedrich *Lexicon Platonicum: Sive, Vocum Platonicarum Index.* Bonn: Habelt, 1956.

Aurobindo. Bhagavad Gita *and Its Message.* Twin Lakes, Wis.: Lotus Light, 1995.

Averroes. *On Plato's* Republic. Trans. Ralph Lerner. Ithaca: Cornell University Press, 1974.

Ballard, Edward G. *Socratic Ignorance: An Essay on Platonic Self-knowledge.* The Hague: Nijhoff, 1965.

Belfiore E. "Plato's Greatest Accusation against Poetry." *Canadian Journal of Philosophy,* suppl. 9 (1983), pp. 39–62.

―――. "A Theory of Imitation in Plato's *Republic.*" *Transactions of the American Philological Association* 114 (1984), pp. 121–46.

Benardete, Seth. *Socrates' Second Sailing: On Plato's* Republic. Chicago: University of Chicago Press, 1989.

―――. "Some Misquotations of Homer in Plato." *Phronesis* 8, no. 2 (1963), pp. 173–78.

Bernal, Martin. *Black Athena: The Afroasiatic Roots of Classical Civilization.* 2 vols. New Brunswick, N.J.: Rutgers University Press, 1987, 1991.

Berti, Enrico. *Aristotele e il Novecento.* Rome: Laterza, 1992.

Bidez, Joseph, and Franz Cumont. *Les mages hellénisés: Zoroastre, Ostanès et Hystaspe d'après la tradition grecque.* Paris: Belles-Lettres, 1938.

Blanchot, Maurice. *The Infinite Conversation.* Trans. Susan Hanson. Minneapolis: University of Minnesota Press, 1993.

Bloom, Allan, trans. *The* Republic *of Plato.* New York: Basic Books, 1991.

Bluestone, Natalie Harris. *Women and the Ideal Society: Plato's* Republic *and Modern Myths of Gender.* Amherst: University of Massachussetts Press, 1987.

Boeft, J. den. *Calcidius on Demons.* Leiden: Brill, 1977.

Bonner, Robert Johnson. *Studies in Greek History and Legal Antiquities.* N.p., 1920.

Boswell, John. *The Kindness of Strangers: The Abandonment of Children in Western Europe from Late Antiquity to the Renaissance.* New York: Vintage, 1990.

Boter, Gerard. *The Textual Tradition of Plato's* Republic. Leiden: Brill, 1989.

Boyce, Mary. *A History of Zoroastrianism.* Leiden: Brill, 1975.

Brague, Rémi. *Concepts et catégories dans la pensée antique.* Paris: Vrin, 1980.

———. *Du temps chez Platon et Aristote.* Paris: PUF, 1982.

———. *Le Restant: supplément aux commentaires de Platon.* Paris: Belles-Lettres, 1978.

Brandwood, Leonard. *The Chronology of Plato's Dialogues.* Cambridge: Cambridge University Press, 1990.

———. *A Word Index to Plato.* Leeds: W. S. Maney, 1976.

Brann, Eva T. H. "The Music of the *Republic.*" *St. John's Review* 39, nos. 1–2 (1989–90), pp. 1–103.

———. *The World of the Imagination: Sum and Substance.* Savage, Md.: Rowman and Littlefield, 1991.

Bréhier, Emile. *The Philosophy of Plotinus.* Chicago: University of Chicago Press, 1958.

Brisson, L. *Platon, les mots, les mythes.* Paris: Maspéro, 1982.

Bruell, Christopher. "On Plato's Political Philosophy." *Review of Politics* 56, no. 2 (1994), pp. 261–82.

Brumbaugh, Robert Sherrick. "A New Interpretation of Plato's *Republic.*" *Journal of Philosophy* 64 (1967), pp. 661–70.

———. *Plato's Mathematical Imagination: The Mathematical Passages in the Dialogues and Their Interpretation.* Bloomington: Indiana University Press, 1954.

Brunt, P. A. *Studies in Greek History and Thought.* Oxford: Clarendon, 1993.

Burckhardt, Jacob. *The Age of Constantine the Great.* Trans. Moses Hadas. Garden City, N.Y.: Doubleday, 1956.

Burkert, Walter. "Itinerant Diviners and Magicians: A Neglected Element in Cultural Contacts." In R. Hägg, ed., *The Greek Renaissance of the Eighth Century B.C.*, pp. 115–19. Stockholm: Lund, 1983.

———. *Lore and Science in Ancient Pythagoreanism.* Cambridge, Mass.: Harvard University Press, 1972.

———. *The Orientalizing Revolution: Near Eastern Influence on Greek Culture in the Early Archaic Age.* Cambridge, Mass.: Harvard University Press, 1992.

Burn, A. R. *Persia and the Greeks: The Defense of the West, c. 546–478 B.C.* Stanford: Stanford University Press, 1984.

Burnet, John. *Early Greek Philosophy.* London: Black, 1930.

Cacciari, Massimo. *L'Angelo necessario.* Milan: Adelphi, 1994.

Cantarella, Eva. *Pandora's Daughters: The Role and Status of Women in Greek and Roman Antiquity.* Trans. Maureen B. Fant. Baltimore: Johns Hopkins University Press, 1987.

Capizzi, Antonio. *The Cosmic Republic: Notes for a Non-peripatetic History of the Birth of Philosophy in Greece.* Amsterdam: Gieben, 1990.

Càssola, Filippo, ed. and trans. *Inni Omerici.* Milan: Mondadori, 1994.

Castoriadis, Cornelius. *World in Fragments.* Trans. D. Ames Curtis. Stanford: Stanford University Press, 1997.

Cavarero, Adriana. *Nonostante Platone.* Rome: Editori Riuniti, 1991.

Charles-Saget, Annick. *L'Architecture du divin: mathématique et philosophie chez Plotin et Proclus.* Paris: Belles-Lettres, 1982.

Cherniss, Harold F. *The Riddle of the Early Academy.* New York: Garland, 1980.

Cornford, F. M. *From Religion to Philosophy.* Princeton: Princeton University Press, 1991.

———. *Plato and Parmenides: Parmenides' Way of Truth and Plato's* Parmenides. London: K. Paul, 1939.

———. *Plato's Cosmology: The* Timaeus *of Plato.* London: K. Paul, 1937.

———. *Plato's Theory of Knowledge: The* Theaetetus *and the* Sophist *of Plato.* London: K. Paul, 1935.

———. *The* Republic *of Plato.* Oxford: Oxford University Press, 1945.

———. *The Unwritten Philosophy and Other Essays.* Ed. W. K. C. Guthrie. Cambridge: Cambridge University Press, 1950.

Craig, Leon H. *The War Lover: A Study of Plato's* Republic. Toronto: University of Toronto, 1994.

Cumont, Franz Valery Marie. *Astrology and Religion among the Greeks and Romans.* New York: G. P. Putnam's Sons, 1912.

———. *L'Égypte des astrologues.* Brussels: Fondation Égyptologique Reine Elisabeth, 1937.

Deleuze, Gilles, and Giorgio Agamben. *Bartleby: la formula della creazione.* Macerata: Quodlibet, 1993.

Demand, N. "Plato and the Painters." *Phoenix* 29 (1975), pp. 1–20.

Denniston, J. D. *The Greek Particles.* Oxford: Clarendon, 1954.

De Quincey, Thomas. *Historical and Critical Essays.* Boston: Ticknor, Reed and Fields, 1853.

Derrida, Jacques. "Donner la mort." In Jean-Michel Rabaté and Michael Wetzel, eds., *L'Éthique du don: Jacques Derrida et la pensée du don,* pp. 11–108. Paris: Transition, 1992.

———. "Force de loi: le 'fondement mystique de l'autorité'"/"Force of Law: 'The Mystical Foundation of Authority.'" Bilingual presentation. Trans. Mary Quaintance. *Cardozo Law Review* 11, nos. 5–6 (1990), pp. 919–1045.

———. "How to Avoid Speaking: Denials." In H. Coward and T. Foshay, eds., *Derrida and Negative Theology,* trans. Ken Frieden, pp. 73–142. Albany: SUNY Press, 1992.

———. "*Khora.*" In *On the Name,* trans. Ian McLeod, pp. 87–127. Stanford: Stanford University Press, 1995.

———. *Memoirs of the Blind: The Self-portrait and Other Ruins.* Trans. Pascale-Anne Brault and Michael Naas. Chicago: University of Chicago Press, 1993.

——— "*Ousia* and *Gramme.*" In *Margins of Philosophy,* trans. Alan Bass, pp. 29–67. Chicago: University of Chicago Press, 1982.

———. "Plato's Pharmacy." In *Dissemination,* trans. Barbara Johnson, pp. 61–171. Chicago: University of Chicago Press, 1981.

————. *Politics of Friendship.* Trans. G. Collins. London: Verso, 1997.

————. *The Postcard.* Trans. Alan Bass. Chicago: University of Chicago Press, 1987.

————. *Spectres de Marx.* Paris: Galilée, 1993.

————. "Tense." In K. Maly, ed., *The Path of Archaic Thinking: Unfolding the Work of John Sallis,* trans. D. F. Krell, pp. 49–74. Albany: SUNY Press, 1995.

————. "White Mythology: Metaphor in the Text of Philosophy." In *Margins of Philosophy,* trans. Alan Bass, pp. 207–71. Chicago: University of Chicago Press, 1982.

Desai, Mahadev. *The Gospel of Selfless Action, or: The* Gita *According to Gandhi.* Ahmedabad: Navajivan, 1946.

Des Places, Eduard. *Études platoniciennes, 1929–1979.* Leiden: Brill, 1981.

Dicks, D. R. *Early Greek Astronomy to Aristotle.* Ithaca: Cornell University Press, 1970.

Diehl, Ernst, ed. *Anthologia lyrica graeca.* 3 vols. Leipzig: Teubner, 1925.

Diels, H. *Fragmente der Vorsokratiker.* 3 vols. Berlin: Weidmann, 1922.

Diès, A. *Autour de Platon: essais de critique et d'histoire.* New York: Arno, 1976.

————. *Platon.* Paris: Flammarion, 1930.

Dixaut, M. *Le Naturel philosophe: essais sur les dialogues de Platon.* Paris: Belles-Lettres/ Vrin, 1985.

Dobbs, Darrell. "The Piety of Thought in Plato's *Republic,* Book I." *American Political Science Review* 88, no. 3 (1994), pp. 668–83.

Dodds, E. R. *The Greeks and the Irrational.* Berkeley: University of California, 1964.

Dupréel, Eugene. *La Légende socratiques et les sources de Platon.* Brussels: Sand, 1922.

Edelstein, L. "Platonic Anonimity." *American Journal of Philology* 83 (1962), pp. 1–22.

Edmonds, John Maxwell. *Greek Elegy and Iambus.* 2 vols. Cambridge, Mass.: Harvard University Press, 1979.

————, ed. and trans. *Lyra graeca: Being the Remains of All the Greek Lyric Poets from Eumelos to Timotheus Excepting Pindar.* 3 vols. Cambridge, Mass.: Harvard University Press, 1952–58.

Else, Gerald Frank. *Plato and Aristotle on Poetry.* Chapel Hill: University of North Carolina Press, 1986.

————. *The Structure and Date of Book 10 of Plato's* Republic. Heidelberg: C. Winter, 1972.

Farabi. *Philosophy of Plato and Aristotle.* Trans. Muhsin Mahdi. New York: Free Press, 1962.

Ferguson, John. *Socrates: A Source Book.* London: Macmillan, 1970.

Festugière, A. J. *Artemidorus: la clef des songes (Onirocriticon).* Paris: Vrin, 1975.

————. *Contemplation et vie contemplative selon Platon.* Paris: Vrin, 1950.

————. *Études de religion grecque et hellénistique.* Paris: Vrin, 1972.

————. *Freedom and Civilization among the Greeks.* Trans. Patrick T. Brannan. Allison Park, Penn.: Pickwick, 1987.

————. *Hippocrate: l'ancienne médecine.* New York: Arno, 1979.

————. "Les Mystères de Dionysos." *Revue Biblique* 44 (1935), pp. 192–211, 366–96.

Findlay, J. N. *Plato and Platonism.* New York: Times Books, 1978.

————. *Plato: The Written and Unwritten Doctrines.* New York: Humanities, 1974.

Finley, M. I. *The Ancient Greeks: An Introduction to Their Life and Thought.* New York: Viking, 1963.

Flew, A. G. N. "Responding to Plato's Thrasymachus." *Philosophy* 70, no. 273 (1995), pp. 436–47.

Foster, Michael Beresford. *The Political Philosophies of Plato and Hegel.* New York: Garland, 1984.

Freud, Sigmund. "Why War?" In James Strachey, ed., *Standard Edition of the Complete Psychological Works,* vol. 22, pp. 197–215. London: Hogarth, 1964.

Freydberg, Bernard. *The Play of the Platonic Dialogues.* New York: Lang, 1997.

Friedländer, Paul. *Platon.* 3 vols. Berlin: De Gruyter, 1964–75.

Fritz, Kurt von. *Hesiode et son influence: six exposés et discussions.* Genève: Fondation Hardt, 1962.

Frutiger, Perceval. *Les Mythes de Platon: étude philosophique et littéraire.* Paris: Alcan, 1930.

Fustel de Coulanges, Numa Denis. *The Ancient City: A Study on the Religion, Laws, and Institutions of Greece and Rome.* Baltimore: Johns Hopkins University Press, 1980.

Gadamer, H.-G. *Dialogue and Dialectic: Eight Hermeneutical Studies on Plato.* Trans. P. Christopher Smith. New Haven: Yale University Press, 1980.

Gallop, David. "Image and Reality in Plato's *Republic.*" *Archiv für Geschichte der Philosophie* 47 (1965), pp. 113–31.

Garratt, Geoffrey Theodore. *The Legacy of India.* Oxford: Clarendon, 1937.

Gerson, Lloyd P. *God and Greek Philosophy: Studies in the Early History of Natural Theology.* London: Routledge, 1990.

———. *Plotinus.* London: Routledge, 1994.

Goldschmidt, Victor. *Les Dialogues de Platon: structure et méthode dialectique.* Paris: PUF, 1963.

———. *Le Paradigme dans la dialectique platonicienne.* Paris: PUF, 1947.

———. *Questions platoniciennes.* Paris: Vrin, 1970.

Grenet, Paul Bernard. *Les Origines de l'analogie philosophique dans les dialogues de Platon.* Paris: Boivin, 1948.

Griswold, C. "The Ideas and the Criticism of Poetry in Plato's *Republic,* Book 10." *Journal of the History of Philosophy* 19, no. 2 (1981), pp. 135–50.

———, ed. *Platonic Writings / Platonic Readings.* New York: Routledge, 1988.

Gross, Barry, ed. *Great Thinkers on Plato.* New York: Putnam, 1968.

Guénon, René. *Formes traditionnelles et cycles cosmiques.* Paris: Gallimard, 1970.

Guthrie, K. S., ed. and trans. *The Hymns of Zoroaster, Usually Called the Gathas.* London: Bell, 1914.

———., ed. and trans. *The Pythagorean Sourcebook and Library: An Anthology of Ancient Writings Which Relate to Pythagoras and Pythagorean Philosophy.* Grand Rapids, Mich.: Phanes, 1987.

Habermas, Jürgen. *Communication and the Evolution of Society.* Trans. Thomas McCarthy. Boston: Beacon, 1979.

Hadot, Pierre. *Philosophy as a Way of Life: Spiritual Exercises from Socrates to Foucault.* Ed. Arnold I. Davidson. Trans. Michael Chase. Oxford: Blackwell, 1995.

Halliwell, S. "Plato and Aristotle on the Denial of Tragedy." *Proceedings of the Cambridge Philological Society* 30 (1984), pp. 49–71.

———. *Plato: Republic 5.* Warminster: Aris & Phillips, 1993.

———. *Plato: Republic 10.* Warminster: Aris & Phillips, 1988.

Hammond, N. G. L. *Studies in Greek History.* Oxford: Clarendon, 1973.

Haslam, Michael. "On Ancient Manuscripts of the *Republic: The Textual Tradition of Plato's* Republic by Gerard Boter." *Mnemosyne* 44, nos. 3–4 (1991), pp. 336–46.

Havelock, Eric Alfred. *The Greek Concept of Justice: From Its Shadow in Homer to Its Substance in Plato.* Cambridge, Mass.: Harvard University Press, 1978.

——. *The Liberal Temper in Greek Politics.* New Haven: Yale University Press, 1957.

——. *The Literate Revolution in Greece and Its Cultural Consequences.* Princeton: Princeton University Press, 1982.

——. *The Muse Learns to Write: Reflections on Orality and Literacy from Antiquity to the Present.* New Haven: Yale University Press, 1986.

——. *Preface to Plato.* Cambridge, Mass.: Belknap, 1963.

Hawtrey, R. S. "ΠΑΝ-Compounds in Plato." *Classical Quarterly* 77 (1983), pp. 56–65.

Heath, Thomas Little. *Aristarchus of Samos, the Ancient Copernicus: A History of Greek Astronomy to Aristarchus, Together with Aristarchus' Treatise on the Size and Distance of the Sun and Moon.* Oxford: Clarendon, 1966.

Hegel, G. W. F. *Vorlesungen über die Philosophie der Geschichte.* Leipzig: Reclam, 1924.

Heidegger, Martin. *Aristotle's* Metaphysics *Theta 1–3: On the Essence and Actuality of Force.* Trans. W. Brogan and P. Warnek. Bloomington: Indiana University Press, 1995.

——. *Early Greek Thinking.* Trans. D. F. Krell and F. A. Capuzzi. San Francisco: Harper & Row, 1984.

——. *Einführung in die Metaphysik.* Tübingen: M. Niemeyer, 1953.

——. *Logik: Die Frage nach der Wahrheit.* Frankfurt am Main: V. Klostermann, 1976.

——. *Nietzsche.* 2 vols. Pfullingen: G. Neske, 1961.

——. *Parmenides.* Trans. A. Schuwer and R. Rojcewicz. Bloomington: Indiana University Press, 1992.

——. *Phänomenologische Interpretationen zu Aristoteles: Einführung in die phänomenologische Forschung.* Gesamtausgabe 61. Frankfurt am Main: V. Klostermann, 1985.

——. "Platons Lehre von der Wahrheit." In *Wegmarken,* pp. 109–44. Frankfurt am Main: V. Klostermann, 1967.

——. *Platon:* Sophistes. Gesamtausgabe 19. Frankfurt am Main: V. Klostermann, 1992.

——. *Der Ursprung des Kunstwerkes.* Stuttgart: P. Reclam, 1960.

——. *Vom Wesen der Wahrheit: Zu Platons Höhlengleichnis und* Theätet. Gesamtausgabe 34. Frankfurt am Main: V. Klostermann, 1988.

——. *Was heißt Denken?* Tübingen: M. Niemeyer, 1954.

Hermann, K. F. *Geschichte und System der Platonischen Philosophie.* Heidelberg, 1839.

Hesiod. *The Works and Days. Theogony. The Shield of Herakles.* Trans. Richmond Lattimore. Ann Arbor: University of Michigan Press, 1991.

Howland, Jacob. *The* Republic: *The Odyssey of Philosophy.* New York: Maxwell Macmillan, 1993.

Huffman, Carl A. *Philolaus of Croton: Pythagorean and Presocratic: A Commentary on the Fragments and Testimonia with Interpretive Essays.* Cambridge: Cambridge University Press, 1993.

Iamblichus. *The Exhortation to Philosophy. Including the Letters of Iamblichus and Proclus' Commentary on the Chaldean Oracles.* Grand Rapids, Mich.: Phanes, 1988.

Irigaray, Luce. *Speculum de l'autre femme.* Paris: Éditions de Minuit, 1974.

Irwin, Terence. *Plato's Ethics.* New York: Oxford University Press, 1995.

Jaeger, Werner Wilhelm. *Paideia: The Ideals of Greek Culture.* 3 vols. New York: Oxford University Press, 1939–44.

Jonas, Hans. *Gnosis und spätantiker Geist: Von der Mythologie zur mystischen Philosophie.* Göttingen: Vandenhoek und Ruprecht, 1993.

———. *The Gnostic Religion: The Message of the Alien God and the Beginnings of Christianity.* Boston: Beacon, 1963.

Julianus (the Theurgist). *The Chaldean Oracles.* Leiden: Brill, 1989.

Kahn, Charles H. *Anaximander and the Origins of Greek Cosmology.* New York: Columbia University Press, 1960.

———. "The Greek Verb 'Be' and the Concept of Being." *Foundations of Language* 2 (1966), pp. 245–65.

———. "The Meaning of 'Justice' and the Theory of Forms." *Journal of Philosophy* 69 (1972), pp. 567–79.

———. "Proleptic Composition in the *Republic,* or Why Book I Was Never a Separate Dialogue." *Classical Quarterly* 43, no. 1 (1993), pp. 131–42.

———. "Some Philosophical Uses of 'to be' in Plato." *Phronesis* 26, no. 2 (1981), pp. 105–34.

Keegan, John. *A History of Warfare.* New York: Knopf, 1993.

Kerenyi, Karl. *The Religion of the Greeks and Romans.* Trans. Christopher Holme. New York: Dutton, 1962.

———. *Prometheus: Archetypal Image of Human Existence.* Trans. Ralph Manheim. New York: Bollingen Foundation, 1963.

Kern, Otto. *Orphicorum Fragmenta.* Berlin: Weidmann, 1922.

———. *Die Religion der Griechen.* 3 vols. Berlin: Weidmannsche Buchhandlung, 1926–38.

Keuls, Eva. *Plato and Greek Painting.* Leiden: Brill, 1978.

Kingsley, Peter. *Ancient Philosophy, Mystery, and Magic: Empedocles and Pythagorean Tradition.* Oxford: Clarendon, 1996.

———. "Artillery and Prophecy: Sicily in the Reign of Dionysius I." *Prometheus* 21 (1995), pp. 15–23.

———. "Empedocles in Armenian." *Revue des études arméniennes* 24 (1993), pp. 47–57.

———. "From Pythagoras to the *Turba philosophorum:* Egypt and Pythagorean Tradition." *Journal of the Warburg and Courtauld Institutes* 57 (1994), pp. 1–13.

———. "The Greek Origin of the Sixth-Century Dating of Zoroaster." *Bulletin of the School of Oriental and African Studies* 53 (1990), pp. 245–65.

———. "Greeks, Shamans, and Magi." *Studia Iranica* 23 (1994), pp. 187–98.

———. *In the Dark Places of Wisdom.* Inverness, Calif.: Golden Sufi Center, 1999.

———. "Meetings with Magi: Iranian Themes among the Greeks, from Xanthus of Lydia to Plato's Academy." *Journal of the Royal Asiatic Society,* 3rd series, 5 (1995), pp. 173–209.

Klein, Jacob. *A Commentary on Plato's* Meno. Chapel Hill: University of North Carolina Press, 1965.

———. *Greek Mathematical Thought and the Origin of Algebra.* Trans. Eva Brann. Cambridge, Mass.: MIT Press, 1968.

Klibansky, Raymond. *The Continuity of the Platonic Tradition during the Middle Ages.* Millwood, N.Y.: Kraus, 1982.

Klonoski, Richard. "The Preservation of Homeric Tradition: Heroic Re-performance in the *Republic* and the *Odyssey.*" *Clio* 22, no. 3 (1993), pp. 251–71.

Kofman, Sarah. *Seductions*. Paris: Galilée, 1990.

———. *Socrate(s)*. Paris: Galilée, 1989.

Kojève, Alexandre. *Essais d'une histoire raisonnée de la philosophie païenne*. 3 vols. Paris: Gallimard, 1968–73.

Koyré, Alexandre. *Introduction à la lecture de Platon*. Paris: Gallimard, 1962.

Krämer, Hans Joachim. *Plato and the Foundations of Metaphysics: A Work on the Theory of the Principles and Unwritten Doctrines of Plato with a Collection of the Fundamental Documents*. Trans. John R. Catan. Albany: SUNY Press, 1990.

Kraut, R., ed. *Plato's Republic: Critical Essays*. Lanham, Md.: Rowman and Littlefield, 1997.

Krell, David Farrell. *Daimon Life: Heidegger and Life-Philosophy*. Bloomington: Indiana University Press, 1992.

Kuhn, H. "The True Tragedy: On the Relationship between Greek Tragedy and Plato." *Harvard Studies in Classical Philology* 52 (1941), pp. 1–40.

Lachterman, David Rapport. *The Ethics of Geometry: A Genealogy of Modernity*. New York: Routledge, 1989.

———. "What Is 'The Good' of Plato's *Republic*?" *St. John's Review* 39, nos. 1–2 (1989–90), pp. 139–71.

Lacoue-Labarthe, Philippe. *Typography: Mimesis, Philosophy, Politics*. Cambridge, Mass.: Harvard University Press, 1989.

Lacoue-Labarthe, Philippe, and Jean-Luc Nancy. "The Nazi Myth." *Critical Inquiry* 16 (1990), pp. 291–312.

Lamb, W. R. M., trans. *Lysias*. Cambridge, Mass.: Harvard University Press, 1988.

Lamberton, Robert. *Homer the Theologian: Neoplatonist Allegorical Readings and the Growth of the Epic Tradition*. Berkeley: University of California Press, 1986.

Larisch, Sharon. "Old Women, Orphan Girls, and Allegories of the Cave." *Comparative Literature* 40, no. 2 (1988), pp. 150–71.

Lattimore, Richmond Alexander. *Themes in Greek and Latin Epitaphs*. Urbana: University of Illinois Press, 1942.

Levinas, Emmanuel. *Basic Philosophical Writings*. Ed. R. Bernasconi et al. Bloomington: Indiana University Press, 1997.

———. *Collected Philosophical Papers*. Trans. A. Lingis. Dordrecht: M. Nijhoff, 1987.

———. *Otherwise Than Being: or, Beyond Essence*. Trans. A. Lingis. Dordrecht: Kluwer, 1991.

———. *Totality and Infinity: An Essay on Exteriority*. Trans. A. Lingis. Pittsburgh: Duquesne University Press, 1969.

Lilly, Reginald, ed. *The Ancients and the Moderns*. Bloomington: Indiana University Press, 1996.

Loraux, Nicole. *The Children of Athena: Athenian Ideas about Citizenship and the Division between the Sexes*. Trans. Cardine Levine. Princeton: Princeton University Press, 1993.

———. *The Invention of Athens: The Funeral Oration in the Classical City*. Trans. Alan Sheridan. Cambridge, Mass.: Harvard University Press, 1986.

———. *Né de la terre: mythe et politique à Athènes*. Paris: Seuil, 1996.

Lycos, Kimon. *Plato on Justice and Power: Reading Book I of Plato's Republic*. Albany: SUNY Press, 1987.

MacDowell, Douglas M. *The Law in Classical Athens*. Ithaca: Cornell University Press, 1978.

Maritain, Jacques. *Man and the State*. Chicago: University of Chicago Press, 1951.

Mattéi, J.-F. *L'Étranger et le simulacre*. Paris: PUF, 1983.

Mauss, Marcel. *A General Theory of Magic*. Trans. Robert Brain. London: Routledge and K. Paul, 1972.

McEwen, Indra Kagis. *Socrates' Ancestor: An Essay on Architectural Beginnings*. Cambridge, Mass.: MIT Press, 1994.

McGahey, Robert. *The Orphic Moment: Shaman to Poet-Thinker in Plato, Nietzsche, and Mallarmé*. Albany: SUNY Press, 1994.

Merkelbach, R., and M. L. West, eds. *Fragmenta Hesiodea*. Oxford: Clarendon, 1967.

Merlan, Philip. "Form and Content in Plato's Philosophy." *Journal of the History of Ideas* 8, no. 1 (1947), pp. 406–30.

———. *From Platonism to Neoplatonism*. The Hague: Martinus Nijhoff, 1960.

Merleau-Ponty, Maurice. *The Visible and the Invisible*. Ed. Claude Lefort. Trans. Alphonso Lingis. Evanston: Northwestern University Press, 1968.

Momigliano, Arnaldo. *Alien Wisdom: The Limits of Hellenization*. Cambridge: Cambridge University Press, 1975.

Montet, Danielle. *Les Traits de l'être: essay sur l'ontologie platonicienne*. Grenoble: Millon, 1990.

Moravcsik, J., and P. Temko, eds. *Plato on Beauty, Wisdom, and the Arts*. Lanham, N.J.: Rowman and Littlefield, 1982.

Moreau, Joseph. *La Construction de l'idéalisme platonicien*. Hildesheim: Olms, 1967.

———. *Réalisme et idéalisme chez Platon*. Paris: PUF, 1951.

Morrison, J. S. "Parmenides and Er." *Journal of Hellenic Studies* 75 (1955), pp. 59–68.

Murdoch, Iris. *The Fire and the Sun: Why Plato Banished the Artists*. Oxford: Clarendon, 1977.

Murphy, N. R. *The Interpretation of Plato's* Republic. Oxford: Clarendon, 1951.

N. Viljoen, G. van. "Plato and Aristotle on the Exposure of Infants at Athens." *Acta Classica* 2 (1959), pp. 58–69.

Naas, Michael. *Turning: From Persuasion to Philosophy: A Reading of Homer's* Iliad. Atlantic Highlands, N.J.: Humanities, 1995.

Nancy, Jean-Luc. *Le Partage des voix*. Paris: Galilée, 1982.

Nettleship, R. L. *Lectures on the* Republic *of Plato*. London: Macmillan, 1901.

Nicgorski, Walter. "Cicero's Focus: From the Best Regime to the Model Statesman." *Political Theory* 19, no. 2 (1991), pp. 230–51.

Nitzsche, Jane Chance. *The Genius Figure in Antiquity and the Middle Ages*. New York: Columbia University Press, 1975.

Ogilvie, John. *The Theology of Plato, Compared with the Principles of Oriental and Grecian Philosophers*. London: 1793.

O'Meara, Dominic J. *Structures hiérerarchiques dans la pensée de Plotin: étude historique et interprétative*. Leiden: Brill, 1975.

Onians, Richard Broxton. *The Origins of European Thought about the Body, the Mind, the Soul, the World, Time, and Fate*. Cambridge: Cambridge University Press, 1951.

Ophir, Adi. *Plato's Invisible Cities: Discourse and Power in the* Republic. Savage, Md.: Barnes & Noble, 1991.

Osborne, C. "The Repudiation of Representation in Plato's *Republic.*" *Proceedings of the Cambridge Philological Society* 33 (1987), pp. 53–73.

Otto, W. F. *Dionysus, Myth and Cult.* Trans. Robert B. Palmer. Bloomington: Indiana University Press, 1965.

Owen, G. E. L. "Plato and Parmenides on the Timeless Present." *The Monist* 50, no. 3 (1966), pp. 317–40.

Panofsky, Erwin. *Idea: A Concept in Art Theory.* Trans. Joseph J. S. Peake. Columbia: University of South Carolina Press, 1968.

Paton, William Roger, trans. *The Greek Anthology.* 5 vols. London: Heinemann, 1916–18.

Pauly-Wissowa. *Pauly-Wissowa Realencyclopädie.* 24 vols. Stuttgart: Metzler, 1894–1963.

Pavese, Cesare, trans. *La* Teogonia *di Esiodo e tre inni omerici.* Turin: Einaudi, 1981.

Peperzak, Adriaan. "Appearance, Myth, and Art in Politics." *Research in Phenomenology* 21 (1991), pp. 48–61.

Plotinus. *The Enneads.* Trans. Stephen McKenna. Ed. Paul Henry. London: Faber & Faber, 1956.

Proclus. *Commentaire sur la* République. Trans. A. J. Festugière. 3 vols. Paris: Vrin, 1970.

———. *Commentary on Plato's* Parmenides. Trans. Glenn R. Morrow and John M. Dillon. Princeton: Princeton University Press, 1987.

———. *Théologie platonicienne.* Ed. H. D. Saffrey and L. G. Westerink. Paris: Belles-Lettres, 1968 ff.

Reale, Giovanni. *A History of Ancient Philosophy.* Albany: SUNY Press, 1985 ff.

Reeve, C. D. C. *Philosopher–Kings: The Argument of Plato's* Republic. Princeton: Princeton University Press, 1988.

Reinhardt, Karl. *Parmenides und die Geschichte der grieschischen Philosophie.* Frankfurt am Main: V. Klostermann, 1985.

Reitzenstein, Richard. *Studien zum antiken Synkretismus aus Iran und Griechenland.* Leipzig: Teubner, 1926.

Richardson, Hilda. "The Myth of Er (Plato, *Republic* 616 B)." *Classical Quarterly* 20 (1926), pp. 113–33.

Ricœur, P. *Être, essence et substance chez Platon et Aristote.* Paris: CDU, 1957.

———. *Platon et Aristote.* Paris: CDU, 1954.

Robin, Léon. *Platon.* Paris: PUF, 1968.

———. *La Théorie platonicienne des idées et des nombres d'après Aristote: étude historique et critique.* Hildesheim: Olms, 1963.

Rohatyn, D. "Struktur und Funktion in Buch X von Platons *Staat.*" *Gymnasium* 82 (1975), pp. 314–30.

Rohde, Erwin. *Psyche: The Cult of Souls and Belief in Immortality among the Greeks.* New York: Harper & Row, 1966.

Rose, Gilbert P. *Plato's* Republic Book I. Bryn Mawr, Penn.: Department of Greek, Bryn Mawr College, 1983.

Rosen, Stanley. "The Role of Eros in Plato's *Republic.*" *Review of Metaphysics* 18, no. 3 (1965), pp. 452–75.

Rosenstock, Bruce. "Athena's Cloak: Plato's Critique of the Democratic City in the *Republic.*" *Political Theory* 22, no. 3 (1994), pp. 363–90.

———. "Rereading the *Republic.*" *Arethusa* 16 (1983), pp. 219–46.

Russon, John, and John Sallis, eds. *Retracing the Platonic Text.* Evanston: Northwestern University Press, 1999.

Sallis, John. *Being and Logos: The Way of Platonic Dialogue.* Atlantic Highlands, N.J.: Humanities Press, 1986.

Samter, Ernst. *Die Religion der Griechen.* Leipzig: Teubner, 1914.

Sargeant, Winthrop, trans. *The Bhagavad Gita.* Albany: SUNY Press, 1984.

Sarri, Francesco. *Socrate e la genesi storica dell'idea occidentale di anima.* Rome: Abete, 1975.

Savinio, Alberto. *La Nostra anima.* Milan: Adelphi, 1981.

Sayre, Kenneth M. *Plato's Literary Garden: How to Read a Platonic Dialogue.* Notre Dame: University of Notre Dame Press, 1995.

Schaper, Eva. *Prelude to Aesthetics.* London: Allen & Unwin, 1968.

Schleiermacher, Friedrich. *Platons ausgewählte Werke.* Munich: Müller, 1918.

———. *Platons Staat.* Leipzig: Durr, 1907.

Schmitt, Carl. *The Concept of the Political.* Trans. George Schwab. New Brunswick, N.J.: Rutgers University Press, 1976.

Schuhl, Pierre-Maxime. *La Fabulation platonicienne.* Paris: Vrin, 1968.

Servais, Jean, et al., eds. *Stemmata: mélanges de philologie, d'histoire et d'archaeologie grecques offerts à Jules Labarbe.* Liège: L'Antiquité Classique, 1987.

Sheppard, Anne D. R. *Studies on the 5th and 6th Essays of Proclus' Commentary on the Republic.* Göttingen: Vandenhoeck und Ruprecht, 1980.

Shiner, R. A. "Soul in *Republic* X 611." *Apeiron* 6 (1972), pp. 23–30.

Shorey, Paul. *The Unity of Plato's Thought.* New York: Garland, 1980.

———. *What Plato Said.* Chicago: University of Chicago Press, 1933.

Sinaiko, Hermann L. *Love, Knowledge and Discourse in Plato: Dialogue and Dialectic in Phaedrus, Republic, Parmenides.* Chicago: University of Chicago Press, 1965.

———. *Reclaiming the Canon: Essays on Philosophy, Poetry, and History.* New Haven: Yale University Press, 1998.

Skemp, J. B. *The Theory of Motion in Plato's Later Dialogues.* Cambridge: Cambridge University Press, 1942.

Souilhé, J. *Étude sur le terme* Dúnamis *dans les dialogues de Platon.* New York: Garland, 1987.

———. *La Notion platonicienne d'intermédiaire dans la philosophie des dialogues.* New York: Garland, 1987.

Stefanini, Luigi. *Platone.* Padua: CEDAM, 1932.

Stewart, J. A. *The Myths of Plato.* London: Macmillan, 1905.

Strauss, Leo. *The City and Man.* Chicago: University of Chicago Press, 1964.

———. *Natural Right and History.* Chicago: University of Chicago Press, 1965.

———. *On Tyranny.* Including the Strauss-Kojève Correspondence. New York: Free Press, 1991.

———. *Persecution and the Art of Writing.* Chicago: University of Chicago Press, 1988.

Sun Tzu. *The Art of War.* Trans. Thomas Cleary. Boston: Shambhala, 1988.

Swift Riginos, Alice. *Platonica: The Anecdotes Concerning the Life and Writings of Plato.* Leiden: Brill, 1976.

Szlezák, T. A. "Unsterblichkeit und Trichotomie der Seele in zehnten Buch der *Politeia.*" *Phronesis* 21 (1976), pp. 31–58.

Tarrant, Harold. *Thrasyllan Platonism.* Ithaca: Cornell University Press, 1993.

Taylor, A. E. *Commentary on Plato's* Timaeus. Oxford: Clarendon, 1928.

Taylor, Thomas. *Thomas Taylor, the Platonist: Selected Writings.* Princeton: Princeton University Press, 1969.

Thesleff, Holger. *Studies in Platonic Chronology.* Helsinki: Societas Scientiarum Fennica, 1982.

Thucydides. *History of the Peloponnesian War.* Trans. C. Forster Smith. 4 vols. Cambridge, Mass.: Harvard University Press, 1956.

Tuana, Nancy, ed. *Feminist Interpretations of Plato.* University Park: Pennsylvania State University Press, 1994.

Vermeule, Emily. *Aspects of Death in Early Greek Art and Poetry.* Berkeley: University of California Press, 1979.

Vernant, Jean-Pierre. *Mythe et pensée chez les Grecs: études de psychologie historique.* Paris: Maspero, 1965.

———. *Myth, Religion and Society.* Cambridge: Cambridge University Press, 1981.

Vernant, Jean-Pierre, and Pierre Vidal-Naquet. *Myth and Tragedy in Ancient Greece.* Trans. Janet Lloyd. New York: Zone Books, 1988.

Vlastos. G. "Degrees of Reality in Plato." *New Essays on Plato and Aristotle.* Ed. R. Bambrough. New York: Humanities, 1965.

———. *Platonic Studies.* Princeton: Princeton University Press, 1973.

———. *Plato's Universe.* Seattle: University of Washington Press, 1975.

———. *Socrates: Ironist and Moral Philosopher.* Ithaca: Cornell University Press, 1991.

Voegelin, Eric. *Order and History.* 5 vols. Baton Rouge: Louisiana State University Press, 1956–87.

Wallis, R. T. *Neoplatonism.* London: Duckworth, 1995.

West, M. L. *The Orphic Poems.* Oxford: Oxford University Press, 1983.

White, John. "Imitation." *St. John's Review* 39, nos. 1–2 (1989–90), pp. 173–99.

White, Nicholas P. *A Companion to Plato's* Republic. Indianapolis: Hackett, 1979.

Williamson, Robert B. "*Eidos* and *Agathon* in Plato's *Republic.*" *St. John's Review* 39, nos. 1–2 (1989–90), pp. 105–37.

Wind, Edgar. *The Eloquence of Symbols: Studies in Humanist Art.* Oxford: Clarendon, 1983.

Xenophon. *Memorabilia* and *Oeconomicus.* Trans. E. C. Marchant. Cambridge, Mass.: Harvard University Press, 1979.

Zimbrich, Ulrike. *Bibliographie zu Platons* Staat: *Die Rezeption der* Politeia *im deutschprachigen Raum von 1800 bis 1970.* Frankfurt am Main: V. Klostermann, 1994.

Zuckert, Catherine H. *Postmodern Platos: Nietzsche, Heidegger, Gadamer, Strauss, Derrida.* Chicago: University of Chicago Press, 1996.

General Index

GREEK INDEX

Greek Index

CLAUDIA BARACCHI is Assistant Professor of Philosophy in the Graduate Faculty of Political and Social Science, The New School. She holds doctoral degrees from the University of Bologna and Vanderbilt University.